THE MAGIC GARMENT

Second Edition

I don't want realism. I want magic! Yes, yes, magic! I try to give that to people.

A Streetcar Named Desire, Tennessee Williams

THE MAGIC GARMENT

Second Edition

Principles *of* Costume Design

REBECCA CUNNINGHAM

Professor Emerita, Brooklyn College

WAVELAND

PRESS, INC.

Long Grove, Illinois

For information about this book, contact:
Waveland Press, Inc.
4180 IL Route 83, Suite 101
Long Grove, IL 60047-9580
(847) 634-0081
info@waveland.com
www.waveland.com

10-digit ISBN 1-57766-613-5
13-digit ISBN 978-1-57766-613-4

Printed in the United States of America

7 6 5 4

To my daughter, husband,
colleagues, past and future students,
and all those who love the theater

Contents

Foreword
by Sylvia Hillyard Pannell

To work magic is to weave the unseen forces into form; to soar beyond sight; to explore the uncharted dream realm of the hidden reality.

—Starhawk (born Miriam Simos)

C. Rebecca Cunningham's splendid book is at once a thorough, practical, and well-written costume design textbook and an insightful acknowledgement of the enchanting aspect of well-designed theatrical costumes. Should you study her text carefully and the essays and designs of the prestigious costume designers whose work she has featured in this, her newly edited text, your costumes too can transcend the world of sketches, cloth and dye, to become Magic Garments!

Let me illustrate the value of a strong text that examines and analyzes in detail the principles of costume design as I invoke some traditional ideas. Consider, for example, that aspect of the costume designer's sleight of hand explained by the old saying "a picture is worth a thousand words." An audience will see, and thus apprehend, volumes of information about an actor's character before he or she can utter one word, let alone a thousand! Therefore, the work of the costume designer is potentially the most powerful visual communication tool in theatrical and entertainment design. In our culture it is expected, and indeed the law, that people wear clothing in public; audiences take it for granted that performers in almost every entertainment arena will be dressed. It is only when they are not that the audience is truly startled. When actors are clothed, audience members are lulled by a sense of order and security. Thus audiences sometimes don't even note the work of the costume designer on a conscious level, which allows the performer's "look" to communicate subliminal messages—"a thousand words" of emotional and/or cognitive information that can inform or deliberately mislead the audience in order to heighten the effect of the drama.

At one end of the theatrical costume design spectrum are costumes so realistic and believable that it is a compliment to the designer should the work go unnoticed. At the other, there are fantastical costumes that delight, fool, and/or stagger the imagination. In any case, the theatrical costume designer's career and work seem to be at once fascinating and inexplicable.

The art of theatrical costume design—so unfamiliar to so many—is actually comprised of the very same thoughts, concerns, hopes, choices, and occupational needs that confront each of us as we get dressed every day of our lives. Indeed, whether it is one's chosen career, everyone is a costume designer. While audience members do not typically rearrange their living room, office, or landscape daily (as does the scenic designer), nor do they regularly control their ambient lighting in or out-of-doors from moment to moment (as the lighting designer does), most do accumulate their personal wardrobes and make daily and carefully considered clothing selections. Age, gender, occupation, style, personality, socioeconomics, religion, aspiration, occasion, and self-expression interrelate to produce individual wardrobe choices. The resulting look—your own daily costume design—is the conscious effort to establish visual persona.

The professional costume designer must consider the same matters that each of us does when we dress, yet the cast of characters is almost always greater than one, and the agenda and historical time frames change with each new play. With these character details examined, the costume designer's choices are made carefully, striving to provide an accurate visual depiction, to achieve a heightened reality, and to serve the mise-en-scène.

Professor Cunningham's new and updated edition of *The Magic Garment* is an artistic and practical guide for students, instructors, and professional costume designers who wish to explore the many complexities and solutions of the costume designer's art and craft. This valuable text weaves the myriad considerations and choices that individuals make daily into a visual tapestry that blends with, supports, informs, and then transforms into what occurs in each new theatrical production.

Twentieth-century U.S. theater saw designers changing from generalists to specialists. In the first half of the century it was expected that the same designer would accept a commission for theatrical costumes, scenery, and/or lighting as well as poster design, fashion design, jewelry, or architecture. Designers designed. A striking example of such versatility was the great Russian artist and designer Erté whose artistry spanned costume design, fashion design, poster design, sculpture, seriography, book and magazine illustration, and interior design to name a few. As the century progressed, as occurred in other fields, designers narrowed their focus to become closely associated with a certain specialty area and were trained as such.

Paralleling this movement, traditional training methods for artists and craftspersons, "apprenticeship" systems and specialty schools, receded into the background as American college and university drama and theater programs emerged. Fine-arts colleges were created and degrees acknowledging education in creative areas became available. As these degrees gained traction and respect, the demand for artists holding the BFA and MFA increased. The entertainment industry was growing exponentially, and demands for graduates holding undergraduate and graduate degrees in costume design, scenic design, or lighting design grew in parallel.

In answer to this trend toward specialization, in 1989 Cunningham published the first edition of *The Magic Garment: Principles of Costume Design.* It was among the first textbooks of its kind, addressing the unique art and craft of costume design. Those teaching costume design in university settings at the time, as I was, were clinging to Lucy Barton's every word for dear life. Barton's invaluable but traditional work *Historic Costume for the Stage,* published in 1935 with new material added in 1961 and 1963, was the primary costume design text available. While I am confident that Lucy Barton's book remains a staple in the research and reference libraries of costume designers of my generation, the need for textbooks in our field has continued. Professor Cunningham responded to that need by writing a comprehensive and precise guide to the art, craft, and business aspects of becoming a costume designer. The first edition of *The Magic Garment* provided a systematic overview of the principles and process of costume design for the stage.

The second edition of *The Magic Garment* has had an impressive face-lift. The fresh and stylish new illustrative material not only serves to reinforce the ideas being presented but also introduces the reader to many new and exciting theatrical productions from professional, regional, and university theaters geographically far-flung. These fresh, bold choices support the text and, at the same time, present new and current trends in sketching and rendering that use traditional methods and materials, computer-generated designs, and exciting combinations of both.

Another hallmark of this edition is the addition of Holly Cole's exceptionally interesting and informative chapter on designing costumes for film. Film is a major sector of the entertainment industry and one that employs many costume designers and legions of costume personnel. Cole thoroughly illuminates an aspect of the costume design profession that has very different requirements from those of stage costume design. Film design is not as frequently considered in college and university theater training programs outside the nation's film hubs and heretofore rarely covered in such depth in stage costume design texts.

Recent technological advancements have changed and streamlined the work of the costume designer in very significant ways. The technological revolution of the late twentieth century, in particular the mainstreaming of computer usefulness to the costume designer, is considered throughout the new edition of *The Magic Garment.* Cunningham has added timely information and instruction for using the computer in the design and production process. Possibilities range from developing sketches and renderings, to engaging in long-distance production conferences, to organizing the costume building and production process. She has approached the usefulness of the computer with care, extolling its value in many areas yet cautioning of pitfalls that lurk within this facile tool. She repeatedly and rightfully warns the reader of property issues associated with readily accessible images and videos. She advises designers to be wary of Internet research that is not juried, as it can be erroneous and misleading. In the new final chapter of the second edition, "Preparing for a Costume Design Career," she underscores the critical role that the computer plays in job searches and career development. From resumes to digital portfolios, personal Web sites, and online placement services the computer provides endless paths to jobs in costume design.

In sum, this book is an important new contribution to the existing literature on costume design. It offers a convincing road map for students, teachers, and professionals alike that advances our understanding of the principles and processes of this unique art form. All of us in this field are indebted to Rebecca Cunningham for her fine work and dedication in advancing the frontiers of our profession through producing a text that has become a standard for a generation of students and instructors.

For many years the first edition of *The Magic Garment* was required reading in my undergraduate and graduate costume design classes at the University of Georgia. My students and I found it a comprehensive and invaluable text. It is a distinct honor to be asked to offer commentary on this exciting second edition of *The Magic Garment* and to be given the opportunity to write the foreword. This book is remarkably detailed and lovingly written and produced by a celebrated costume designer, educator, and author—Rebecca Cunningham. May you use it for enlightenment and enjoyment as I plan to!

Sylvia Hillyard Pannell
Professor of Drama Emerita, University of Georgia,
and Immediate Past President, USITT

Preface

When the first edition of *The Magic Garment* was originally published in 1989, I never dreamed it would enjoy such longevity; I have been thrilled and humbled by its acceptance as a textbook. However, I have been aware for some time that technology has impacted our field and that revisions in the text were needed. I hope this new edition will address the needs of costume design students today and tomorrow. Although I recognize the great contribution technology makes to our work as costume designers, I still believe the basis of the theater designer's work is the understanding of the artistic principles that apply to all art forms. Building on this understanding the designer adds specific knowledge of dramatic literature, theater techniques, costume history, styles of visual presentation, costume fabric/materials, and skills in research, drawing, painting, conceptualizing, interpretation, communication, and collaboration—all topped with great dollops of imagination.

These design fundamentals and many personal variations are presented here in the hope that students will develop the foundation needed to support their own approach to costume design.

I would like to thank all those who very generously shared their time and talent in the production of this second edition: the esteemed Broadway designers who shared their sketches and thoughts on costume design in the included interviews, Greg Barnes, Judith Dolan, William Ivey Long, Martin Pakledinaz, Paul Tazewell, and Catherine Zuber; my respected colleagues in regional and educational theater who permitted me to use their sketches to illustrate the text, Bill Brewer, Laura Crow, Joel Ebarb, Sheila Hargett, Eloise Kazan, Mathew LeFebvre,

Margaret Mitchell, Michelle Ney, C. David Russell, and Shima Ushiba; the author of the film chapter, Holly Cole; the contributors who assisted me with new sections of text and new illustrations, Vivianne Galloway, Shahrzad Haghjoo, Jeanette Aultz Look, and Kristen Vaughan; my fellow design professor Sylvia Hillyard Pannell for her beautiful foreword; and last, but by no means least, my dear husband Jack Cunningham for his moral support and many critical and technical contributions. I would also like to gratefully acknowledge the support and assistance of Don Rosso of Waveland Press in the preparation of this edition and extend my gratitude to Patricia White and Jim Hurley of the Theatrical Wardrobe Union Local 764 I.A.T.S.E. for their help and expertise.

Rebecca Cunningham

Chapter 1

Understanding Stage Costumes

Lend me thy hand,
And pluck my magic garment from me.

The Tempest, William Shakespeare

A costume is a "magic" garment—a garment that enables an actor to become, for a time, someone else. Like Prospero's cape, which concentrated his supernatural powers over the winds and sea, an actor's costume helps concentrate the powers of imagination, expression, emotion, and movement into the creation and projection of a character to an audience.

This magic has a long history. Theatrical costume is one of the oldest art forms known to humanity. Prehistoric cultures used animal heads and skins as masks and costumes for ritual dances. These dances were created to relive and retell experiences. They were used to invoke the spirit world and were thought to favorably influence the hunt, weather, and fertility. Long before plays were written, and probably before paintings were painted, costumes and makeup magically transformed dancers and actors. Modern costumes still have this aura of magic.

Costumes have come a long way from animal heads and skins, yet each time an actor dons a costume, some vestige of that ancient magic is called upon to trans-

Figure 1.1 *The Wizard of Oz*. The Scarecrow. Designed by Bill Brewer for the Orlando Repertory Theatre. This costume is based on a tradition of illustration and costume design for *The Wizard of Oz* established through literature, movies, and stage.

form the actor into the character portrayed. Sometimes this magic works subtly by affecting the posture, walk, and presence of the actor and by touching the store of cultural information in the collective memory of audience. Other costume images are so well known within a culture that the appearance of an actor in that costume immediately identifies that character and evokes a suitable attitude or frame of mind in the audience. Costumes of this type may be based on traditional theatrical characters like Harlequin (figure 2.4), or they may draw on familiar associations from outside the theater. *The Wizard of Oz* has been a popular tale in literature, movies, and on the stage for over 100 years. The costume for the Scarecrow in figure 1.1 is based on that tradition of illustrations and costumes.

Basic Functions

What is a stage costume? A stage costume may be defined as anything worn on stage. The real question is, "What is an *effective* stage costume?" An effective costume engages the audience's attention and enhances the production and the actor's performance. It performs two basic functions: (1) it *visually* defines and supports the character developed by the actor, and (2) it helps establish the overall theme (idea) and mood (atmosphere) of the production as interpreted by the director. An effective costume speaks to the audience's subconscious store of knowledge and experience, helping them to identify the individual characters even before they speak and even if they are silent.

Defining the Character

Differences between characters must be clearly visible, enabling all members of the audience to distinguish them and to understand the action. Even when other characters in the play are confused about the identity of certain characters, the audience should usually have no doubts. Shakespeare's *Comedy of Errors* involves two sets of twins and depends on the confusion of one twin brother for another. Costumes for these characters must be similar enough for the confusion to be logical, but different enough for the audience to understand which character is on stage. (See color plate 1.)

How does the costume visually define a character? What does the audience need to know? The costume must (1) set the character in time (historical period) and space (geographical or imaginary place), (2) establish the approximate age and gender of a character, (3) establish the rank or social status of the character, (4) establish the personality of the character, and (5) reflect any changes in time, space, age, status, and personality that the character goes through during the play.

Setting a Character in Time and Space

When and where did this character live? Often the playwright specifies the date and locale of the play either by a statement at the beginning of the script or by specific reference to a person or historical event. When a period or date is specified, the playwright usually has a reason for setting the play in that time. Perhaps the ambience or mystique of the period or place enhances the theme. By setting *Macbeth* on the misty moors of Scotland in a time distant even to his own day, Shakespeare added mystery and magic to his comment on the violent nature of man (and woman). Perhaps a historical incident allows safe comment on a current, parallel situation. *The Crucible,* by Arthur Miller, is set in seventeenth-century Salem, Massachusetts. This play about the witch trials in early America reflects Miller's views on the McCarthy hearings taking place in his own time. If no reference to date can be found, the designer may assume the play was set in the time in which it was written. Sometimes, however, the style, theme, and mood of the play may suggest a historical period different from that in which it was written or set by the playwright.

A director may choose to move the play into a different time period. A new emphasis or fresh point of view on a classic play may be gained by changing its traditional period and locale or by establishing a fantasy world in which to place the production. A designer may suggest an appropriate change of period to the director. Shakespeare's plays may be produced in Elizabethan costume, modern dress (see figure 1.2), and many other periods and styles, each contributing a slightly different point of view.

Establishing Age

An audience usually needs a clear idea of the age of each character. A major part of the responsibility for projecting age falls on the actor, but the costume must support that characterization. A costume can suggest age through the length of the garment, the length or type of sleeve, the shape of the neckline, and many other design considerations. The hairstyle and makeup may also be designed by the costume designer.

Figure 1.2 *Coriolanus.* Coriolanus. This design uses modern dress to create a bridge to a contemporary audience. Designed by Joel Ebarb for Texas Shakespeare Festival. Photo by Tony Galaska.

Figure 1.3 *Twelfth Night.* The youth and innocence of Olivia and Sebastian are emphasized by the choices made by the costume designer. Designed by the author for Brooklyn College. Photo: Richard Grossberg.

In figure 1.3 the youth and innocence of Olivia and Sebastian in *Twelfth Night* are emphasized by the use of white and pastel colors, lightweight fabrics, the cut of the garments, and the type of accessories.

Appropriate age projection in the costume is especially important when the actor and the character being portrayed are far apart in age. In almost every production of *Romeo and Juliet,* actors older than Shakespeare's characters play the young lovers, as few thirteen-year-old actresses have the understanding and skill to portray the thirteen-year-old Juliet. Careful handling of the costumes helps the actors project the youth and immaturity so essential to these characters.

Establishing Rank or Social Status

In most historical plays (also called period plays) a hierarchy of characters is established and is basic to the action. The primary action often centers on conflict between characters or groups of *different* rank or social status—rich versus poor, ruler versus subject(s), church versus secular government, servant versus master. For example, the cast of characters for *The Marriage of Figaro* by Jean-Pierre de Beaumarchais includes a count and a countess (nobility), a doctor and a music master (middle class), household servants, and various peasants. The plot matches the wit of the servants against the power of the nobility. Figure 1.4 shows another example of class differentiation through costuming from *The Caucasian Chalk Circle.*

Even in plays that do not feature kings, queens, counts, or bishops, some element of class, ethnic or regional origin, lifestyle, occupation, or income level is necessary to define all characters. These elements create variety and make us draw on our own experiences to help us understand the characters. George S. Kaufman and Moss Hart's *You Can't Take It with You* features an odd assortment of characters including the Vanderhof-Sycamore family: Grandpa, a philosopher; Penny, a middle-aged mother, painter, and playwright; Penny's husband, Paul, a part-time fireworks manufacturer; Mr. DePinna, a boarder, formerly the iceman; Penny and Paul's daughter, Essie, an amateur ballet dancer and candy maker; Essie's husband, Ed, a printer and xylophone player; Alice, Penny and Paul's second daughter, a secretary; two black household servants; and the Kirbys: Tony, Alice's beau; Mr. Kirby, Tony's millionaire businessman father; Mrs. Kirby, Tony's mother and uptight socialite; plus a Russian countess working as a waitress; a Russian dance instructor; an inebriated actress; and a pair of FBI agents. The social or economic status (real or imagined) of each character contributes something to understanding the play's meaning. The conflict between the free lifestyle of the Sycamores and the luxurious but staid existence of the Kirbys must be supported by the contrast in their styles of dress.

Modern plays tend to focus on inner conflicts, conflicts between a character and his/her own social or economic group, or conflict between closely associated groups. Regardless of the nature of the conflict, correct establishment of the social milieu in which the play takes place is an important part of the designer's job.

Figure 1.4 *The Caucasian Chalk Circle.* Grusha, Azdak, and the Fat Prince. These costumes reflect the differing social positions of the characters. The low social status of Grusha and Azdak are expressed in their simple, worn costumes that contrast with the elaborate uniform and mask of the Fat Prince. Designed by Sheila Hargett for Texas State University.

Establishing Personality

The costume designer must assist the actor in projecting the character's personality. In television and films the camera can move in for close-ups to catch facial reactions that reveal character; on stage, however, broad gestures and large-scale visual clues often are needed to make the point. From the moment of Nora's entrance in *A Doll's House* the audience must know that she is the doll about whom Henrik Ibsen is writing. Her costume should suggest the pampered innocence in which she is living. The cut of a garment, the color, the fit, the type of trim, the accessories—*all* aspects of the costume can express something about the character's personality.

Sometimes the costume must reveal something about the character in contrast to what that character pretends to be. In figure 1.5 the character Lenck, in order to visit one of his mistresses, disguises himself as a nursemaid. When he gambles away almost everything he owns including his clothes, he resorts to wearing his maid's clothes, revealing something of his inner character as well as his physical one.

Reflecting Changes

One of the easiest ways to reflect a change in a character is to change costumes. A new costume clearly and dramatically demonstrates that something has occurred. However, not all changes of character condition are dramatic or obvious. Some take place gradually and subtly. These changes must be reflected by slight variations in appearance: opening a blouse, loosening a tie, changing shoes. Not all characters in a play go

Figure 1.5   *Bach at Leipzig.* Lenck in his nursemaid's clothes. Designed by Mathew J. LeFebvre for The Milwaukee Rep.

through a change of condition, but major characters almost always progress or regress as a result of the conflicts in the plot. The changes in Eliza Doolittle are the major focus of George Bernard Shaw's *Pygmalion* and her costumes obviously should parallel the improvements in her speech and behavior. The changes in Higgins, barely perceptible, are not acknowledged by him and should scarcely be reflected in his dress. The two costumes for *Crimen contra la humanidad* (*Crime against Humanity*) illustrated in figure 1.6 show a character in two different conditions. First Carota appears in a crisp day dress; later she reappears in tatters after imprisonment and both physical and emotional torture.

Figure 1.6 *Crimen contra la humanidad* (*Crime against Humanity*). Carota. These two costumes show a character in two conditions. Designed by Eloise Kazan for Teatro UNAM.

Supporting Theme, Concept, and Mood

A play exists because a playwright has one or more ideas to express. A play may be based on an existing story, but the playwright has some comment or point of view on that story that forms the *theme*. He or she consciously or unconsciously transmits that theme to the audience through what is included or omitted from the story, the order and way the incidents are presented, and the language that is used to tell the story. The director of each production is responsible for interpreting the playwright's theme anew. This is referred to as the *director's concept*. The costumes of a given production collectively express the director's interpretation of the theme for that production. Concepts that evolve from the study of the script and are based on either the action or the language of the play are said to be *organic*. These interpretations are triggered by ideas found in the play itself, not found elsewhere and applied to the surface of the play. Setting *Julius Caesar* in Nazi Germany may sound like a great idea, but what elements in the play support this change and will the play work well in its new setting? The concept should enhance the play, not smother it.

Many plays lend themselves to a variety of valid interpretations. *Hamlet* has been interpreted in many ways, some stressing the political aspects of the play and some stressing the psychological aspects.

The *mood* of a play is the emotional feeling that pervades the experience. Mood may be part of the playwright's theme or imposed by the director's concept. Melancholy, joy, terror, anger, humor, and disorientation are all moods that can be found in plays. In some plays the mood varies between different feelings; in other plays one prevailing mood gradually builds throughout the play.

The theme, concept, and mood of a production are supported by the costumes through (1) style, (2) color, (3) scale, and (4) texture.

Style

Style is the manner or mode in which a designer creates the costumes in order best to interpret the mood and concept. It is the result of decisions and choices made by the designer. The two basic styles are *realism* and *stylization*. Costumes done in a realistic style are as close to actual dress as the demands of the play and theatrical values will allow. Stylized costumes are those that depart from real clothes in some obvious way. The designer may choose to exaggerate shape, silhouette, color, trim, or other aspects of the costume. The more realistic a production is, the more subtle the coordination of the costumes can be; the more stylized the production is, the more obviously coordinated the costumes can be. Within these two approaches, hundreds of variations are possible.

Color

After choosing an overall color scheme for the production, colors appropriate to each individual character must be determined. The designer must consider how all the costumes will look together, and what the overall effect will be when all the costumes in a given scene are on stage together. Do the major characters stand out against the crowd or blend into the group? Do the colors project the mood or feeling desired? Do the colors express comedy or tragedy?

Scale

The scale of an object is its size relative to a norm or to other related objects. Realistic productions call for realistic or slightly exaggerated scale (depending on the size of the theater). More stylized productions may exaggerate scale (larger or smaller) for humor, horror, or other effects. The costume for Solinus, Duke of Ephesus in *Comedy of Errors* (figure 1.7) incorporates an enormous hat, very large scarf, very long coattails, and very full pants for humorous effect.

Texture

All materials have texture, smooth to rough. While contrast between textures is desirable, the proportion of one to the other affects one's perception of the whole group. A costume of predominantly rough materials suggests a primitive or earthy character. If all the costumes are constructed of rough materials, then the whole group shares these characteristics. The designer uses textures to tell the audience something about the character and relationships between the characters in the play. The overall textural feeling of costumes and scenery helps project the feeling or mood of the play.

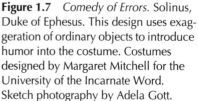

Figure 1.7 *Comedy of Errors.* Solinus, Duke of Ephesus. This design uses exaggeration of ordinary objects to introduce humor into the costume. Costumes designed by Margaret Mitchell for the University of the Incarnate Word. Sketch photography by Adela Gott.

How Does the Costume Designer Work?

. . . What are these
So withered and so wild in their attire,
That look not like the inhabitants o' the earth,
And yet are on't . . .
   You should be women,
And yet your beards forbid me to interpret
That you are so.

Macbeth, William Shakespeare

The costume designer's art lies in effective interpretation, collaboration, and execution. The designer must be able to interpret visually and verbally the action, style, and characters of the play, the costumes and manners of the historical period, and the elements of the style of presentation. Collaboration involves the ability to communicate and compromise with the director, the actors, and the other designers. Critical to real success is the costume designer's ability to effect not just the execution of a sketch, but also the translation of the sketch to a final costume that serves both the actor and the production in visual and practical terms.

Designing costumes for a play is thus a very complex project. How does the designer begin? What steps need to be taken and in what order? Each designer develops an individual approach to attacking the myriad tasks of designing, but most follow the same basic outline.

Reading and Studying the Play

The script usually indicates directly or indirectly most of the basic information needed by the designer: historical period, character information, special problems (quick changes, broad action, disguises), and mood or style. Several careful readings may be needed to find this information. The stage directions give some insight into the action and personality of each character. Even more valuable, however, will be the character's dialogue and what others say about that character. The comment by Banquo on the witches in *Macbeth* that opens this section is very revealing. Bearded, withered, and wildly dressed, they appear unearthly to him. Along with other lines, his observations suggest the eerie mood and pervading sense of evil on the moor. If the script does not give enough information, the designer, director, and/or actor will need to decide on the points in question. Notes on all pertinent information are then organized into various lists known as "plots," which express visually the information needed to design the show.

Collaboration between Designers and Director

Collaboration is a key word in the success of most theatrical productions. Careful discussion of ideas, effects, images, concepts, schedules, and other pertinent information helps to keep all participants working toward the same goals. Asking exploratory questions and responding without taking or giving offense to the collaborative team are keys to effective collaboration. As the guiding force behind the production, a good director knows how to give the design team an indication of the style desired without squelching their creativity. To be an effective participant in this collaboration, the costume designer must know enough about the tasks of the director, the scenic designer, and the lighting designer to discuss the overall production intelligently and to understand how a decision in one area might affect another area of the production. A detailed understanding of the script is helpful to a designer before design conferences begin. Attendance at rehearsals and discussions with the actors about the characters they play also give the designer insights into the total production.

The designer must also have sufficient understanding of construction and cost factors to design within budget limitations. He or she must be prepared to adjust, make changes, and even start completely over in some situations. Communication, coordination, and cooperation are essential to good collaboration.

Research

The designer needs a basic knowledge of costume history to even begin researching a period play. The type and amount of research required for a show vary considerably from play to play. Modern plays may require visits to places where people similar to the characters can be found. Plays set in historical periods may require extensive study of the painting, literature, and existing artifacts of that period. Some research material is readily available; some must be fer-

Figure 1.8
A research collage. Samples of Greek traditional dress assembled by computer on a collage board to facilitate discussion. By the author.

reted out with great diligence. Some research is primarily to inspire the designer and may be abstract in nature. After collecting stacks of research material, the designer must sort, evaluate, and develop it for effective use. Many designers use their research to develop a collage board to express their concept. The resulting board may actually have no costume pieces on it, but images of color, form, texture, and mood.

Developing the Costumes

Using the ideas expressed in designer–director discussions and the collected research, the designer develops a series of quick sketches called *roughs*. In these sketches the designer begins to work out the overall look of the show as well as individual character approaches. These sketches then serve as the basis for further discussions with the director. These roughs may also be presented as a collage.

Analysis of the costume roughs should indicate if major characters stand out from subordinate characters, if character delineation is clear, and if relationships between characters are indicated. Many rounds of roughs may be necessary before the various problems of a specific costume are solved.

Unifying the Whole

The designer constantly works to unify the production, to establish the feeling that all parts belong to the whole. Collaboration with the director and other designers should bring a clear concept and approach into focus. Comparison of the costume designs with the set designs and the plans of the lighting designer should determine if all approaches agree. Adjustments in all areas of the design may be needed.

Rendering the Costume Sketches

When most of the decisions have been made concerning each costume's design, the designer creates a series of color illustrations for the costumes. These *renderings* may be done in watercolor, ink, pastel, pencil, gouache, tempera, or any combination of suitable media or using computer rendering techniques. The drawing should be done carefully so that a pattern can be made for the costume. As in figure 1.9, additional notes may be added to indicate fully the intentions of the designer. Color samples or *swatches,* small samples of selected fabrics, may be attached with indications where each is used. Swatches may come from the designer's collection or from the shopper's research, or they may be attached after the fabric is purchased.

With the wide availability of color photocopying and computer scanning, designers can now provide color copies of their original sketches for the director, actors, and shop personnel. This practice saves wear and tear on the original sketches. These images can also be sent by e-mail to directors and costume shops from the designer's studio.

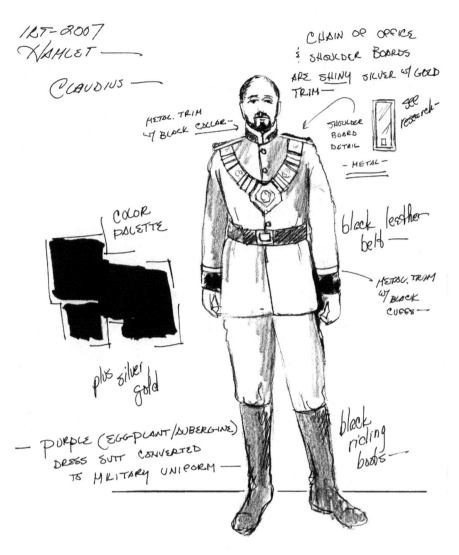

ILT-2007
HAMLET ——

CLAUDIUS ——

METAL. TRIM
w/ BLACK COLLAR ——

COLOR PALETTE

plus silver gold

— PURPLE (EGGPLANT/AUBERGINE) DRESS SUIT CONVERTED TO MILITARY UNIFORM ——

CHAIN OF OFFICE
& SHOULDER BOARDS
ARE SHINY SILVER & GOLD
TRIM ——

SHOULDER BOARD DETAIL
— METAL —

see research

black leather belt ——

METAL. TRIM w/ BLACK CUFFS ——

black riding boots ——

Figure 1.9 *Hamlet.* Included on this costume sketch for Claudius are details of the construction, trim, and accessories of this design for the king. Designed by Joel Ebarb for Indiana Repertory Theatre.

Choosing Fabrics for Costumes

The painter's medium is paint; the sculptor's medium may be metal, wood, or clay; and the costume designer's medium is fabric. The choice of fabric is a major influence on the final look of each costume and the overall look of the production. The same garment, cut of different fabrics, can suggest characters of very different ages, personalities, or economic levels. A group of costumes designed in a variety of fabrics has an interesting, and usually realistic, feeling. A set of costumes that uses only a few fabrics, on the other hand, tends to be very strongly unified and stylized. Fabric choice must be suitable for the garment, period style, character's personality, concept of production, budget allotments, and maintenance requirements of the production.

Getting the Show Together

The designer's responsibility to the show does not end with the completion of the sketches. Different situations require different types of involvement. For some productions the designer also must locate, rent, buy, or build the costumes. In other situations the costume shop manager is responsible for the delegation of portions of the work to the various staff members, leaving the designer to supervise details. The designer must attend rehearsals; supervise costume use for dress rehearsals, photo calls, and previews; and instruct wardrobe crews regarding special problems of quick changes and maintenance. The designer also is responsible for keeping the show costs within the budget. Some of the designer's work may be delegated to design assistants. These stages of the design process often overlap or reverse order depending on the design problems of a given production or the approach of a particular designer.

While a successful costume design effort should substantially contribute to the total effect of the production, the scenery, lights, and costumes should complement and balance each other and provide support for the acting and direction of the play. The importance of the costumes in a given play is relative and subjective. Some plays make strong visual statements; others stress verbal or psychological meanings. Some directors are interested in strong visual effects; others stress emotion and movement. While many lavish and spectacular productions are remembered for their beauty or extravagance, the visual and technical trappings of a production should enhance, not overshadow, the audience's understanding of the theme of the play.

The art of the costume designer lies in the ability to weave all aspects of costuming into a seamless and unified production. The following chapters examine the basic skills and information the designer needs in order to approach and coordinate these aspects of costume design.

Chapter 2
Understanding the Play

Yes, I have tricks in my pocket, I have things up my sleeve. But I am the opposite of a stage magician. He gives you illusion that has the appearance of truth. I give you truth in the pleasant disguise of illusion.

The Glass Menagerie, Tennessee Williams

What Is a Play?

A play is a playwright's version of some truth, an illusion often more real or penetrating than reality. A play is a live representation of selected actions. Plays "happen" in the present no matter what time they represent. The stage is a magic time machine on which we view events from other eras and from the minds and imaginations of other men and women. The script for a play is but a blueprint for these events, not a finished product. It contains dialogue, character information, and directions for action. The script is the playwright's attempt to reveal a personal vision to the audience.

Before the task of designing a play can begin, a thorough study of the script is necessary. The designers must seek the playwright's vision and combine with it their own and that of the director and actors in order to reveal that vision to the audience.

In order to read and understand a play, to discuss it intelligently with the director, and to design suitable and effective costumes, a designer must understand the various types of drama and their characteristics.

What Kind of Play Is It? Forms of Drama

The actors are come hither, my lord . . . the best actors in the world, either for tragedy, comedy, history, pastoral, pastoral–comical, historical–pastoral, tragical–historical, tragical–comical–historical–pastoral, scene individable, or poem unlimited. . . . These are the only men.

Hamlet, William Shakespeare

A list of forms of drama creates not a series of specific types, but a spectrum of forms, some shades broader than others, some with undefined edges, and some tones flecked with contrasting hues. To understand the classification of various plays takes study and experience in reading scripts. Many plays can easily be interpreted in more than one way, leaving the final classification to be determined by the director's contribution.

Tragedy

A dramatic form centering on themes of great philosophical importance, *tragedy* explores the individual's purpose and destiny, one's relationship to forces greater than oneself, and the nature of good and evil. Usually tales of kings, queens, and gods, tragedy has a scope and scale beyond the daily experience of the average human being. The playwright seeks to arouse pity and fear in the audience and to provide catharsis and moral enlightenment. Despite staggering adversity, the humanity, spirit, and integrity of the human race (in the person of the protagonist) remain intact. The most formal theatrical form, *classical tragedy* dates from the Greek Golden Age. Tightly structured and written in verse, Greek tragedy explored profound questions regarding humanity's existence through the retelling of Greek myths of men, women, and the gods. Examples of Greek tragedies are *Medea* by Euripides and *Oedipus Rex* by Sophocles.

In the seventeenth century, French playwrights turned to Greek tragedies as models for inspiration and style. *French classical tragedies* include *Polyeucte* by Pierre Corneille and *Phaedra* by Jean Racine.

Although written in blank verse and with a less formal construction than Greek tragedy, *Elizabethan tragedies* also explore questions of power, good and evil, purpose, and destiny. However, these plays tend to focus on extraordinary human beings and their failings rather than on the influence of fate or the interference of the gods. Shakespeare's *Othello* and *Hamlet* are among a long list of great Elizabethan tragedies.

Modern tragedies explore the dilemmas of ordinary persons caught in situations that test their morals, strength of character, and sanity. Arthur Miller's *Death of a Salesman* is an example of modern tragedy.

Serious modern plays, *dramas,* share many aspects of tragedy but lack the profundity and universality of traditional tragedy. Usually featuring ordinary people, these plays explore ideas, social and philosophical issues, and behavior under the stresses of modern life. Dramas look for meaning in a rapidly changing world, often with tragic results. Henrik Ibsen's *A Doll's House,* Clifford Odets' *The Country Girl,* and Tennessee Williams' *Summer and Smoke* are examples of this form.

Costumes for tragedy have traditionally been elaborate and designed in grand scale. The Greeks and Romans used masks and thick-soled boots to make the actors "larger-than-life." (See figure 2.1.) Costumes for classical tragedy may stress universality over the specifics of historical time and place. Modern tragedies and dramas are usually costumed in realistic or nearly realistic, historically accurate dress.

Figure 2.1   Tragedy mask. From Pompeii, this fine marble sculpture represents a theater mask of the type found in Greek and Roman tragedy. Photo: Westair Surveys.

Melodrama 情景剧

This popular form of escapist drama got its name in the late eighteenth century when music was used to heighten the effect of stage action. Often exaggerated, this form of play emphasizes suspense, action, and the contrast between good and evil. Usually ending happily, melodrama is the form of detective stories, soap operas, and adventure plays in the theater, in film, and on television. Perhaps the most well known melodrama of the nineteenth century is *Uncle Tom's Cabin,* based on the novel by Harriet Beecher Stowe. (See figure 2.2.) Robert Sherwood's *Petrified Forest* is a twentieth-century example of this genre.

Melodrama may depend rather heavily on stereotypes. The characters are often recognized by their costumes: Heroine in sweet white dress, Villain in black, Hero in white. The closer to drama the melodrama is, the more realistic the costumes tend to be.

Comedy

On the lighter side of the spectrum is found a broad selection of comic plays. Primarily entertaining, comedies are usually funny and end happily. Most comedies do not question values, but explore behavior. The characters of comedy may be fairly realistic, but they are caught in compromising circumstances that reveal their humanity.

High comedy is a form of comedy based on wit and subtle, intellectual observation. Usually dealing with characters in polite society, these plays deal primarily with language rather than action. *Private Lives* by Noel Coward is an example of this type of comedy.

A sophisticated comedy set in court circles or upper-class society is sometimes called a *comedy of manners.* This dramatic form displays the contrast between parlor etiquette and the real nature of people. These comedies reveal and ridicule pretentious and hypocritical behavior. Examples of this type of play are *She Stoops to Conquer* by Oliver Goldsmith, *Lady Windermere's Fan* by Oscar Wilde, and *The Misanthrope* by Molière. *Restoration comedies* are comedies of

MARKS   ELIZA'S ESCAPE ON THE ICE.   UNCLE TOM.

LEAVITT & PASTOR'S
THIRD AVENUE THEATRE.

POSITIVELY ONE WEEK ONLY,
COMMENCING
MONDAY, MARCH 30th, 1885.

MATINEES MONDAY, WEDNESDAY AND SATURDAY.

JOHN   P.   SMITH'S

GRAND MAJESTIC REVIVAL OF THE NEW VERSION OF
THE GREAT MORAL DRAMA OF

UNCLE TOM'S CABIN

WHICH WILL BE PRODUCED WITH

New and Beautiful Scenery ! New and Charming Music, with over One
Hundred People in the Cast.

Introducing Jubilee Singers, Shout Singers, Banjo Players, Castinet Players, Tambo Players
all Colored people.

Seats for Uncle Tom, will be on sale at the Theatre Ticket Office, on and after Thursday,
March 26th. Secure your seats in advance and avoid the crowd at Box Office at night.

ADMISSION 15 & 25 CENTS.   MATINEES MONDAY, WEDNESDAY & SATURDAY.

Figure 2.2 *Uncle Tom's Cabin.* This extremely popular nine-teenth-century melodrama was often lavishly produced. The Theater Collection; Museum of the City of New York.

manners written in England in the latter half of the seventeenth century (after the restoration of the monarchy). *The Country Wife* by William Wycherly is from this period.

When action and situation are of primary importance and language is unimportant, except for the use of vulgarities, the play is said to be an example of *low comedy.* Emphasis is placed on physical deformities, malfunctions, and mishaps sometimes called "comic bits." Characters tend to be personifications of one or two characteristics. The comedians of early films were particularly adept at physical forms of comedy. Laurel and Hardy, Buster Keaton, and Abbott and Costello were all masters of this genre. Low comic scenes may be included in other types of drama for *comic relief.* The "gatekeeper's scene" in *Macbeth* and the "grave digger's scene" in *Hamlet* are scenes of comic relief.

By coloring the tragic aspects of human life with irony and humor, *black comedy* enables us to look at situations that might otherwise be too painful to contemplate. Plays such as *A Day in the Death of Joe Egg* by Peter Nichols help us consider the plight of those in circumstances we may never personally know.

Tragicomedy also blends elements of tragedy with humor, irony, and pathos. More bittersweet than black comedy, tragicomedy is about characters that are more recognizable and approachable. Tragicomedy can touch an audience deeply. Lanford Wilson's *Fifth of July* is such a play.

Originally *burlesque* was a kind of satire or mockery of a well-known figure or type of person. In the twentieth century burlesque came to mean bawdy humor. In vaudeville, for example, a series of comic skits was combined with dance acts featuring female dancers in provocative costumes.

Based on ridiculous and improbable situations, *farce* has laughter as its sole purpose. An extremely active form of theater, farce builds at a frantic pace, piling one outrageous action on top of another until everything collapses in a hysterical heap. Plays in the farcical form include Shakespeare's *Comedy of Errors* and Michael Frayn's *Noises Off.*

Costumes for comedy span a very wide range. High comedies and comedies of manners are usually done in appropriate period dress, elegant and beautiful, although exaggeration of dress or decoration is frequent. Low comedy, farce, and burlesque costumes often feature distortion of body shapes, bold colors, and large size decoration. Comic costumes are developed through the same *comic devices* used by writers.

Comic Devices

Comic writers work with four basic "comic devices" when creating funny situations. The costume designer should understand these devices.

Derision is a form of criticism aimed at pomposity, hypocrisy, and sanctimoniousness. Derision must be leveled at symbols of authority to be funny; deriding the weak or pathetic becomes cruel and humorless.

Physical deformity is a very old comic device. Many comic characters are intentionally distorted and exaggerated in appearance through the use of masks, padded costumes, phallic symbols, or makeup. The spirit in which this is done and how far the device is taken determine the humor of the device.

Incongruity, the juxtaposing of two contrasting objects, situations, people, or other elements of a scene, creates a humorous effect. A large woman wearing a very small hat, speech inappropriate to the speaker or occasion, a character in unfamiliar surroundings, and action contrary to the expectations of a character all produce laughter.

When a character loses his/her human flexibility and behaves mechanically, when situations repeat themselves as if a machine is at work, or when dialogue becomes repeated for comic effect, the playwright is making use of the device of *automatism.*

Many scenes illustrate more than one comic device. Identifying the comic devices used by the playwright gives the costume designer clues to costuming the characters.

Many playwrights have felt free to mix elements of several dramatic forms in the same play. This freedom provides a broad variety of plays for us to enjoy. Still, the predominant form should be identified to guide the direc-

Figure 2.3 *Still Life with Iris.* Flower Painter. Incongruity (flower pot hat and flowers growing from the toes) and exaggeration (large sleeves) create a gently comic costume. Designed by Bill Brewer for the University of Minnesota, Duluth.

tor and designers in making artistic decisions about the production. The choice of color, texture, and scale as well as the relative importance of the visual elements in the total production will vary according to the form of the play.

How Is the Play Structured? Elements of Drama

Plays are composed of certain elements, the proportion of which differs in each play, providing endless variations. These elements are *plot, character, theme, audio elements,* and *visual elements.*

Plot

The plot is the skeleton or armature on which the playwright molds the play. The plot is not the story, but the arrangement in which the events of the story are told, the form of its actions, dialogue, and characters.

Most plays are organized into "acts," which may be divided into "scenes." The action takes place in a series of interchanges between characters that are grouped together for a purpose: to give the audience background information, to establish circumstances, to demonstrate a challenge or problem, to find a solution, or to resolve the situation. Act divisions may indicate a passage of time, change of scene, or a turning point in the action. Blackouts, intermissions, or scene breaks mark time lapses and provide the opportunity to change scenery and costumes. Scenes can be organized in two basic ways: *climactic* and *episodic.*

A play with *climactic* structure follows a linear sequence of events, in chronological order, leading to a specific result. The plot begins late in the story, near the climax, and is shown in only one or two locales. Past incidents affecting the action are revealed by the dialogue. The number of characters is limited and the action is compressed into a brief time period. Some tightly constructed climactic plays are referred to as "well-made" plays. *Antigone* by Sophocles and *Of Mice and Men* by John Steinbeck are two examples of plays with climactic structure.

Plays written with an *episodic* structure exhibit many opposite characteristics, such as short, fragmented scenes; many threads of action; various locales; and numerous characters. The plot may begin early in the story and skip large segments of time or may be told in flashback or simultaneous scenes. Examples of episodic plays are *Peer Gynt* by Henrik Ibsen and *The Caucasian Chalk Circle* by Bertolt Brecht.

The structure of a play influences the design concept. Plays with climactic structures take place within a specific time frame. Logic, unity, and realism within the costumes may be indicated by this type of structure. Episodic plays usually give the designer more freedom because of their looser structure.

Character

The beings that inhabit the play are the characters through which the playwright presents a point of view and then challenges that view. Characters can be humans, animals, spirits, even concepts and normally inanimate objects. Characters in a play differ from characters in a novel because the audience rarely hears what the former are thinking. Occasionally a playwright uses a special device, such as a *soliloquy* or *monologue,* to give the audience insight into the character's mind. However, that knowledge is more commonly gained from a character's dialogue, actions, and reactions. Much must be read "between the lines." Actors and directors refer to such information as the *subtext.*

Play characters tend to fall into certain categories that are useful for designer/director discussions.

Those roles through and around which the primary action in a play is built are called *main characters* or *major characters.* They provide the focus of the plot and either precipitate the action or find themselves the recipients of it.

Supporting characters are smaller parts intended to support the action of the main characters. The playwright uses these characters—often very interesting roles—to provide balance and counterpoint to the main characters. Just as a composer repeats a theme on different instruments or introduces contrasting rhythms to a piece of music, a playwright may use supporting characters to emphasize a theme either by subtle variation, strong harmony, or sharp contrast.

The additional characters needed to complete the picture and populate the world of the play are called *extras.* Many playwrights specify who these people are—policemen, waiters, peasants; other playwrights leave that decision up to the director. A designer should be prepared to assist in designating the individuals in a crowd.

The *chorus* is a special group of extras. The original chorus in Greek drama spoke in unison to set the scene, comment on the action, and express the moral of the play. The Greek chorus was an anonymous group (townspeople, old men), not a group of individuals. The use of a chorus in contemporary drama is primarily found in opera and musical theater. Here the singing chorus may represent large groups of similar people (sailors, schoolgirls, nuns), or may be represented as individuals within a large group (a street scene including peddlers, newsboys, a taxi driver, rich "swells," a baby nurse with carriage, sailors on leave, schoolgirls, businessmen and women, and so on). In some modern plays the chorus has been reduced to one actor, the narrator; now the chorus becomes a supporting role or even major character.

Many modern plays are constructed for *ensemble* acting, where almost equal importance is given to all characters. The focus shifts from one character to another and back again throughout the play. Certain types of characters have long traditions in the theater, some dating back to Greek and Roman theater. *Stock characters* symbolize a particular type of person or an outstanding characteristic of human behavior to the exclusion of almost everything else. Found particularly in comedy, these characters develop surefire combinations of physical attributes, idiosyncrasies, and "comic bits" that have become linked to them for hundreds of years. Often known by the name given them during the development of the *commedia dell'arte,* these characters can be traced from Greek and Roman drama through Molière and Shakespeare and up to modern TV situation comedies. Two of the most familiar of these characters, Harlequin and Pantalon, are found in figure 2.4 in their traditional attire.

Similar to stock characters, *stereotypical characters* are recognizable types and express only two or three characteristics, often based on ethnic models. Lacking

Harlequin.   Zany Corneto.   Il Segnor Pantalon.

Figure 2.4 Commedia dell'arte. Sixteenth century. Wearing their traditional costumes, the patched and torn Harlequin and the bearded Pantalon in his robe sing to the accompaniment of the Zany Corneto. Drottningsholms Teatremuseum, Stockholm, Sweden.

depth as written, these characters depend on the actor and director to provide the human dimension neglected by the playwright.

Theme

As works of art, plays express the artist's vision or concept of the world. The playwright's vision includes not only the story to be told, but also the point of view from which it is told and the style (mode) in which it is told. Some playwrights support the prevailing philosophy of their age; some challenge the mores and morals of their time. Some plays are intended to enlighten us, some to entertain us.

The director searches the play for its theme and for ways to transmit that essence to the audience. The designer needs to understand this essence when conceptualizing the costumes, so the visual messages do not conflict with the underlying themes. Themes are rarely stated directly by the playwright. Careful reading and discussion with all members of the design/directing staff may be needed to determine the playwright's point of view.

Sometimes a shift in emphasis by the director can alter the overall concept of a play. The designer needs to be aware of the director's concept as well as the playwright's intent. A designer should ask for a clear statement of theme from the director. What aspects of the play does the director wish to stress? When directing George Bernard Shaw's *Major Barbara,* for example, a director might choose to emphasize the domestic situation (father–daughter conflict), the boy–girl relationships of the younger characters, the moral-political questions raised by the manufacture of munitions, or the religious questions of charity and salvation.

Audio Elements

Communication through sound is fundamental to drama. Except for mime or pantomime, all plays include audio elements. Character, ideas, and emotions are expressed through *dialogue,* from great poetic verse forms to common street language and even meaningless sounds. Verbal communication between characters reveals to us their situation, social standing, and education or intelligence, as well as information about other characters. Not only the lines as written, but the shades of meaning given them by the actor, reveal to us the nature of the character speaking. Is this a great man or a charlatan? Is this a prince or a pauper? Is this a warm or cold person? Does this character speak in down-to-earth language or elevated rhetoric?

The rhythms of the dialogue create a subtle feeling of music and movement that add to the understanding of the characters and the situations the playwright presents to us. Short, clipped speech moves us along rapidly with the action, whereas fluid, undulating speech creates a languid, romantic aura and touches us emotionally. The playwright uses choice of words, metaphors, and rhythms of speech as the designer uses fabric, color, and line. The designer should study the language of the play to find its appropriate visual expressions.

Many plays are enhanced with background *music* even though the script may not actually specify its use. Music can underscore the action or ease transitions; it can express the mood of the scene or provide clues to the characters or situations. Music can range from simple sound effects to complete musical scores for musicals, operettas, or operas. The more important the music becomes in a production, the more the costume designer must take it into consideration. In musical theater and opera the style of the music becomes the main consideration in one's visualization of the style of the production. Figure 2.5 shows how the decadent qualities expressed in the music for *The Threepenny Opera* can be reflected in the style of the costumes.

Visual Elements

Scenery, costumes, and lights produce the physical environment for the play. The set suggests the place, time, and atmosphere that combine to create the world of the play; it provides the areas for action, the arenas for the conflict required for the play. Stage lighting illuminates the action and intensifies the atmosphere. Like music, lighting can create strong emotional reactions in an audience. The costumes define the characters and relate to the other visual elements. The total impression conveyed by

Figure 2.5 *The Threepenny Opera.* The decadent qualities of Kurt Weill's music are suggested in use of fabric and textures in this costume. Designed by the author for Brooklyn College. (See also color plate 5.)

these visual elements must support the theme and concept of the play and set the mood intended by the playwright.

Movement and dance introduced into a play create interest, express moods and feelings, and help set the atmosphere for scenes and events. Many plays call for crowd scenes, parades, battle scenes, and other large gatherings on stage to provide contrast to the more intimate scenes and to show the relationship of a character to the surrounding community.

Modern productions often introduce slides, film, and other special effects to advance the play rapidly and effectively by providing information visually.

The proportions of these elements in each production depend on the purpose of the playwright, the concept of the director, the budget, and the audience for which the production is intended.

Most plays are written with stress on one or two of these elements. Some plays, like *The Italian Straw Hat* by Eugene Labiche and Marc-Michel, stress plot and action, leaving the characters two-dimensional and underdeveloped. Other plays, like Arthur Miller's *Death of a Salesman,* are deep character studies with little action or spectacle. Most plays are open to numerous interpretations and variations. One production might stress the philosophical or political ideas inherent in a script by stripping away the audio and visual elements. Another production of the same play may use the visual and audio elements to stress the poetry and romance also embodied within the text. The question to be answered is not, "Is this right or wrong?," but, "Does this work for *this* production?"

The balance of the elements can shift and change, but no element should be overemphasized to the detriment of the meaning of the play or the playwright's intention.

In What Mode (Style) Is the Play Written?

. . . for style is for the writer, as for the painter, a question, not of technique but of vision. It is the revelation—impossible by direct and conscious means—of the qualitative differences in the way the world appears to us, differences which, but for art, would remain the eternal secret of each of us.

Remembrance of Things Past, Marcel Proust

The style and manner of expression chosen by the playwright to convey the play's meaning is referred to as the *mode of drama.* Effective costumes may depend on the designer's understanding of the play's mode or style. Plays written within a historical period and cultural milieu usually share many characteristics reflecting the prevailing philosophy and morals of that age. Playwrights have often been among the vanguard of artistic movements that have included visual artists, philosophers, architects, and writers of other literary forms. To fully understand a given play, the designer may need to examine the historical context and the prevailing philosophies of its period, and to study the visual arts and other literary works of its time.

All theatrical styles have certain *conventions* that have developed to assist in their presentation. A stage whisper is accepted by the audience as an intimate comment, unheard by the other characters on stage, even though hundreds of audience members heard it quite clearly. The conventions of musical theater allow the characters to burst into song whenever the mood strikes them. Once the style of the play is established, the audience can accept spotlights, masks, voice projection, and many other "tricks of the trade."

Broadly speaking, plays can be divided into two styles, *representational* and *presentational*. Representational plays propose to show events from life as they happen and allow the audience to "overhear" the action. The goal of a representational production is to have the audience forget it is in the theater and, to that end, the actors never acknowledge their presence. A presentational performance seeks to challenge the audience directly, to heighten the experience by making the audience participate in the event. The conventions of a presentational play allow the actors to step out of character and address the audience, leave the stage and mingle with the audience, and otherwise break the audience/stage barrier. Plays of both styles can be found among the plays in the following modes. Since artists from all aesthetic forms may share the philosophical and social milieu of specific movements, their work may also be labeled as the same mode or style.

Classicism

The word "classic" has many shades of meaning. The mode of "classic" drama is derived from the style of Greek plays. Usually describing tragedies, classicism stresses order, clean line, and a formal structure, the same values reflected in classic sculpture and architecture. Written in verse, classical plays emphasize dialogue, emotion, and ideas, and minimize action. Violence is rarely seen: only the result of violence is displayed or discussed. *Classical tragedies* stress universal concepts and explore humanity's relationship to the gods or the forces of fate. The main characters of classical tragedies are extraordinary people—kings, queens, or children of the gods—who are caught in some kind of monumental struggle. *Classical comedies* are based on Greek and Roman models and explore the follies of man.

Sometimes a play may be referred to as a "classic." This use of the word does not refer to its style, but to the fact that it is an outstanding example of its type, whatever style or form that may be, and that it deserves to be produced for and enjoyed by audiences of all times.

Later playwrights, admiring the great Greek classical plays, attempted to write new plays in the same style. These *neoclassic* plays were written in verse and followed the same general construction as their models.

Costumes designed for plays in the classic or neoclassic mode usually stress clean, flowing lines; simple shapes; and formal grace.

Romanticism

Plays in the romantic style glorify love, exaggerate emotion, and tend to suffer from an excess of "prettiness" and a lack of depth. The various meanings of the word "romantic" can be misleading to a designer. "Romantic" can describe any play that is about tender feelings and sweet emotions and that has a basically optimistic, happy ending. The term "Romantic" is also used to designate a style of literature from the early nineteenth century. This entire period is sometimes called the Romantic Period and some costume history authors designate clothing from this period as Romantic Costume. When a designer or director uses this term, the meaning should be made absolutely clear.

Romantic costumes tend to be in pastel or floral tones; to make excessive use of ribbons, lace, and trim; and to have a generally frothy and youthful effect.

Sentimentalism

An unembarrassed appeal for pity or sympathy and an unquenchable optimism may signal an excessive dose of *sentimentalism* in a play. An intensely good or innocent character, like a child or animal (whose sole or primary claim to the attention of the audience is being intensely pathetic), may be the central character, seen struggling against seemingly insurmountable odds. A style associated with melodrama, sentimentalism has broad appeal but little depth. *The Streets of New York* by Dion Boucicault is typical of the nineteenth-century sentimental melodrama.

Realism

The predominant mode of modern drama is realism. Realism seeks to show life as it is. Influenced by the philosophies of Darwin, Marx, and Freud, playwrights began in the late 1800s to write plays about ordinary men and women caught in familiar dilemmas. While still carefully constructed, the plays of the realists minimized the histrionics and artifice of the prevalent nineteenth-century styles and eventually influenced acting and directing profoundly. Using everyday language, playwrights built plays stressing ideas rather than action, and revealing the emotions and motivations of the characters. The audience was allowed to look "through the keyhole" at the everyday lives of the characters. For the realistic style, every attempt is made to reproduce correctly the details of dress and accessories, allowing for the requirements of the theater. Examples of realistic drama are *The Little Foxes* by Lillian Hellman and *Cat on a Hot Tin Roof* by Tennessee Williams. Figure 2.6 is a costume for *Pride and Prejudice* with realistic period details.

Selective realism is an approach that chooses or "selects" certain aspects of a play (usually the costumes and props) and represents them realistically while treating other aspects of the production (the set and lights) in a fragmentary, abstract, or stylized manner.

Naturalism

An extreme form of realism, naturalism was an effort to present in the most direct and immediate way, through the language and the physical aspects of the play, the utmost in reality. Also emerging in the late 1800s, naturalism gave way to other forms, in part because of the difficulties of production. Stage representations of a tenement, for example, were no longer adequate for the naturalist; a *real* tenement would be reassembled on stage. Plots emphasized the predestination of man as shaped by his heredity and environment. The form produced some notable works such as Maxim Gorky's *Lower Depths* before its proponents drifted away into other styles.

Stylization

In the twentieth century many movements sought effective modes of theatrical expression. The term *stylization* has come to mean some departure from realistic presentation. The key to stylized presentation is to find a visual expression of the spirit and meaning of a play. These modes of presentation are often related to movements in the visual arts and are also important in opera and dance presentation.

Symbolism

Plays in this style deal not with intellect and logic, but with the spiritual aspects of life. The significance of silence and the duality of objects, personality, actions, and situations are explored. Whereas the realist holds up a mirror to reflect the reality of life for the audience, the symbolist offers the audience a window through which to view the spirituality of life. One such play is *The Blue Bird* by Maurice Maeterlinck.

The word "symbolism" in common usage has come to mean any partial representation of objects or actions, or an action, object, or decorative motif that represents an idea, person, or other action. Since all literary works contain some metaphors or symbols, the director or designer may decide to stress one of these literary devices to conceptualize the playwright's theme for the audience.

Symbolic costumes take many forms. Some may represent an inanimate object like a "rose" or a concept like "love." In fact all costumes are symbolic in some way since their function is to help the actors represent people or things other than themselves.

Figure 2.6 *Pride and Prejudice*. Caroline. Realistic details give great depth and texture to a costume and to a production. Designed by Mathew J. LeFebvre for The Guthrie Theater. Photo by Michal Daniel.

Constructivism

Not a style of play, but an approach to visual interpretation, constructivism was developed by Vsevolod Meyerhold. He rejected pictorial realism and naturalism and laid bare the machinery of the stage for the audience to see. Ramps, stairs, platforms, and other structural elements were combined, with the primary purpose of maximum mobility for the actor through various kinds and levels of acting space. Illusions were banned, and decorations were eliminated or minimized. The resulting skeletal assemblage emphasized an individual's position in the mechanized world in a bold and dynamic way. Many plays that are written in other styles have been produced in this mode.

Expressionism

A very subjective style, expressionism forces the audience to view the action through the eyes of the central character. Distortion and repetition are substituted for character development. An expressionistic play presents a mental landscape.

Emerging from the turmoil of World War I and the Russian Revolution, expressionistic plays were a reaction to the mechanization and dehumanization of humanity. These plays are harsh and provocative, pointing out the limits of human morality and sanity. Some plays in this genre are *The Adding Machine* by Elmer Rice and *The Skin of Our Teeth* by Thornton Wilder. Figure 2.7 depicts a scene from *The Adding Machine* showing the machine as an enormous apparatus almost beyond human control.

Related to the works of constructivism and expressionism are the theater works of the Dada art movement and the dance designs by the painters of cubism and the Bauhaus school. These works often emphasize the concept of "man as machine." Figure 2.8 shows costumes done by the artist Sonia Delaunay in the cubist style.

Figure 2.7 The Expressionistic mode (style) is usually more evident in scenery than in costumes, as in this scene from the 1923 production of *The Adding Machine.* Billy Rose Theater Collection, The New York Public Library at Lincoln Center; Astor, Lenox and Tilden Foundations.

Figure 2.8 An emphasis on geometric shape reflects the cubist style of these costumes by Sonia Delaunay. (*Rythmes et couleurs,* Hermann, editeurs des sciences et des arts, Paris, 1971)

Epic Theater

Epic theater, a very presentational style, was developed by Bertolt Brecht. Generally episodic in structure, Brecht's plays make no effort to disguise the fact that an actor is "playing a role." Often the actors sit on the stage until called upon to present themselves in a scene. The audience is to be aware of being in a theater at all times. Visual elements are very theatrical, not necessarily realistic. *Mother Courage* and *The Caucasian Chalk Circle* are two of Brecht's best-known plays.

Documentary

The documentary is a dramatization in a "news format." Declaring itself objective, a documentary basically has an educational purpose. This mode was used by the Federal Theater Project for *The Living Newspaper* during the Great Depression.

Absurdism

Believing the modern world to be absurd, playwrights in this genre stress a sense of alienation in an illogical, unjust, ridiculous world. Representing an existentialist point of view, these plays are peopled with characters devoid of personal motivation and past history. Absurdist plays defy logic, traditional beliefs, and common understandings. They challenge the audience with nonsense, non sequiturs, and contradictory statements, as in the excerpt from *The Bald Soprano* in Box 2.A. Many of these plays are written with a climactic structure, but the result of the series of actions is illogical. Absurdists are fond of using comic devices for ironic effects and poking fun at sacred ideas. Samuel Beckett's *Waiting for Godot* and Eugene Ionesco's *The Bald Soprano* are two celebrated absurdist plays.

Costumes for constructivist, expressionist, and absurdist plays range from rather realistic to exaggerated and distorted variations of dress.

Box 2.A   Absurdist dialogue: *The Bald Soprano* by Eugene Ionesco

Mrs. Smith: Poor Bobby.

Mr. Smith: Which Bobby do you mean?

Mrs. Smith: It is his wife that I mean. She is called Bobby too, Bobby Watson. Since they both had the same name, you could never tell one from the other when you saw them together. It was only after his death that you could really tell which was which. And there are still people today who confuse her with the deceased and offer their condolences to him. Do you know her?

Mr. Smith: I only met her once, by chance, at Bobby's burial.

Mrs. Smith: I've never seen her. Is she pretty?

Mr. Smith: She has regular features and yet one cannot say that she is pretty. She is too big and stout. Her features are not regular but still one can say that she is very pretty. She is a little too small and too thin. She's a voice teacher.

(The clock strikes five times. A long silence.)

In the late twentieth and early twenty-first centuries, even realistic plays have often been presented in the mode of the more stylized theatrical forms. Scenery is now often focused on "playing spaces" and visual decoration is limited or omitted. Mood is established by music and lighting effects; locale is produced by projections. Visual icons are developed to represent the theme of the play and not the location. Little attempt is made to hide the fact that the audience is in a theater.

Establishing the Mode

When producing plays from other periods, the director and the designer are first faced with the question, "Should this play be produced in its original style or be reinterpreted?" Some plays can be successfully interpreted in many ways, while others depend so heavily on their mode for substance that they are extremely difficult to successfully reinterpret in any major way. Many plays originally presented in the realistic style can be reinterpreted in a selective realism or other stylized concept. A play written in the expressionistic style, however, depends heavily on that mode for its meaning and loses its impact in too realistic a production.

One of the first important functions of collaboration between designers and directors is the discussion of the style or mode of the play. However, the director is the final authority on style for any given production and makes the decision either to follow the playwright's intention, to give a historically accurate interpretation, or to reinterpret the script from a new point of view. Establishing the mode or style of a play gives the designer a point from which to conceptualize and visualize the play.

Reading the Play

> . . . 'Tis not alone my inky cloak, good mother,
> Nor customary suits of solemn black,
> Nor windy suspiration of forced breath,
> No, nor the fruitful river in the eye,
> Nor the dejected 'havior of the visage,
> Together with all forms, moods, shapes of grief,
> That can denote me truly. These indeed seem,
> For they are actions that a man might play.
> But I have that within which passeth show;
> These but the trappings and the suits of woe.
>
> *Hamlet*, William Shakespeare

The *first reading* of a script establishes an overall sense of the story and characters. Reading the play in one sitting also should provide a good sense of its flow and movement. The designer should try to find pleasure in this first reading and should resist the temptation to take extensive notes. *After* the first reading, the designer might make notes on the structure, form, and mode of the play. What themes were apparent from the first reading? The designer should try not to prejudge and impose personal taste on the play.

During the *second reading* the designer's attention should focus on the language and imagery of the play. What kind of language does the playwright use? Poetry? Street talk? Dialect? Witty repartee? Does it vary with the characters? What rhythms are established? What words or phrases are repeated often? How do they relate to the central theme? What are the most meaningful phrases in each scene and who says them? Does one image represent the central theme or the soul of the play?

While these questions should be considered, the designer must remember that the primary responsibility for the interpretation of the script and development of the production concept belongs to the director. The designer must be prepared, however, to participate intelligently in discussions with the director. The director's concept may be stated in nonvisual terms, and the designer may need to translate the concept into a visual idea. A central part of the collaborative process is the exchange of ideas about the visual and conceptual needs of the play.

Some ideas come to the designer spontaneously while he or she is reading the script. The designer should be open to impressions, ideas, and flashes of inspiration that come during the first and second readings, without stopping to analyze or work them out.

After a designer has a clear understanding of the general outlines of the script and of the director's thoughts on the play, a meticulous *third reading* should provide answers to specific questions. All possibilities and all limitations should be sought. Many designers mark references to costumes, entrances, exits, and pertinent action in the script with a pen or yellow marker. A designer should be prepared to do as many readings and referrals to the script as necessary to answer whatever questions arise.

Determining the historical period of the play is a necessity for the costume designer. Some plays clearly indicate the time in which the play is set, either in a foreword or by reference to historical characters or events. What purpose did the playwright have for setting the play in a specific period? In what way does the essence of the time affect the characters or the action? If the playwright has not specified a date, the style of the play may suggest a time period. A strongly romantic play may suggest to a designer a period in which the costumes are particularly soft and flowing or light in hue. Some plays take place in a fantasy time, either in the past or in the future. The designer and the director must carefully discuss the aspects of the "time" in which these plays take place.

Careful study of a play may suggest relationships to other periods that the designer may wish to suggest for consideration. Some directors want to move plays out of the time in which they are written in order to point out these relationships or the universality of the theme of the play.

Many plays are thus transferred to the present or "no period." An unspecific time, "no period" sometimes is a combination of long dresses (of no particular period) for women and long pants, shirts, and coats for men. At other times, a complete abstract world may be constructed to provide an imaginary time and place in which to set the play. Here again it is necessary to collaborate completely with the director and other designers.

If no reference to the date can be found, the designer may assume the play was set in the time in which it was written. Even with a historical play, the date it was *written* may be as important to a designer as the period in which it is set. The influence of the playwright's world will be reflected in any play, even if set in another period. Many plays have been set in a historical period either to disguise or to reveal the playwright's view of a contemporary situation. For example, *The Resistible Rise of Arturo Ui* by Bertolt Brecht draws a frightening parallel between Hitler and the crime lords of Chicago.

From the second and successive readings of the play, the costume designer makes detailed notes on each character. How many characters are there? Are they male or female? What kind of characters are they? Main characters? Chorus members? Stock characters? How are they used? To present information? To focus attention? To state the playwright's point of view? What specifics are known about each one? Some playwrights give detailed descriptions of each character in the stage directions; others give no specific description. The designer ferrets out the needed information from what the character says or from what is said about the character. Specific facts and adjectives are sought. A character's actions reveal important information, but what he or she fails to do may be equally revealing. All other conditions suggested by the playwright must be considered as well—occasion, time of day, climate or weather conditions, specific action requiring costume accessories.

In box 2.B, an excerpt from *Pygmalion,* Bernard Shaw gives us a complete description of Liza. While the designer is not in all cases bound by the playwright's description, careful consideration should be given to the playwright's intent. More binding to the designer is information about a character that is found in the dialogue. In box 2.C, an excerpt from *Twelfth Night,* Maria describes Malvolio as wearing yellow, cross-gartered stockings, information that the costume designer should not overlook.

Box 2.B   Costume description in stage directions:
***Pygmalion* by Bernard Shaw**

The Flower Girl (picking up her scattered flowers and replacing them in the basket): Theres menners f' yer! Te-oo banches o voylets trod into the mad. (She sits down on the plinth of the column, sorting her flowers, on the lady's right. She is not at all a romantic figure. She is perhaps eighteen, perhaps twenty, hardly older. She wears a little sailor hat of black straw that has long been exposed to the dust and soot of London and has seldom if ever been brushed. Her hair needs washing rather badly: its mousy color can hardly be natural. She wears a shoddy black coat that reaches nearly to her knees and is shaped to her waist. She has a brown skirt with a coarse apron. Her boots are much the worse for wear. She is no doubt as clean as she can afford to be; but compared to the ladies she is very dirty. Her features are no worse than theirs; but their condition leaves something to be desired; and she needs the services of a dentist).

Act I

Box 2.C   Costume description in dialogue:
***Twelfth Night* by William Shakespeare**

Maria: If you will see the fruits of the sport, mark his first approach before my lady: he will come to her in yellow stockings, and 'tis a color she abhors, and cross-gartered, a fashion she detests; and he will smile upon her, which will now be so unsuitable to her disposition, being addicted to a melancholy as she is, that it cannot but turn him into a notable contempt. If you will see it, follow me.

Act II, Scene V

The designer should try to visualize the action in each scene as if sitting in the middle of the theater. Is the same actor who was the last character on stage in one scene also the first one on stage in the next scene? Is there a time lapse? Is a costume change indicated? Will that costume need to be rigged for a "quick change"? What physical activities are required of the actors? Dancing? Acrobatics? Bike riding? Tricks? Is anyone in disguise? Does the audience know about the disguise? Are the other characters fooled?

Boxes 2.D and 2.E are sample designer checklists for play analysis and character information. Answering these questions helps the designer focus on the information needed to design the show.

Arranging pertinent information in a *costume plot* (figure 2.9 on pp. 36–37) provides a visual reference that helps set the play in the designer's mind and facilitates quick retrieval of information. The costume plot is a chart that helps organize the structure and needs of the play by providing a box for each character and each division of the script—act, scene, or musical number. In each box are listed the costume items needed and pertinent information about entrances,

Box 2.D   Designer checklist I: Play analysis

1. What form of drama is this play? Could it be interpreted any other way?
2. What type of structure does it have? What is the basic story?
3. In what style (mode) is it written? Could it be interpreted in other ways?
4. Where and when does this play take place? What are the climatic conditions? Are there other possibilities?
5. What is the mood of the play? Does this vary with scenes or characters? What are the pivotal scenes (turning points in the course of events)?
6. What colors and textures are suggested by the mood, style, and form of drama of this play?
7. What images are evoked throughout the play? Do they reoccur? To whom are these images related? Which images are central to or represent the soul or spirit of the play? List words that evoke visual images. Do images change from scene to scene?
8. What is the time sequence of the play? In what season(s) do the scenes take place?
9. Can the images in the play be visualized? Do they relate to characters specifically?
10. How does the playwright use the various characters in the play? To which other characters does each character relate? With what other characters is he or she in conflict?
11. What comic devices does the playwright use?
12. Outline the action of each scene.
13. Combine information in a chart and/or costume plot that graphically illustrates the action and costume needs of the play.

Box 2.E   Designer checklist II: Character information

1. What kind of character is this—major, minor, stock, abstract, allegorical?
2. What are the character's physical characteristics?
    a. Age?
    b. Physical appearance?
    c. Carriage and bearing? Vitality?
    d. Ethnic background?
    e. Mannerisms or affectations?
    f. Speech patterns or dialect?
3. What are the character's mental characteristics?
    a. Education? IQ?
    b. Artistic accomplishments or tendencies?
    c. Ability to relate to reality?

4. What personality traits does this character exhibit? What is the character's emotional state? Does it change as the play progresses? Introvert or extrovert?

5. What is the character's social status or rank?

    a. Economic status?

    b. Moral viewpoint?

    c. Religion?

    d. Profession?

    e. Political viewpoint?

    f. Social standing with peers?

6. What is the character's objective? Does this character represent the playwright's point of view?

7. How should the dress of this character reflect this analysis?

8. What events in the life of this character have had lasting effects on his or her character?

9. What specific references are made in the script to this character's clothing? What action does this character perform that might affect the clothing? For what occasions is this character present in the play? In what scenes does this character appear; is he or she the focal point or supporting character?

10. Will the actor cast in this role need special padding, shoes, or other items to "look the part"?

11. Do the characters dress in agreement with all aspects of their personalities and roles or do they attempt to hide, disguise, or deny the reality of their personalities from the other characters and/or the audience?

exits, costume business, and quick changes in that scene. The first version of the costume plot is usually done by hand, but most designers quickly set up the plot as an Excel spreadsheet or Word table. The computer makes changes and updates quick and easy all the way up to opening night. Brief descriptions of time-of-day, scene action, or setting are also helpful. The costume plot should be updated as needed throughout the design process. It helps to focus designer/director discussions and to simplify the designer's research and planning. Some designers develop the costume plot in depth to facilitate their understanding of the play. Ultimately, the final version of the plot can be given to the wardrobe crew as a valuable guide for the organization of quick changes.

Collaboration: Director–Designer Discussions

At some point during the process of reading and studying the play, the designer has a first conference with the director. Each director has an individual

COSTUME PLOT

DESIGNER: _R. CUNNINGHAM_

PRODUCTION: _MEMORY OF WATER_

SET: VI'S BEDROOM – LONG ISLAND – 1980'S

CHARACTERS - ACTORS	ACT I– SC 1 P. 1-15	P. 16-27	P. 28-40	P. 41-42	P. 43-45	P. 46-48	INTERMISSION	ACT II– SC 1 P. 49-50	SC 2 P. 5-59	SC 3 P. 60-89	P. 90
J. AULTZ **MARY** (01)	PLATE #1-0101 SUNGLASSES, PAJAMA PANTS, BL. SWEATER, PINK SLIPPERS,	PLATE #2-0102 (FROM SUITCASE) SAND-COLORED SWEATER, JEANS, TUBE SOCKS, BLUE SNEAKERS,	SAME	SAME	0103- DUPLICATE OF VI'S GREEN DRESS (0201) **ONSTAGE CHANGE** ☆	SAME		SAME	PLATE #2 -SAME AS ACT I SC I SAND- COLORED SWEATER, JEANS, TUBE SOCKS, BLUE SNEAKERS **QUICK** ☆ **CHANGE**	PLATE #3-0104 BLK PANTS, BLK TOP, BLACK BELT, PEARL NECKLACE, PEARL PIN & EARRINGS, BLK JACKET, BOOTS	PLATE # 4-0105 WOOL COAT, GLOVES, WHITE KNIT HAT, RED PRINT SCARF, BLACK PURSE
K. SQUITIERI **VI** (02)	PLATE #5-0201 GRN TAFFETA DRESS, CROSS, SILVERSHOES, EARRINGS, WATCH, PANTY HOSE, PETTICOAT	X	X	X	X	SAME		SAME	X	PLATE #6-0202 PINK DRESS, PINK SLIPPERS, GRAY WIG, PANTY HOSE	X
D. HERTZBERG **TERESA** (03)	PLATE #7 –0301 STRIPED SWEATER, WHITE CARDIGAN, GREY SKIRT, BROWN SHOES, BLK HOSE, BEADED BELT, NECKLACE, EARRINGS, HAIR ORNAMENT	SAME	SAME	SAME	SAME	X		X	SAME	PLATE #8-0302 BLACK TURTLENECK, NECKLACE, EARRINGS, BLACK SKIRT, GREY SUIT JACKET, BOOTS, BLK PANTY HOSE	PLATE #9-0303 GLOVES, TWEED COAT, TWEED HAT, PURSE, STRIPED SCARF
V. GALLOWAY **CATHERINE** (04)	PLATE #10-0401 WHITE COAT, KNIT PINK HAT & GLOVES, DENIM JACKET, PK/WH PURSE, "ELTON JOHN" SHOES, WH. JEWELED TOP, JEANS, HOSE, SILVER/BLK. EARRINGS, COLORFUL SCARF, EXTRA SCARF	BLACK VELVET JACKET SAME AS PLATE # 12-0403	SAME	SAME	SAME	SAME		X	SAME	PLATE # 11-0402 DRESSING GOWN P. 87 – PLATE 12 #0403 WHITE LONG- SLEEVE TOP, BLACK VELVET JACKET (SAME AS 0402, BLACK MINI-SKIRT, OPAQUE BLK TIGHTS, BOOTS	WHITE COAT KNIT PINK HAT & GLOVES, DENIM JACKET, PINK/WHITE PURSE, SILVER/BLK EARRINGS, SAME AS PLATE # 10- 0401 BOOTS SAME AS PLATE 12 #0403
J. HILTON **MIKE** (05)		X	X	PLATE #13-0501 COLORFUL TIE, BLUE SHIRT, SILK SCARF, GRAY SUIT, GRAY OVERCOAT, GRAY SOCKS, BLK GLOVES, GRAY HAT, WEDDING RING, WATCH, PINKY RING	SAME	SAME		X	PG. 58- TOWEL WRAP PLATE #14-0502 WOMAN'S ROBE	SUIT, ETC. SAME AS PLATE #13-0501 BUT WITH SOLEMN TIE	COAT, ETC SAME AS PLATE #13-0501 BUT WITH SOLEMN TIE
M. ARMSTRONG **FRANK** (06)		X	X	X	X	PLATE #14-0601 BRN COAT, BOOTS, WATCH, TAN GLOVES TWEED HAT & SCARF, SOCKS, GR. TWEED JACKET. WEDDING RING, TAN STRIPED SHIRT, KHAKI PANTS, WH. COTTON SWEATER, GREEN TIE		X	SAME	PLATE #15-0602 TAN STRIPED SHIRT, SWEATER VEST, CHARCOAL PANTS, BLK JACKET, RD/BL TIE, SAME WATCH, BOOTS, WEDDING RING	BR. COAT, TWEEDY SCARF AND HAT, GLOVES, SAME AS PLATE #14
PROP CLOTHES	SUITCASE OF EXTRA CLOTHES	X	X	8 EXTRA DRESSES TO PACK, COCKTAIL DRESS, PINK HAT	MORE CLOTHES, HAIR PIECE, HAT, DAYWEAR	X		GREEN DRESS	X	X	X

Figure 2.9A Costume plot. Analyzing and arranging information about the play in the plot helps the designer to visualize the whole play and its costume needs at a glance. This plot has been updated mid-production as more detailed information became available.

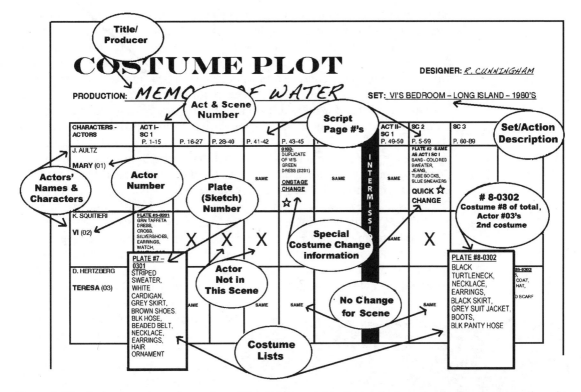

Figure 2.9B   A close-up view of a portion of the costume plot indicates the way the designer arranges the relevant information in the plot.

approach to directing a play. Some directors present the designers with a complete plan and specific requirements at the first meeting; others speak in very abstract terms at first and more specifically later. Some never give the designer specifics. Some directors are nonvisual; they do not have or cannot express visual ideas. The designer must learn to interpret and translate the director's verbal concepts into visual ideas.

Ideally, the designer and director develop a working relationship that stimulates the best ideas and work from both of them. This type of relationship occurs more easily with an atmosphere of mutual respect and a spirit of cooperation.

Because the amount of pre-production time varies with each producing organization, the length and scope of these meetings also varies. The more "homework" a designer has done, the more productive the director–designer conferences should be.

The designer may return many times to the script for further information and inspiration. Any unanswered questions the designer has from reading the play should be addressed to the director. If the director cannot answer the question, the final clue may come from the actor's interpretation of the character. Because the rehearsal period is an exploratory time, many discoveries are made and new ideas are continually being tried out. The designer must be prepared for some revisions in concepts as the actors and the director explore the script together. The director and/or stage manager should inform the designer of innovations that affect the costumes, but the wise designer makes time to attend rehearsals periodically to evaluate the situation personally. On the other hand, the wise director realizes that major changes in concept are extremely costly and time-consuming once construction of costumes has begun and prepares thoroughly in advance to minimize the necessity for major changes.

Other questions for the director include: Will any roles be double cast (two actors in one role) or doubled (same actor playing two roles)? How many extras are planned and how are they to be used? What budget has been allotted to costumes? What are the director's priorities? How will the costumes be used? Are the pockets, closures, or other costume features practical (do they need to be real or can they be faked)? Learning to formulate good questions is an important skill for the designer. Questions that begin with, "How do you see . . . ?," What do you have in mind for . . . ?," or, "What would you like for . . . ?" are good discussion openers.

The costume designer may at this time meet the scenic and lighting designers. Their plans may affect the final approach to the costumes. Often the scenic designer is hired before the costume designer. The style of the scenery may already be established and the costume designer may need to work within that framework. Usually the lighting designer will wait until certain work on the scenery has been completed before making a lot of decisions, but he or she may have ideas about what color light would establish the correct mood in each scene. Questions of the scenic designer include: How high and wide are the doors? Are there stairs? Ramps? Rough textures? Will the stage floor be flat or raked? Will there be adequate room for backstage changes? What kind of furniture will be used? Will there be tables on stage on which characters may place accessories, or will the actors have to carry them throughout the scene?

Some designers find it helpful to prepare a visual representation of their understanding of the play and/or the director's concept of the play. This might be a paper and paste or computer collage or a painting of the visual ideas developing in the reading and discussion of the play. Figure 2.10 is a conceptualization done by computer for *The Tempest* expressing the influence of nature and its forces on Prospero.

Figure 2.10 Concept board. This computer collage for *The Tempest* expresses the influence of nature's forces on Prospero. Designed by the author.

Developing this concept board helps the designer organize his/her thoughts and present them more clearly to the director.

Not all of this information may be available at the first designer/director conference, but the sooner these questions are answered, the better the planning and the fewer problems there will be as the production progresses. With the availability of e-mail, cell phones, and text messaging, the designer and director have the ability to ask and respond to questions immediately. An agreement on the use of e-mail communication should be arranged early in the process between the design team members and the director. However, even with electronic communication, face-to-face collaboration is still necessary and meaningful.

Good collaboration among director, designers, and actors takes patience, experience, and skill. The designer must understand that the production of a unified whole is the goal. Some personalities work better together than others, but all members of the team must learn to cooperate and make concessions to accomplish the goal. The key to good collaboration is respect for the talents of all parties involved in the production. Box 2.F is a designer checklist to assist the designer in conferences with the director.

Box 2.F   Designer checklist III: Director–designer conference

1. What does the director see as the mode (style) and form of the drama of the play?

2. What theme or concept has the director developed for the play? Is the concept clearly stated?

3. Can the play be described in one word? Innocent? Decadent? Frivolous? Does that word express the *essence* of the play?

4. How does the director see the characters? How many male and how many female? What physical types are they? What psychological types? What image does the director wish projected by each character?

5. Will any roles be doubled or double cast? How many costumes will need to be duplicated for additional cast, for stress, or for other practical considerations?

6. How many extras are planned? How are they to be used?

7. How many changes of costume for each character does the director envision?

8. How elaborate is the production to be? What is the budget?

9. What are the director's priorities?

10. When is casting to be completed?

11. When do dress rehearsals begin? Are any pieces needed before dress rehearsals (rehearsal props)?

12. What deadlines need to be set?

13. Set up a production calendar. Include dates for dress rehearsals, dress parade, fittings, measurements, final sketch approval, preliminary sketch conference, and first blocking rehearsals.

The Production Schedule

At the first or second meeting the designer and director should establish a set of deadlines for the production. Many producing organizations have guidelines for the production schedule already established. If not, the director, stage manager, and producer should develop a production schedule with the agreement of the technical staff involved in the production. The costume designer should take the established production schedule and add dates pertinent to the costume design process. Starting from opening night and working backward, dates are set for dress rehearsals, measuring actors, discussing finished sketches and roughs for the costumes, and all other director–designer and designer–actor meetings. As the work proceeds, more deadlines are added to the production schedule. The schedule varies according to the length of time available for a specific production. Some productions have six to nine months to develop; others are pulled together in days. The essential meetings and deadlines are spread out or compressed as allotted time requires.

Keeping Organized

Using the general production schedule as a guide, the costume designer should keep a personal calendar with day-to-day appointments, general notations (shopping day), and meetings. A notebook binder with schedules, calendars, copies of sketches, actor measurements, swatches, shopping lists, and meeting notations should be with the designer at all times. The designer must take notes on everything. (See sample production schedule, figure 2.11.) Setting up the schedule as a calendar on a computer makes adjustments easy and quick.

Developing and Stating a Concept

Fair ladies—shine upon us like the sun,
Blossom like flowers around us.

Cyrano de Bergerac, Edmond Rostand

A major goal of the director–designer conferences is to state a specific approach to, or concept for, the entire production. Doing this may take several discussions, with time for research and thought in between. Not every production of every play can have a new and exciting concept. However, every production of every play should make a *clear statement*. Usually, a concept emerges naturally and organically from studying the script and conferring with the director.

Here are some suggestions for developing concepts:

1. Study notes made from the script. What visual images are expressed? Are they related? Play word games with the recurring adjectives. For examples: airy—light—angel—wings—feathers. Can these words be translated into a visual concept?

DESIGNER'S PRODUCTION SCHEDULE						
	SUNDAY	**MONDAY**	**TUESDAY**	**WEDNESDAY**	**THURSDAY**	**FRIDAY**	**SATURDAY**
WEEK 1	•MEETING DIRECTOR, COSTUMES, LIGHTS, & SETS	•MEETING SHOP CREW •RESEARCH	•RESEARCH	•SWATCHING •RESEARCH	•SKETCHING	•SKETCHING •MEETING: DIRECTOR	•SKETCHING
WEEK 2	•SKETCHING	•MEETING: ROUGHS, DIRECTOR •SKETCHING	•CHECK STOCK	•MEETING: ☆ FINALS WITH DIRECTOR •SWATCHING	•SWATCHING •SKETCHING	•MEETING: REWORKS WITH DIRECTOR	•SHOPPING
WEEK 3	•SHOPPING	•READ THRU ☆ •PRESENT SKETCHES •SHOPPING	•MEASUREMENTS	•PRODUCTION MEETING	•PULL STOCK •PATTERN SUPERVISION		•PUBLICITY PHOTO CALL
WEEK 4	•SHOPPING		•ALL FABRIC ☆ DUE IN SHOP	•PRODUCTION MEETING •MUSLIN FITTINGS	•MEETING: DYER •DUMMY (RACK) SHOW	•SEE FIRST RUN THRU	
WEEK 5		•APPOINTMENT RENTAL HOUSE ☆	•SHOPPING	•PRODUCTION MEETING •MEETINGS: HAIR/WIGS	•MEETING: FABRIC PAINTER	•SHOPPING ACCESSORIES	•SEE RUN THRU
WEEK 6	•FINAL ☆ FITTINGS	•RENTALS ☆ DUE IN SHOP	•MEETING: WARDROBE	•PRODUCTION MEETING	•DRESS PARADE •RUN THRU	•NOTES •ORGANIZE WARDROBE	•FULL DRESS ☆
WEEK 7	•NOTES •FULL DRESS •PHOTO CALL	•PRODUCTION MEETING •DRESS REHEARSAL	•DRESS REHEARSAL	•PREVIEW	•PREVIEW	☆ ☆ OPENING NIGHT ☆ ☆	

Figure 2.11 Designer's production schedule. The calendar varies, depending on the length of time available. This example is based on a six- or seven-week production period.

2. Catchwords and phrases from the script may lead off in many directions. Free associate. Drift with the images. Eliminate restrictions or judgments. Do seemingly unrelated images emerge? Does the quote from Cyrano bring up images of ladies in flower-toned gowns? Are there supporting phrases for the idea?

3. What will the set look like? Imagine the play as it might be played on stage.

4. What feelings and emotions are evoked by the play? Express the emotion of the play in a collage or doodle. Does this exercise suggest the kind of color, line, texture, or rhythm that is appropriate for the play?

5. Can the play be described in one word? Is it innocent? Decadent? Intellectual? Flamboyant? Poetic? Does that word capture the *essence* of the play?

6. Research may take the designer down many streets, looking for connections between the play and other elements of the period or milieu of the play. What painters, musicians, sculptors, philosophers, scientists, authors, and famous figures were contemporary with the period of the play? What other works express the same ideas as the play?

7. Discovery of interesting materials may stimulate the designer's thinking in new directions. Costume designers have found ways to use foam, Mylar, latex, Plexiglas, and various materials never intended for clothing or costumes.

The design concept should be stated briefly and concisely. Here are some examples of concepts.

Comedy of Errors.   An Elizabethan circus inspired by Miró. A fast-moving farce. Stylized period costumes. (See color plate 1.)

The Marriage of Figaro.   An unfinished painting viewed by candlelight. A work in progress. An earthy, romantic comedy inspired by Goya tapestry cartoons. Not rigidly period. (See color plate 8.)

Room for One Woman.   A drama in realistic, modern, nonspecific time. Space also represents time. The set is not only a room, but also a time or period of life. Images of plant life: mature, blooming; aging, autumnal; dying, barren. The costumes reflect the life cycles of the plants referred to in the script: green and blooming for the younger woman; brown, orange, and autumnal for the aging woman; and gray, beige, and barren for the old woman.

The designer must have a clear approach to the project, stated in meaningful terms, against which to evaluate the costume decisions for each character.

Interview I.
Concept, Research,
and Practice.
A Conversation with
Catherine Zuber.

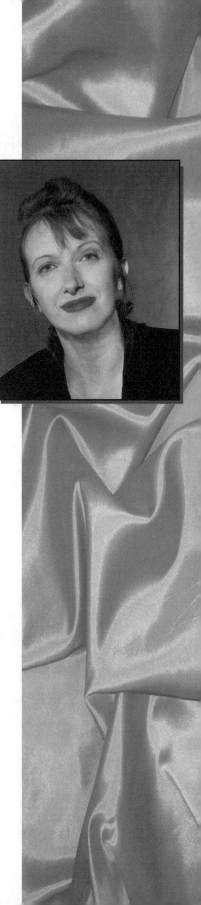

At the time of this interview with the author Broadway designer Catherine Zuber had received multiple design awards including four Tony Awards and an Outer Critics Circle Award. (See bio, page 422, for career details.)

RC: How do you develop a visual concept for a theatrical piece?

CZ: The beginning of a visual concept initially develops from meetings with the director and the other designers, particularly the set designer. We start to talk about what we feel the play or the opera is about and what story we want to tell.

Each production team is different. Sometimes a producer or director repeats a team, but new collaborators keep things interesting. The first time that you work with someone, you are learning how to develop a visual vocabulary together.

I can be inspired by a certain time or place, or a reference from a visual source. At times a novel can be a source—a novel by a writer with a certain descriptive style that sociologically or emotionally seems right for the play. Inspiration can come from portraits, or a fashion layout in a magazine—photography, editorial pages that have captured an essence that seems right for the play. I study fashion archives, photos, and films to learn how different time periods have interpreted dress—a designer needs to learn to recognize the influence of the aesthetic of the moment. I look at what the couture collections are showing. Their freedom of expression is inspiring. I also take my own photos of situations I find interesting or relevant to the production.

SOUTH PACIFIC
Produced by Lincoln Center Theater
Directed by Bartlett Sher
Costumes by Catherine Zuber
Thanksgiving Follies
Sketch #007.2, 008.2

Figures I.1 and I.2   Sailors. Bloody Mary. Some of Catherine Zuber's Tony-award winning costumes for *South Pacific* at Lincoln Center Theater.

SOUTH PACIFIC
Produced by Lincoln Center Theater
Directed by Bartlett Sher
Costumes by Catherine Zuber
Bloody Mary
Sketch #002.1

Then I attempt to understand the nuances of the play or opera. Sometimes the piece gives me a direction and tells me what it needs to be. Sometimes the conclusion is that an overly artistic approach can overburden a piece that would be better served with simplicity. I try to determine *what its essence is.*

RC: What were some of your most unusual research sources?

CZ: The *National Geographic* magazine [1940s] had a lot of information for *South Pacific*. The photographs had a candid quality.

In the library, a designer should rummage in the stacks and picture collections and hopefully stumble on an unexpected treasure of information. *Invite serendipity.*

I was in a market in France when I was working on *The Barber of Seville.* There was a vendor displaying burlap bags full of spices. The colors were so beautiful; I took some photographs and used them to create a wonderful palette of colors for the chorus. A designer can enjoy inspiration from so many varied sources. Carry a camera and snap away.

Students should know—*not everything is on the Internet.* There are many "Internet shy" books in bookstores. I always look for old books, magazines, photo albums, postcards, etc. in used bookstores. Going to the Metropolitan Museum of Art, the MOMA, attending fashion shows, parades, exhibitions, etc. can all be sources of inspiration!

RC: What does the designer do after the sketches have been approved?

CZ: Even after one has researched, collaborated, and sketched, it is better not to feel "that's it," that the creative door is closed and now it's just a matter of producing the costume. The actors are getting to know their characters and they may make discoveries that require departures from the approved sketches. The director may have a new take on a scene or a character. So keep the process alive and moving forward, be as flexible as possible as you move towards tech.

It's the same when you have a fitting with the performer. Because of the actor's body type or his persona, you may need to make adjustments to the initial concept to move in a slightly different direction. You may find that you want to distress the costumes more than you anticipated, or change the choice of accessories, for example. You may find the need to experiment with style and color with the wig maker and/or make-up artist.

RC: Where do all these things come from?

CZ: It depends on the period. If you are doing a modern dress play, you need to wrap your head around where that person would shop. What choice would they make? What is their budget? A person in modern dress wouldn't have their clothing designed and made for them. Would they go to Kmart, Target, Saks Fifth Avenue, Gap, Nord-strom's, Macy's, or boutiques and thrift shops? Would they be Internet shoppers? Are they up-to-the-minute fashionable? Do they care about comfort? Are they practical? Do they dress inappropriately for their age?

When shopping for period dress, sometimes you can find existing things, but be careful that they not look *too* used, that could give the wrong information about characters that are supposed to be well dressed.

RC: How important do you think it is for a designer to have skill and experience of costume construction?

CZ: Even if you don't actually make the clothes, you need to understand what different shapes and fabrics will do in terms of creating the correct silhouette. Is it or isn't it on the bias? What corset is the best shape for the period and for the character? What materials are the costumes made of? What are the best fabrics needed in order to create the right sculptural quality for the garment? What are the linings? The interfacings? Is there too much interfacing or not enough? What's the lining choice? Having the knowledge of all those things can only help the designer be more pleased with the result.

RC: Do you ask the actor's opinion before you've drawn the sketch?

CZ: It depends; the actor usually sees the sketches for the first time in the rehearsal room. It is wonderful to get their reaction and feedback at that time.

However, I like to be open to the contribution of the actor. I think the performer always takes ownership of the character, becomes the dramaturge of the character, and usually has great instincts about the details of what the character should be wearing.

I am currently working on a production of *The Cherry Orchard*. I did a group of sketches working only with the director. After a week of rehearsal, we had individual meetings with the actors. We had ten minutes with each actor, showing them their sketches, getting their reactions and making adjustments. Having a "one-on-one," a sort of private interview with each person, was

Figures I.3 and I.4 Figaro. Rosina. Examples of Catherine Zuber's costumes for *Il Barbiere di Siviglia* at The Metropolitan Opera.

Figure I.5 Almaviva. Example of Catherine Zuber's costumes for *Il Barbiere di Siviglia* at The Metropolitan Opera.

quite informative. You could see whether the costume was supporting the idea they had of themselves. In two cases the performers said, "I really didn't see it like that." I talked to them about *why* they didn't see it like that and I decided to sketch *their* version. I showed alternative ideas. We then discussed the advantages and disadvantages of the alternative direction. To be able to do this on paper is not only reassuring to the performer, but ultimately so much more practical than cutting it out and stitching it together, and *then* realizing you have gone down the wrong road. It's much harder to backtrack. If you start to go in one direction and someone needs to be more flamboyant or conservative or more pulled together or disheveled, it is a little harder if you have set your journey off on the wrong path.

For modern dress I usually display research in the rehearsal hall. Most performers really understand the nuances of the period they are living in, and understand what different articles of clothing mean. We usually have discussions before the fittings. They see me at rehearsals and they'll say, "Oh, I thought my character would have this or that in their wardrobe." The difference between actors is interesting. Some actors are so into what their costumes are that they really need those additional elements to help them be their characters. Then, there are other actors that just say "you know what, just put me in whatever you think is right."

Shoes are really important. In *Farragut North*, one of the actors decided the character needed to be supported by "duck boots." They enabled him to walk a certain way that felt like his character to him. It's wonderful how different shoes can really change the body language of the performer.

RC: What advice would you give to a young designer?

CZ: I recommend *travel*—a designer must have interest in the world, in different cultures. Travel helps a designer to experience cultures that are different than those he/she knows well.

Always *be open to experience, and delight in the pursuit of research*. Learn to tell a story—have delight in what makes that story unique. What is that life like? That house? That day? Those clothes? Always, when working on plays of the past, the designer should become immersed in the details—"channeling" what that world would be like.

Chapter 3
Doing Research

. . . There's my pretty darling Kate! The fashions of the times have almost
infected her, too. By living a year or two in town, she's as fond of gauze and
French frippery as the best of them. Blessing on my pretty innocence! drest out
as usual, my Kate. Goodness! What a quantity of superfluous silk has thou
got about thee, girl! I could never teach the fools of this age, that the indigent
world could be clothed out of the trimmings of the vain.

She Stoops to Conquer, Oliver Goldsmith

Extensive research is absolutely necessary to the successful designing of almost every play. For the professional costume designer, research is a way of life. The designer needs a background in literature, world history, art, architecture, costume, and theater history. Seeing plays; visiting museums; nosing around antique shops; searching out both new and old books with information about costumes, manners, and etiquette of different periods; exploring the Internet; and reading biographies and period novels are all activities that become part of a designer's lifestyle and help provide a rich background of information from which to draw.

Goals: What Are We Searching For?

A costume designer seeks two types of research: *factual* for information and *evocative* for inspiration. Factual research consists of studying sources of history, current events, science, and craft for a range of facts. Evocative research involves seeking stimuli for creative interpretation. These stimuli may come from many sources: music, fabrics, art, travel, literature, and the language of the play. Some sources may be suggested during the course of factual research. Factual research involves diligent effort; evocative, sometimes called *lateral* research (see box 3.A), requires being actively open and receptive to all experiences and seeing connections to design problems.

Box 3.A   Lateral research

Laura Crow, Director of Design, University of Connecticut says:

> The process of creativity has long puzzled scientists. After tracking artists at Harvard and encouraging them to verbalize all of their visual ideas, scientists discovered that a sort of pattern evolved, but it was not driven by logic. Since science and education have (always) been logic-oriented, it was hard to accept that there was a totally different approach to problem solving. I call this process "lateral thinking."
>
> We know that the left-brain is our logical side and the right brain is our creative side. With lateral thinking the right brain is isolated and picks up random often visual ideas and somehow the brain creates a cohesive whole. The creative process is hard to rush. It takes its own time and makes its own patterns. What the rest of the world sees as procrastination is a very important part of the creative process. There has to be time to make all of these disparate elements into a creation that is thematically connected on some level.

Factual research for each production should provide a general understanding of the period and culture in which the play takes place and specific information on the types of garments suitable for each character in the play. Evocative research seeks sources that share, illuminate, and project the essence of the play, characters, and theme.

Understanding the period and culture is extremely important and too often overlooked by the novice designer. What social mores of the time or place affected dress and manners? What were the views on courtship and marriage and the roles of men and women? What were the erogenous zones (areas of the body considered sexually provocative)? What colors were used and why? What materials and dyes were available? What kinds of work were performed? What leisure activities were enjoyed or permitted? Were special garments worn for work or play? What differences were established between age groups—married and unmarried, rich and poor? What was the political system under which the characters lived? What religious beliefs were held? How did these beliefs affect dress and manners? What assumptions were made about people based on their dress? How did they view themselves in relation to the world? How can these mores be translated to our own time? The answers to these and other questions give the designer a context in which to consider the design choices.

Sources: Where to Look?

Research material falls into two basic categories. *Primary sources* are original materials or copies and translations of original materials. Paintings (or reproductions of paintings) representing the time in which they were painted, novels representing the author's contemporaries, and original artifacts from a period or place are all primary source materials. *Secondary sources* are materials that represent or discuss a subject in more general terms, are based on primary sources, and draw broad concepts and conclusions. Encyclopedias, textbooks, and general reference books are very valuable as distilled sources of information.

Internet research is very popular with students and designers. Online searches turn up general sources and specific sources. Unfortunately, these searches frequently offer a large number of inappropriate sources, mostly secondary research. Without the background knowledge to sort through the tremendous amount of erroneous information that can be found on the Internet, an inexperienced designer may be misinformed and misled. A list of both primary and secondary sources can be found in the bibliography at the back of this text.

Secondary Sources: Where to Begin?

The appropriate secondary sources give the designer a beginning, overall view of the costumes needed. For the novice designer a good costume-history textbook provides basic information. Several general texts might be consulted for a broad understanding against which to evaluate other material uncovered by more extensive research. (One such basic outline of fashion history is in appendix II.) The designer should find several areas of further research suggested by these texts. Because costume texts usually concentrate on the fashionable dress of the period, characters requiring ethnic, peasant, or occupational costumes may not be represented. A list of special topics of research should be started as the needs for specific information are noted.

Since many costume texts present composite or redrawn examples of period dress, care should be taken to check these drawings against primary source materials. Secondary sources may vary from the original as a result of the artist's drawing style, the taste of the period in which the drawing was done, or the conscious or unconscious taste and editing of the artist or author. The original artist may also have flattered the subject or stylized the presentation, further complicating the designer's task.

Distinguishing primary research from secondary research may be difficult. In figure 3.1 a number of similar garments are analyzed.

A   B

Figure 3.1   Primary and secondary research. Distinguishing primary research from secondary research may be difficult. (A) and (B) are modern photos of eighteenth-century gowns. They are considered primary research because the gowns are period originals. At first glance, (C) appears to be an eighteenth-century gown, but in fact is a 1920s design for "fancy dress" that echoes the bodice and sleeves of (A) and the skirt of (B); fabric and fit are influenced by 1920s fashion. Compare it with (D), a fashionable tea dress of the 1920s. Both (C) and (D) are primary sources for the 1920s, but (C) is a secondary source for the eighteenth century. (E) is a nineteenth-century gown by the famous designer Worth that also looks like an eighteenth-century gown (embroidered underskirt, lace collar) but is in reality an evening gown of the 1880s. (F) is also an 1880s evening gown with eighteenth-century influence. These gowns are primary research for the 1880s, not the eighteenth century.

C

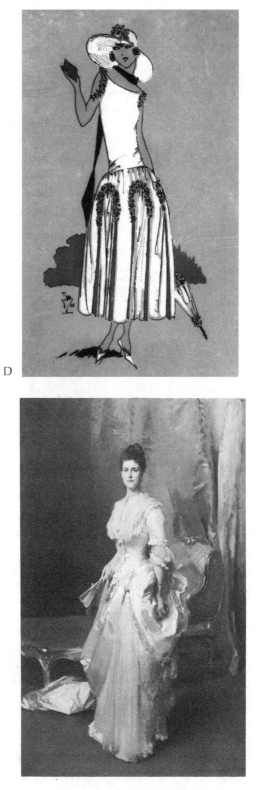

D

E

F

The closer one gets to modern times, the more important careful dating of research material can be. Changes may occur in the basic look of garments within a relatively short period of time. In figure 3.2 a series of nineteenth-century fashion plates illustrates some of the differences in silhouettes during that century.

Understanding the basic look of the period is essential when the designer is approaching such primary source material. Much of this material carries no date. In some cases only the birth and death dates of the artist or the century in which the painting was created may be available. Transition garments, "fancy dress," fashion aberrations, and even flights of artistic fantasy are often represented in the art of a period. While these garments may be far more interesting and exciting to the costume designer, they would be inappropriate in many plays.

Primary Sources: Where to Go from Here?

After the designer has studied the play, developed the costume plot, and reviewed costume textbooks, a list of specific areas of research should emerge. (See chapter 2.) These areas should be investigated in primary sources.

> . . . *He might have been a model for Callot—*
> *One of those wild swashbucklers in a masque—*
> *Hat with three plumes, and doublet with six points—*
> *His cloak behind him over his long sword*
> *Cocked, like the tail of strutting Chanticleer—*
> *Prouder than all the swaggering Tamburlaines*
> *Hatched out of Gascony. And to complete*
> *This Punchinello figure—such a nose!—*
> *You cannot look upon it without crying: "Oh, no,*
> *Impossible! Exaggerated!" Then*
> *You smile, and say: "Of course—I might have known;*
> *Presently he will take it off" But that*
> *Monsieur de Bergerac will never do.*

Cyrano de Bergerac, Edmond Rostand

Box 3.A (on p. 54) is a list of areas of research identified for *Cyrano de Bergerac* from information about the play and from the quote above. Careful study of the entire script would certainly add many other topics to the list.

After checking secondary sources like costume texts, the designer may proceed with an online search for primary and other secondary research. For the most varied and interesting information, research areas beyond standard costume sites may be required. Image sites may be helpful for nineteenth, twentieth, and twenty-first century research. Special-topic books may be ordered online. Internet research should constitute only the beginning, never the full extent of the designer's research. Because this research is often incorrectly dated or not dated at all, it should be carefully checked against other texts (secondary sources) for appropriateness.

Primary source material may be found in museums and museum libraries and in art sections and picture collections in libraries. An examination of the art of the period in an art history text or general art reference should provide the

Figure 3.2 Fashion silhouette. The 1807 silhouette (A) is high-waisted, soft, narrow, and vertical. The 1833 silhouette (B) has a natural, tight-fitted waist, broad sloping shoulders with large sleeves, and a short, very wide skirt. The 1850 silhouette (C) retains the horizontal effect with sloping shoulders, modest sleeves, and a long, very full skirt. The 1870 silhouette (D) shows the movement away from the broad shoulder line; it has a narrower shoulder and the skirt now has a bustle. The 1891 silhouette (E) has a long, pointed bodice, narrow shoulders, and trumpet-shaped skirt that create a strong, vertical feeling.
(A) The collection of the author. (B) Courtesy of the Picture Collection, Cooper-Hewitt Museum Library: Smithsonian Institution, New York. (C) Picture Collection, The Branch Libraries, The New York Public Library. (D) Courtesy of the Picture Collection, Cooper-Hewitt Museum Library: Smithsonian Institution, New York. (E) Picture Collection, The Branch Libraries, The New York Public Library.

> **Box 3.A   Sample research list for *Cyrano de Bergerac***
>
> ### French Costumes 1640–1655
>
> **French History**
>   Louis XIII, r. 1610–1643
>   Louis XIV, r. 1643–1715
>   Richelieu, Cardinal, 1624–1642
>
> **Mentioned in Script**
>
> | | |
> |---|---|
> | Actors/costumes 1640s | Pastry cooks |
> | Paris street life | Cardinals |
> | Swashbucklers | Nuns |
> | Theater performances 1640s | Plumed hats |
> | Doublets (with six points) | Masques |
> | Chanticleer | Capuchin monk |
> | Spanish officers | Tamburlaine |
> | Cadets of Gascoyne | Punchinello |
> | Spanish ruffs | |
>
> **Artists**
>
> | | |
> |---|---|
> | Peter Paul Rubens | Jacques Callot |
> | Phillippe de Champaigne | Diego Rodriguez de Silva y Velasquez |
> | Pierre Mignard | Francisco de Zurbaran |
> | Charles le Brun | Franz Hals |
> | Rembrandt van Rijn | Cornelius de Vos |
> | David Teniers, Elder | Cornelius Johnson |
> | David Teniers, Younger | Abraham Bosse |
> | Adriaen Bouwer | Wenceslaus Hollar, engraver |

names of painters, engravers, illustrators, and other visual artists to add to the research topic list. (See the bibliography and appendix I.) The designer then investigates volumes that treat the period in depth, and books or folios of reproductions of the pertinent artists. William Ivey Long's costumes for a couple in *Steel Pier* (C-2) were designed after the work of the artist Reginald Marsh.)

As useful garments are found in the research, the designer should make sketches, photocopies, or scans. Being well organized at this point is essential to effective research. If photocopying is not possible, a tracing-paper pad is a handy way to record details quickly. To protect the volumes or folios, the designer should place a sheet of acetate over the page before tracing the garment from an illustration. Notations on the tracing should include the name of the book or folio, artist's name, page number, date, library, and character for which the garment or detail might be useful. While this approach may seem unnecessarily time-consuming, it will make relocating the source much easier should additional information be needed later. Abbreviations can be used for noting information, but a key should be included in the sketchbook. Some research may be interesting even though its use may not be immediately clear. Sorting and eliminating should be done later. It is better to have more than can be used than to make several trips to the same source.

Most libraries permit photocopies to be made of source material. These work extremely well for line drawings and lithographs, but photocopies of paintings and photos are not always clear enough to be useful. Experience will indicate when to try photocopying. The cost of this type of reproduction adds up quickly and may limit its use for many designers. Again, labeling is important. Some libraries require that the library staff do all photocopying, and for this service the library charges a fee.

Some libraries and museums may permit the designer to take photographs of research material. Permission to photograph *must* be obtained from the librarian or curator. Digital camera technology is a quick way to record research. A flash is necessary for clear pictures but may not be permitted. Even so, these quick photos of source material may be distorted and unclear. Photos thus taken are limited for personal and educational purposes only and may *not* legally be used for publication. *Special permission is required to use photos of museum and library materials in books, articles, ads, posters, or any other printed material.* Documenting and making notes regarding the source may still require a pad and pencil or a notebook computer.

Permission to photograph original garments in costume collections may be difficult to obtain. The heat and light required for photography are damaging to delicate fabrics. Some museums will photograph items in their collections for a fee. Photographing museum garments is often impractical for the beginning designer because of the expense, the difficulty in obtaining permission, and the level of photography skill required. Sometimes the garment has already been photographed for exhibit catalogs or other museum purposes, and slides or prints may be available through the museum archives. *Having the photo does not mean that permission to print it has been granted,* and a special fee is usually required for reprint permission.

Scanning imagery from books to use for personal reference is very helpful, but may not be possible in a library. Again, having a copy of the picture does not mean permission is granted to reprint it.

The designer must be able to sketch elements of the research in a sketchbook freehand. For some sources, this may be the only way to record information. This approach also provides excellent practice in drawing garments. Most libraries and museums require researchers to use pencils for all sketching and notations, since ink can cause serious damage to books and other research materials.

Museum bookstores are valuable sources of art books, reproductions, postcards, posters, and slides. Old magazines and photos can be found in used bookshops, thrift stores, and flea markets. Some of these sources can also be found online. (See figures 3.3, 3.4, and 3.5 on pp. 56–58.)

Care should be taken to identify each research item properly with as much information as can be determined. Accurate identification may be very difficult with some items of research. Portraits were often painted in "fancy dress," garments with details from other periods, or costumes assembled by the artist. Information on the artist's approach to the work may indicate if this is the case, and comparison with other sources is helpful. The correct title of the painting may offer a clue.

Figure 3.6A (on p. 59) is an example of an *eighteenth-century* portrait painted in "fancy dress." In this painting by Gainsborough, the designer might be confused by the seventeenth-century details of the costume if the lady had not retained her fashionable eighteenth-century wig. A comparison with figure 3.6B

Figure 3.3 Ads in period magazines are excellent sources for sports attire and unusual accessories. *The Theatre,* January and June 1910. From the collections of the author.

(on p. 59), a *seventeenth-century* portrait by Rubens, painted in the dress of the day, reveals a marked difference in certain details, such as the hair style, bodice length, collar, and weight of the fabrics. Further research would confirm the eighteenth-century popularity of dress styled after the seventeenth-century paintings of Rubens or Van Dyke during the eighteenth century.

Special Problems

Research into special groups like Amish communities, early American settlements, Native American tribes, various ethnic groups, and East Asian cultures should follow the same approach. Secondary sources give some answers and may indicate other questions and other places to look. Some possibilities are *National Geographic* and *Smithsonian* magazines; restoration villages such as Williamsburg, Virginia; museums such as the Museum of the American Indian; and the embassies or consulates of foreign countries. The designer must be prepared to request specific information from such sources, however, and not expect to be sent volumes of general material. Obviously, this type of research is very time-consuming and must be undertaken well in advance of a production. Much of this material may be found on the Internet. Documentaries and independent films often offer interesting cultural research materials.

When a play includes characters based on "stock characters," such as *commedia dell'arte* characters, the designer should be familiar with their traditional costumes, even if a decision is made to approach these characters from some other point of view. (See figure 2.4.) Research into the theater conventions of a period, including costuming practices, can only enrich the designer's work.

Research for contemporary plays can sometimes be difficult. Even in this age of mass media and rapid, continual movement of people from place to place, differences can be noted in the dress of persons from different Western European cultures and even different areas of the same country. In large cities, different socioeconomic or ethnic groups gravitate to specific areas of the city and influence the type of clothes worn in that area. This situation is particularly pronounced in cities that are ports or points of entry for immigrants.

Research for contemporary plays may involve visiting areas where persons similar to the play's characters live. An afternoon on the street or in the park with sketchbook or digital camera may prove very productive (figures 3.7 [p. 60] and 3.8

Figure 3.4
"Homemaker" magazines are brimming with suitable styles for housewives, adolescents, and young adults. "The Modern Priscilla," May 1914. From the collections of the author.

[p. 61]). Magazines, newspapers, Web sites, and documentary studies of the area or lifestyle under research are all useful, as are mail-order catalogs and Web sites that are designed to appeal to particular social, regional, or occupational groups. Ads for these catalogs may appear in the backs of other current magazines. Trade and special-interest magazines (sports, crafts, etc.) usually have ads from clothing manufacturers whose products appeal to the group targeted by the magazine. These ads and catalogs might clue the designer to a "look" for certain characters. These magazines can be found in the periodicals sections of large libraries. Keywords for particular interests (hunting, fishing, tennis, etc.) will turn up Web sites that feature clothing for those interests.

A designer should also collect a personal library of books, magazines, and other resources that can serve as a quick reference for future design projects.

A

B

C

Figure 3.5   Photos (first appearing in the mid-nineteenth century) are very useful research material for the designer. Photos reveal the way clothes were actually worn, not just the fashion ideal. (A) A couple in their wedding finery. (B) A lovely woman in a simple print frock and brooch. (C) A middle-class or working-class woman in her best suit, obviously bought "off the rack," with sleeves too long and less-than-subtle fit. From the collections of Hilary Sherred and John Scheffler.

Authenticity

How much research is enough? How authentic must designs for a play be? These questions have no fixed answers. The solution to each design problem is different. In general, the more realistic the production, the more precise and exact the research should be. Decisions should be based on information, not ignorance. The kind of hat, purse, or glasses should be chosen from the range of correct possibilities, not from contemporary experience or the lone historical source found. The more options available, the more interesting the final choices will be. Even in productions that are simplified or stylized, a thorough understanding of the appropriate period allows the designer to make the most meaningful choices. One perfect detail may make the complete statement. Research does not limit creativity, but stimulates it. Designers who limit their research also limit their flexibility, scope, and creativity.

A.   B

Figure 3.6   (A) *The Honorable Frances Duncombe*, a portrait in "fancy dress" painted by Gainsborough in the eighteenth century. (B) An authentic seventeenth-century portrait by Rubens. (A) Copyright, The Frick Collection: New York. (B) Courtesy of Calouste Gulbenkian Foundation Museum, Lisbon, Portugal.

Organization:
What to Do With the Research?

By this point in the designer's work ideas should begin falling into place. The next step is to organize the research into categories based on the assembled research. Categories for this stage of organization might be: inspiration, character names, chorus, extras, mood, concept, details, style, construction notes. Some garments may be perfect as found in the research. Sometimes the cut is good but the fabric wrong. Perhaps the colors of a painting suggest the feeling, mood, or style of the play even though there are no costumes represented. Dif-

ferent details from several garments may be combined in one costume, provided they are compatible in period and style and appropriate to the character.

Each designer develops a personal approach to dealing with the tons of research collected for a large project. Stick-on labels or Post-It notes are very useful for labeling research. Folders, brown envelopes, or accordion files make it easier to organize the material. Nothing is so distressing as not being able to locate that perfect piece of research in all the clutter. A bulletin board is handy for displaying important finds. As the project progresses, new research may be needed to supplement the original information.

Analysis: What Does It Mean?

Several problems may arise when the designer is interpreting research material. With primary source material, the artist's style may affect the interpretation of the garments represented. The great masters frequently created illusions to flatter the subjects of their paintings or interpreted the model in their own artistic style, not realistically representing the costume. Less gifted and less well-known artists often lacked the skill for these illusions and repre-

Figure 3.7   Photos of street life. Research for contemporary theater may require a field trip. Photos by Kristen Vaughan.

Figure 3.8 *Stand-up Tragedy*. Lee. Costume design based on street research. Designed by Paul Tazewell for Arena Stage Ensemble.

sented the details of dress more precisely. These artists were more apt to distort the proportions of the figure, however, and so comparison of many sources is important. Personal style, the fashion of the day, and contemporary ideas of beauty influence each artist in the presentation of a subject. Figure 3.9 shows two paintings of approximately the same date. The unknown artist who painted *Dr. Hezekiah Beardsley* (3.9A) carefully and precisely reproduced the detail and costume information of his subject, while in the Gilbert Stuart painting of *The Skater* (3.9B) less importance is given to the costume and more emphasis is placed on the body and presence of the model.

To further complicate the task, the modern designer brings a current view of fashion and beauty as well as a personal taste and style to the evaluation and interpretation of period research. Beauty truly *is* in the eye of the beholder. Current ideals of beauty and sex appeal, the fashionable figure type and fashion silhouette, and the designer's personal taste all influence the choice, use, and interpretation of period research.

The influence of contemporary fashion on the interpretation of period costumes can be seen by comparing primary source material with costume interpretations from a later period (secondary sources) and with fashion plates of that later period. (See again figure 3.1.) Several things happen to a garment when it

A

B

Figure 3.9 Variety of sources. Often the less sophisticated painter will show more costume information. (A) Unknown artist, *Dr. Hezekiah Beardsley*, Yale University Art Gallery, gift of Gwendolen Jones Giddings. (B) Gilbert Stuart, *The Skater (Portrait of William Grant)*; National Gallery of Art, Washington; Andrew W. Mellon Collection 1950.

is interpreted in a later period. Almost always it is worn over currently fashionable undergarments. These undergarments produce the currently fashionable figure that may or may not relate to the silhouette of the earlier style. In many fashion periods a corset was used to alter the natural body shape. In figure 3.10A Geraldine Farrar wears a fashionable 1910 corset (figure 3.10B) under

A

B

Figure 3.10   (A) Foundation garments. *Ladies Field,* 1911. (B) Corset. *The Theatre,* January 1910.

Figure 3.10 (C) Medieval statue. The Metropolitan Museum of Art, The Cloisters Collection, 1947. (47.101.12ab)

her medieval costume. Figure 3.10C is a statue of a medieval saint in a similar garment, but without a structured undergarment. The effect of the foundation garment on the silhouette is clearly visible. Without the corset the garment is a medieval gown; with the corset it becomes a nineteenth-century stage costume.

Reproducing a garment in currently fashionable fabrics may also substantially alter its period look. (See figure 7.5A.) A stiff period silhouette reproduced in a soft fabric has a different feeling from that of the original. Often subtle changes in the shape or depth of the neckline, length of the sleeve, and fullness of the skirt are sufficient to distort the period essence of a costume. Trim, color, and decorative design may be strongly influenced by contemporary styles as well. Almost always, shoes, makeup, and hairstyles are strongly influenced by current trends. These interpretations are not necessarily inappropriate for their original use, but the designer addressing the research must be aware of those influences. (See figure 3.11.)

Concurrent research into the cut of period garments is important even if the designer is not responsible for making the garment. The designer should understand the way patterning, tailoring,

Figure 3.11 Contemporary influence. Sara Bernhardt wore this Elizabethan doublet over a 1907 corset as "Jacasse" in *Les Bouffons* by Zamacoïs. From the collection of Hilary Sherred.

Figure 3.12 Men's artificial silhouette. Women's fashion is not alone in altering the natural shape of the body. From the author's collection.

undergarments, and padding affect the costume. In figure 3.12 precision cutting, extra padding in the chest area of the vest and coat, and tight lacing of the vest combine to produce the small waist and large chest of the 1860s fashionable male silhouette. The costumer is better able to reproduce the desired effect if the designer can give detailed construction information. As each project is completed, research should be filed for future use.

Developing Personal Research Sources

A serious designer develops a personal collection of research material. A library of basic books on costumes, art, history, decorative styles, pattern making, costume construction, and crafts is essential. (The bibliography in this book might serve as a guide.) Additional volumes collected for work on specific shows can be added as needed.

A file of magazine clippings, postcards, posters and art reproductions, period patterns—anything that might prove useful—should be developed. Clippings from magazines or newspapers should be mounted on heavy paper or index cards, or slipped into plastic sleeves to prevent deterioration. Each research piece should be identified as clearly as possible: period or date, subject, and, if a clipping, the original source. File folders, envelopes, or file boxes properly identified should be used to keep the information in order by play, period, or subject. Scanned or downloaded computer research can be transferred to computer files under specific topics or for specific periods and organized in categories on a hard drive or transferred to CDs labeled by category.

When the show is finished, research material should be sorted and filed for future use. Some designers store their research according to the play for which it was done; others find filing material by date or period is more useful. Good research may be reused and redeveloped many times; research should never be discarded. The unused detail may be perfect for the next show in the same period. Much time can be saved on future productions if the designer has a head start on the research.

In addition to research sources, many designers keep files of fabrics, patterns, and sources. A swatch of fabric is attached to a card labeled with the fiber content, use, source, and price. Patterns should be filed with a line drawing of the garment and a description on the outside of the envelope. A source file should contain information on how to locate needed items. (See figure 7.6.)

A personal research library saves the designer time in the early stages of the design process, but should not be relied on exclusively.

Chapter 4
The Designer's Tools
The Elements and Principles of Design

. . . O that I were a fool!
I am ambitious for a motley coat.

As You Like It, William Shakespeare

All visual artists work with the same elements of design whether they are working on a painting, a sculpture, an advertisement, or a costume. These elements are combined according to certain principles of design. Each element has both physical and psychological effects on the observer. The particular choices made by a designer in a given situation produce a design with specific characteristics and effects. All elements can be manipulated to the designer's purpose. Knowledge of the elements and principles of design is necessary for one to design costumes effectively and to discuss design concepts with the director and the scenic and lighting designers.

Elements of Design

The basic elements of design are space, line, shape, form, light, color, and texture.

Space

Space is defined as the area between or within shapes. The painter works on a canvas; the sculptor works in abstract space; the costume designer works with two specific spaces: (1) the area of the actor's body and costume, and (2) the total area of the stage or screen space.

The Silhouette

The space of the actor's body and/or the outline of the garment is called the *silhouette*. The costume designer establishes the shape of the silhouette and sub-divides that space to accomplish the desired effect for each character. Manipulation of space by division results in both physical and psychological effects. Physically, these divisions affect the perception of weight, height, and size. Psychologically, these divisions can affect the emotional response of the audience.

The "Stage Picture"

Almost all theaters can be divided into one of three basic types: proscenium theater, thrust theater, or arena theater. (See figure 4.1.) These designations are based on the relationship between the audience and the stage.

The *proscenium theater* is an arrangement in which the audience faces the stage, most of which is behind a "picture frame" structure. The actors are seen in a shadow box effect. A curtain can be raised and lowered or pulled from the sides to close off the stage and hide the set and actors. Because of the distance (physical and psycho-

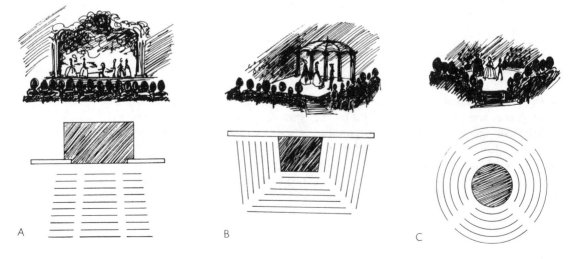

Figure 4.1   Types of theater arrangements. (A) proscenium, (B) thrust, and (C) arena or theater-in-the-round.

logical) and the relationship between the audience and the stage, the "stage picture" can be more precisely controlled in the proscenium theater than in other theaters. By manipulating the areas of light and shadow on stage, controlling the colors of sets and costumes, and using the scenery in various ways, the director and designers can very carefully control the division of space and the image the audience sees.

In the *thrust theater* (also called *three-quarters round*) the stage is built out into the audience area. In some thrust theaters the fourth side provides a proscenium area where some effects and scenery can be played. These areas, however, are not generally used for acting. The thrust section of the stage is the main acting area. The actors and the audience may be extremely close and have a sense of sharing the space.

Arena or *theater-in-the-round* is presented with the audience surrounding the acting space on all sides and with entrance aisles dividing the audience.

In a proscenium-style production the acting space is flattened in the audience's perception to an almost two-dimensional picture; in a thrust or theater-in-the round presentation, the costume designer works like a sculptor in a three-dimensional space. The arrangement of actors on stage is the responsibility of the director, and the spatial relationships between them result from the action. However, in plays with crowd scenes the costume designer should be aware of the spatial relationships between the various groups of actors on stage. The division of space that results from costuming members of the group either differently or alike alters the total effect of the stage picture. In plays like *Oedipus Rex,* the chorus may be seen as a unified, moving mass. In other plays the chorus may be seen as a group of individuals. In Act II of Giacomo Puccini's opera *La Bohème* the chorus is seen as participants in a great Christmas Eve crowd in Paris's Latin Quarter. Various chorus members are depicted as vendors, entertainers, and street urchins—individuals, rich and poor.

In films or television the image is controlled within specific shapes (the screens). The figure and the costume on the screen may be seen only in a close-up or as a fragment of the total. When the designer knows how scenes are to be shot, he or she should consider how the divisions of the garment relate to the screen shape.

Pleasing Divisions of Space

Uneven divisions of space are generally the most pleasing. Equal divisions or extremely unequal divisions are generally less pleasing. (See figure 4.2.) However, an unpleasing effect may be exactly what the designer is obliged to produce for certain characters or scenes, particularly comic or evil ones. Also, the uninteresting division may gain interest if it is unusual in the context in which it is seen. Characters like the trolls in *Peer Gynt* may require a design based on unusual divisions of space.

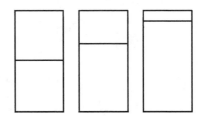

Figure 4.2   Divisions of space.

Line

I don't like that underslung line. It cuts her across the fanny. Makes her look positively duck-bottomed.

The Women, Clare Booth Luce

An elongated mark connecting two points or defining the edge of a shape is called a *line*. The line of a costume may be expressed by the cut of the garment, the seaming, the application of trim, and/or the overall silhouette of the period.

Aspects of Line

There are eight aspects to a line: (1) path, (2) thickness, (3) continuity, (4) sharpness, (5) contour, (6) consistency, (7) length, and (8) direction. Within each aspect are numerous variations, each conveying its own psychological and physical effects. These effects of line are based on associations with objects from our experience or from nature.

The costume designer uses line to accent psychological traits of a character and to emphasize or minimize the actor's physical characteristics. Figure 4.3 and box 4.A show examples of the aspects of line, the basic effects of using each aspect, the psychological characteristics that each stresses, and the way to incorporate each in a garment. The effect of each type of line can be modified

---

Box 4.A   Aspects of line

Aspect	Physical Effects	Psychological Effects	Ways to Use
Path			
Straight	Emphasizes angularity, tends to conceal body contours	Stiffness, directness, tension, stubbornness, masculinity, self-assurance, austerity	Seams, darts, hems, pleats, belts, stripes, geometrics, tucks, ribbons
Straight variations (zigzag)		Sharpness, abruptness, instability, nervousness, excitement	Garment edges, trim
Curved	Emphasizes roundness	Flexibility, grace, femininity, fluidity, ease, subtlety, youth	Seams, garment edges, scallops, patterns, draping
Width			
Thick	Adds weight	Forcefulness, self-assurance, aggressiveness, masculinity	Borders, trims, cuffs, fabric patterns, belts
Thin	Minimizes weight	Delicateness, daintiness, gentleness, serenity, passivity, subtlety	Seams, darts, pattern, trim
Continuity			
Unbroken	Smoothness, emphasizes bumps and curves	Constancy, elegance, smoothness, grace	Seams, pleats, gathers, trim, draping
Broken	Emphasizes irregularities	Less rigidity, playfulness, informality, casualness, busyness	Trims, buttons, edgings, pattern

Sharpness

Sharp	Emphasizes contours it follows	Assertiveness, boldness, precision, hardness	Seams, darts, edges, trims, stripes
Fuzzy	Softens contour, gently increases area, reduces definition of edge or shape	Softness, indecisiveness, femininity, gentleness, ease	Fringe, fur, feathers, patterns, translucent fabrics, trims

Contour

Smooth	Reinforces smoothness or accents shapes	Straightforwardness, simplicity, boldness, assertiveness, hardness, definitive precision	Seams, darts, edges, trims, stripes
Shaped	Effect varies depending on elements of shape	Complexity, informality, deviousness	Lace, trim, pattern

Consistency

Solid	Advances boldly	Smoothness, self-assurance, strength	Stripes, binding, piping, braid, belt, borders
Porous	Does not advance, may recede	Openness, delicacy, weakness, refinement, uncertainty	Lace, crochet, fringe, eyelet trim

Length

Long	Emphasizes its direction, smoothes and elongates	Evaluation relative to figure, stress on continuity, grace	Seams, darts, trims
Short	Breaks up spaces	Possibly busyness, agitation	Any of the above

Direction

Vertical	Lengthens, narrows	Dignity, strength, poise, elegance, superiority, grandness, alertness, austerity	Any of the above
Horizontal	Shortens, widens	Tranquility, repose, calmness, serenity, passiveness	Any of the above
Diagonal	Near vertical—lengthens Near horizontal—widens 45 effect—influenced by other factors	Dramatic, vivacious, unsettled, active, unstable, dynamic	Any of the above

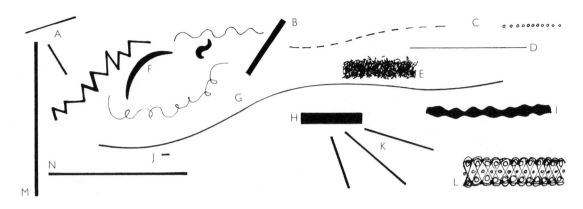

Figure 4.3   Aspects of line. (A) straight; (B) thick; (C) broken; (D) thin, sharp; (E) fuzzy; (F) curved; (G) long, unbroken, smooth; (H) solid; (I) shaped; (J) short; (K) diagonal; (L) porous; (M) vertical; (N) horizontal

by the effect of other elements used with it. The designer chooses those aspects of line that most clearly reflect the character's traits (figure 4.3). The basic line of most costumes is vertical since the actor is seen primarily standing or sitting. The effect of the various aspects of line can reinforce or modify the verticality of the actor.

Shape and Form

Your lord does know my mind; I cannot love him.
Yet I suppose him virtuous, know him noble,
Of great estate, of fresh and stainless youth;
In voices well divulged, free, learned, and valiant,
And in dimension and the shape of nature
A gracious person. . . .

Twelfth Night, William Shakespeare

Shape is flat space enclosed by a line; *form* is a three-dimensional area enclosed by surfaces. Hollow forms are perceived as volume; solid forms are perceived as mass. Shapes and forms are *defined* space. They assume the effects of the lines surrounding them and the space separating those lines. For example, rectangles and squares, constructed of vertical and horizontal lines, suggest stability, confidence, and assertiveness. Triangles, pentagons, and other shapes with diagonal sides suggest drama and action, but less stability. Shapes with curved sides project the attributes of curved lines with vertical or horizontal effects, but more subtly expressed. The way in which the designer subdivides a shape can alter the audience's perception of that shape (figure 4.4A). Lines inside a shape, subdividing it into smaller shapes, can help the designer create a variety of moods and illusions. The Roustabout costume in figure 4.4B uses different types of line—straight, shaped, diagonal, smooth, thick, thin, and solid—to divide the shape of the silhouette into smaller divisions.

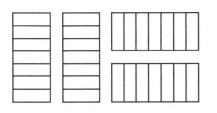

Figure 4.4A Dividing shapes. Different ways of subdividing a shape alter the perception of that shape.

Figure 4.4B *Carnival.* Roustabout #1. This costume uses different types of line to divide the shape of the silhouette into smaller divisions. Designed by Paul Tazewell for the Kennedy Center.

Most shapes have corresponding forms. The human body, and garments designed for it, can be translated into simple two-dimensional forms and yet are understood to be three-dimensional. Basic shapes and forms have names that are useful when one is discussing designs. (See figure 4.5 on the following page.)

Structural Shape and Form

The units that make up an object contribute to and are inherent in its structural shape or form.

The Human Body.   The first form the costume designer must deal with is that of the human body. The separate shapes and forms of the body (head, arms, torso, legs) combine to create the individual's body structure. The structural shape of a specific actor is a given part of the design formula that the designer must use, and the costume must ultimately work on that actor. In addition to

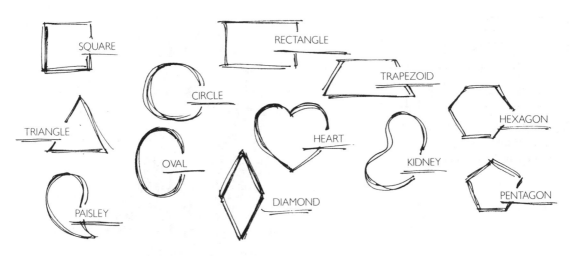

Figure 4.5   The names of the basic shapes. Knowing the names of basic shapes and forms is useful when discussing design.

taking measurements, the designer should analyze the effect of the actor's figure. Is it well-proportioned? Tall, thin, and angular? Short, round, and stout? Broad-shouldered, narrow-hipped? Stooped? The designer must ask, "Does the actor's body correspond to the character type required or should physical or visual alterations in the figure be attempted?" Figure 4.6 and box 4.B demonstrate the visual effects of shape in costume.

Box 4.B   Visual effects of shape in costume

1. A silhouette (shape) emphasizes the direction of its dominant lines. (4.6A)

2. Subdividing a shape vertically visually lengthens and narrows it. Subdividing a shape horizontally shortens and widens it. (4.6B)

3. Shapes standing away from the body add apparent weight and bulk to the figure. (4.6C)

4. Tightly fitted costumes emphasize body contours and may increase the apparent size of the figure. (4.6D)

5. Body-skimming shapes seem to add weight and bulk, but they may also disguise the exact shape and size of the body, making it easier to visually modify the too-heavy or too-thin figure. (4.6E)

6. A shape tends to emphasize the part of the body at its edge. (4.6F)

7. A shape conveys the psychological effect of the line enclosing it and the space within it.

8. Impressions of size and shape are initially established by the overall silhouette and its relationship to the surroundings, and then the internal subdivisions become related to the silhouette.

Figure 4.6   The visual effects of shape. Compare with box 4.B.

C

D

E

F

In the design for Pa Ubu (figure 4.7) line and shape (structural and decorative) combine to express character. The bold simple shapes and the horizontal lines on the pants and sleeves emphasize his bulk and his childlike character.

The Costume Silhouette.   Throughout history people have been extremely inventive about the shape and division of the space surrounding and including the human body. As such, preferred silhouettes have changed over time. The silhouette of the historical period in which the costumes are to be designed is thus a given part of most design projects. Historical silhouettes and modern clothes can be analyzed in their structural shapes. Analyzing silhouettes in this way (figure 4.8) helps the designer to determine the effects of the finished costume. Seeing basic shapes and forms is also key to translating research to sketch, sketch to pattern, and pattern to costume.

Figure 4.7 *Ubu the King.* Pa Ubu. The bold simple shapes and the horizontal lines on the pants and sleeves of this costume emphasize Pa Ubu's size and immaturity. (A) Designed by Cynthia Turnbull for Denison University. (B) Photo by Robert Gander.

Figure 4.8   Analyzing garment shapes.

A careful look at a costume resource reveals basic shapes and forms. The total effect suggested by the combination of these shapes is either horizontal or vertical. Although the combination of shapes may vary, in most periods the majority of garments give a similar effect. Between the extremes of vertical and horizontal periods are transitional periods that show some characteristics of both the earlier costume styles and the later styles. The designer needs to keep in mind the effects the shapes will suggest on the bodies of the actors and the desirability of these effects in projecting character traits for each role. Adjustment of the silhouette shapes may be necessary to counter undesirable effects.

Decorative Shape

Once the basic silhouette and the structural shapes of a garment are determined, and designer begins to deal with decorative shapes and forms within the silhouette. Dividing the silhouette into smaller shapes with trim, patterns, seams, and other design devices produces variety and subtlety of effect.

Smaller areas within a silhouette are usually perceived as shape, and larger areas as space. A design is generally more pleasing if there is enough contrast between the size of decorative shape and the size of surrounding space to clearly define each. When seen on stage, costumes that lack sufficient difference between space and shape within the silhouette may be perceived as merely textured or may create a busy, fussy effect. A motif (decorative shape) that must be recognized as a symbol by the audience may need to be large with much surrounding space to compensate for the distance from stage to audience. A cross or fleur-de-lis on a tunic for St. Joan, for example, has strong character significance and must be readily recognized by the audience. The need to clarify the symbol may lead the designer to simplify other aspects of the garment.

Light

Don't look at us like we are, sir. Please. Remove ten pounds of road dust from these aged wrinkled cheeks. See make-up caked, in glowing powder pink! Imagine a beard, full blown and blowing, like the whiskers of a bear! And hair! Imagine hair. In a box I've got all colors, so I beg you—imagine hair! And not these clothes. Oh no, no, no. Dear God, not rags like any beggar has. But see me in a doublet! Mortimer, fetch the doublet. There—Imagine! It's torn: I know—forget it. It vanishes under light. That's it! That's the whole trick; try to see me under light! . . .

The Fantasticks, Tom Jones and Harvey Schmidt

The portion of the electromagnetic or radiant spectrum that is visible to the human eye is called *light.* This radiant energy results from the vibration of electrons and includes x-ray, ultraviolet, infrared, and radio waves. The source of the energy is called the *stimulus* and the visual perception or sensation is termed the *response.* Visible rays are only a tiny part of the electromagnetic spectrum.

Light waves vary from other radiant energy only in wavelength and frequency. *Wavelength* is the distance between the highest point of one wave and the highest point of the next. *Frequency* refers to the speed of the wave vibrations. *Brightness,* or *level of illumination,* depends on the amount of energy radiating from the stimulus.

Light makes the visual perception of all other design elements possible. It provides illumination, defines lines and forms and locates their position in space, and identifies the textures and colors of surfaces. Light is perceived in two ways: *direct light* (from the source, i.e., sun, lamp, candle) or *reflected light* (reflected from the surfaces of objects).

As in almost no other situation, light on stage can be controlled and manipulated for an aesthetic purpose. While the responsibility for the direct light belongs to the lighting designer, the manipulation of reflected light is affected by the choice of materials, fabrics, and trims made by the costume and set designers. The figure on stage may appear different from moment to moment as it moves from one area of light to another. The costume designer must be aware of the lighting possibilities of any given moment in a play and choose fabric and trims that reflect light in suitable ways.

Physical Effects of Light

If our visual perception of an object depends on the reflection of light off its surface, then a designer must understand the effects produced by the manipulation of the aspects of light. The visual effects on costumes or scenery vary depending on the direction of the light, angle of light incidence, level of illumination, quality of light, and texture of reflecting surface.

The *direction* of light is generally controlled by the lighting designer. Light can be focused on the stage from the front, sides, top, back, and floor. Lighting for the thrust and arena theaters is generally balanced to produce a similar image to the audience on all sides of the stage. Lighting from the different areas of the proscenium stage produces specific effects: front light provides basic illumination, side light gives the actors and the scenery dimension, and back light separates the actors from the scenery and provides depth. Side lighting and back lighting also help eliminate or control shadows on the actors and the scenery.

The *angle of incidence* refers to the angle at which the light hits an object. A low angle of incidence produces low angle reflection off the surface of the object and long shadows behind the object. A high angle of incidence produces high angle reflection off the surface of the object and short shadows behind it.

The *level of illumination* refers to the degree of brightness of the light. The lighting designer uses the brightness and dimness of the light in a given area of the stage to create focus (helping the audience know where to look), to establish the time of day or climate, and to create a mood.

The *quality of light* on stage may be soft and diffused or sharp and focused, depending on the lighting instruments used and the effects desired. Diffused light is atmospheric; it reduces the contrast between surfaces and softens the contours of objects. Sharp light emphasizes surface quality, accents differences in textures, and stresses dimension. The use of sharp focused light heightens drama by creating strong highlights and dark shadows. (See box 4.C.)

Box 4.C   Aspects of stage light and their effects

Aspect	Effect
Direction	Produces highlights and shadows, creates or eliminates distortion, varies importance of objects or actors
Front	Gives general illumination; puts emphasis on areas or specific actors
Side	Defines figures and scenery, mood, atmosphere, and time
Back	Separates figures from scenery, sets mood, creates environment
Down	Reduces shadows on scenery, creates distorted effects on figures
Up	Creates dramatic effects on scenery and figures, is used for lighting drops and cycloramas
Angle of Incidence	
Low angle	Produces low angle reflection, long shadows
Sharp angle	Produces sharp angle reflection, less visible shadows
Level of Illumination	
Higher (brighter)	Reflects more light from the surface; offers higher temperature of radiant energy; directs audience's attention
Lower (dimmer)	Gives less light and less heat; creates atmosphere; draws less attention
Quality of Light	
Sharp	Emphasizes surface quality; accents differences in textures; stresses 3-D quality; heightens drama; creates brighter highlights; produces sharper, harder, darker shadows
Diffused	Reduces contrast; softens contours; creates mood

Surfaces react to light by *reflecting* (bouncing off), *absorbing* (intercepting light rays), or *transmitting* (passing light through a medium) the light rays. Using fabrics and trims that react to light in all three ways helps create variety, depth, and interest in both the individual costume and in groups of costumes. Although the lighting designer is responsible for the type and placement of the stage lighting, the costume designer can create many special effects by controlling the surfaces on which the light falls. Box 4.D lists some commonly used costume materials and their responses to light.

Box 4.D   Material responses to light

High Reflection	Medium Reflection	High Absorption	Transmission
Mirror	Raw silk	Velveteen	Organza
Sequins	Brocade	Velvet	Chiffon
Lamé	Taffeta	Wool	Organdy
Vinyl	Crepe	Cotton	Scrim
Satin	Chintz	Velour	Net
Mylar		Knits	Tulle
Polyester			Lace
Lurex			
Glitter cloth			

Hard, smooth surfaces are highly reflective. Fabrics with fuzzy or irregular surfaces absorb most of the light rays. Fabrics that transmit light have spaces between fibers that permit some light rays to penetrate or they are made of materials that are translucent or transparent. Highly reflective materials applied in small shapes, such as sequins, reflect light differently than similar materials used in large flat surfaces because of the size of the surface and different angles of incidence provided by the movement of the wearer. Combining the two types of reflection is demonstrated to good effect in figure 4.9.

Psychological Effects of Light

The more light in a space, the more spring-like, cheerful, happy, and youthful the perception of that space will be. Conversely, a space with less light is perceived as sadder, more melancholy, older, and more winter-like. Sharp, bright, crisp, warm light in a space gives the feeling of joy, glory, or hope. Soft, diffused, cool light projects grief, melancholy, or romance. Harsh, strong light may suggest anger, violence, or power. The color of the light may suggest the time of day, the weather or climatic conditions, and the mood of the scene.

Color Perception

Strictly speaking, objects do not *have* color. They have pigmentation. A *pigment* is a material with the ability to reflect certain light waves. The perception of color in an object is the result of light reflected from the pigmentation of that object to the eye of the viewer. The color observed in an object depends upon the color pigmentation of that object, the color of the light rays illuminating the object, *and* the beholder's ability to discern the difference in the rays.

So-called "white light" appears white because it contains all colors of the visible spectrum in balanced proportions. When this light strikes a surface, two effects may result: the light may be reflected unchanged as sharp white highlights (such as are reflected off satins, vinyls, and water) or the white light may slightly penetrate the surface of the object, where the pigment in that surface absorbs all the wavelengths but one. That unabsorbed wavelength is reflected to the viewer's eye and the object is perceived as the color of *that wavelength*. The color we perceive is the color *not* absorbed by the surface pigment of the object. If balanced white light is focused on an object with no pigmentation, all the wavelengths are reflected and the object is perceived as white. If a surface contains pigments to absorb all the

Figure 4.9 *The Comedy of Errors*. Courtesan. A glittering and beautiful effect is produced by the combination of highly reflective (sequins) and transmissive (chiffon) materials chosen for this costume. Designed by Margaret Mitchell. Sketch photography by Adela Gott.

wavelengths, few are reflected and we perceive the object as black. The perception of black costumes on stage often depends on the color of the area surrounding the actor. The reflection of light from surrounding areas defines the black costume against those areas and compensates for the absorption of light by the black of the costume.

In practice, however, pure white light is seldom used for stage. The lighting designer develops a plan using various colors of light to create a mood or environment for each of the hundreds of moments in a play. The use of dozens of lighting instruments focused on the acting area enables the lighting designer to subtly (or dramatically) direct the audience's attention to important points of action and to reflect or enhance the mood of the moment.

Color Theory for Light

Isaac Newton used a prism to separate white light into a spectrum and thereby made visible the magic of light and color. He devised the first *color wheel* (a device for showing relationships between hues) by bending his spectrum into a circle. Other color theorists have since developed the color wheel and theory more completely. Physicists agree that the primary (basic) colors of light are red, green, and blue. These basic colors cannot be mixed by combining any other colors of light, but among them they can create all other light colors. Overlapping red and green light produces yellow; overlapping red and blue light produces magenta; overlapping blue and green light produces blue-green or cyan. Therefore the secondaries in light are yellow, magenta, and cyan. (Pigment colors behave differently from light colors. Color theory for pigments is discussed in the *Color* section in this chapter.)

Combining all three primaries produces white light; thus, adding colors of light together is called the *additive theory.* White is the presence of all light and color; black is the absence of all light and color.

Colored lights for stage are produced by inserting a sheet of color medium into a frame that is placed in front of the lighting instrument. This plastic medium (sometimes called *gel)* screens out all wavelengths except that of the medium. Because a pigmented surface can reflect *only* the colors that are in the light that strikes it, colored light can seriously alter the perception of the color of objects on stage. Box 4.E indicates the *probable* effects of colored light on costume colors. Further complicating matters, stage light usually combines several colors, with the dominant color changing as the play progresses. Variations in the colors of light on stage are designed to give objects and figures dimension, create mood, and stimulate emotional responses from the audience.

Not only is the color of stage light controlled, but the levels of illumination are constantly varied. The level of illumination affects the perception of the object, and some colors may darken more quickly than others as the light dims. Colors with longer wavelengths (reds and oranges) lose their reflecting ability faster and therefore look darker sooner as the lights dim. Colors with shorter wavelengths (blues and violets) retain their reflecting ability longer and darken more slowly. This phenomenon might be an important consideration when scenes overlap and one area of the stage dims as lights go up in another area. Actors in costumes in the darker area should disappear quickly as the lights dim so as not to be "ghosts" moving offstage—unless, of course, this is the desired effect.

In bright, white light, colors seem warmer and tend toward yellow; at low light levels, the same colors seem cooler and tend toward blue. The costume designer may need to compensate for low levels of illumination in certain scenes. For example, if a red fabric is chosen for a dimly lit scene, a red-orange will appear warmer and richer than a pure red or a red with blue undertones. Greens might need to be more yellow to keep from looking too cool in lower illuminations. A moonlight scene such as the balcony scene in *Cyrano de Bergerac* requires some careful thought. Cyrano's black costume will make it easy for him almost to disappear under the balcony as he coaches Christian in the art of wooing, but will he disappear completely? What colors should Roxanne and Christian wear? What light will they be seen in? The usual colors of moonlight (blues)

Box 4.E   Probable effects of colors of light on colors of fabric

Fabric Color	Colors of Light						
	Amber (Yellow)	Orange	Red	Violet	Blue	Blue-green (Cyan)	Green
Yellow	Bright yellow	Yellow-orange	Red	Scarlet	Yellow-green	Yellow-green	Yellow-green
Orange	Orange	Bright orange	Bright red-orange	Scarlet	Light brown	Light brown	Light brown
Red	Bright red	Red-orange	Bright red	Scarlet	Purple-black	Dark maroon	Maroon
Violet	Dark brown	Dark brown	Dark gray	Deep violet	Dark violet	Dark violet	Violet
Blue	Dark blue-gray	Black	Gray	Light blue	Dark blue	Light blue-gray	Light blue
Blue-green	Green-blue	Dark green-blue	Black	Dark blue	Very dark blue	Dark blue-gray	Dark green
Green	Bright green	Dark green	Dark gray	Bluish brown	Light olive-green	Light green-gray	Strong green

Note: The effect of colored lights on fabric is difficult to anticipate. This chart suggests the probable effects of various colors of light on fabric colors. The exact shade, tint, or intensity of each color, however, may react in an unexpected way. For example, a dark red that has been lowered in intensity because its complement, green, has been added may turn black under red light as the green pigment *absorbs* the red light.

will make blue costumes more intense. Orange-based tones will gray out. Reds with too much blue will appear to vibrate. The costume will appear darker in the lower light levels than it actually is. What effect is desired?

Color

Beautiful ribbons, Count! That color, now,
What is it—"Kiss-me-Dear" or "Startled-Fawn"?
I call that shade "The Dying Spaniard."
Ha. And no false colors either. . . .

Cyrano de Bergerac, Edmond Rostand

The most exciting, powerful, and provocative element of design is color. As a purely physical phenomenon, we have seen that color is the result of the reflection of specific wavelengths of light from an object and the perception of those wavelengths by the observer. The physical understanding of this element, however, is only a small part of the story. The emotional or psychological response elicited by color is the result of both a vast store of cultural associations shared by a society and associations unique to each individual. The costume designer must learn to manipulate both the physical and psychological aspects of color in order to produce the desired audience response.

Color Theory for Pigments

Planning pleasing color schemes for sets of costumes, mixing paint for rendering sketches, and mixing dyes and paints to be used on fabrics for costumes all require that the designer understand basic color theory for pigments.

Many color theories have been developed for working with pigments. They do not behave in the same way that light waves do. The color wheel for pigments identifies red, yellow, and blue as *primaries,* that is, as basic colors that cannot be mixed from any other colors but, when combined, produce other hues. Red and yellow combine to make orange, blue and yellow combine to make green, and blue and red combine to make violet. Thus orange, green, and violet are identified as the *secondary* colors. *Tertiary* colors are produced when a secondary and a primary color are combined. These colors are named red-orange, yellow-orange, blue-green, red-violet, and blue-violet, expressing the influence of the primary color first. (See color plate 3.)

Colorless objects, such as glass and surfaces with no identifiable hue (white, black, or gray), are called *achromatic.* Objects with identifiable hue are called *chromatic.* Substances that produce color are called *colorants.* For light, the colorant might be a colored filter or gel. For surfaces, the colorant might be paint, dye, or ink.

Dimensions of Color.
To discuss color properly, one needs to understand its different aspects or dimensions. *Hue* is the general term or family name applied to a color, the location of the wavelength on the light spectrum. A pure hue is a color as it appears in the spectrum or on the color wheel. *Value* is the lightness or darkness of a hue. Colors with white added to them are called *tints* and are said to have *high values.* Colors with black added to them are called *shades* and are said to have *low values.* The values of colors can be compared to a gray scale shading from white to black. Every pure hue has its own *home value.* Yellow, the lightest hue, has the highest home value. The next color in descending value is orange, then red and green at similar home values, then blue, and at the lowest and darkest home value is violet. Changing the value of a hue can alter the psychological effect it produces. Lighter values tend to be purer, clearer, more youthful colors; darker values appear more serious, rich, and meaningful. However, the addition of white or black to some colors tends to alter the hue of that color. Black added to yellow, for example, pushes yellow toward a green hue. Some violets begin to appear pink when white is added. Black, white, and grays are *neutrals* because they express no hue.

Intensity is the brightness or dullness of a hue. Intensity is also referred to as saturation, chroma, purity, or vividness. Colors of high intensity are bright, clear hues; colors of low intensity are dull, slightly grayed hues. A hue is its brightest, therefore at its full intensity, only at its home value. To reduce the intensity of a hue with the least alteration in its value, a small amount of its complement can be added. Equal strengths of complementary colors combine to form a neutral gray. Because pigments are not all of the same concentration, and because different hues are of differing intensities, adjustments in the *amount* of pigment may be needed in order to mix equal *strengths* of two complementary hues. To produce a true neutral, complements must be of equal *strength.*

Physical Effects of Color

Single colors produce certain physical effects, but colors are rarely seen alone. Most are seen in relation to other colors. Colors next to one another or superimposed on one another are said to be juxtaposed. Colors in costumes are juxtaposed within the costume, with the hair and skin tone of the actor, with other actors' costumes, and with the scenic elements against which they play.

Each dimension of a color makes a contribution to the physical effects produced by that color.

Physical Effects of Hue.   The effects produced by a color on stage may be altered by the color of stage light. The effects described here assume the use of balanced or white stage light. Juxtaposing colors creates many effects. The following effects are most pertinent to the problems of the costume designer.

1. *The same color will look different against two contrasting background colors.* Two costumes of the same color may appear to be different hues if played in front of set areas of greatly differing colors.

2. *Two juxtaposed complements intensify one another.* A green costume on a red-haired actor has the effect of intensifying the hair color.

3. *Two closely related (but not adjacent) juxtaposed hues tend to repel each other.* When the "middle" color is added, a link is provided to draw the colors together by emphasizing their similarities. A character in a red costume and one in a violet costume might appear quite independent of each other until a third character in red-violet completes the color group.

4. *A color gives the effect of its complement to colors juxtaposed with it.* A neutral, tint, or shade will tend to take on the character of the complement of the juxtaposed color. An orange costume may cause a neutral gray backdrop to have a cold blue feeling. The exception: Bright colors may reflect onto juxtaposed colors.

5. *Reds, oranges, and white tend to spread and merge with each other and with other colors; greens, blues, violets, and black tend to separate and delineate colors.* Shapes outlined in white look lighter and merge with one another and surrounding space. Shapes outlined in black are sharp and distinct. A costume with skirt ruffles outlined in white will look lighter and more delicate; a costume with skirt ruffles outlined in black will look heavier, crisper, and more distinct.

6. *Edges between adjacent hues of like value and intensity tend to fade.* Groups of chorus or crowd members who need to be nonspecific will be less distinct if costumed in adjacent colors of similar value and intensity—for example, medium-value, low-intensity blues; medium-value, low-intensity greens; and medium-value, low-intensity blue-greens.

Visual mixtures are blendings of color that occur in the eye and brain rather than on the surface of objects. Dots of color placed next to one another are blended by the eye and brain. Visual mixtures are particularly interesting for stage use because the distance from stage to audience is a necessary ingredient in the process. With the addition of multicolored stage light, the richness of visual mixtures is enhanced. Visual mixing is achieved through choosing fabrics with small flecks, dots, or patterns of color or by spattering or spraying the garment with paint or dye. The colors produced by visual mixing have more depth, richness, and vibrancy than colors achieved through pigment mixing.

7. *Visual mixtures of points or dots of two primary colors produce vibrant secondary or tertiary colors.*

8. *Visual mixtures of all three primaries and/or black and white tend to mix more quickly and are muted.* These visual mixtures provide rich neutrals for background or chorus colors.

9. *Color points of similar value and intensity mix more easily than those of extremely contrasting values or intensities.*

10. *Smaller dots of color blend visually at shorter distances than larger dots of color.* The closer the audience is to the acting area, the smaller the points of color need to be for complete visual mixing.

Physical Effects of Value.   Contrast in value is one of the most powerful principles of visual design. The stronger the value contrast, the bolder and more severe the effect is; the softer the value contrast, the gentler and more subtle the effect is.

1. *Light values advance and enlarge; dark values recede and reduce.* Lighter values tend to make individuals stand out from large groups on stage. A main character dressed in a lighter value should be clearly visible standing in front of the chorus.

2. *Value affects apparent density.* If two shapes are the same size and are seen against a neutral background, the dark one will appear to weigh more. This effect explains the top-heavy feeling given by some garments when the upper portion is dark and the lower portion is light.

3. *Light and dark values juxtaposed push each other apart, stressing their differences.* Light values make dark values seem darker; dark values make light colors seem lighter. The stronger the contrast in value between costumes, the less the characters will seem to be related. This effect can be overcome by the use of different values of the same hue.

4. *When value contrast is extreme, the hues involved are less noticeable; when values are closer together, the hues are more apparent.* The audience is more aware of the strong contrast in hue than in the colors involved. When costumes are closer in value, the variety of hue becomes more important.

Physical Effects of Intensity.   The careful manipulation of color intensities provides an infinite variety of color effects for the costume designer's use.

1. *Brighter intensities demand more attention.* In general, the brighter the intensity of a hue, the less of the color is needed for effect. A strong accent of bright red draws attention on a black dress, even if it is rather small.

2. *Bright intensities advance and enlarge; dull intensities recede.* Bright intensities worn by important characters make them stand out from low-intensity group colors. With stage lighting, however, a group of similar intensities

can be lowered by reducing the amount of light or altering the color of the light on them. Spotlighting one member of a group makes that character's costume color a brighter intensity than the rest of the group in a lower light level.

3. *Large areas of unrelieved, bright-intensity color can become tiring to the observer.* This effect, too, can be altered with stage lighting; variations in light color and level of illumination create different intensities of color on large areas of the same hue.

4. *Different intensities intensify each other regardless of hue.* Any differences in color will be emphasized when there is contrast in intensity. A high-intensity red and a low-intensity blue used together visually separate and delineate each other. Medium intensities of these colors used together tend to be less distinct and the edges between the two may blur at a distance.

5. *Small areas of bright intensity balance larger areas of dull intensity.* Conversely, large areas of bright intensity tend to overpower smaller areas of low-intensity color (face, hair). Scenes with many characters in low-intensity colors can easily be accented with small areas of bright-intensity color (scarves, flowers, hats, ties). More difficult may be very colorful scenes (musical numbers, dance, crowd scenes) where focus may wander from the actors' faces. Potential solutions include careful variation of hue and intensity and introduction of neutrals.

Psychological Effects of Color

Our emotional response to a color is the result of a triggering of some subconscious association we have with that color. These associations begin to accumulate when, as very small children, we first perceive and respond to colors. Researchers have shown that red, yellow, green, and blue at bright intensities and normal values are the first colors to attract the attention of young children. As a child grows and develops, colors become associated with the objects of everyday experience. Blue sky, brown earth, and green trees are almost universal associations. Colors of the changing seasons become associated with the concepts of time passage, age, temperature, and climate. Groups of people with similar experiences of the world share the same color associations. Religious concepts have for centuries been expressed in symbolic colors. (See box 4.F.) Citizens of most countries have such strong associations with the colors of their country's flag that the colors themselves elicit patriotic feelings even when the flag is not present. Colors are powerful symbols and can communicate to large groups of people in a common language.

Some color associations come from experiences unique to the individual. These experiences can be either negative or positive and may alter the expected viewer response. The costume designer cannot anticipate these associations in the individual audience members. Some thought should be given to those personal associations that may affect the designer's *own* color responses, however. Such associations may lead to the use of personal color preferences that are unrelated to the mood or character. Personal color prejudices limit the designer's ability to succeed in a broad range of theater work.

The various dimensions of color all contribute to the emotional responses and associations of the observer.

Box 4.F Historical color symbolism

West and Middle East

	Red	Yellow and Gold	Green	Blue	Purple	White	Black	Other
Egypt	Mortals	Sun, universal power	Nature	Heaven, sacred	Earth			
Classical Greece	Love and sacrifice		Learning	Truth, integrity, altruism		Divinity, purity		
Druids			Wisdom	Truth		Supremacy, purity		
Judaism	Sacrifice, love, glory, salvation, sin	Heavenly	Earthly	Glory of the Lord	Divine condescension, splendor	Purity, victory		
Cabalism	Strength	Beauty	Victory	Mercy	"The Foundation"	"The Crown"	Understanding	Orange: glory Gray: wisdom
Christianity	Holy Ghost, human body, blood of Christ, suffering, Hell, martyrdom, charity, sacrifice	Glory, power, God the Son, the human mind, earth	Immortality, faith, contemplation	Hope, deity, serenity, heaven, God the Father, the human spirit, sincerity, love of divine works, the Virgin Mary	Penance, suffering, repentance, self-sacrifice, faith, endurance, affliction, melancholy	Purity, innocence, chastity, joy, glory	Death	

Far East

	Courage, zeal	Loyalty	Youth, hope	Piety, sincerity	Sacrifice, patriotism, royalty	Faith, purity	Grief, penitence	Orange: strength, endurance / Orange: engineering Pink: music
Heraldry	Courage, zeal	Loyalty	Youth, hope	Piety, sincerity	Sacrifice, patriotism, royalty	Faith, purity	Grief, penitence	Orange: strength, endurance
Academics	Theology	Science	Medicine	Philosophy	Law	Arts and letters		Orange: engineering Pink: music
Brahmanism	Sacred	Universal understanding		True hue of the sun			Evil	
Confucianism		Sacred to Confucius		Sacred, the Ultimate				
Buddhism	Love, sin	Sun, universal power, sacred to Buddha					Sacred	
Shintoism	Blood of life		Wisdom				Mystery	
Persia		Glory	Immorality			Eternity	Sin	
Islam	Sacred		World mother, sacred to Mohammed			Infinite joy / Salvation		

Psychological Effects of Hue. In human experience certain colors have become associated with sources of light and heat. The red glow of burning coals, the yellow flicker of a candle flame, and the orange of molten metal are subconsciously related by the observer to those colors in other forms. Because of these associations, these colors are referred to as *warm colors*. Colors from the opposite side of the color wheel—blue, green, and violet—are associated with the sky, mountains, and water in various forms, all of which have cool, refreshing connotations, and these are called *cool colors.* Yellow-green and red-violet have warm effects juxtaposed to cool colors, but they behave like cool colors when combined with warm colors. On the color wheel warm colors have cool colors as complements.

Warm colors appear to advance and cool colors appear to recede. Because we associate distance with size of objects, shapes in advancing warm colors seem larger and shapes in receding cool colors seem smaller.

The perception of colors as "warm" and "cool" has a great deal to do with the associations attached to those colors. Box 4.G shows the major color associations of Western European and American cultures. Some colors have opposing connotations depending on the context in which the color is seen. Green, for example, has associations with summer, growth, and naturalness when seen in a costume, but might suggest disease or terror if used for skin tones. The designer should not ignore the prevalent associations with specific colors, nor be restricted by them. The designer should be aware, however, that these associations operate in the audience primarily on a subconscious level.

Psychological Effects of Value. The effects of value can alter the effect of hue. A lighter value (*tint*) of a color dilutes the associations made with the pure color. A darker value (*shade*) deepens or controls the emotional response to the pure color. For example, a light pink (a tint of red), while still warm, is not considered passionate or loud but may still express love or quiet sacrifice. A dark garnet red (a shade of red) might still express passion or danger, but with control and sophistication.

Because light colors *reflect* more light, light-colored surfaces *absorb* less light and therefore less *heat.* For centuries, societies in warm climates have preferred light-colored garments for their comfort. Because dark colors absorb *more* light, therefore more *heat* from the radiant source, people in cold climates have leaned toward darker colors. These associations have been transferred to seasonal clothing and, in spite of air conditioning and central heating, persist today in psychological associations.

Lighter values of naturally low-value colors (tints of blue or violet) appear less dense than the pure hues, and light values of cool colors begin to advance. Low values of naturally high-value colors (shades of red, yellow) appear denser than the pure hues, and low values of warm colors begin to recede.

Psychological Effects of Intensity. Since a color appears in its full intensity on the color wheel, its intensity can only be lowered from that level. Lowering the intensity of a color subdues the effects of its hue. Lowering the intensity of orange, for example, quiets and stabilizes its effects. As a color is neutralized, its effects become more neutral.

Box 4.G   Major color associations of Western European and American cultures

Color	General Appearance	Associations
Red	Brilliant, intense, enlarging, masculine, active, opaque, dry	Fire, heat, strength, love, passion, power, danger, primitiveness, excitement, patriotism, sin, fierceness, sacrifice, vitality, loudness, impulsiveness, blood
Red-orange	Intense, bright, dry, enlarging, masculine	Autumn, energy, gaiety, impetuousness, strength, spirit, boldness, action, warmth, loudness
Orange	Bright, luminous, dry, enlarging, masculine, glowing	Autumn, warmth, cheer, youthfulness, vigor, exuberance, excitement, extremism, earthiness, satiety, loudness, charm
Yellow-orange	Bright, radiant, dry, enlarging, masculine	Autumn, happiness, prosperity, hospitality, gaiety, optimism, openness
Yellow	Sunny, incandescent, radiant, feminine, enlarging, dry	Spring, brightness, wisdom, enlightenment, happiness, kindness, cowardice, treachery, ill health, warmth, sunlight
Yellow-green	Tender, bright, enlarging	Spring, friendship, youth, sparkle, warmth, restlessness, newness
Green	Clean, moist, reducing	Summer, youth, inexperience, growth, envy, restlessness, newness, quiet, naturalness, wealth, coolness, water, refreshing, ghastliness, disease, terror, guilt
Blue-green	Quiet, clean, moist	Summer, quietness, reserve, relaxation, faithfulness, smoothness, discriminating, rational
Blue	Transparent, wet, deep, reducing	Winter, peace, restraint, loyalty, sincerity, youth, conservatism, passivity, honor, purity, depression, melancholy, sobriety, serenity, gentleness, innocence
Blue-violet	Deep, soft, reducing, moist	Tranquility, spiritualism, modesty, reflection, somberness, maturity, aloofness, dignity, fatigue
Violet	Deep, soft, dark, misty, atmospheric, reducing	Stateliness, royalty, drama, dominance, mystery, dignity, pomposity, supremacy, formality, melancholy, quietness, mourning, loneliness, desperation, profundity, art, philosophy
Red-violet	Deep, soft, dark, warm	Drama, enigma, intrigue, tension, remoteness, intensity
Brown	Warm, dark, deep	Autumn, casualness, friendliness, naturalness, earthiness, tranquility, honesty, security, substance, stability, humility
White	Spatial, light, deep	Winter, snow, youthfulness, virginity, joy, purity, cleanliness, honesty, hope, innocence, spiritualism, enlightenment, forgiveness, worthiness, delicacy, love, day
Black	Spatial, dark, deep	Night, mourning, ominousness, death, formality, sophistication, gloom, uncertainty, evil, mystery, dignity, sorrow
Gray	Neutral, misty	Calmness, dignity, serenity, versatility, resignation, death, ghastliness, obscurity, penitence

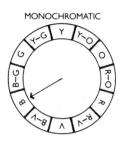

MONOCHROMATIC

ADJACENT

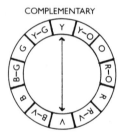

COMPLEMENTARY

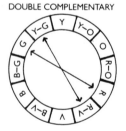

DOUBLE COMPLEMENTARY

ADJACENT COMPLEMENTARY

High-intensity colors are simple, youthful, and dynamic; low-intensity colors are mature, sophisticated, and complex, hinting at associations instead of shouting them.

Some color effects have been overused and run the risk of being trite or stereotyped. The designer must look for a variety of color choices to express the range of associations desired.

Color Schemes

Some basic formulas for combining colors have been developed through the use of the color wheel. These color schemes are guides for the designer who is choosing colors for costumes, but they should not be viewed as rules. The basic color scheme can be further developed by the use of a wide range of values and intensities of each color and by the addition of neutral colors. (Some popular schemes such as red, white, and blue do not fall under these formulas.)

A *monochromatic* color scheme is based on one hue and is developed with a range of tints, values, and intensities of that hue. An example of a monochromatic scheme is light blue, royal blue, and navy blue.

Analogous or *adjacent* color schemes are based on two to four hues that lie next to each other on the color wheel. Yellow, yellow-orange, orange, and red-orange represent an adjacent color scheme.

Complementary color schemes are based on two hues opposite one another on the color wheel. Violet and yellow are complementary colors.

A *double complementary* scheme would include two adjacent hues and their complements. Yellow-orange and orange with blue and blue-violet make a four-hue base for a double complementary scheme.

An *adjacent complementary* scheme is made up of two complements and a color next to one of them. Green, red, and red-orange combine for an adjacent complementary scheme.

Single split complementary schemes start with a pair of complements, take the hues on each side of one of the complements, and then omit *that* complement. Yellow, red-violet, and blue-violet (omitting violet) form a single split complementary scheme.

A *double split complementary* scheme starts with a pair of complements, takes the hues on each side of the complements, and then omits *both* complements. The resulting four-hue base includes two sets of complements that are not adjacent to one another. Yellow, orange (omitting yellow-orange), violet, and blue (omitting blue-violet) combine for a double split complementary color scheme.

Triad color schemes are based on three hues equally spaced on the color wheel. The primaries—red, yellow, and blue—are an example of such a color scheme.

Tetrad color schemes are based on four hues equally spaced on the color wheel. Yellow-orange, red, blue-violet, and green form a tetrad color scheme.

A *neutral* color scheme makes use of black, white, and gray. Sometimes low intensities and very high or very low values of other colors are called neutral because their hue is difficult to determine. A color like navy blue, tan, or cream can vary a neutral color scheme or contribute beautifully to a scheme including its home value.

These formulas offer only a guide for developing pleasing combinations of color. To find suitable combinations the chosen hues might be lightened, darkened, or dulled. A carefully balanced contrast in both value and intensity is needed in order for a color scheme to be harmonious and to produce the desired physical and psychological effects. The emotional quality of a given color will differ as its forms differ. The greater the contrast in values and intensities in a scheme, the stronger and more dramatic the physical effects and the bolder or more severe the psychological effects are in that scheme. Subtle combinations are more difficult to achieve, but they offer intricate variations in meaning. Harmony is generally perceived in color combinations that either are closely related or are opposites. Color experiments indicate that more pleasing effects result from either very small or very large differences in color. The distinction between colors that are very close in value or intensity is easily lost on stage, however. Stage lighting tends to blend similar values and intensities together.

Texture

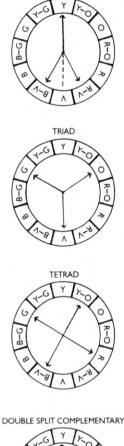

> *I think you're nuts.*
> *No, I ain't. George says I ain't. I like to pet nice things with my fingers.*
> *Soft things.*
> *Well, who don't? Everybody likes that. I like to feel silk and velvet. You like to feel velvet?*

Of Mice and Men, John Steinbeck

The *texture* of an object is its tactile surface characteristics or a visual representation of a tactile surface. There is a tendency to associate texture with "rough," but the word "texture" applies to a quality of all surfaces. Tactile sensations tell us a fabric is smooth, rough, fuzzy, or nubby. By the time we are adults, we have vast experience with textures. We no longer need to touch a surface to understand and relate a sensation to a given texture. Just as we relate colors to experiences of the world around us, so we may relate textures to objects we have experienced: "smooth as glass," "rough as gravel," "soft as fur." We experience these textures vicariously when we see them *visually* represented.

Fortunately for the costume designer, fabric (the basic medium of costumes) comes in an almost endless variety of textures. In addition, the designer can add textural interest to costumes with trims, paint, and design details such as tucking, pleating, shirring, ruching, ruffles, smocking, embroidery, appliqué, or quilting. In figure 4.11 (on the following page) a variety of textural materials are used to create the armor for War in *The Horseman*.

Figure 4.10 The most common color schemes (see text for definitions).

Aspects of Texture

Structural texture is the result of the elements of a substance and the method of its construction. Each medium used by an artist has unique textural qualities. The basic ingredients in paint produce certain textural effects. The method of application produces additional effects. The surface to which the paint is applied may add another textural element. Fabrics, like other media, have unique properties

Figure 4.11 *The Horseman* (short film). War. Textural materials and metallic paint were combined to create the armor for War. Designed by Cynthia Turnbull for Room 101 Productions. Photo by Chad Dutka.

that need to be understood for effective manipulation.

The basic structural elements of fabric are *fiber, yarn, construction,* and *finish.* Varying these elements produces fabrics each with a different "hang" (draping quality), "hand" (the way a fabric feels when handled), and surface effect. Further discussion of fabric can be found in chapter 7.

Visual texture refers to the visual and mental response to structural texture, or the impression of a tactile surface created by visual representations of actual textures or by decorative pattern. The use of textures (fabrics) by the costume designer creates variety in the individual costume and relates or contrasts the whole group of costumes. By varying the type of textures employed, the designer can produce totally different design concepts. Similar structural textures (similar fabrics) with varying decorative textures (motifs or trims) provide one approach. Varying structural textures (different fabrics) can be unified with related decorative textures.

In addition to fabric and trim in the costume, the designer must consider the relationship of textures in the actor's hair and skin, in the costume accessories, and in the scenery as components of a total composition.

Fabrics span the range of textures from smooth–hard to rough–soft. Some other descriptive terms for both structural and visual texture are:

scratchy	heavy	crisp	fuzzy
satiny	pebbly	papery	bristly
velvety	sandy	furry	

Physical Effects of Texture

Textures can either alter or support the physical perception of the effects of light, color, line, and form. Rough textures soften the edges of forms and create irregular outlines. They break up light and diffuse it. Rough textures tend to enlarge shape, but small even textures do not necessarily reduce shape. Smooth, hard textures present forms distinctly and reflect light in sharp highlights. Rough textures soften the effect of strong line; smooth textures strengthen the effects of line. Rough textures soften or dull the effects of color; smooth, hard textures emphasize color. Medium-textured fabrics provide neutral background spaces for textural effects in decorative trim. Extreme contrasts in texture may have harsh or severe effects, whereas lack of contrast in textures becomes uninteresting unless contrast is provided by some other design element. The costume designer uses texture to modify or strengthen effects of other design elements in the costume and to assist in creating variety and interest.

Psychological Effects of Texture

Textures express moods or associations that modify or support the psychological effects of color, line, and form. Texture is a strong tool for the designer. The use of various textures can suggest character, status, personality, sophistication, age, occasion or season, or fragility or strength. We associate fragile-looking fabrics with occasions that put no stress on garments and with characters that do no hard physical labor. A costume for Laura in *The Glass Menagerie* might make good use of a soft, smooth, almost sheer fabric to express her delicate, fragile quality. Sturdy textures are associated with more vigorous occasions and characters. Box 4.H describes the physical and psychological effects of some basic textures.

When planning textures for the stage, the designer must take into consideration the distance between the audience and the stage. More delicate textures

---

Box 4.H   Effects of texture

Texture	Physical Effect	Psychological Effect (Mood)
Smooth, crisp	Sharp silhouette, much reflected light	Refined, hard, cheerful, perky, sophisticated
Smooth, soft	Sharp silhouette, much reflected light	Sensuous, relaxed, luxurious
Velvety soft	Enlarging, but less defined, dense, less reflected light	Rich, luxurious
Fuzzy	Enlarging, but less defined, dense, less reflected light	Luxurious, cuddly, primitive, untamed
Rough	Softer silhouette, less reflected light	Sporty, natural, uncouth, coarse, primitive, casual
Coarse	Enlarging, less reflected light	Uncouth, earthy, uncivilized
Medium (regular)	Neutralizing, medium reflected light	Businesslike, mature, stable, conservative
Medium (irregular)	Neutralizing, medium reflected light	Stable, active, warm

tend to disappear over long distances and their effects may be lost on the audience. The effect of visual mixing (see p. 85) may eliminate the texture but enhances the color and the three-dimensionality of the costume.

Pattern

A special form of visual texture is *pattern*. Made up of other elements (line, form, color, and space), pattern creates a special kind of texture from the stage. Smaller patterns are indistinguishable at a distance and behave like medium or small textures. Medium to large patterns, however, have stronger effects than their counterparts in structural texture. Identifiable pattern creates psychological responses in the viewer and sends messages about the character that are stronger than those sent by any other element except color.

Patterns are derived from four sources: *nature, made objects, imagination,* and *symbolism* (see figure 4.12). Patterns derived from nature are pleasing and calming and, unless severely distorted, suggest positive associations. Patterns based on made objects have strong associations to time, place, gender, and events. Patterns derived from imagination fall into two categories: geometric and freeform. Few perfectly geometrical forms appear in nature (visible to the naked eye), but artisans for centuries have decorated clothing, everyday objects, and ritual accoutrements with geometric designs. Many of these motifs may have originated in the weaving of baskets or cloth and later been applied to other objects with paint. Free-form pattern can be inspired by nonvisual sources and may suggest feelings or moods rather than objects. Symbolism uses pattern based on any source and gives that motif a specific and widely accepted meaning. Symbols identify large, complex ideas in quick immediate ways. They are very useful to the costume designer, making possible quick identification of characters and the ideas with which they are associated. The problem for the designer is to use symbols in ways that are not simplistic, cliché, or anachronistic.

No matter what the source of pattern inspiration, it must be interpreted in some way. The choice of presentation form is determined by the effect desired. Patterns may be presented in realistic, stylized, and abstract forms. The costume designer's choice depends on character interpretation, period, and production style and concept.

The arrangement of pattern on a costume is an important consideration for the costume designer. The distance between audience and actor may alter the perception of pattern. Small spaces between pattern repeats may merge and reduce definition. Detail between repeats may be lost and cause central motifs to advance, creating a spotty effect.

Pattern repeats can be arranged in any of six ways (see figure 4.13 on p. 98):

1. *All-over:* Patterns that have the same effect from any direction.

2. *One-way:* Patterns that have the same effect from one direction only.

3. *Two-way:* Patterns that have the same effect from top to bottom and bottom to top.

4. *Four-way:* Patterns that have the same effect from top to bottom, bottom to top, left to right, and right to left.

5. *Border:* Patterns arranged to place main motifs along one or both selvages of fabric.

Figure 4.12 Types of pattern. (A) natural sources, (B) made objects, (C) geometrical designs, (D) free-form pattern, and (E) symbolic pattern. Photos by Jack H. Cunningham.

A

B

C

D

E

Figure 4.13 Arrangements of pattern.
Six ways printed or woven motifs repeat:
(A) all-over, (B) one-way, (C) two-way,
(D) four-way, (E) border, and (F) panel.
Photos by Jack H. Cunningham.

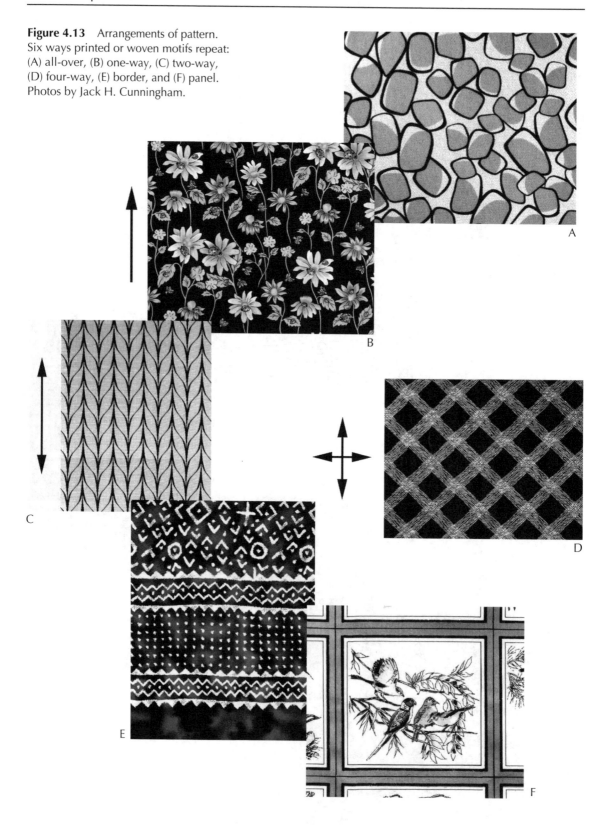

6. *Panel:* Self-contained motif that may repeat only once within the garment and is designed for specific usage; for example, a scarf or a decorative neckline.

Physical Effects of Pattern. Since a pattern combines the elements of space, shape, line, and color, it is subject to all the physical effects of the design elements used to develop it. In addition, the following effects follow:

1. Pattern accents the area in which it is used.

2. Pattern complements simple structural design.

3. Pattern adds visual interest.

4. Pattern attracts attention away from silhouette, distracting the eye from less pleasing body contours.

5. Larger patterns are enlarging, but smaller patterns do not necessarily reduce.

6. Sharply outlined motifs are more emphatic, dramatic, and enlarging than fuzzy-edged motifs.

7. Patterns that create optical illusions quickly become distracting and visually tiring.

Psychological Effects of Pattern. Pattern is also subject to all the psychological effects of the design elements used to develop it. In addition, the following effects of pattern seem prominent in Western cultures:

1. Closely spaced motifs may create a crowded, pressured feeling. Widely spaced motifs may create a spotty impression.

2. Flattened motifs (those without shading or dimension) suggest youth, simplicity, casualness, or humor.

3. Plant, floral, and flowing motifs are viewed as feminine; animal and geometric motifs are considered more masculine.

4. Large motifs are viewed as dynamic and bold; small motifs are viewed as dainty.

Generally, the patterns used in a production should be related in scale and style. The use of multiple patterns in one costume can suggest carelessness, naiveté, or in some cases extreme sophistication, depending on the context of the costume. In figure 4.14 (on the following page) the use of several stripes and plaids gives Dean from *Once Upon a Forest* an air of innocence and youth. Effective use of pattern makes a set of costumes interesting and varied.

Principles of Design

The theatre . . . should be a perfectly pure juxtaposition, a series of precise concatenations, each element gauged to its exact value. Beauty resides in the power of suggestion inciting the spectator's participation. Creation is incomplete without his contribution and spirit. Beauty refuses to bow to the limitations of meaning or description.

Sonia Delaunay

DEAN AS
DUMBLING

Figure 4.14   *Once Upon a Forest*. Dean as Dumbling Brother. Effective use of pattern makes a set of costumes interesting and varied. Designed by Laura Crow for The Children's Theater Company.

If the elements of design are the components with which designers work, the principles of design are the techniques or guidelines for using those components. A principle of design is both the *method* of manipulating the elements and the *effect* of successfully applying that method. The sixteen principles discussed here fall into three groups: *directional, highlighting,* and *synthesizing* principles (see figure 4.15). All principles can be used either structurally or decoratively. Each principle is intricately related to the other principles and an example of one may also involve the use of others.

Directional Principles

Generally the simplest, directional principles lead the eye from one place to another, build to a climax, and emphasize a direction.

Repetition is the use of a design unit more than once. A color repeated in two areas of a costume, rows of trim on the skirt and cuff of a garment, a series of buttons on the front of a vest are all examples of repetition. *Regular* repetition repeats identical elements; *irregular* repetition repeats related but slightly different elements. Irregular repetition weakens direction but increases interest. Repetition causes the eye to follow the repeated elements, thus strengthening the direction of the line between them or of the space they occupy. Repetition is a strong tool for creating unity in a costume or group of costumes.

Parallelism is the use of equidistant units on the same plane. Parallelism applies to line, shape, and space. Effective use of parallelism creates interest and emphasis. Like repetition, which it closely resembles, parallelism causes the eye to follow the direction of the parallel elements. In figure 4.16 (on p. 102) parallel divisions of space (stripes, tucks, trim) emphasize the height of the actor.

Sequence is one unit following after another in a particular order and in regular succession. Sequences build to a climax, relax, then build up to a climax again. They are less flowing than other directional effects, but they can be versatile and playful while establishing a sense of order.

Figure 4.15 Principles of design. (A) repetition; (B) transition; (C) parallelism; (D) concentricity; (E) gradation; (F) radiation; (G) sequence; (H) alternation; (I) rhythm

Alternation is the sequence of two units changing back and forth. The alternation of two things causes the eye to follow the direction of the sequence. Primarily decorative in its application, alternation is usually calming but may become boring.

Gradation is the sequence of adjacent units, identical in all respects but one, which changes in specific steps from one unit to the next. Gradation may reverse at the climax and return to step one of unit one, or it may repeat as in a sequence, or it may end at a climax. Gradation has powerful potential for costume development because its use heightens and intensifies the psychological effects of the element gradated.

Transition is the smooth, continuous movement from one position or condition to another. Lines, shapes, colors, spaces, and textures can make smooth transitions within a costume design. These transitions sweep the eye along in the direction of the movement with graceful, gentle, but powerful force.

Radiation is a sense of movement outward from a central point (visible or implied). It produces strong directional effects of outward movement.

Rhythm is the perception of organized movement. Design units organized to create the feeling of movement may have either calm, soothing beats, or sharp, staccato beats. The psychological responses to rhythm can be casual, playful, sensuous, stately, or militant. Some types of rhythm are:

flowing	looping	sweeping	syncopated
jerky	marching	swinging	undulating
lilting	stately	swirling	vibrating

Highlighting Principles

Highlighting principles focus attention on the differences between one unit and another.

Figure 4.16 *On the Open Road.* Monk. Parallel divisions of space (stripes, tucks, trim) emphasize the height of the actor. Designed by Mathew J. LeFebvre for Penumbra Theater Company.

Concentricism is the layering of shapes, each progressively larger and each having the same center. Concentric shapes lead the eye inward to the next smaller shape and finally to a visual climax in the center.

Contrast is the juxtaposition of unlike units. The more unlike the units are, the sharper the contrast. The sharper the contrast is, the stronger the pull on the eye to the spot where the contrast occurs. Strong contrast is invigorating and dramatic, whereas subtle contrasts are desirable for delicate effects. Contrast is required in each costume and between different costumes that will be grouped together on stage. Box 4.I (on the following page) shows ways to create contrast between various aspects of the design elements.

Contrast creates interest and emphasis. The eye is drawn to the different element in a costume and to the different costume in a group. Figure 4.18 (on p. 105) shows how contrast is used in a series of costumes. In (A) the costume contrasts the curved line of the collar with the straight line of the gown. In (B) the patterned body of the gown is contrasted with the solid undergown. In (C) a tucker of a high-value color (light tone) contrasts with a gown of low-value color (dark tone). In (D), the small shapes of the hood and shoulder cape contrast with the larger shape of the cape.

Figure 4.17 *The Winter's Tale*. Autolycus. This sketch illustrates several principles of design. The stripes of the cape are *parallel* from neck to hem. The ribbon tassels on the edges of the cape are in a *sequence* and are *repeated* throughout the costume. The patterns on the pockets of the cape *alternate* for interest. Designed by Joel Ebarb for Purdue University.

Emphasis is the placement of focus on a point or area of the design—the center of interest to which all other areas are subordinated. Emphasis implies organization and complementary relationships of dominant and supporting elements.

In costume design the area of the garment emphasized also draws attention to that part of the body. By controlling emphasis, the designer can focus attention to the appropriate areas of the character's body. In theater, focusing on face and neck facilitates communication between audience and actor. In dance, how-

Box 4.1   Ways to contrast design elements

Elements	Contrast
Space	
Filled	Unfilled
Large	Small
Line	
Thick	Thin
Smooth	Rough
Solid	Broken
Vertical	Horizontal
Straight	Curved
Shape	
Straight-edged	Curved
Large	Small
Light	
Harsh	Diffused
Bright	Low (dim)
Reflected	Absorbed
Color	
Pure (saturated)	Low intensity
Hue	Complement
High value	Low value
Hue	Neutral
Texture	
Smooth	Rough
Soft	Hard
Patterned	Plain
Shiny	Dull

ever, the emphasis might be preferred on the feet or line of the body, not on the expression of the face.

Figure 4.19 demonstrates how each element of design can be manipulated to create emphasis in a costume and bring attention to a specific part of the body. *Space:* in (A) an area of filled space (the patterned bodice) emphasizes an area of open space (the neck and chest). *Line:* in (B) a strong line (the baldric) emphasizes the areas of the costume adjacent to it. *Shape:* in (C) a prominent shape (the triangular stomacher) focuses the viewer's eye on the areas around it (the waist). *Color:* in (D) a bright splash of color, like this bandanna, focuses the attention on the face. *Light:* in (E) reflective materials used on a costume draw attention to the area of "glitz." *Texture:* in (F) the texture created by a mass of curly hair successfully focuses attention on the face.

Figure 4.18 Contrast between aspects of elements. In (A) the costume contrasts the curved line of the collar with the straight line of the gown. In (B) the patterned body of the gown is contrasted with the solid undergown. In (C) a tucker of a high-value color (light tone) contrasts with a gown of low-value color (dark tone). In (D) the small shapes of the hood and shoulder cape contrast with the larger shape of the cape.

Figure 4.19 Emphasis. Each element of design can be manipulated to create emphasis in a costume and bring attention to a specific part of the body.

Emphasis can diminish undesirable physical attributes by drawing attention to more desirable ones. The eye naturally tends to seek out and differentiate between similarities and differences. The advancing, assertive effects of an element usually provide the best means of creating emphasis: warm colors; sharp, bold lines; shiny, reflective surfaces; contrast in elements. Basically, the *odd* element attracts the eye and creates emphasis at that point.

The edges of a garment emphasize neighboring parts of the body. Structural lines leading to a point create emphasis, as do unusual closings, seaming, and draping. When carefully manipulated, garment decoration can provide emphasis, but, if overdone, it merely creates confusion and fussiness. In figure 4.20 a white ruff creates primary emphasis at the neck of this design for Stephano in *The Tempest,* drawing the eye to the face of the actor, but smaller white ruffs on the sleeves provide secondary emphasis on the hands.

Figure 4.20
The Tempest. Stephano. The white ruff places primary emphasis at the neck, and the smaller sleeve ruffs provide secondary emphasis on the hands. Designed by Sheila Hargett for Texas State University.

A major problem for the production team is controlling the focus on stage at all times. In films and television the camera focuses our attention on the important action, reaction, or character in a scene. We see only what the camera sees and can only take the point of view of the camera. With stage productions the attention of the audience must be subtly directed to the important characters and action. On stage the director may move an actor to a more prominent stage position. The lighting designer may spotlight important characters or dim the light on less important ones. The costume designer works with line, shape, color, and texture to create emphasis (focus) on a character. In the musical *Little Mary Sunshine,* Mary is not much different in age and general appearance from the young ladies of the chorus, but she must not be lost among them.

Synthesizing Principles

Synthesizing principles guide the total combination of elements in a design to relate and integrate the parts.

Proportion is the result of the comparative relationships of distances, sizes, amounts, degrees, or parts to the whole. These relationships work in four ways:

1. *Within each part,* as in comparing the length with the width of a rectangle or silhouette.

2. *Between parts,* as in comparing the area of one shape with that of a neighboring one, such as the sleeve to the bodice.

3. *Part to whole,* as in comparing the area of the whole garment with that of the bodice.

4. *Whole to environment,* as in comparing the area occupied by the figure with that of the full stage.

The proportions of the elements appropriate in a given costume are relative to the effects of all the design elements in that costume. Figure 4.21 shows shapes divided in various proportions. Proportions of one-third to two-thirds (A) or two-fifths to three-fifths (B) are generally considered pleasing. The strength and number of the colors, patterns, textures, spaces, lines, and reflective surfaces (light) must be balanced for suitable effects (C–F). A designer must experiment and learn to evaluate the visual impact of the proportions of elements chosen.

Evaluation of pleasing proportion is culturally influenced. Many cultures have developed guides for pleasing proportions, usually expressed in mathematical formulas. However, the most pleasing proportions are often slightly off the mathematical formulas and related to a personal aesthetic sense. Application of proportion follows the same general guideline as all principles and elements of design do: enough variety for interest, but not so much as to create confusion or conflict. Basic relationships

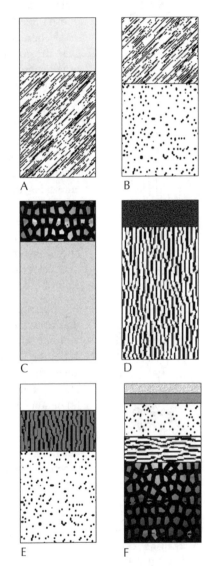

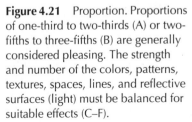

Figure 4.21   Proportion. Proportions of one-third to two-thirds (A) or two-fifths to three-fifths (B) are generally considered pleasing. The strength and number of the colors, patterns, textures, spaces, lines, and reflective surfaces (light) must be balanced for suitable effects (C–F).

A

B

C

Figure 4.22 Scale.
(A) Realistic scale.
(B) The same style
garment is reinter-
preted in a theatri-
cal scale for a
medium-size
theater. (C) The cos-
tume is exagger-
ated in scale for a
humorous effect.

of two-thirds to one-third, or two-fifths to three-fifths, are generally viewed as pleasing. There are, however, always those artists with the sensitivity and skill to push proportion to extremes and still present pleasing relationships in a design.

Functionally, the proportions of a costume must agree with the proportions of the actor's body to allow for movement and comfort. Arms, legs, heads, waists, and feet must be able to function as the action requires. A mermaid doesn't need to walk, but most characters do!

When considering proportion, we think first of the division of space. However, the consideration of proportions applies also to color, texture, and pattern. Smaller proportions of more advancing elements work well against larger proportions of receding elements.

Scale is the relative size of shapes to the whole and to each other, or comparative proportional size relationships. The scale of theatrical designs is often exaggerated to make the costumes visible to the audience throughout the theater. The less "real" the style of presentation is, the more exaggerated the scale can be. In figure 4.22 the same style garment has been interpreted in three different scales for realistic, theatrical, and humorous effects.

Larger-scale shapes are more aggressive and advancing than smaller-scale shapes. The sizes of decorative shapes, motifs, patterns, or accessories must be adjusted to relate to the part of the garment to which they are applied or to the body as a whole. "Out-scaled" (very large) or "under-scaled" (very small) shapes or accessories are often used for comic costumes. The circus clown with the too-small hat and too-large shoes is a well-known example.

Balance is the sense of evenly distributed weight, size, density, or tension that results in stability. Balance in a design is achieved when each part interacts with all others and with the whole to achieve stability. When the right side balances the left side, designs are said to have *horizontal balance*. When the top balances the bottom, designs are said to have *vertical balance*. When the whole is balanced around a central point, designs are said to have *radial balance*. Horizontal balance is necessary if the figure is to appear sober, stable, and upright. Vertical balance is necessary if the figure is to appear to rest firmly on the ground without looking top-heavy or weighed down. This type of balance is generally desirable. An exception might be dance costumes, particularly ballet costumes, where every effort is made to buoy the figure to enhance the feeling of weightlessness and flight.

There are two types of horizontal balance: *symmetrical* and *asymmetrical*. Designs balanced symmetrically have identical right and left sides. The determination of one side automatically is mirrored on the other side. Asymmetrical designs are different on each side of the central dividing line but still have a feeling of equally distributed weight. A skillful combination of elements is required to create a design that is balanced asymmetrically. Balance is crucial to a psychological feeling of security and stability. Symmetrical balance is stately and dignified, but obvious, static, and unassuming. Characters with formal, stable, or dignified traits would be well defined by costumes with symmetrical balance. Asymmetrical balance is casual, dramatic, complex, lively, and rhythmic. Characters with erratic, flamboyant, eccentric, or comic traits might be well defined with asymmetrically balanced costumes. In figure 4.23 a series of costumes illus-

FIGURE 4.23 Horizontal and Vertical Balance.

Figure 4.23   Horizontal and vertical balance.

trates the effect of the different approaches to balancing a garment. A symmetrical garment (A) tends to give a conservative or formal look to the figure, whereas an asymmetrical garment (B) tends to be less formal and suggests youth and vitality and sometimes sophistication. When one considers vertical balance, large areas of *dark color* at the bottom of a figure (C) give it a solid, feet-on-the-ground feeling. Large areas of *light color* at the bottom of the figure (D) will balance a smaller area of dark color at the top of the figure but may suggest a character with a streak of dandyism or happy-go-lucky traits. Figure 4.24 (on the following page) shows a design for Romeo that takes advantage of the dynamic movement of an asymmetrically balanced garment to focus on the head and shoulders and to create the impression of a spirited personality.

Symmetrically balanced garments emphasize irregularities of the figure, while asymmetrically balanced garments disguise irregularities.

Garments and figure must also balance in profile. The size and shape of the hat or hair are an essential element in balancing both front and profile views of the figure.

Harmony is a pleasing combination of elements, a consistency of feeling, mood, and function. Harmony demands an agreement among the functional, structural, and decorative aspects of the design. Harmony is strongly influenced

Figure 4.24 *Romeo and Juliet.* Romeo. The asymmetrical design of this costume sweeps the eye up to the face of the actor and helps creates the impression of a spirited personality. Designed by Bill Brewer for the British Resident International Theatre, University of South Florida.

by culture, fashion, and time. Some ideas of harmony pass quickly and others become classic. The determining factors in this process are (1) how broadly recognized and accepted a mood or idea is, (2) how well that idea or mood is interpreted by the design elements and the principles used, and (3) how well the functional, structural, and decorative aspects of the design agree.

Advancing qualities agree with other advancing qualities, and receding qualities agree with other receding qualities, but skillful combining of receding and advancing qualities provides complex and engaging costume designs that reflect the complexities of the characters portrayed. (See box 4.J.)

The perception of harmony in individual costumes and groups of costumes is not exclusively a visual perception. Harmony must be established between the visual aspects of the costumes themselves and between costumes and the concept of the play. Beautifully designed costumes and sets that do not support the concept of the play are not in harmony with the production.

Box 4.J   Advancing and receding effects of design elements and principles

	Receding	Advancing
Space	Small, closed, broken	Large, open, unbroken
Line	Curved, broken, thin, fuzzy, horizontal, short, porous	Straight, continuous, thick, sharp, solid, diagonal, vertical, long
Shape	Small, concave, porous	Large, solid, straight-edged, convex
Light	Dim, cool, diffused	Warm, brilliant, focused
Color	Cool hues, dark values, dull intensities	Warm hues, light values, bright intensities
Texture	Smooth, supple, porous, sheer, fine, delicate	Rough, bulky, stiff, thick
Pattern	Dainty motifs, soft edges, subtle shading, muted colors, small all-over or directional patterns	Bold motifs, sharp edges, flat and bright colors, geometric shapes, borders, spaced motifs, figure and ground distinct
Direction	Transition	Gradation, concentricism, emphasis
Rhythm	Smooth, flowing, gentle	Staccato, dynamic, dramatic
Contrast	Subtle, close	Bold, extreme
Balance	Formal, simple	Informal, complex
Scale	Small, dainty	Large, bold

Unity is the feeling of wholeness, of all parts complete and necessary to the totality. Harmony and unity are closely related; unity without harmony is impossible, but harmony without unity is possible. Unity integrates all aspects of the design but cannot truly be separated from them. Unity is subtle. It is the result of design elements used well and design principles applied well. Structural, functional, and decorative elements all must work toward a unified result.

In the theater, unity and harmony must be evaluated by a different set of functional standards from those used for other art forms. As one develops costume design skills, one must also develop the standards by which to judge harmony and unity on stage.

These principles of design provide basic guidelines for the use of design elements, but the designer must decide what effects are *desired* and must choose the elements and principles accordingly. The final question asked about any costume design is, "Does it work?"

Interview II.
Bringing Everyday Dress to the Stage.
A Conversation with Paul Tazewell.

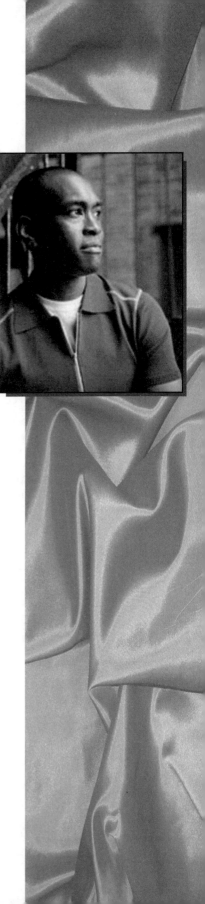

At the time of this interview with the author Broadway designer Paul Tazewell had received multiple honors and awards including three Tony Award nominations, three Helen Hayes Awards, and the Lucille Lortel Award. (See bio, page 422, for career details.)

RC: How did you become known as the go-to designer for contemporary street dress and how do you do research for street wear?

PT: My last year at NYU I met director Tazewell Thompson (no relation) and he recommended me for a production at Arena Stage called *Stand Up Tragedy,* a play about a young Puerto Rican guy from a broken home who relied on the world of comic books and its heroes to deal with life. That was the first time I was asked to design a production that was reflective of street life.

All along I was doing it by the book, what I was taught—you go to the library and do your research. But for *Tragedy* my research started on the street—riding the subway back and forth, just looking at people, taking note of what they wore, and *making up reasons* why they were wearing what they were wearing. Young people were beginning to wear clothes to give signals—signals of being part of a gang, signals of cache, the idea of "label." That was a world that was completely foreign to me. I am from Akron, Ohio. I grew up in a city neighborhood of separate homes with yards and gardens. I wasn't a part of that kind of street life, so I didn't know that vocabulary.

Figures II.1 and II.2 Paul Tazewell's Tony-award winning costumes for two town Gossips from *The Color Purple,* Broadway.

I never try to make it up. Taking the images that I saw in the subways, on the street, in magazines featuring rap artists—using all that, applying what I had learned and what was intuitive for me—that was the way I went. *Making character choices* is really what it comes down to, making specific character choices *that help to tell the story*.

That's really my strength, being as true as I *can be* to the character and how the character represents himself through clothing. And using clothing from character to character to create a *poetic moment*, to create an arc to say something about the piece as a dramatic moment, to say something large about the piece as a whole—all the things I learned in school that would apply to a Chekhov, or Shakespeare, or other classic piece.

My hope is that you experienced the piece, not really thinking about the clothes. That you got the feeling it was right and all the pieces were there, appropriate for the different characters, and it all felt seamless with the rest of the production. But I know in my head what I am doing. I'm setting up characters so that when you first see them, when they walk down the street, they give you a certain impact. Much of that is *intuition* in the fitting room.

My associates, assistants, and I will go out shopping and bring in a load of things. We have a whole rack of clothes to try on the actor, and just for one reason or another, something is just not right—either through getting feedback from the actor, or just having it not quite be a match. It might be the color I asked for, the kind of pattern I've asked for, the cut I asked for, all those things might have been fulfilled, but when it all comes together with the actor in the clothes—it just doesn't do what I want it to do.

So, really, contemporary clothes are for me more work, and more challenging than doing period clothes. With period clothes you can draw it out, and you can choose your fabric because you know it's going to be built, and you follow though all the steps, and as long as you have a draper or tailor that's talented—you know it will pretty much work as you would like it to.

You have a lot of knowledge about your own period and what means what. Even to the point in the language of urban clothing that when a pair of sneakers is out, they're out! You're passé and you've got to get the thing that's hot! The young performers know what's in and they don't want their friends to e-mail or text them, "what was that your designer had you in?" I appreciate that, but it's maddening. That's just what it is to do contemporary street costumes.

RC: Are you happy with being known for doing street dress?

PT: I've been fortunate to be able to balance solely contemporary work with pieces that are more classical, or new pieces set in periods, and fantasy pieces. I've had a good balance. Most of my work in NY tends to be pieces that involve stories about people of color, but I have developed strong relationships with directors who have seen beyond that.

However, I love, love, love my culture, and everything about it. One of my favorite designs and productions was *The Color Purple* because it was so vast—covering a period of time that really speaks to me (1912 to the forties). There are beautiful photographs of black people in that period. It was a great period of style and fashion for everyone, but definitely for Afro Americans in America. I would look at those photographs over and over again, maybe because I saw so much of my family in them. To be able to investigate that more directly was very gratifying.

Even being able to figure out the design in street clothes has also been exciting. To be nominated for a Tony for *In the Heights* was a shock and a surprise because somebody took note and saw what I did. I wasn't just putting clothes on people, I was trying to design something, a moment—saying something.

We always draw from our experience; that's what you start from—you see the world through you lenses, with the fog of your own experience.

Specifically as an Afro American designer, when I am doing a Black show, I have a more direct bank of images, actual people and characters that I remember from growing up that I can draw on, that feel like the characters that are being portrayed—an uncle or aunt, or a man down the street, the church congregation. . . . I know that they had access to the Sears and Roebuck catalog or whatever.

Also, there is what I call the "feeling." You remember going into a room in your friend's home when you were ten. You remember what the walls were like, and the smells. The mother came into the room and she had on a caftan, and you are trying to get all of that experience to happen on a character. The pattern for the caftan is chosen to put all those senses together—to give some kind of *impact* that feels like what you remember in your specific experience.

RC: That is the kind of experience any designer might have had of his/her own culture and can apply to a costume project.

PT: Exactly. I might need it to be a Jewish woman's home and character. I still want it to feel something like this. So I

Figures II.3 and II.4 Paul Tazewell's Tony-award winning costumes for a town Gossip and Celie from *The Color Purple*, Broadway.

Figure II.5 Paul Tazewell's Roustabout #2 designed for *Carnival at* The Kennedy Center.

choose certain patterns and colors for her that are appropriate for that character and her culture, that feel something like what my experience was.

RC: What advice do you have for young designers?

PT: Go and make use of the library. Do your research. You find so much going to the library, looking at one book and finding something else next to it that you didn't know to look for. You don't know what it's about, and you open it up, and you flip through it, and it takes you in a new direction.

I do a lot of computer research, too, because it offers up different kinds of possibilities. There are images that you would never come across if you weren't on the Internet.

But the computer is not the end of your search. It might be where you begin, but you can't feel you have covered it all if you just sat at your computer and did a search. *That's not everything that's out there.* You have to get off your duff and pound the pavement. That's what this job is about, *pounding a lot of pavement.* That's how you do it effectively.

Chapter 5

Developing the Costume

. . . Costly thy habit as thy purse can buy,
But not expressed in fancy; rich, not gaudy;
For the apparel oft proclaimes the man . . .

Hamlet, William Shakespeare

For the purpose of discussion, the different steps of the costume design process have been separated here, but one should understand that these steps are intricately interwoven and cannot in fact be separated completely. Nor is their order rigidly set. No two designers work exactly alike and the same designer may work in different ways on different productions. In one situation a strong overall concept may evolve from reading the play and individual characters are based on aspects of the concept. In other cases strong characters provide the starting point for the design approach and the overall concept develops outward from the decisions made about those characters. In some cases the design concept is developed before doing research; in others, the research leads to the unifying element. In some productions the historical period is part of the unifying element; in other productions the theme may be a deliberate confusion of time. Consistency is the key—even if it means being consistently inconsistent!

Some theatrical forms (dance, performance art, avant-garde, nonverbal theater) approach costumes from a purely thematic or conceptual point of view. These costumes are based not on period or character, but on ideas. Designers seek to create the "essence," not the "reality" of a character, play, or period.

In producing organizations that provide long developmental periods (workshops) for new scripts or experimental approaches to established works, the costume designer may be asked to participate in the process. After attending rehearsals, the designer helps develop the costumes through collaboration with the actors and director. The actors may bring in garments and objects to incorporate, and the designer assists in refining the look and locating desired pieces. Emphasis is placed on the process of discovery rather than on the finished project. Sketches may not be involved. The production may be presented to the public as a "work-in-progress," may be remounted as a full production incorporating ideas from the workshop, or may not be presented at all.

In a majority of productions, however, once the overall concept is agreed upon, the designer proceeds to develop ideas about the individual characters, gradually refining both theme and character projection.

Developing Character Concepts

Many inexperienced designers don't know where to begin when they sit down to sketch. They may know what ideas to express, but not how to express them. Using the information provided by the script and the director, the designer should be able to describe each character in specific terms. (After the show is cast, adjustments in character concept may be necessary if the director has cast against type or if exaggeration or de-emphasis of physical attributes is desirable.) A written statement about each character helps to focus the designer's thoughts on the desired effect of the costume, the ideas to be projected to the audience. What elements or principles of design could assist in projecting these ideas? (Refer again to the boxes in chapter 4.)

Sorting out the accumulated research according to the characters for whom it seems appropriate helps the designer get started. Which examples seem to suit each character? What elements or principles of design are demonstrated by these examples? Do they project appropriate concepts for the character? What modifications are needed? Just as lines, colors, and textures have associations, costume features such as accessories, fit, and cut have cultural associations that the designer can tap for character definition. A costume need not be consistent in all aspects, but the majority of design features should agree with one another if a clear message is to be sent to the audience.

Boxes 5.A, 5.B, 5.C (on p. 120), and 5.D (on p. 121) offer broad outlines for suggesting age, social status, personality, and character traits. The notes in these charts are *not* rules, but general associations that the designer can use or adjust to specific needs. These associations may change with current fashion or taste. Obviously, the requirements of a given historical period affect the choices made by a designer. The more complex the character, the more subtle and complicated the costume may become. There will be dozens of reasons for going against

Box 5.A   Expressing age in costume features (subject to period and personality)

Feature	Old Age	Maturity	Youth	Childhood
Cut				
Skirt/pant length	Long	Long	Short	Shortest
Sleeve	Long	Medium to long	Long or short	Long or short
Neckline	High or medium	Low or high	Low or medium	Medium or high
Hair				
Female	Coiffed (outdated) or frazzled	Coiffed, specific	Loose	Long, loose or braided
Male	Balding, frazzled	Tightly controlled	Freer style	Loose, longer
Colors	Low intensities, low values	Secondaries, lower intensities	Stronger pastels, primaries, secondaries, high intensities, high values	Pastel or primaries
Fit	Body fitting or sagging	Body fitting, relative to period	Neat, but may be loose	Loose, not figure fitting
Silhouette	Complex or simple	Most complex	Simple to medium complex	Simplest

Box 5.B   Expressing rank or social status in costume features (subject to period and personality)

Feature	Rich	Middle Class	Poor
Cut			
Skirt length	Longest	Long	Shortest
Style	Most complex	Simple to complex	Simple
Color	Vibrant, intense	Lower intensity, lower value	Low intensities, low values
Fit	Proper fit	Neat, proper fit	Poorly fitted
Silhouette	Fashion silhouette	Not latest silhouette	Outdated silhouette
Texture	Smooth, shiny, napped	Medium textures, low shine	Rough, bold textures
Condition	New, clean	Worn, clean	Worn, ragged, dirty

Box 5.C	Expressing personality in costume features (subject to period)	
Feature	**Extrovert**	**Introvert**
Cut	Lavish, low neckline, shorter skirt, bare arms or short sleeves	Modest, high neckline, longer skirt, long sleeves
Fit	Body revealing	Body concealing
Texture	Hard, shiny	Medium to fine
Hair	Loose, bold style	Tight, close to the head
Colors	Warm colors, high intensities, high values (See also *Color* in chapter 4)	Cool colors, low intensities, low values
Silhouette	Simple and dramatic, or complex	Simple
Line	Exaggerated curves, zigzags, diagonals	Gentle curves, straight lines

these associations in specific situations, but they serve as a guide for evaluating research and for developing the rough sketch. As an example, figure 5.1 shows how simple differences in a garment cut can affect the projection of age in four female characters. Variations in skirt length and fullness, depth of neckline, length of sleeve, and waistline treatment alter a simple costume style to suggest childhood, youth, maturity, and age.

Design features are judged in relation to the fashion ideal of the historical period. If straight skirts were in fashion, then fuller skirts might be desirable for less fashionable characters (more room for activity for the peasant or working class). If very full skirts were considered chic, skirts with less fullness would be worn by peasants and the working class because less fabric, and therefore less

Figure 5.1 Variations on a simple costume style project different ages.

Box 5.D   Expressing character traits in costume features (subject to period)

Feature	Loving	Sensuous	Innocent	Evil	Miserly	Severe
Cut	Open, flowing, modest	Full cut, open, lavish	Full cut, modest	Tight, straight cut	Tight, straight cut	Tight, straight cut
Fit	Body revealing	Body revealing	Body concealing	Body revealing	Body revealing	Body revealing
Texture	Soft, fuzzy	Soft, shiny, smooth	Soft, fine	Harsh, rough, hard, shiny	Hard, rough or medium	Hard, rough
Hair	Soft, generous volume	Elegant, generous volume, or severe, sexy	Soft, loose	Severe or frazzled	Severe or frazzled	Severe, tight style
Colors	Warm, medium intensity, high or low values	Warm, medium intensity, high or low values	Cool, medium intensity, high value	Warm, high or low intensity, low value	Cool, medium or low intensity, medium to low values	Medium or low intensity, medium to low values
(See also *Color* in chapter 4)						
Silhouette	Round or oval shapes	Round or oval shapes	Round or oval	Straight shapes	Straight shapes	Straight shapes
Line	Wide curves, soft edged	Undulating lines	Gently curved lines	Hard, straight or zigzag lines	Hard, straight lines	Hard, straight or zigzag lines

cost, would be required to make them. In any fashion period, the working and middle classes and the elderly are the last to give up older fashions. Furthermore, these groups will usually choose the more conservative elements of the newer styles when they do adopt them.

Adjustments may be made for periods that do not offer all the alternatives, but research should be sought for all the characters. Keep in mind that persons with different personalities, ranks, and ages have existed in all periods and have found ways of expressing themselves in dress. Modern associations sometimes interfere with an accurate projection of period information. Ordinarily, the costumes should not require program notes for clarification. The designer must decide if certain style information will be understood by the audience or if modifications are necessary. One aspect of costume that often deviates from the specified period is the neckline. To help a modern audience understand the sensuality of a character, for example, a deep décolletage may be developed in a period of basically modest necklines.

Few plays are meant to be exact historical recreations. *Theatrical license* is the term used for liberties taken with historical accuracy. These liberties are usually taken to clarify the spirit or essence of the theme and to make it work aesthetically in the theatrical setting. Elaboration, exaggeration, and even fantastication may be necessary for theatrical dress. The objective is effective interpretation, not simply precise historical representation.

No two designers are likely to solve a design problem in exactly the same way. Designs could vary considerably because of different production concepts, different actors playing the role, and different ways designers approach the work. Figure 5.2A shows a costume for Lady Sneerwell in *The School for Scandal*, designed by Michelle Ney; figure 5.2B (left figure), a costume by Bill Brewer, is for the same character. The interpretations differ, but many similarities remain.

Historical research must be adapted in some way for all productions. Rarely can a period garment be used without some modifications. The pattern or trim may need to be in a larger scale in order to be seen in the theater. The construction may be too confining for the action, or the color may be inappropriate.

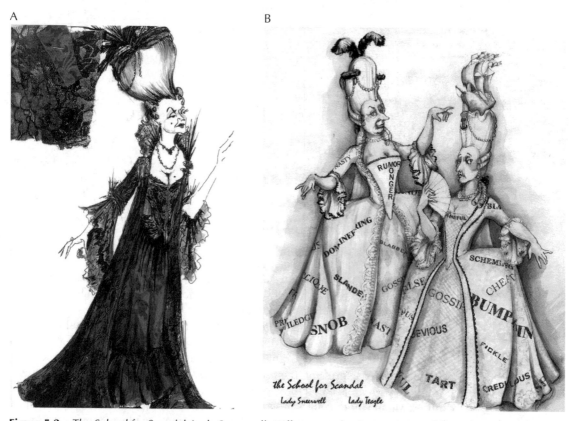

Figure 5.2 *The School for Scandal.* Lady Sneerwell. Different production concepts, different actors in the role, and different designer approaches to a work produce two different design solutions. (A) Design by Michelle Ney for the University of Idaho; (B) Design by Bill Brewer for the University of Minnesota, Duluth.

Modern clothing places fewer restrictions on movement. Authentically cut period garments may seriously limit a character's movement, however. The importance of recreating period movement in a given production is determined by the director and is of fundamental importance to the costume designer. The designer should point out to the director the advantages and restrictions that the use of authentic garments would create. If authentic costumes severely restrict the projected movement, is that movement appropriate to the play? Would characters of the period move in that way, or have too many modern ideas been applied to the script and not enough research? The more accurate the movement must be, the more accurate the costume should be. Bodice construction, skirt length, corset, and shoes *all* affect movement. Modifications should be made to permit the projection of character, theme, mode, and form of drama, and to allow for required or desired action.

Rough Sketches and Collage Boards

Roughs are quick sketches, usually in pencil or pastel, which suggest the main ideas of the costume for each character. Some roughs indicate color. Some designers work in thumbnail size (two to three inches); others use larger-size figures (six to eighteen inches). (The novice designer will find that sketching in a larger size is good practice for the rendering process to come.) Using the costume plot, research, and character statements as guides, the designer sketches one or more roughs for each required costume. By determining the shape of the silhouette, the division of the silhouette space, and, finally, the accessories and trim, the designer works to create the desired effect

Many designers concurrently develop a series of *collage boards* using research, items torn from magazines, or scanned or photocopied images. These boards may represent the overall concept for the design of the production, the color palette, the period research, or the individual characters. Sometimes they are rather abstract; sometimes they are specific. They may be produced with illustration board and glue or developed in a computer art program. Collage boards are especially useful for modern dress, shopped, or rented productions where the precise garment need not be shown, only the type of garment and a suggestion of its style and color are needed. These boards are used in film and television design as well. See figures 2.10, 3.13, and 9.11 for examples of collage boards.

A simple approach to roughs is to use tracing paper over a basic figure. Until a designer is comfortable and fast at figure drawing, this approach saves time in the early design stages. Meanwhile, the basic figure proportions are becoming set in the designer's subconscious mind. A variation of this approach is to photograph the actors, paste their figures into Photoshop files, and create the garments on them on a computer. Unless the designer has good computer skills the approach may take more time than is expected.

Some designers develop rough sketches by observing rehearsals and sketching the actors as they develop the posture and physicality of the character. Unfortunately, not all production schedules allow for this approach. However, a sense of the type of character, overall silhouette, posture, and presence should be considered in the rough-sketch stage no matter how these sketches are derived. The overall feeling is more important than the detail at the early stages. Once this basic look of the character is established, the designer proceeds to develop and refine the costume.

A designer may develop a series of sketches for a costume before the final choice is made. Figure 5.3 shows two sketches by Mathew LeFebvre illustrating early thinking and a final costume design. The preliminary pencil sketch was used in early discussions with the director. When agreement on the costume was reached, the sketch was photocopied on cardstock and colored with markers and watercolor.

Figure 5.3 *Cyrano de Bergerac*. Ragueneau. A "rough" sketch (A) and the final design sketch (B). Designed by Mathew LeFebvre for the Milwaukee Rep.

Individual Focus (Emphasis)

Each costume design should have a focal point. For most characters the head and face are emphasized. There are times, however, when other areas of the figure are more important; legs or feet for dancers, hands for magical characters, or stomachs for fat, jolly characters. One trick for checking focus is to view the color sketch turned upside down. What area commands attention? Is this area relative to the character's action or personality? More than one area of emphasis may be developed in a costume. In figure 5.4 the plunging neckline and heavy necklace of this costume for Anna in *Burn This* creates emphasis at the neck and face when the character is facing forward, but as she turns to the side and back, the sweep of the train and the crossed straps create back interest.

Figure 5.4 *Burn This.* Anna. Emphasis is not always on the face. Designed by Laura Crow for Plymouth Theatre, Broadway. Jewelry designed by Jane Nyhus.

Focus can be created in many ways. Strong lines pointing to the same point or strong shapes relating to an area provide emphasis on that area. An advancing color carefully placed on an area is one of the most effective focus devices. A large white collar on a costume usually focuses our attention on the face of the actor. However, in color plate 6 the white collar and hat blend with the white face makeup, and the exuberant patch pattern of this Harlequin draws attention to the body of the dancer. (See also figure 4.19.)

Considering the Actor's Physicality

When the actor for a character is cast, consideration must be given to that actor's physical proportions in relation to the character ideal. When the physical characteristics are important to the role, a designer may wish to underscore those characteristics visually. In figure 5.5 the character's bulk has been emphasized by the use of an over-scaled jacket, a diagonal belt with large patch pockets, and jodhpur-style pants. Not infrequently, a director chooses to ignore obvious physical differences between the actor and the character and to cast for a desired voice quality or superior acting ability. Particularly in operas and musicals, the voice requirements are always considered first and visual requirements second. The designer is then called on to create a costume that brings the actor as close to the desired visual interpretation of the character as possible. The designer must make a careful study of the period garments and all the effects of the elements and principles of design to create a garment with the most appropriate visual effect. Even if historical accuracy must be nearly abandoned, certain characters must be costumed in becoming garments.

Conversations with the cast members give the designer insight into the physical problems, preferences, and character interpretations of each actor. A designer may not be able to meet all the requests of the cast members and still serve the whole production, but if a designer ignores an actor's strong point of view (hated colors, styles) trouble could develop later. Fitting problems are best dealt with in the planning stage as well. An actor with unusual proportions cannot be ignored! Dealing with figure problems and special sizes requires tact and diplomacy. If special effort is needed to meet special needs, extra time must be allowed for handling the problem. Remember that the actor must feel comfortable, self-assured, and confident to perform well, and the ultimate goal is a unified, quality production.

Accessories

Careful consideration should be given to shoes, hats, gloves, handbags, canes, and other accessories. These small items add visual interest and character detail and provide possibilities for stage business. Some items may be required in the script; others may be requested by the actors; still others may be suggested by the designer or director for visual or practical purposes. In figure 5.6 (on p. 128) Abby's carefully chosen accessories complete her elegant look.

Shoes are extremely important to the character's walk and posture and contribute to the sense of period. The heel height, general weight, and type of shoe should be indicated in the rough sketches and discussed with the director and the

EXIT THE KING

THE GUARD

Figure 5.5 *Exit the King.* The Guard. The character's bulk has been emphasized by the use of an over-scaled jacket, a diagonal belt with large patch pockets, and jodhpur-style pants. Designed by Shima Ushiba for Connecticut Repertory Theatre. Photo by Shima Ushiba.

actor. In general, the heavier the shoe is, the heavier the walk of the character wearing it. Shoes with soft soles create a lighter, more resilient step; hard-soled shoes, especially those with heavy heels, produce a more authoritative walk. High-heeled shoes create a walk with more swing in the hip, and the posture and balance of the figure must be adjusted. The full weight of the body descends on the heel, and the pelvic section is thrust forward as the wearer walks. High heels also alter the shape of the calf muscle and produce a more curvaceous leg. "Com-

Figure 5.6 *Arsenic and Old Lace.* Abby in mourning. Care has been taken with the accessories for this character—hat, fur collar, button-up boots, and walking stick all support her elegant look. Designed by Judith Dolan for Alley Theatre, Houston, Texas.

C-1 *Comedy of Errors.* These identical twin servants are costumed as mirror images. To help the audience identify them, different but related colors (pink and orange) were used for corresponding sections of their costumes. Designed by the author for Brooklyn College. Photo by Richard Grossberg.

C-2 William Ivey Long's costume designs for a dance couple in *Steel Pier* were based on the work of the artist Reginald Marsh. Broadway.

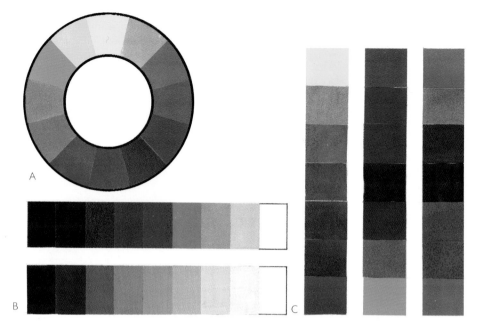

C-3 Color basics. (A) Basic color wheel—primary and secondary colors. (B) Value chart—adding white to a color raises its value; adding black to a color lowers its value. (C) Intensity chart—adding a color's complement lowers its intensity.

MISS CAROLINE BINGLEY

SC. 5 STROLLING w/ DARCY @ LONGBOURNE PARK.

C.D. 4342
COSTUME DESIGNER
SIGNATURE MJL

C-4 *Pride and Prejudice*. Caroline. The period details on this Regency gown add authenticity, depth, and texture. Designed by the Mathew J. LeFebvre for the Guthrie Theater. Photo by Michal Daniel.

C-5 *The Threepenny Opera*. Jenny. The decadent qualities of Kurt Weill's music are suggested in the use of the textures and torn fabric in this costume by the author for Brooklyn College. Photo by John Ricasoli. (See also figure 2.5 for costume sketch.)

C-6 *Harlequinade*. In Rouben Ter-Arutunian's costume multicolored patches emphasize the dancer's movement. Designed for the New York City Ballet.

C-7 *Tons of Money.* Jean. This sketch gives a series of costume views including a cape and hat, handbag, back view, and notes about details. Designed by Margaret Mitchell for the University of the Incarnate Word. Sketch photo by Adela Gott.

C-8 *Blind Man's Bluff.* This painting by Goya inspired the color scheme for a Brooklyn College production of *The Marriage of Figaro.* Prado Museum.

C-9 Swatch board. A collection of swatches based on the Goya painting (figure C-8) helps the designer visualize the show and present ideas to the director.

C-10 *The Lion, the Witch, and the Wardrobe.*
Aslan. This costume is based on the designer's lateral
research into the ritual costume of Bali, Thailand, and
India. Designed by Laura Crow for Children's Theatre
Company, Minneapolis. Photo by Peter McCoy.

C-11 *The Hypochondriac.* Beline. This sketch demonstrates the interesting use of shapes to create a costume by combining triangles, ovals, hearts, and a dome shape. Designed by Joel Ebarb for the Texas Shakespeare Festival.

C-12 *Central City Nights.* Including copies of research with the sketch is useful to the pattern maker. This 1930s sketch for "Attitudes" by Robert Edmond Jones includes a photo of the original source (circa 1900). Courtesy of the Department of Theater, Brooklyn College.

C-13 *Lucky Duck.* Queen. Gregg Barnes' design for the pompous queen of poultry incorporates feathers, feather-like shapes, a large bustle and a large bosom to suggest the profile of an elaborate duck. Designed for the Old Globe Theatre, San Diego.

C-14 *Candide.* Judith Dolan's sketch for The Baron (A) wittily expresses his pomposity and arrogance, and the sketch for Cunegonde in Lisbon (B) reflects her decision to "Glitter and be Gay." The humor in the music is reflected in the color and detail of the costumes. Designed for The New York City Opera.

C-15 *Cyrano.* DeGuiche. Good presentation helps the designer "sell the costume" to the director and the actors. The careful placement and modeling of the figure, the supportive background, and the artful addition of fabric swatches combine to give this sketch visual impact. Designed by Mathew J. LeFebvre for the Milwaukee Repertory Theater.

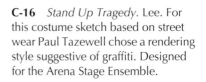

C-16 *Stand Up Tragedy.* Lee. For this costume sketch based on street wear Paul Tazewell chose a rendering style suggestive of graffiti. Designed for the Arena Stage Ensemble.

mon-sense" shoes (oxfords with thick heels) produce a "common-sense" walk. Sandal and slipper wearers tend to shuffle. Characters that must dance need shoes appropriate to the type of dance they do, regardless of period considerations.

Novice designers tend to overlook the importance of shoes. Early decisions about shoe styles are important because the actors should rehearse in the type of shoes that they will be wearing in the role and because shoe purchases are a major budget item.

The style and size of handbags and other hand-held props must also be determined early and should be included in the rough sketches. Similar rehearsal versions of these items will be required so the stage business can be developed and so that the actor can become familiar with their size, closures, and manipulation.

Hats, too, must be considered for the rough sketches. Until the middle of the twentieth century, head coverings were an essential part of dress for both men and women, rich and poor alike. The size, scale, and style of a hat are major elements of the complete costume design. Because the execution of millinery is frequently time-consuming and may become a major budget item, hats should be considered at the same time as other aspects of the costume.

Outerwear (coats, capes) is another aspect of the costume often overlooked by beginning designers. The script may give only scanty references to these items, but they represent major budget and construction considerations and should be included in the rough sketches.

Achieving Balance

As roughs develop for each character, sketches should be compared with one another. Are the costumes different enough? Are they too dissimilar? Are they designed in the same style? Are they done in the same scale? Which characters become most important as groups are combined and recombined? Is the focus in each scene on the important person in that scene? By taking advantage of the advancing and receding effects of the various elements of design, the costume designer can go a long way toward establishing the important character in a scene. Because light or warm colors advance and dark or cool colors recede, characters in light or warm colors usually stand out from those in dark or cool colors. Because shiny, smooth textures advance and dull textures recede, an actress in a satin gown usually stands out among costumes made of wool. One effect overrides these guidelines, however: the *odd* element in a design usually attracts the most attention. One black costume on an all light, bright stage will draw the most attention. One cool-colored costume against all warm colors may draw the eye to itself. And . . . a spotlight overrules everything!

Relationships between characters can be suggested by similarities in the color, cut, or texture of their costumes. The more realistic the style of presentation, the more subtle these relationships need to be. The more stylized or abstract the play, the more obvious the relationships can be. Costumes for comedy, farce, or dance are often very strongly related. Adversaries, particularly opposing armies, must be clearly differentiated for audiences. Uniforms of different cut and/or colors are the obvious choice. Opposing forces of good and evil should be similarly identified for the audience. In *Romeo and Juliet* the members of the two feuding households, the Montagues and the Capulets, are often designed in complementary colors, each family in its own hue.

Planning Color

A color layout may be developed before, during, or after the rough stage of design work, but it is usually shown to the director when the roughs are discussed. Groups of swatches, chosen to represent types of fabric and colors, are taped or stapled to a sheet of stiff paper as a representation of the colors and textures in the costumes. These swatches may be from the designer's collection or fabrics swatched specifically for the show. Starting with colors dictated by the script or color impressions from the script, an overall color scheme and textural plan evolves in the swatch layout. This plan may be based on a painting, a print fabric, art objects, or other sources that suggest the mood of the play. Goya's *Blind Man's Bluff,* shown in color plate 8, inspired the color scheme for a production of *The Marriage of Figaro;* the next step toward developing the color for the production was to organize a swatch board (color plate 9) to help the designer and the director visualize the show.

When textures are less important, a color plan may be more efficient and can assist the designer with specific character choices. Soft pastels are a quick, useful medium for working out a color plan.

Budget

At the early stages of design some consideration should be given to budget restrictions. All designers must work within the budget limitations set by the producing organization. No matter how wonderful a set of designs may be, if there is no way to realize them, a designer will need to change the approach.

A simple rule of thumb for evaluating costume cost is to divide the total budget by the number of costumes to arrive at an average cost per costume. Then, the process of "robbing Peter to costume Paul" begins. When the number of costumes is figured, each change and each outer garment must be considered a separate costume. Considering the cost of shoes, hats, and undergarments, is it reasonable to expect to assemble a costume for the amount proposed?

In addition to the actual costume budget, a designer must know what facilities and staff are available for the production. Is costume stock available for use? How extensive and in what condition is the costume stock in the required period? Is rental of costumes possible? How much time is allowed? Are the actors to provide any personal items? The designer should consult with the costume shop manager or costume director to answer these and other budget questions. (Further budget considerations are discussed in chapter 8.)

Financial restrictions sometimes stimulate very creative and theatrical solutions to costume problems, but budget limitations should be recognized and faced early in the design process. A simple approach, well executed, is more effective than an elaborate design that is uncompleted because it was too expensive, was beyond the skill level of the staff, or was too time-consuming. Remember that the audience sees only what is actually on stage, not the designer's unfulfilled sketches.

Special Considerations

While the general principles of costume design apply to all situations, each production presents special problems to the designer. The designer is constantly challenged to anticipate and solve the problems unique to each situation.

The Theater Structure

The type of theater in which a production will be seen must be considered in the development of the costumes. For the costume designer the proscenium stage has both advantages and disadvantages. A major disadvantage is the psychological barrier produced between the audience and the actors by the proscenium arch. The distance between actor and audience created by the apron (forestage) and orchestra pit becomes difficult to bridge. Much detail is lost if that distance is great. If detail is desired, the designer must anticipate the problem and enlarge the scale of the detail to read (be seen) from a distance. On the other hand, costumes that are shabby and worn often look wonderful under lights on the proscenium stage. Poor construction and cheap fabrics are less likely to read from this type of stage. Cheap baubles and fake jewelry often give an effect superior to that of the real thing. Fantasy effects and tricks also are easier to achieve behind the proscenium.

Regardless of the type of structure, a larger theater requires a larger scale in which the designer must work in order for the costumes to read, but care must be taken to stay within reasonable limits of the style of the production. Constructing the costume with cording in the seams or trimming the edges of garments with braid or ribbon will help carry the line of the garment over long distances, but may also further remove the garment from reality. In figure 5.7 (on the following page) decorative cording delineates the lines of the doublet and pumpkin hose for the Masquer in *The Rover.* Even when there is little contrast between the braid and garment colors, the added texture creates highlights and shadows that help the costume read throughout the theater.

Making the different pieces in slightly different colors, or shades of the same color, will also help project the costume. Instead of a three-piece suit, for example, a combination of solids, stripes, and textures in the same colors, while appearing the same from a distance, will be read as three pieces instead of a gray or brown blob. Careful shading with an airbrush or spray paint under collars, lapels, pocket flaps, and cuffs can emphasize details and add highlights and shadows to costumes that might otherwise fade over long distances.

For film and productions in small, "black-box" type theaters the audience viewpoint is very close to the actors, and costumes must generally be more "real." Subtle aging, quality workmanship, and careful makeup become even

Figure 5.7   *The Rover*. The Masquer. Decorative cording delineates the lines of the doublet and pumpkin hose. Designed by Sheila Hargett for Texas State University.

more important in these situations, as in figure 5.8.

Because actors are seen from all sides in thrust and arena theaters, often also in close proximity to the audience, special problems arise. Zippers, Velcro, and other modern closures used in period clothing are more readily seen and may become distracting. The over-scaled trims that might be desirable on the proscenium stage may become comic when used on a small thrust or arena stage. The quality of the fabric, trim, and workmanship is much more obvious to the audience in these theaters. Also the rumpled, soiled costume can be clearly seen. Since the costume is being seen from all sides at once, the back must be as interesting and well thought-out as the front. The designer must think specifically of the three-dimensional, sculptural characteristics of the costume. Accessories like shoes and handbags are even more important than in proscenium productions.

In addition to all these problems, arena theaters are often temporary arrangements with limited support spaces (dressing rooms, workshops). Pageants, street theater, and tent theaters for summer stock are often done in the round. There is usually no place for special effects and tricks and no wall against which to disguise a costume change or create an illusion.

The Outdoor Theater

The outdoor theater can be based on any type, but the fact that the production is outdoors leads to special problems. Obviously, weather is the main consideration. The costume designer must understand the variations in temperature to be expected in the particular locale. Extremes of heat and cold as well as excess humidity or rain can adversely affect the actors, costumes, makeup, and wigs. Costume materials should be suitable for the climatic conditions even if these materials are unusual choices for the period or style of production. Easy maintenance of costumes also is important.

In some areas afternoon performers could be cooked with broiling heat and evening performers could be frozen with a chilling mountain breeze. Costumes designed with removable pieces or layers allow for adjustment to heat or cold. Capes, shawls, robes, or coats can be added or removed. Special undergarments might be needed to adjust for temperature. Thermal underwear for warmth is relatively easy to provide; undergarments with coolants are more difficult and must be specially made.

Almost all outdoor theaters must battle insects. The costume designer may need to limit the exposed areas of the actors' bodies. In addition to stage makeup the costumes must tolerate sunscreen and insect repellant!

Figure 5.8   *What I Did Last Summer.* Anna. Productions in small "black-box" theaters generally require costumes to be more "real." Designed by the author for Retro Productions. Photo by Kristen Vaughan.

Productions with Music

Music is a major influence on the style of a production. It creates both limitations and possibilities for the costume designer.

Musicals

Much of American theater is dedicated to the production of musicals, and they present the costume designer with a few special problems. Musicals usually have large casts of singers and dancers. While there is generally an element of fantasy present in a musical that allows the designer leeway in interpreting period, finding ways to allow for sufficient movement for dancers and room for singers to breathe and sing may take some ingenuity.

Costumes in musical numbers are under extreme stress and must be well constructed of sturdy fabric and backing. A dancer should never be worried about losing part of the costume on stage. Special stretch fabrics or special construction techniques may be required for long-running productions or energetic dancing.

Trained singers may expand their chest several sizes when singing. Care should be taken to allow for this expansion in the fitting of their costumes. Garments should not restrict the throat.

In many musical numbers all the dancers or singers are costumed alike. Since these parts will generally be cast for voice or dance ability, the shape and size of the individuals may vary considerably. An attempt should be made to choose a style that will flatter as many of the group as possible. If such a style cannot be found, different costumes might be designed for each chorus member, perhaps in related colors and fabrics.

For most musicals the costumes are designed in bright, cheerful colors and in strong, bold shapes. Some exaggeration of scale lifts the musical out of the realm of reality.

Musicals are often conceived as spectacles with what seems like (and sometimes is) hundreds of costumes. Quick changes are numerous and frantic, so expert organization is essential. Some quick-change problems can be solved with costumes that can be worn over or under other costumes. Breakaway costumes using Velcro or large snaps may be necessary. Sometimes complete ensembles must be mounted onto one base garment and treated like a jumpsuit. With this solution, other costumes can be worn underneath and an almost miraculous costume change results.

Opera

Opera, like tragedy, explores emotions, passions, and themes that are often profound and larger than life. Most operas require a sense of grand scale: an exaggerated, highly theatrical, visual approach. The form and feeling of the music are major factors in determining the visual style. Regardless of the period of the story, the period and style in which the music is written should be the major influence. In color plate 14 the humor in Bernstein's music is reflected in the color and detail of the costume for *Candide,* and in figure 2.5 and color plate 5 Brecht's music influences the design of *The Threepenny Opera.* Although traditionally operas have been designed in a grand scale, many contemporary productions are presented in a more streamlined, less ornate style.

Because the music is the primary consideration, the roles in an opera are cast by voice, not by the visual considerations of the character. All the optical tricks of color, line, and form are needed to provide the most becoming and workable costume for the singer who does not physically look the part.

In established opera companies, productions are performed in repertory, each opera playing once or twice a week and alternating with several other operas. Costumes for each production are stored together and not used for other operas. This system simplifies maintenance and turnaround time from one production to another.

Costuming large groups of extras and chorus singers is very time-consuming. These costumes are built to allow for much alteration or designed as "one size fits all" to allow for many cast changes.

Dance

Costumes designed for dance must be approached from the choreographer's point of view. In traditional ballets and some other works there is a story line and specific characters to interpret. In other dance forms the dancers may be expressing feelings, interpreting the music, or exploring movement in abstract ways. In the former, the designer may have the help of period research and traditional interpretations of the dance piece. In the latter, the designer must become familiar with the choreography, attending rehearsals and discussing the work with the choreographer at all stages of development. The movements, shapes, and forms as well as the relationship of the dancers to the music must be explored for clues to the visual style. What parts of the body are emphasized in the movement? Are the movements circular? Angular? Rhythmical? Do the dancers act in unison or in opposition? Do they express emotions and relationships or abstract movement? What does the music express? What physical attributes of the dancer should be emphasized or modified?

Dancers view their costumes as their "skin." They want to feel the garment as a part of their body, as an extension of the gesture and movement, not an addition to it. Dance costumes should emphasize, complement, and complete the movement. In practical terms the costume must allow the dancer the freedom of movement needed to perform the dance. A formal period dance may require less mobility in the upper torso and may permit the use of a stiff, fitted bodice, whereas a jazz or modern dance piece may need to be done in stretch leotards. Specially cut sleeves, gussets, and stretch fabrics open up possibilities for movement in garments that appear to be close fitting, as in figure 5.9. Skirt lengths are modified for dance even in period pieces to permit the dancer to move and to allow the audience to appreciate the choreography. In the costume from *Persephone* in figure 5.9 the skirt is cut to lower-calf length and bodice is made of stretch fabric to allow for maximum movement while remaining elegant.

Figure 5.9   *Persephone.* Dancer. Choreography by Michael Foley. (A) Sketch. Costumes by Bill Brewer for the School of Theatre and Dance, University of South Florida. (B) Photograph by Bill Brewer.

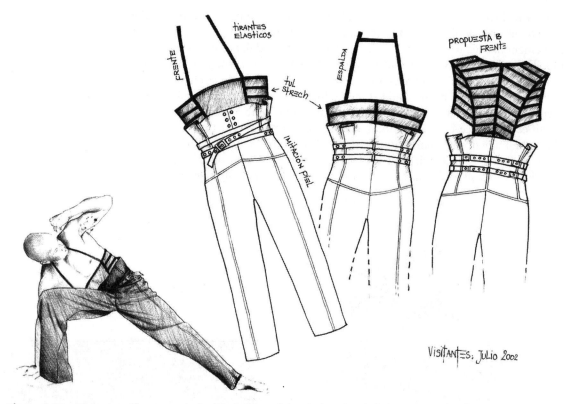

Figure 5.10   *Visitantes.* Choreography by Tania Pérez-Salas. In her sketch for *Visitantes,* the designer anticipates the areas of stretch needed in the dance costume. Designed by Eloise Kazan for the Mnemosine Dance Company.

The designer must think through all areas of stretch required by the dancer and plan the costume to accommodate those needs, as in figure 5.10. Designing garments that move well is the dance designer's primary responsibilities. Cutting garments on the bias; using variations of the circular skirt; or choosing fluid or floating fabrics like tulle, crepe, and chiffon are popular approaches to dance costumes. Generally speaking, dance costumes should be lightweight and fluid, allowing for the full appreciation of the work of the choreographer and dancers.

Inspiration

No rules or guidelines produce inspired costumes. Sometimes inspiration defies all guidelines. It cannot be taught. The designer learns with experience when to trust that inspiration. Inspiration, however, rarely flashes like a comet across the sky. More often than not, it is uncovered like a buried treasure after much strenuous effort. The more information (research) assembled, the more likely the rubbing together of ideas will set off a creative spark. Either a designer *is* creative or *isn't, has* vision or *doesn't,* but no designer exists or works in a vacuum. Constant stimuli and raw materials for the creative fires are required. The script is the basic source for the designer's inspiration, but seeing plays; reading novels and poetry; visiting art exhibits, museums, and junkyards; studying architecture, decorative objects, and street scenes; traveling; and countless other experiences provide raw material for the creative process. The costume designer cannot sit and wait for inspiration; it must be eagerly sought.

The rough-sketch phase should be a period of exploration. The designer should keep an open mind toward all possibilities. Sometimes the most unrelated object or experience will stimulate a wonderful idea or approach to a design problem.

Director–Designer Conferences

A meeting should be scheduled to show the research, collage boards, and roughs to the director. Roughs should be presented with a purpose in mind. Usually, major characters in major scenes are dealt with first and minor characters and chorus members are considered later. Two approaches are possible. One, the characters can be shown, scene-by-scene, starting with Act I. The alternative approach is to show all costumes for a character together, then all costumes for the next character, and so on. The choice of approach is a personal one, but the first method seems more appropriate for realistic and ensemble-type plays, and the second approach may work better for plays centering on a few main characters. The director is looking to see the *character* appear in the sketch, not just a nice drawing or beautiful costume.

The designer must be prepared to explain the roughs to the director carefully and completely. The designer should accept graciously, and note in writing, all directorial comment, without becoming defensive or taking criticism personally. Collaboration is difficult, and much information must be read between the lines. Often a negative reaction from the director is based on misunderstandings, misinformation, poor sketch presentation, inadequate research, misreading of the sketch, or preconceived ideas that can be discussed and modified. Remember that the director has the final word on how the production is to look. Coordination of the scenery, costumes, lighting, and acting style into a unified whole is the director's responsibility.

Asking meaningful questions is the key to communication with the director. The designer should ask for specifics. "She looks too old" is a more meaningful statement from a director than "I don't like it." Always ask, "Do you know why (you don't like it)?" Sometimes the reaction is to the posture or figure in the sketch, not the costume itself. Some alterations can be made on pencil sketches during the conference or on tracing paper over the sketch to show possible variations.

This is the time to fill in any blanks from earlier discussions. Perhaps the sketch does not explain the character because of inadequate analysis of the script or because the script or the director was unclear. Perhaps the designer has not done adequate research. Has the casting of a specific actor clarified the role or changed the director's ideas about the character?

Many designers and directors are conferencing via phone and/or Internet. Roughs, collage boards, and sketches can be scanned and e-mailed to the director, and questions and answers can be e-mailed back and forth saving travel time and expenses. Video conferencing is available to more and more designers and directors. While the technology speeds the process, the basic techniques are the same. Relevant questions and thorough answers are necessary.

After the conference the designer should analyze the result. Which costumes met with the director's approval? What further work is needed on them? Which costumes were rejected? Why? Is more research needed? Is the concept carried throughout? Will another conference on the roughs be needed? What is happening with the scenery? How does the look of the set affect the direction of the costume design? A checklist for this stage of the work is provided in box 5.E. This information can be used in making revisions and redesigning. If corrections are relatively minor, the designer may proceed to do finished costume sketches as described in the next chapter. Work may proceed on certain costumes while designing others.

Box 5.E   Designer checklist IV: Roughs

1. Does each costume define the character's age, social status, and personality? Does this costume fit within the historical period or concept of this production?

2. Can the actor perform the required actions in each costume?

3. Have the costume accessories been considered? Are they appropriate? Will they help the actor or get in the way?

4. How will this costume look on the actor cast in this role? Is corsetry or padding required? Is this costume becoming to the actor?

5. Is it interesting? Imaginative? Dramatic?

6. Are the proportions pleasing? Is the scale dramatic?

7. Are the parts logically combined? Do they relate to each other?

8. Do the parts of the costume logically surround the body on all sides? Do they connect in the back or on the other side? What does the back look like?

9. Where is the focus in each sketch? On whom will the focus be in each scene?

10. Is more research needed? Are other accessories needed?

11. Do all costumes appear to be for the same production?

12. Do important characters stand out from the group as a whole?

13. Can we see important relationships among characters?

14. Do the costumes reflect the form and mode of drama of the play?

15. Do the costumes and scenery work together effectively? How will the colors of the costumes work against the colors of the set?

16. Is any character operating on contradictory levels? What aspects of the costume could represent each level?

17. Does the costume reveal *too much* about the character?

18. Do the silhouette (shape), cut and trim (line), fabric (texture or pattern, and hang), and color of this costume reflect important aspects of the visual definition of this character?

Interview III.
Collaboration.
A Conversation with Judith Dolan.

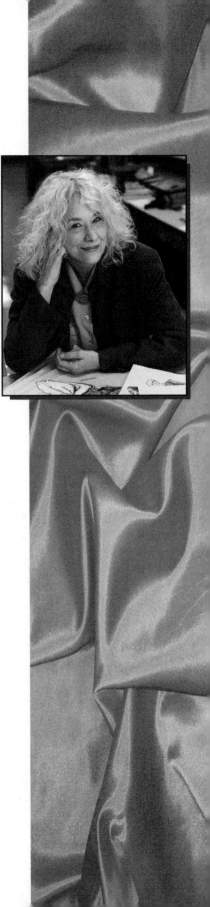

At the time of this interview with the author Broadway designer Judith Dolan had received a Tony Award, the Lucille Lortel Award, and two Drama Desk Award nominations. (See bio, page 421, for career details.)

RC: Tell me about your approach to collaboration with the director and other members of a production.

JD: I believe there is the very strong crossover between directing and designing. I tend to approach a text as if I were directing it. That's not to say I *want* to direct it, I want to be really clear about that! It does require that I work with strong directors who enjoy the dialectic with designers who have strong ideas. They can tell you "no"; they can pull you back if they think you have gone too far, but that exchange is really important to me.

So the text, that's everybody's anchor, and beyond that it's the fun of the unknown—playing in the minds of the director and the other designers. The rift of ideas, the back and forth—everything is possible! You are all going to get together to create a world that individually you couldn't do by yourself—it's the happiest part.

That is, philosophically, the most exciting thing—to come up with a world that is completely specific, that will *never happen again* because those collaborators will never again be together in that time, in that place, that moment. To come up with an artistic expression that could not exist in another time or place—that's something that I love, *really love* about live performance, and why I'm a theater artist.

Figure III.1   Judith Dolan's costume for Teddy II, "Panama" for *Arsenic and Old Lace* at the Alley Theatre, Houston, Texas.

Figure III.2   Judith Dolan's costume for Polly in the Broadway of *LoveMusik.*

RC: Do you have advice for young designers who have difficulty developing that level of communication and collaboration?

JD: I think it is important to *respect your instincts*. You can begin your research anywhere. I remember doing *Parade*, a musical at Lincoln Center. It was based on a true story about the rise of vigilantism and the Ku Klux Klan in the early part of the 20th century in the Deep South.

That's quite a load! Where do you begin? I actually started at the Stanford University Law Library, because I found out that this was a very important judicial case. That research led me to all sorts of artists, and cultural and historical artifacts. I looked at old newspapers—at what was happening in the African-American community, the kinds of music, the photography of Lewis Hine, and how child labor was being dealt with. I embedded myself in the culture of the moment. I didn't start with images.

There are other times when my instincts [say] just find an artist or a work of art that resonates in some way with you. But don't worry if you can't explain it. Go with your gut; let it sit with you, keep looking at it.

[I tell my students], "Don't tell me what you 'think' or what you 'like,' tell me what you *see*." That allows everybody to open up and not to worry about criticism, but to care about each other's approach to the material. Simple description is very much underrated as an artistic tool. Just go with your instincts; just look at an image and—say exactly what you *see*.

While learning to see is very important, you should not divorce yourself from reading about the time, about the period. If it's a 20th-century moment, look at films and documentaries from that period. It's almost like you become a visual dramaturge. But we shouldn't think that we are just image-driven artists. I think of a theater artist as a kind of poet. We use images and words to create a *poetic space* . . . an aesthetic space to say things in real time—a real event, with a real effect for the audience.

RC: So you take all those things to the director?

JD: Yes, everything. I create entire notebooks of background cultural information. I remember sending African-American song fragments to Harold Prince. I thought having an African-American point of view about lynching was key to understanding *Parade*. I found contemporary articles about Mexican children working as field workers, under the wire, unseen, and I thought, my gosh, a hundred years ago they were using child labor and we haven't changed any! Hal had not asked for that, but with really good directors, they absorb it—they absorb it in terms of what you are trying to say about creating a look on stage.

I also write letters to accompany my research, so [the images] are not seen in a vacuum. Actually, I prefer sending material ahead to bombarding a director in person with a whole lot of words and images, without giving time to absorb the information. First send the words, and then have a meeting.

RC: How has a PhD in directing changed your work?

JD: It sort of validated the way I work. I discovered that only other theater artists really understand what we do and appreciate all the avenues of research and the collaborative spirit.

I found that the artistic springboard could be anything as a director. My springboard is design. As a costume designer I work all the time with actors—very intimate, very specific, very detail-oriented interaction. Costume designers are so detail-oriented that I found it quite easy to take all that experience and couple it with the techniques of text analysis that a director might use, then to break it down and bring it all together again. They enhance one another.

I am a stronger designer as a result of being a director. I find I don't go about directing in the traditional way. It's a much more collaboratively driven and much more open process for me.

RC: Do you have any advice for young directors and designers?

JD: Before I start anything, directing or designing, I do a character breakdown, *by hand*. I refuse to use the computer. I look at it not just as a costume plot, but as [mapping] the structure of the play and how I am orchestrating it. I see it as *a musical exercise*. At the bottom I put my questions, notes, character notations, and ideas.

The computer isn't just a tool; you have to be aware that it *alters your perceptions*. Doing plots by hand—with pencils and rulers and pasting together papers—slows the designer and director down, allows them to think about the play more carefully and thoughtfully, instills pride of ownership, and gives them a strong handle on the piece.

I give each scene on the plot a name or a title. That is another way of finding out dynamically where the director and the designer are thinking in common and where

Figures III.3 and III.4 Judith Dolan's costumes for the Conley Chain Gang and The Governor's Wife for the Broadway production of *Parade*.

Figure III.5   Judith Dolan's costume for Newt, Courtroom for the Broadway production of *Parade*.

they can build on each other. It's a very practical exercise. It keeps the focus on the work, not on each other.

It's not unusual for me to take three or four days to properly read a Shakespeare, to think specifically about the language or metaphors, and to create a character chart. I would encourage young directors and young designers to give themselves the benefit of time when they begin working. That can be really hard, [but] the first step is extremely important. You don't get to be a genius right away! Staying open to other designers' input, the back and forth of the process—these are important elements.

RC: What about collaborating with performers?

JD: You do your research, you come up with your renderings, you find the fabric, but it's really just a *blueprint* for working with those actors.

Designers should recognize that they have had time— hours, days, months, even years – to discuss and evolve the piece. The actor doesn't have that benefit. Actors are walking in quite vulnerable, and they have to stay open to all this background and pre-production work that has been going on between the director and the designer. It's new information to them. I think the costume designer is a very important bridge between the directorial approach to a piece and the actor. It is important to identify with the actor, not because you want to give in to every whim, but because it is *extremely important* that they can get up on that stage and do what they have to do, and be in their comfort zone.

That's why the rendering is only a blueprint. Working with the actor, the discovering of what is going to be individually represented in that person is very important to a successful design and a successful production. The actors are truly collaborators with the costume designer.

I really love actors. After you have gone though all this designing, you have this person coming in and you have this creative exchange on a *whole other level*. Staying open to it—I find that exciting and fun.

Costume designers create moving sculptures that are extremely ephemeral and specific. I think we are *incredibly lucky*. We make a garment very specifically for a production, for one actor, custom-made. It is very exciting to have that sort of privilege. I feel fortunate, really fortunate.

Chapter 6

Rendering the Sketch

You need to interact with the choice you make. There is a conversation that goes on between you and your media when you are in the zone at the drawing table. It helps you slow down and think. Watercolor—sliding down the page—you have to be free and light. Sometimes I realize that I am drawing too small and I get out big sheets of newsprint. It's liberating!

Judith Dolan, costume designer

Of all the skills required of a costume designer, the ability to draw figures and illustrate garments meaningfully is one of the most essential. The designer must be able to work out ideas and convey to the director, the actors, and the costumer the real proportion, emotional content, and construction detail necessary for each to understand the aspects of the costume that most affect them. Designers need to study figure drawing, anatomy, and painting. Such study is a lifelong involvement. This chapter provides some basic drawing and painting instruction for the beginning costume designer.

Setting Up a Work Area

The costume designer needs a reasonable amount of well-organized workspace. A table or desk large enough to spread out palette, paints, water container, drawing board, and other equipment is adequate, but a drawing table set at an appropriate angle and a side table to hold equipment is more desirable. A comfortable chair and a good incandescent light are essential. (Fluorescent light distorts color.) A bulletin board is useful for roughs, swatches, and research material. A large wastebasket should be kept handy for rejects. Right-handed persons should place water and paints on their right side so as not to drip across their work; left-handed persons should set up materials on the left side. Materials should be kept well organized and in good condition. The time spent keeping the work area neat is repaid many times in efficiency and speed.

Art Supplies

The following list of supplies covers the basic techniques used by costume designers as described in this chapter. However, artists are constantly experimenting, and costume designers are no exception. Almost any relatively fast technique can be used for costume designs, provided the end result is substantial enough for the extensive handling to which costume sketches are subject. Most designers experiment with many approaches until they find a medium that best suits their own personal style. Versatility is desirable, however, to allow the designer to choose a medium that expresses the concept or mood of the play.

Pencils

Drawing pencils: B (soft) and 2B (softer) are used for sketching. Experiment with 2H (hard) and HB (medium) for different effects. Some designers like mechanical pencils, which can be filled with the desired lead. *Colored pencils* are popular with designers for details or shading, especially in white. Some designers find grease pencils in black and white useful. *Conté crayon* and *charcoal pencils* can be used but require more experience.

Sharpeners

Small metal *pencil sharpeners* with containers for catching shavings are handy. Special sharpeners are required for mechanical pencils. *Sandpaper pads* shape pencils and pastels.

Erasers

Art-gum erasers clean up drawings without damaging the surface of the paper. *Kneaded erasers* are used for chalk, charcoal, conté crayon, pastel, and soft pencil and can be formed into shapes to erase small areas. An *ink eraser* can lighten mistakes, but may damage the finish of soft papers.

Pens

Drawing pen holders and *nibs* (points), and *felt* and *fiber-tipped pens* can be used by the costume designer. The designer should experiment with a variety of pens to express different types of line. Look for pens that produce lines of varying width and character. Felt-tip and fiber-tip pens should have permanent ink. Metallic felt-tip pens are very useful for decorative detail.

Paints

Watercolors: A designer needs a set of assorted colors or a group of separate tubes. Basic colors are Cadmium Yellow Pale, Naples Yellow, Yellow Ochre, Raw Sienna, Burnt Sienna, Raw Umber, Van Dyke Brown, Sepia, Cadmium Red Light, Cadmium Red Medium, Scarlet, Alizarin Crimson, Violet, Ultramarine Blue, Cerulean Blue, and Chinese White.

Gouache or *designer colors:* These assorted colors can be used for various opaque effects. White is especially useful for adding detail and for touch-ups.

Metallic paints: Water-base metallic paints add flash and glitz to costumes. Do not use oil-base metallic inks on watercolor sketches, since oil resists further wash techniques (transparent layers). Wash is discussed later in this chapter under "Basic Watercolor Techniques." These inks can also leave an oily "halo" on some papers.

Acrylic paints: A set of assorted colors or individual tubes can be used for wash and opaque techniques.

Pastels

A set of hard or soft pastels (chalk) or pastel pencils offers the designer another useful medium. They can be sharpened with a mat knife and sandpaper block. Paper stumps of various sizes, degrees of hardness, and types of points are used for blending. *Oil pastels* are used for resist techniques and a "crayon look."

Ink

Black waterproof *drawing ink* is used for line and wash. Assorted *colored inks* allow for intense wash techniques.

Papers

Papers are available in pads or loose sheets. Pads of *drawing paper, newsprint, tracing paper,* or *layout paper* are needed for sketches, roughs, and research. For watercolor, ink, or pen and ink, use *Bristol board* (vellum finish), *Murillo board, coquille board, illustration board,* or *watercolor papers* with fine finishes. Do not use plate finish papers for wash techniques. *Charcoal paper, velour paper,* and *mat boards* come in many colors and can be used for pastels. Mat board can also be used for gouache, acrylic, and watercolor painting. *Parchment* and *rice papers* are suitable for quick, simple sketch style with little correction, but are not good for large wash areas.

Papers come in a wide range of weights. For wash techniques, a paper should be at least 80 pounds. If paper is too lightweight, washes will cause them to buckle and crinkle unevenly, distorting the sketch and making painting difficult. Papers with high rag content and of heavier weights make wash techniques and corrections or scrub-outs easier.

The paper surface can be *hot press, cold press,* or *rough.* Hot press papers have a smooth, hard finish and absorb moisture slowly. These papers are used for technical work and illustration. They are good for pen and ink, but washes tend to sit too long on the surface and may run or streak. Cold press papers have a slight texture and absorb moisture more quickly. These papers are good for wash techniques. Rough papers are usually unsuitable for costume sketches as details are difficult to represent.

For computer-created sketches, medium-weight papers like *Bristol board, parchment,* and *matt photograph paper* may be used in sizes that fit the available printer. Lighter weight papers can be used for distribution copies.

Brushes

Only quality brushes should be used for watercolor and ink work. Called "pointed rounds," *watercolor brushes* made of red sable or sablene in sizes #1, 4, and 8 are needed for costume sketches. A large brush that makes a good point will serve the designer's needs better than several small brushes. Sizes of various available brands should be compared. Cheap brushes are only good for gluing. Synthetic fiber brushes are satisfactory for acrylics. A small, flat acrylic or oil painting brush is useful for applying rubber cement.

Drafting or Masking Tape

Tapes are used for securing papers to the drawing board and for masking sections of work for sharp-edged shapes.

Fixative

Spray fixatives are used for fixing charcoal, pencil, conté crayon, and pastel sketches to prevent smearing. Spraying should not be done near an open flame, or spray fumes inhaled. For a temporary spray booth use a large cardboard box on its side and place the artwork inside for spraying. Provide good ventilation.

Acetate

Acetate (.003 weight) can be cut and taped around sketches to protect them from damage. Sketches can also be fitted into acetate or polypropylene protector sleeves, which are available in standard sizes.

Glues/Adhesives/Double-Faced Tapes

Suitable adhesives are: *water soluble white glue*, used for gluing heavy boards or attaching swatches to sketches, and *clear gel glue* with roll-on applicator (neutral pH adhesive—PVA). Mylar adhesive photo tabs can be used to attach items to backings in a portfolio. Spray adhesive and rubber cement are not recommended for original art work because over time they will turn dark and stain the paper.

Water Containers

Large jars or bowls can be used to hold water. Some designers use two containers, one for washing brushes and one to hold clean water for mixing into paints.

Palette

Mixing trays, small dishes or cups, plastic egg cartons, or plastic ice trays all provide suitable containers for mixing inks and watercolors. Palettes should be non-absorbent and white (to prevent visual distortion of paint color during mixing).

Mat Knife

A retractable knife and extra blades are needed for cutting heavy paper and illustration board.

Cutting Mat

A self-healing mat is used to protect table surface when cutting papers with a knife.

Drawing Board

A drawing board, 20 by 26 inches or larger, is needed to support loose paper during painting. A piece of Masonite (with finished edges) or a drawing table can serve as a substitute.

Rulers and T-Square
Metal rulers are needed for measuring and cutting paper for sketches.

Tissues or Clean Rags
A box of tissues should be kept within easy reach for cleaning brushes and blotting up excess paint.

Tool Box or Case
A suitable container to keep art supplies together and organized is needed.

Wastebasket
Don't let sketches become too precious. If it isn't working, throw it out and start over.

Portfolio
The designer will need a string-tied folder for carrying sketches. A presentation portfolio for photos and sketches of shows designed will be needed for job interviews. (See chapter 10.)

Care of Materials

Good art materials are expensive and should be cared for properly. Pens and holders should be wiped clean with a tissue or damp cloth after each use and they should be stored carefully to prevent damage to the points. Fiber-tipped and felt-tipped pens should always be capped.

Good brushes deserve the very best care; poor-quality brushes are not worth having. During painting, brushes should be rinsed often in clean water. They should be washed with cool water and mild soap or commercial brush cleaner occasionally to remove any residue of paint materials. Always dry brush tips with a tissue or cloth and shape into a point. Allow the brush to dry, brush tip up, in a container. Do not put the brush in the mouth or stroke the tip with fingertips. *Never* leave a good brush standing, point down, in a water container. When working, rinse the brush and prop the ferrule (metal collar that holds bristles on handle) on a tissue or brush holder when you are not using it.

Tube paints should be squeezed from the bottom of the tube. Tube tops should be kept clean and tightly capped when not in use. Inks and liquid paints need to be stirred or shaken at each use. Check the labels. Clean the rim of the bottles and put the lids on securely when finished.

Palettes and water containers should be cleaned after each use.

The top of the drawing table can be protected with a sheet of mat board, cutting mat, or other covering. *Always* use an extra piece of heavy cardboard or a cutting mat under the work when cutting with a mat knife, to prevent scarring the tabletop.

Drawing the Figure

To draw, you must close your eyes and sing.

Pablo Picasso, NBC-TV, September 15, 1957

Proportion

Many costume designers use the "fashion figure" for costume sketches. The average adult body is 7 1/2 times the height of the head, whereas the fashion figure is 8 1/2 times the height of the head. This slight elongation of the figure adds grace to the body and shows the garment to advantage. Further elongation of the figure distorts the body proportions and makes the interpretation of the sketch more difficult. The designer should study the people encountered daily and collect pictures of interesting figures in order to understand the visual effects produced by different body proportions. Deviations from the "ideal" provide needed contrast. Directors often cast actors of various shapes and sizes to create a more interesting stage picture. The designer should reflect these differences in the sketches. In figure 6.1 examples of full-front figures demonstrate the relative proportions of the 8 1/2-head male and female fashion figures.

Female Proportions

The female head is egg-shaped and fills the first head space in figure 6.1. This shape represents the head before the hair and headdress are added.

The width of female shoulders is 1 1/2 times the height of the head. The shoulders are drawn on a line at the halfway point of the second head space. The nipples are drawn at the second head line, the waist at the third head line. The top of the leg is drawn along the fourth head line. The kneecaps are centered on the sixth head line, and the legs begin to taper in just above the seventh head. The ankles are drawn at the eighth head line. The feet take up the last half head or a little more, the actual space depending on the position of the foot.

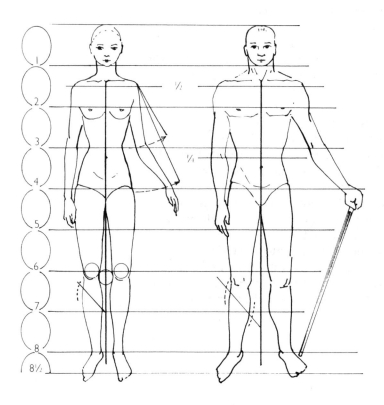

Figure 6.1 Basic fashion figures. Drawn at 8 1/2 times the height of the head.

The arms round off the shoulder points, and the inside of the elbow is even with the waist at the third head line. The outside of the elbow touches the top of the pelvic bone. The wrist lines up with the fourth head line. The hand rests on the thigh down to the fifth head line and is about three-quarters the size of the head.

The upper arm swings from the shoulder in an arc. As long as the arms are in the *same plane* as the body, the apparent length of the upper arm and lower arm does not change as they swing outward.

The leg curves are higher on the outside and lower on the inside of the leg. The ankle is higher on the inside and lower on the outside.

Male Proportions

Male proportions vary from that of the female in several areas. Assuming the two figures are the same height, the following differences exist in the proportions of the male and female fashion figures. The head is wider and more angular. The neck is heavier. The shoulders are the width of two head lengths (figure 6.1) and are drawn at one-third of the second head. The nipples are on the second head line. The male figure's waist is lowered to a line one-fourth of the fourth head. The top of the legs is at the fourth head. The knees are drawn at the sixth head line and the ankles at the eighth head line. The feet take up the last one-half head.

The arms pivot from the shoulder, and the inside of the elbow is in line with the waist. The outside of the elbow touches the top of the pelvic bone. The pelvic area of the male figure is smaller than that of the female figure. Because the waist of the male is lower, the upper arm is longer. The lower arm is also slightly longer, bringing the hand down just past the fifth head line. The angle of the leg curves and ankles are the same as on the female figure.

The male figure is generally drawn heavier, more muscular and angular, and with larger feet and hands.

Balance

The "balance line," an imaginary line representing the pull of gravity on the body, helps the designer draw a figure that appears to be standing securely on the ground. With the body weight evenly distributed on both feet, the balance line falls from the pit of the neck, perpendicular to the bottom of the paper, and falls *between* the ankles of the figure. When the weight shifts to one leg, the balance line moves toward the supporting foot. When all the weight is supported by one leg, the balance line falls from the pit of the neck to the ankle of the supporting leg. Figure 6.2 (on the following page) shows two full-front action figures. Note the sharp curve of the body and the angles produced by the shift of weight. The hip of the supporting leg is higher than that of the non-supporting leg. The shoulders are tilted in the opposite direction for balance. The breasts are in line with the angle of the shoulders. The part of the body that is most flexible is the area between the rib cage and the pelvic bone. This area stretches or contracts for movement.

Eye Level

Most designers sketch costume figures with the viewer's eye level at the chest or waist of the figure. If the eye level is too high, the viewer appears to be looking

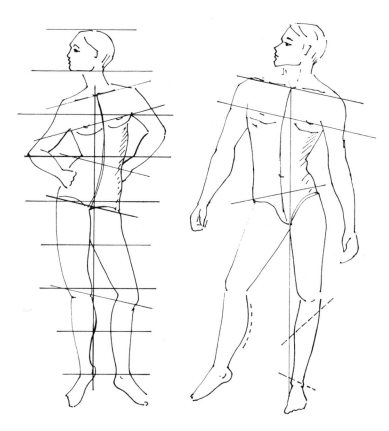

Figure 6.2 Full-front action figures. As the weight is shifted from both feet to one foot, the body compensates to maintain its balance, creating a feeling of movement and action in the figures.

down from the balcony. If the eye level is too low, the viewer seems to be seeing the figure from below stage level.

With the eye level (horizon line) in the chest area, the viewer can logically see under the hat brim and down onto the skirt. A set of sketches should share the same eye level. A full-front figure is drawn in one-point perspective (the sides, top, and bottom of the figure converge at the same point on the horizon line). Figure 6.3 illustrates the effect of one-point perspective on a figure in costume. Relating parts of the costume to circles or ovals in perspective helps the designer draw them properly.

Varying the Pose

Three-Quarter Views

A set of costume sketches should include a variety of poses. The three-quarter view is a good choice for many sketches because the front and part of the side of the costume are visible. Figure 6.4 shows figures in the three-quarter position. Turning the figure places it into two-point perspective. Visualizing the body as a group of geometrical forms helps the designer place it into perspective. Figure 6.5 illustrates a three-quarter figure in two-point perspective. This figure is standing straight with weight evenly distributed, but at an angle to the viewer.

Although a costume should be illustrated in a simple pose, some action adds interest to the sketch. Keep the action appropriate to the character. Select a moment in the play in which the character makes an important entrance, discovery, decision, or characteristic gesture. Figure 6.6A (p. 152) shows King Lear walking on the moor. Figure 6.6B (p. 152) shows the Satyr frolicking in *The Winter's Tale*. These sketches demonstrate poses with character-appropriate action that will help the director "see" the character.

Choose a pose and figure type that suggests the age, historical period, and personality of the character. Study research from the period of the play to find the appropriate posture for each character. The posture and fashionable body shape of a period are controlled by the foundation garments. A suitable pose

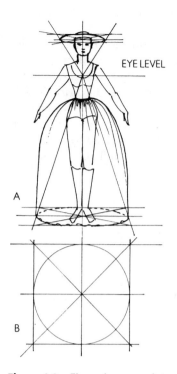

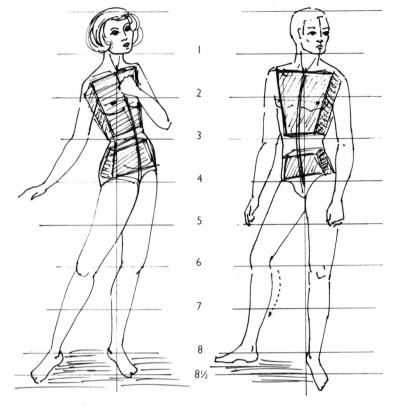

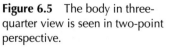

Figure 6.3 Figure in one-point perspective. The skirt, at its bottom edge, and the brim of the hat form a circle. Relating these circles to a box in one-point perspective (B) helps in drawing them correctly.

Figure 6.4 Three-quarter figures. Costume sketches drawn on three-quarter figures show some of the side of the body as well as the front.

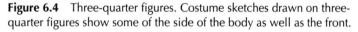

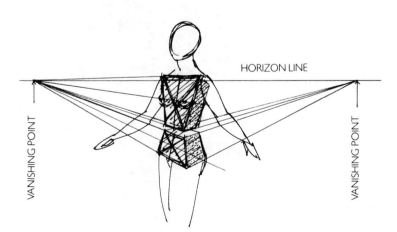

Figure 6.5 The body in three-quarter view is seen in two-point perspective.

will help the director and the actor visualize how the costume will help create the character on stage.

Choose a pose that illustrates the costume to advantage. If a long hanging sleeve is a feature of the costume, extend an arm to display the full sweep of the sleeve. In figure 6.7A the Dragon Lady holds her shawl up to take advantage of the drama in a great drape of fabric. In figure 6.7B the Kalendar Prince's body position suggests action and his cape flies out behind him. Generally, the front of a garment is the most important view and should be completely explained by the sketch. Profile and rear views limit the information provided by the sketch. If profile or rear views are used, small sketches of the front will also be needed.

A

B

Figure 6.6 (A) *King Lear*. Lear. (B) *The Winter's Tale*. Satyrs. These sketches demonstrate poses with movement or character-appropriate actions. (A) Designed by Margaret Mitchell for Shakespeare Festival of Dallas. Sketch photography by Adela Gott. (B) Designed by Joel Ebarb for Purdue University.

Sketches should be large enough for adequate scale and accurate detail. Hold the sketch up to a mirror to check the accuracy of the drawing. If it is drawn on tracing paper, turn the figure over and look at it from the back. Drawing mistakes are often more obvious to the viewer when the sketch is seen in reverse. Before transferring the rough sketch to art paper, give thought to the layout of the final sketch and the placement of labeling and swatches.

Rear Views

With the same proportions maintained, the rear view can be drawn simply as in figure 6.8A (on the following page). Note that the point of the elbow is

A

B

Figure 6.7 *Scheherazade* (A) Dragon Lady. (B) Kalendar Prince. These sketches demonstrate choosing a pose that illustrates the costume to advantage and with a sense of action. Designed by C. David Russell for Enchantment Theatre Company.

below the third head line. The curve of the buttocks is on a line one-quarter head below the fourth head. A figure in three-quarter rear view, as in figure 6.8B, is more interesting than a straight rear view.

Profile Views

Some feature of the costume may require a profile presentation. In figure 6.9A a simple profile figure is illustrated. Proportion remains the same as for the full-front figure. The head in profile is still egg-shaped but is now tilted so that the face plane is almost perpendicular to the first head line. The arm attaches to the shoulder line at one-half the second head space. The nipples are on the second head line. The top of the leg curves downward in the back, and the fullest part of the buttocks is drawn in the lower half of the fourth head space. The knees are drawn at the sixth head line. The upper leg is almost perpendicular to the balance line in front, but the back of the leg tapers in more sharply. The shin is straight and tapers in to the front of the foot. The calf curves out between the back of the knee and the seventh head line. The back of the leg then curves into the heel. More action can be put into the profile view by thrusting the pelvic section forward as illustrated in figure 6.9B.

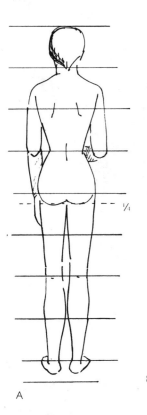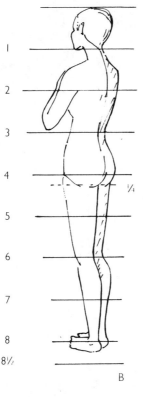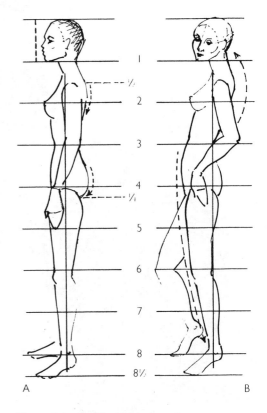

Figure 6.8   Rear view. A rear view figure may be needed occasionally to show the back of the costume.

Figure 6.9   Profile (side) view. Some costumes are more effectively drawn on a profile figure.

Indicating Age

Proportions vary according to the age of the character. Figure 6.10 shows children of several ages. Babies' heads are much larger in proportion to their bodies than are those of adults. As the child grows, the torso, arms, and legs gradually lengthen in relationship to the head until adult proportions are reached. Children tend to be chubby and have prominent tummies, short necks, and no obvious bone structure. (See figure 6.11 on the following page.) An understanding of the adolescent body helps to project the character's age.

As illustrated in figure 6.12 (on the following page), middle-aged characters usually have thicker torsos and less erect posture. Women's breasts begin to sag, and men's muscles become soft and less defined.

Aged characters are drawn at 7 to 7 1/2 heads high. Disease and old age can cause stooping and shrinking of the figure. If the shoulders and back become quite bent, the knees must bend to prevent the figure from falling forward. The head must then be thrust back so the person can see. Extremely old people may be thin and frail with soft muscles and sagging skin. The neck, elbows, knees, and torso, which in youth and middle age have firm muscles and fatty tissue to give them soft, round shapes, become bony with age. In women the breasts sag more and the buttocks become flat.

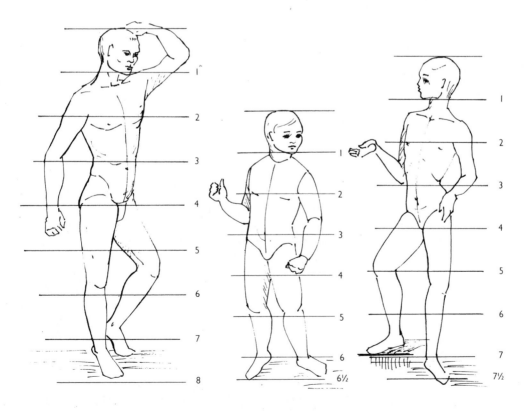

Figure 6.10   Children and young adults. The head of a young child is large in proportion to its body.

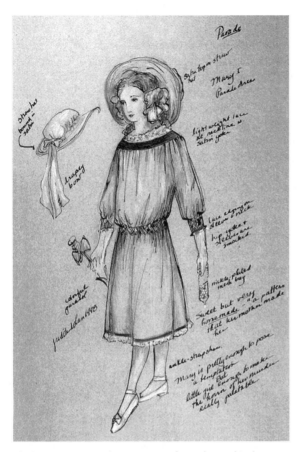

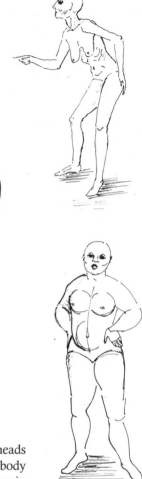

Figure 6.12   Aged and heavy-set characters. The costume designer must learn to suggest the age and physique of all types of characters.

Figure 6.11   *Parade*. Mary, aged 13, dressed in her Sunday best. An understanding of the adolescent body helps to project the character's age. Designed by Judith Dolan for Broadway.

Heavy-set figures can also be drawn 7 to 7 1/2 heads high. Weight settles first in the waist area for most body types. For men this usually means a "belly." Women gain weight in the waist, stomach, hips, and breasts. As weight increases, thighs and upper arms become heavy. Excess weight has the effect of rounding shoulders and shortening the neck. Limbs are rounded, not muscular. Legs appear shorter. In corset periods excess flesh is forced smooth in the torso area and creates large cleavage, round and full hips, and sometimes prominent stomachs.

Drawing Heads

Figure 6.13 shows the basic proportion of the head in various positions. The eyes are drawn on a line at the one-half point of the head. If the width of the head is divided into five equal parts, the eyes occupy spaces 2 and 4, with the width of an eye between them. The nose is drawn on a line three-quarters of a head from the top and is about the width of the space between the eyes. The last one-quarter of the head is divided into three equal parts. The center of the mouth is drawn on the first line, and the shadow under the bottom lip falls on the second line. The mouth width varies, but it is wider than the nose.

The ears are drawn on the side of the head between the eyes and the nose. Eyes should be drawn with the upper lid covering about one-third of the iris of the eye to avoid a surprised look. The bottom of the iris is just touched by the bottom lid. Do not draw in individual eyelashes.

The female neck lines up with the outside corner of the eye and is a straight-sided cylinder. The hairline is drawn on a line about one-sixth of the head.

The male head is angular and more nearly square with a broader jaw and brow. The male neck is thicker. Other proportions are approximately the same.

The head in profile sits at an angle on the neck, which juts out from the shoulders. The vertical divisions of the head are the same as for the full-front view. The nose extends beyond the egg-shape. The jaw line curves up to the ear in the center of the egg-shape. The ear fits between the eye line and the bottom of the nose. The eye in profile is half the size of the eye in full face and is drawn closer to the nose than to the ear.

Heads in Perspective

Heads in three-quarter view are the most difficult to draw. It is helpful to visualize the head in a box, with the face and side of the head as the two visible planes. The center line of the face plane and the center line of the side plane can

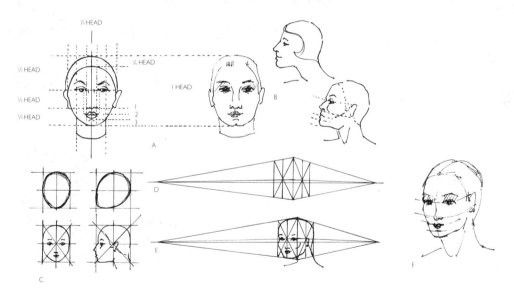

Figure 6.13 Heads. (A) The ideal proportions of male and female heads. (B) The head in profile (note the position of the ear). (C) The head related to a rectangle (face plane) and a square (side plane). (D) and (E) The head related to a box in perspective. (F) Head in three-quarter view.

be located in the same way as the center of any rectangle in perspective. (See figures 6.13C, D, and E.) Remember that the base of the nose is on the centerline, but the nose itself extends beyond the face plane. The ear is drawn from the center line of the side plane toward the back half of the head. The features are widest on the half of each plane nearer the viewer. Less is seen of the features on the half of each plane away from the viewer.

A designer's collection of photos and sketches should include heads in three-quarter view to study and use as models.

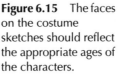

Figure 6.15   The faces on the costume sketches should reflect the appropriate ages of the characters.

Figure 6.16   Hair should be drawn beyond the head, related to the hairline, and indicating the direction in which the hair is combed.

Figure 6.14   Facial details.

Suggesting Age

Some suggestion of wrinkles between the eyebrows and on the forehead, "crow's-feet" and "laugh lines," dark circles or bags under the eyes, and sagging or double chin help indicate middle-aged characters. For aged characters, more wrinkles, puffy eyelids, thin lips, drooping mouth, and splotchy skin are characteristic. Prominent bones, hollows in the neck, and an oversized nose are also common characteristics of age. Varying the proportions of different features creates different character faces. (See figure 6.14.)

Children's faces are more nearly round than those of adults, with larger eyes in proportion to the face. The nose is broader and less defined. Children have small rounded eyebrows, round cheeks, small mouths, and short necks. There is little bone definition. (See figure 6.15.)

Hair

Since the designer must suggest the hairstyle of the character, skill in drawing hair is necessary. (See figure 6.16.) Hair is added *beyond* the head-sized oval, with the hairline as a guide. For hairstyles that cover part of the face, the relationship of the hair to the facial features must be considered. The sketch should suggest the direction in which the hair is combed. Hair should look light and airy, not solid.

Hands and Feet

Graceful hands add to the beauty of the costume sketch, but details of the hands are less important than correct size. The basic shape of the hand is a truncated diamond about three-quarters of the head length. In costume sketches a suggestion of the hand may be more attractive than an overly detailed hand and fingers. Small hand props or accessories are often indicated in the costume sketch. Understanding the basic shapes and divisions of the hands (figure 6.17) simplifies drawing them.

Feet are wedge-shaped and must be large enough to appear to support the body. The actual size depends on the position of the feet in the pose. The feet should be positioned to show the style of the shoe and the height of the heel required for the character. If the shoes do not show because of the length of the costume, working drawings or small detail drawings may be included. (See figure 6.17.)

Once basic proportion is understood, the designer should work for a feeling of movement and style in the figures. A collection of photos and sketches of suitable poses should be assembled to serve the designer as models. Life drawing classes are very valuable for learning about the body structure, but the poses are rarely suitable for costume sketches.

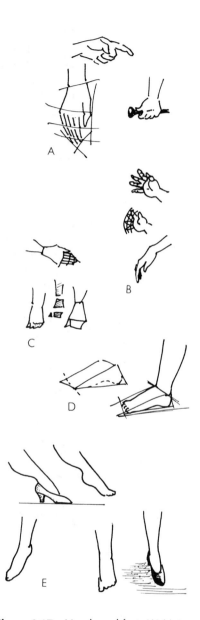

Figure 6.17 Hands and feet. (A) Note the division of the hand at the knuckles. (B) Children's hands are short and round with stubby fingers. (C) Isolate the various shapes in the hand to simplify the drawing. (D) The foot is a wedge shape. (E) The height of the shoe heel affects the shape of the foot and the line of the leg.

Dressing the Figure

Because the body position affects the proportion, hang, and movement of the garment, the designer should not attempt to draw the costume without sketching first the complete figure on which it is worn. To position the garment accurately on the body, the following guidelines should be lightly drawn on the figure: the center of the figure (from the pit of the neck through the navel to the crotch), the base of the neck, the natural waist, the angle of the shoulders and breasts, and the joining of the arm to the torso.

The designer has to analyze the relationship of the period garments to various points of the body. Does the waistline fall at the natural waist? Above or below it? How far from the neck (toward the shoulder) is the neckline? How much chest or bosom shows? What shape does it create? Where on the arm does the sleeve end? Above or below the elbow? At the wrist? How long are pants or skirt? Ankle length? Instep length? Floor length? Does the posture of the period affect the shape of the silhouette? What basic shapes make up the garment? Using the lines blocked out on the figure, the designer draws the garment silhouette and details in correct relationship to specific body points. Figure 6.18 illustrates how the garment relates to the body within it.

If a costume is worn by a corseted figure, the torso is rigid from waist to breast and cannot be twisted or bent except at the exact waist or hip as allowed by the corset. The backbone and rib cage are held together in a solid block so that the whole upper torso must move together as a unit.

Figure 6.18   (A) A corseted figure has a high bosom and the shape of the bosom changes with the shape of the corset. (See also figure 3.8B.) (B) Establish these important lines on the figure to guide the drawing of the costume. (C–F) The garment must relate to the body within it.

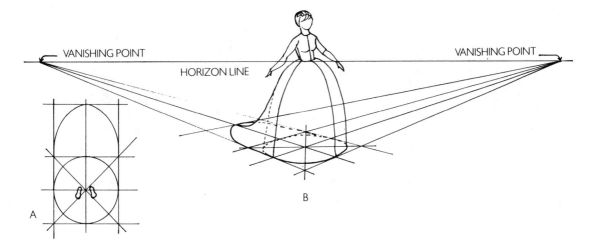

Figure 6.19   The figure in two-point perspective. To draw a garment in three-quarter view correctly, the designer must be able to locate the center front, sides, and center back. These points control costume details and trim placement. Visualizing the skirt in a square or rectangle (A) and placing that shape in perspective (B) will help locate these important points.

Figure 6.19 shows a figure drawn in two-point perspective, showing the position of the center front, side, and center back seams of a large skirt, and how they are established in perspective. The circle that the skirt makes on the floor fits into a square in perspective. The center of the square is formed by the intersection of diagonal lines joining the opposite corners of the square. When this point is connected to each vanishing point, the sides are divided in half. Where these lines touch the outside of the skirt circle, the center front, side seams, and center back can be located. The train is drawn in line with a rectangle extended in perspective, with the center of the train in line with the center back seam.

The designer should study the way garments hang on the body and consider the pull of gravity on different fabrics. Fabric falls from the extended parts of the body or from areas where the fabric has been drawn into the body (points of suspension). Shoulders, breasts, arms, buttocks, waist, and hips can support the fabric. Gravity exerts a downward pull from these points. The density, cut, and hand of the fabric affect its response to the pull of gravity. (See figure 6.20 on the following page.)

The gravitational pull on a garment is modified by the movement of the figure. When a figure is standing with its weight evenly distributed on both feet, the pull of gravity causes the garment to hang evenly around the figure. When the weight of the figure is shifted to one leg, the center of the body is no longer perpendicular to the base of the sketch. This shift is expressed in an "action line," an imaginary line that follows the center of the torso from the pit of the neck through the crotch and down the *non-supporting* leg. The center front line of the garment now relates to the action line of the body. A feeling of motion is also achieved in a sketch if the costume appears to be windblown, and a slight ripple of the fabric toward the back of the figure suggests that the character has been caught in movement.

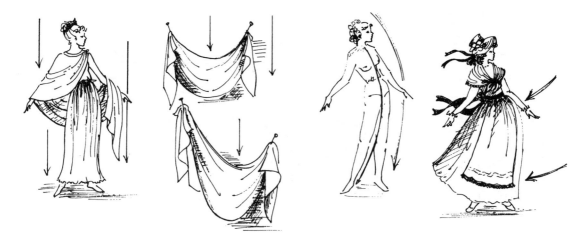

Figure 6.20   Gravity creates a downward pull on the fabric from the points of suspension (head, shoulders, elbows, wrists, breasts, waist, hips, and knees). The movement of the body or a slight breeze will alter the hang of the garment temporarily as the flow of air counters the force of gravity.

Figure 6.21   Proper size of hat. Enough room should be allowed for the head and hair inside the crown of a hat.

Drawing Hats

After drawing in the head and hairstyle, the designer locates the place on the head where the hat actually sits. The crown of the hat usually tilts down in the back, but for some styles it sits flat on the head or forward over the forehead. Enough room should be allowed for the head and hair inside the crown. The brim is added, with its width being judged from the bottom of the crown. Trim is added last. (See figure 6.21.)

Costume Details

Because the costumer must interpret the sketch, an effort must be made to express details accurately. Figures 6.22 and 6.23 show how to illustrate numerous costume details. Note the differences in shapes produced by gathers, pleats, and flares. Trim that is applied to edges of a garment should be drawn parallel to those edges. Aprons and overskirts that are parallel to the underskirt should be drawn to follow its folds and edges. Patterns are illustrated on the basis of a grid as shown in figure 6.24. The scale of the pattern should usually be the same on the top and bottom of the figure and is determined by how many times the motif could be repeated between neck and waist.

Much about drawing garments can be gleaned from the research of the period in which the costumes are being designed. This information should be carefully noted.

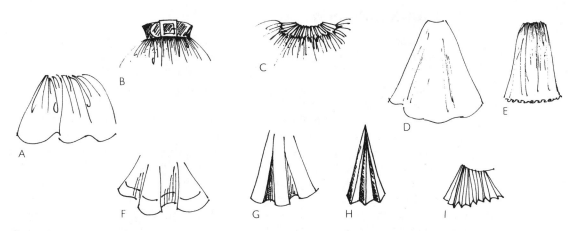

Figure 6.22   Costume details. (A) Gathers in a crisp fabric. (B) Gathered skirt with belt. (C) Cartridge pleats. (D) Flared skirt. (E) Gathered skirt of soft fabric. (F) Circular skirt. (G) Box pleats. (H) Sunburst pleats. (I) Pleated ruffle.

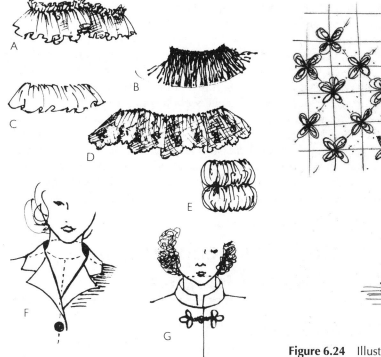

Figure 6.23   Costume details. (A) Gathered ruffle with heading. (B) Fringe. (C) Gathered ruffle set into seam. (D) Gathered lace ruffle. E) Shirred trim forming puffs. (F) Rolled collar. (G) Mandarin or standing collar.

Figure 6.24   Illustrating patterns. Estimate the number of motifs to repeat between the neck and the waist of the figure. Maintain that size over the whole garment. Most motifs repeat on fabric in a staggered pattern. Establish a grid on which to space the motifs, with horizontal lines parallel to the hem and vertical lines radiating from the waist.

Transfer Methods

Ideally, the designer should be able to copy the costume from the rough sketches directly onto the watercolor paper or board with style and ease, but it may not be possible for the novice designer to do this. Because excessive erasing damages the finish of most paper, designers may wish to trace or transfer the corrected roughs to the paper.

Rubbing the back of the sketch with pencil lead or a graphite stick makes it possible to trace the figure onto the painting surface. For sketches on layout or tracing paper, a graphite wash can be used. (After rubbing graphite onto the back of the sketch, the designer paints over it with turpentine. It then has to dry before tracing begins.) The same method can produce a separate graphite tracing sheet.

Trace the lines and shapes of the figure and garment to achieve good proportion and correct shape. Take care not to indent the surface of the watercolor paper when tracing, or the wash will puddle in the groove. Redraw details directly on paper, and clean up tracing smudges with an art-gum or kneaded eraser.

Another method of transferring a sketch is to use a light box or light table. Tape the sketch to the glass of the light box and tape the watercolor paper over it. Redraw the figure, using as a guide the shadow of the sketch produced by the light shining through the paper. If a light box is not available, try taping the rough sketch and paper to a sunny window.

Do not use waxy carbon papers for transferring sketches to be painted in wash techniques, because the carbon resists water. White dressmakers' carbon will work on tinted boards if gouache, pastel, or other opaque media will be used. It can be erased with the warmth from an iron (no steam) or hair dryer, but may leave an oily residue. Some designers photocopy or blueprint the pencil drawings and paint the copies with gouache. The paper used for copies is not suitable for wash techniques, but it will accept paints mixed with little water.

Pencil sketches can be scanned digitally and printed on lightweight watercolor paper, then painted with watercolor or gouache. Many copies can be made for experimenting with various color ideas and the finished sketch can be rescanned, given a background, and printed many times. (See figures 1.4, 6.36, and 6.37.)

Basic Watercolor Techniques for the Costume Designer

And never yet did insurrection want
Such water colors to impaint his cause . . .

Henry the IV, William Shakespeare

General Notes

Always mix watercolor paints with some water. The beauty of watercolor is strongly related to the transparency of the medium. Always mix more paint in the desired color than seems necessary. (Refer to "Color Theory for Pigments" in chapter 4.) A soft matte finish is characteristic of fine watercolor. Work for clean color and flowing line.

Most watercolorists work by painting areas of light color first and adding successive layers of darker color to build up the shadows and darker shapes. They achieve highlights by leaving areas of paper or light wash to show through the darker tones.

To prevent puddling of the paint or visual distortion of the sketch, the drawing board or drawing table should be positioned at about a 30-degree angle. A box, book, or block (1 1/2 to 2 inches high) placed under the board will produce a suitable angle.

Wash

A transparent layer of color on an area of the sketch is a *wash*. Any painting that features large areas of wash must be on paper or board thick enough not to ripple or swell. Watercolor paper should be taped down to a drawing board first. Washes are done with a mixture of paint and water several shades darker than the desired finished color. Watercolor dries two or three shades lighter than the wet color. The paint must be completely fluid and thoroughly blended with the water. (See figure 6.25 on the following page.)

Flat Wash

The area of the wash should be dampened with a brush or sponge dipped in clean water. Water should not pool up on the surface but should leave an even shine over the area to be painted. With a large, fully loaded (but not dripping) brush of paint, strokes are made from left to right (reverse for left-handed persons) across the top of the area. The strokes are repeated down the area, each stroke slightly overlapping. The excess color will collect at the bottom edge of each stroke and be picked up by the next stroke. Excess color at the bottom edge of the last stroke can be picked up with the tip of a clean, barely damp brush. The layer of water on the paper will define the wash area and assist the blending of the strokes. Too much water will cause separation of the pigment, however. Experiment with effects on scrap paper. The layer of water will further dilute the color, so mix a wash tone several shades darker than the desired finished color. (See figure 6.25A.)

Graded Wash

Starting with an intense mixture of paint, stroke across the sketch. Add water to the brush with each successive stroke, blending the wash evenly to the lightest desired tone. (See figure 6.25B.)

Wet-on-Wet Technique

Additional paint applied to an already wet, painted surface produces interesting bleeding and fuzzing effects. (See figure 6.25C.) This technique is frequently used for large areas like backgrounds as in figure 6.26 (p. 167).

Figure 6.25   Sample rendering techniques. (A) Flat wash. (B) Graded wash. (C) Wet-on-wet strokes. (D) Dry brush strokes. (E) Resist techniques: rubber cement, masking liquid, masking tape, and wax. (F) Layered wash, sponge texture, and stippling.

Dry Brush

Rough textured effects are produced by using very little water in the paint and very little paint in the brush. (See figure 6.25D.)

Resist Techniques

Applying a substance to resist the paint or ink when a wash is applied to the area allows the designer to leave areas with sharp outlines or textures. Masking

Figure 6.26 *Good.* Hoess, Freddie, and Elizabeth. The background effect in this sketch is produced by painting color onto damp paper (wet-on-wet), while the harder lines of the uniforms and boots were painted when the paper was dry. Designed by Margaret Mitchell for the University of Texas at Austin. Sketch photography by Adela Gott.

tape, rubber cement, liquid mask, oil pastels, or paraffin (wax) are common resist devices. (See figure 6.25E.)

Layered Effects

Numerous layers of watercolor wash, each allowed to dry before the next is painted, achieve a feeling of transparent depth. Layers of paint can be applied with a sponge over wash or stippled with small brush strokes for textures. (See figure 6.25F.)

Painting the Costume Sketches

Listed below are the steps to follow in the process of painting the costume sketch.

1. Sketch the costumed figure directly onto a board or paper, or transfer it using one of the methods previously described. Determine the direction of light on the figure.

2. Mask off the areas to remain white, if desired. For smaller shows, work (paint) each step on all the sketches at one time. For large shows, work all the sketches for a scene or an act at one time. If a large group of sketches are painted at once, an overall view is maintained. Sketches progress simultaneously to the same level. This approach avoids overworking one sketch at the expense of others. Sketches that do not work can sometimes be spotted and eliminated before too much time is spent on them.

3. Wash in the backgrounds, if desired. Set them aside to dry. Usually by the time the last one is finished, the first one can be taken to the next step. (See figure 6.27.) Backgrounds suggest the mood of the play or the color of the set, if it is known. Avoid excess detail in the backgrounds. A suggestion of a shadow cast by a strong light on the figure is effective. Remember the direction of light on the figure. A graded wash makes an effective background, with the darkest part of the wash used as the shadow behind the figure. Turn the sketch on its side for left to right gradation. Figures done on tinted papers may not need backgrounds to suggest environment, but since stage costumes are almost never seen against white, a wash to tone down white paper is desirable. Intense background colors tend to detract from costumes; neutral colors enhance costume sketches.

4. Paint the flesh tone areas. A basic paint mix for flesh tones consists of Burnt Sienna or Van Dyke Brown, Yellow Ochre, Chinese White, and a touch of Cadmium Red or Alizarin Crimson. Another flesh tone combination includes Raw Umber, Cobalt Blue, and Cadmium Orange. Varying the amounts of each color produces a variety of skin tones. Keep these flesh tones transparent by limiting the use of white and by adding water. Paint all areas of the skin that will be seen, including parts of the body seen through transparent fabrics. Paint the whole head to prevent a hard hairline. Paint the whole foot and add the shoes later, unless the skin tone is quite dark. After painting in flesh tones in all the sketches, set them aside to dry.

Figure 6.27 Painting the costume sketch. Steps 1 through 3. After transferring or drawing the figure onto watercolor paper or board, mask areas that are to remain white, and wash in backgrounds.

5. Paint in large areas of costume using the lightest color wash desired. Test the colors on scrap paper before painting the sketch. Leave unpainted paper for the white highlights of fabrics with a hard shine. Leave unpainted paper also for large white details like collars and cuffs. Paint applied to white paper will never be whiter than the paper itself. Leave the paper unpainted for white garments or large white areas of garments and paint in only the shadows using gray, blue-gray, or other pale wash. Strong background tones play up white costumes sketched on white paper. Sketches on tinted papers or smaller areas of white on colored grounds may be painted in with white gouache.

   Mistakes can be blotted up with tissue or a soft, clean cloth. A clean, damp brush can also remove some color. To produce textures, apply heavy color and blot up some of the paint with paper towels or terry cloth. Some color can be scrubbed out of a dry area with a damp brush or cotton-tipped swab. These techniques can be used for corrections or special effects.

6. After the sketches have dried, paint in the smaller areas: hair, shading, features, and accessories. For shading use darker washes of the same color, use lower intensities of the same color (add complement), or use overlay with wash of contrasting color. Shading can also be done with Payne's Gray, Sepia, or Van Dyke Brown. Experiment with unusual colors in the shadows, perhaps indicating the colors of stage lighting reflected off the costume. (See figure 6.28 on the following page.)

Figure 6.28 Painting the costume sketch. Steps 4 through 6. Paint in flesh tones and large costume areas using the lightest shades of desired colors. When adjacent areas are dry, paint in base tones of all smaller areas and basic shadows.

7. Add details with opaque paint, pencil, pen and ink, or brush and paint. (See figure 6.29.)

8. Label each sketch with the name of the character, the title of the play, act, and scene number. Sign the sketch. Number each sketch consecutively according to the order in which they are seen on stage (consult the costume plot). Add any details or notes to the costumer. If the sketch is on lightweight paper, mount it on mat board or other sturdy cardboard. Attach swatches, if they are available. Cover the sketch with acetate or slip it into a plastic sleeve to protect it from damage by handling in conferences and the costume shop. Alternatively, scan or photocopy and provide copies for the director, actors, and costume shop personnel.

Watercolor effects can be widely varied. The whole sketch can be heavily painted or the watercolor can be used gently to suggest light and delicate tones.

Working Drawings

Additional construction and trim details may be drawn in pencil or pen and ink on a separate board or on layout paper taped to the sketch. These drawings may be needed to clarify the design for the patternmaker or shopper. Painted or stenciled motifs may require actual size or sample drawings in one-half-inch scale for the

Figure 6.29 Painting the costume sketch. Steps 7 and 8. Add details in paint, pen and ink, or pencil. The sketch is then ready for labeling and attaching swatches.

Figure 6.30 *La Pietra Del Paragone.* Marquis Ortensia, Act I. This delicate sketch is primarily pencil with watercolor wash used for light shading and coloring. Designed by Michelle Ney for the Austin Lyric Opera.

painter. Photocopies of pertinent research should accompany the sketches given to the costume shop. Any work the designer must give to someone else to do must be clear and well documented. (See figures 1.8, 4.16, 5.10, 6.7A, and color plate 7.)

Other Techniques

Gouache

Other media can be used for costume sketches, either alone or with watercolor as the base painting. Gouache is a common choice. Because it is opaque, gouache is very useful for adding details over layers of wash, particularly light details over dark colors. Gouache is also good for suggesting heavier fabrics. The colors are slightly duller than watercolor and much less intense than ink colors. Gouache can also be used to paint sketches on colored boards and papers where the transparency of watercolor would allow the paper color to show through and distort the color of the wash. Figure 6.31 is a sketch for the puppet Shalken in *The Painted Rose* done with gouache, watercolor, oil pastel, and collage.

Figure 6.31. *The Painted Rose*. Shalken. A sketch for a puppet done with gouache, watercolor, oil pastel, and collage. Designed by Shima Ushiba for Dramaton Theater.

Acrylic Paints

Acrylic paints can be used as wash or as opaque color. Textures can be built up with acrylics without losing the life of the color. Because acrylics are a form of plastic, some designers find the sheen of the paint harsh.

Inks and Dyes

Many designers use colored inks or bottled dyes. These are handled in the same ways as watercolor, but require careful mixing and pre-testing. Most of the inks and dyes stain the paper immediately. Some correction can be made with bleach, but it must be neutralized with vinegar, and some yellowing of the paper results. Bleach should be applied with an otherwise useless brush or a cotton swab. *Never* use a good sable brush for bleach, since it destroys the natural fibers.

Inks provide an intensity of color not available in many other media. Details in ink can brighten delicate watercolor renderings. Permanent inks can be used to outline figures and costumes before the watercolor is painted in. These lines must be completely dry or else bleeding will occur in the painting process. Figure 6.32 features a figure drawn with a pen and permanent black ink. Some shading and color to the jacket and hat were added when the ink was thoroughly dry.

Felt-Tip Pens

Felt-tip and fiber-tip pens make an extensive range of colors available to the designer. These colors are intense and especially good for adding details. Felt-tip pens are good for expressing modern looks and for quick sketches, but subtle effects are hard to achieve and blending colors is somewhat difficult.

Pastels

Many designers use pastel sticks and pastel pencils. They are particularly suitable for ballet tutus or other airy, frothy-looking costumes, but they can also be blended for other effects.

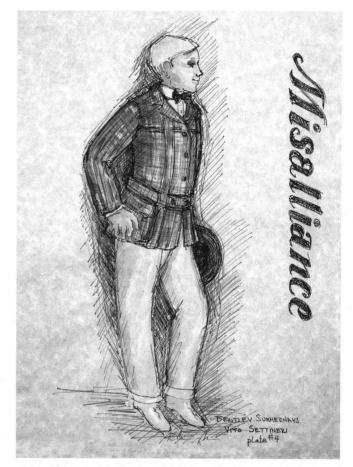

Figure 6.32 *Misalliance*. Bentley Summerhays. The figure is drawn with pen and ink; shading and color were added with watercolor when the ink was thoroughly dry. Designed by the author for Brooklyn College.

Pastels should be used on softer finish papers that absorb the chalk. Paper stumps of various sizes are used to blend the color. For small details rub the pastel onto a sandpaper block, pick up the color on the tip of the stump, and apply the color to the sketch with the stump. Pastels must be sprayed with fixative. In figure 6.33 (on the following page) a gray textured board forms the background for Judith Dolan's pastel sketch for *Lovemusik*.

Mixed Media

Designers often experiment with combining media to produce different effects. A collage of various papers used with compatible paints or ink for details can be very interesting. When combining different color media, keep in mind the type of paper that each needs for best results.

Other collage materials like clip art, photocopied images, paper doilies, glitter, sequins, bits of wrapping paper, fabric, and magazine clippings can produce

Figure 6.33 *Lovemusik.* Lotte. A gray textured board forms the background for this pastel sketch. Designed by Judith Dolan for Broadway.

Figure 6.34 *Learned Ladies.* Belise. Collage materials can produce an interesting costume sketch. Designed by the author for Brooklyn College.

quite interesting sketches. The careful application of glue is necessary to accomplish a neat sketch. A similar product can be produced on a computer by cutting and pasting images into a costume design in an art program. Figure 6.34 is an example of a collaged costume sketch.

The designer should collect and study examples of various painting and illustration techniques and should adapt them to express the different moods or concepts of plays being designed. In figure 6.35 the design for the Nurse in *Hippolytus* is rendered in watercolor, ink, and gouache in a style suggestive of Greek vase painting. See also color plate 2, William Ivey Long's designs for *Steel Pier* after the work of Reginald Marsh.

Figure 6.35 *Hippolytus.* Nurse. The style of this sketch is adapted from Greek vase painting. Designed by the author for Brooklyn College.

Computer Rendering

More and more costume designers are incorporating computer techniques when developing their costume sketches. The extent to which a computer is used depends on the availability of suitable software and on the computer skills of the individual designer. Some ways that computers are used in the costume sketch process are:

1. to develop decorative backgrounds to be repeated on an entire series of sketches (See figure 1.4);
2. to label sketches with decorative computer fonts;
3. to scan, store, and reuse basic figures;
4. to manipulate figures for different sizes, positions, and garments;
5. to scan and manipulate materials for collage boards of research and costumes;
6. to create decorative fabrics for the costumes (figure 1.6);
7. to experiment with different color combinations on the same garment by scanning in the pencil sketch and using a "paint" program to color it;
8. to include "found objects" in the sketches by scanning, trimming, and "pasting" them onto the sketch digitally; and
9. to offer variations of color and style quickly and efficiently.

Even though many designers are incorporating digital techniques into their work, most continue to do some aspects of the sketch by hand—the drawing of the figure, the drawing of the costume, or the decorative aspect of the sketch. Most view it as another tool in their art kit for producing the best possible work within a reasonable time.

Presentation

The completed sketches should again be discussed with the director for final approval. Good sketch presentation helps the designer "sell" the costume to the director. Many sketches in this text demonstrate the dramatic use of line and color, the pose of the figure, its placement on the paper, and the artful addition of fabric swatches combine to create strong visual impact. (See figures C-4, C-7, C-10A, C-13, C-14, and C-15.)

Sketches are important for effective collaboration, whether the show will be built, pulled, or rented. Even with a specialized vocabulary, words are woefully inadequate for describing costumes. Sketches and examples of research make discussions more precise. A clear understanding of the designer's intentions limits expensive changes later. Careful notes should be made on changes or additions requested by the director.

This is also a good time to discuss and draw up a list of rehearsal costumes with projected dates for introducing them into the rehearsal process. (See chapter 8.)

Depending on the schedule and type of producing organization, a designer may be asked to present the finished sketches at the first cast meeting or first

Box 6.A   Designer Eloise Kazan describes her method of working in Photoshop on sketches like figure 6.36:

Step 1. I try to take a photo of the actor, dancer, or singer. If that is not possible, I use a photo of a person from a book or magazine. I always prefer to take a photo of the person I'm designing for, as it allows me to really work with their body and proportion. I can start planning an overall look for that character including hair and makeup. The actors love it!

Step 2. I cut away the background, clean the edges, and print the photo of the figure.

Step 3. I do a rough sketch of the entire outfit on top of the photo in pencil. I then scan the sketch and continue working in Photoshop.

Step 4. I look for images/photos of the right textures and materials. I use combinations that give me the effect I want. I then blend everything together with some wonderful Photoshop tools like special effect, blur and sharpen, brushes, and filters.

Step 5. Sometimes I sketch or look in books and magazines for images of accessories that resemble what I have in mind. I scan and distort them in Photoshop until they "fit" my actor. I add colour, use texturizers, and add details until I get the desired effect.

Step 6. I put in a photo of the real background or at least the scenery colour and texture. I adjust my overall costume colours and contrast levels.

Step 7. I put in the date, show information, a signature and then the work has just begun!

Figure 6.36 *Jenúfa.* Chorus. A computer-generated sketch with figure and background photo scanned in and manipulated. Designed by Eloise Kazan for La Ópera de Bellas Artes and Festival de México en el Centro Histórico. Background photograph by Nicolas Pereda.

rehearsal. The actors will be anxious to know how they are to look and the types of garments with which they must work. Completed sketches may be presented either by character, in order of appearance, or by scene. A designer should be prepared to explain the concept behind the designs, the effects desired by the director and designer, and special skills required to use the costume effectively. Actors may request rehearsal costumes and assistance with special items.

Several sets of photocopies of the approved sketches can be useful (1) for the actors so they can visualize themselves in the actual costume, (2) for the director and stage manager so they can answer costume questions that arise during rehearsals, and (3) for the costume shop, in order to reduce handling of the original sketches and to allow several people to work on the same costume at once. If the approved costumes differ from the costume plot (see p. 36) it should be revised to reflect the changes. Copies of the plot should be made for the director or stage manager and the costume shop. A computer composite of a series of costumes (figure 6.37) makes a useful visual costume plot. As the work progresses, frequent updates and additions may be needed. The final version of the costume plot may be passed on to the wardrobe crew to assist in the show organization. The process of adjusting the sketches and sending upgrades to the director, stage manager, and costume shop is greatly expedited by the use of Internet services.

As sketches are completed and approved, the work of assembling the necessary staff, materials, patterns, trims, and accessories can begin in earnest.

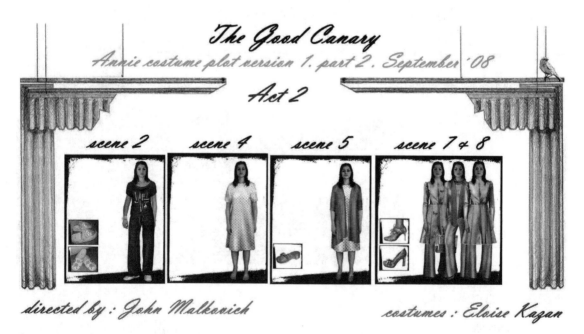

Figure 6.37 *El Buen Canario (The Good Canary).* Anna. A computer composite of a series of costumes for a character makes a useful visual costume plot and presentation tool. Designed by Eloise Kazan for the Teatro Insurgentes.

Interview IV.
Designing for Dance.
A Conversation with
Martin Pakledinaz.

At the time of this interview with the author Broadway designer Martin Pakledinaz had received multiple honors and awards including two Tony Awards, a Drama Desk Award, a Helen Hayes Award, and an Obie Award. (See bio, page 422, for career details.)

RC: How is designing for dance different from designing for other forms of theater?

MP: The one word that always means more to dance design than anything else is *flexibility*. No matter what dance form you're working with, you have to deal with the fact that the body is going to go into positions that we don't expect it to in normal movement. Even if you are using spandex or stretch, you still have to deal with the fact that the arms, for instance, are up vertically as much as they are down. You have to deal with the fact that the legs are going to go higher, or with where the joints really happen on the body—which is not necessarily where you want your design lines to be!

And you have to keep that garment in place. I can just wear my shirt tucked into my pants to go down the street, but if I'm going to go *dancing* down the street I will probably have to add something to the shirt between the legs that holds it in place. There's a certain amount of simple practicality that comes into play.

RC: How do you develop costumes for dance if there is a non-linear story, or no story line or defined characters?

MP: That is always a wonderful, exciting, and scary proposition for any designer. The first thing you do is talk to your choreographer to see if there are any words or images he/she can

THOROUGHLY
MORGEN
MILLIE

"SPEEDTEST"
SUTTON FOSTER

C.D. 230
COSTUME DESIGNER

Figures IV.1 and IV.2 Two of Martin Pakledinaz's Tony-award winning costumes for the Broadway production of *Thoroughly Modern Millie*—Millie (the Speed Test) and Kate Baldwin.

KATE BALDWIN

give you—"freedom," "destruction," any word that you can take away. I usually ask [choreographers] if they have a specific shape in mind, if they're seeing legs all the way up, if they're seeing a skirt. I ask very pragmatic questions—is the dance "traditionally male/female" or does the sexual line need to be blurred?

Then I listen to the music. I listen to the music while I watch the dance, because then I receive some images of emotion. I try to find a three-dimensional symbol for that emotion to take back to the choreographer.

The more abstract the dance becomes, the more abstract your research can become. I remember Patricia Zipprodt talking about Anthony Tudor's *The Leaves Are Fading*. She watched the dance and famously said, "I feel like it's a bouquet of roses whose petals are falling to the ground." That image led her into a color scheme with pastel pinks and roses, and bruised browns—colors like that. She actually had patterns of petals painted on her costumes. So in that case, the design just came from her own emotional response.

RC: What are the major differences between designing costumes for a Broadway musical, a classical ballet, and a modern dance?

MP: Dance being created for a dance company generally has a much longer [time] span than choreography for Broadway shows. With a ballet company, it's not unusual to come in nine months or more before the piece, just for the beginning of the creation.

On Broadway, it all happens within a finite six- to eight-week period. Broadway usually needs a realistic form of costume, so the choreographers tend to be very practical and know exactly what they are going to want.

Modern dance costume, to me, means *flexibility and simplicity,* because the movements are simple with incredible flexibility. The costumes are coming almost from the concept of rehearsal clothes.

For Broadway dance, the designer is often asked to make it look like clothing, and yet, to abstract it. You might have a shoulder pad in a suit coat for a man, but you have to watch the choreography to make sure that it wasn't coming up and hitting his head because of his upward movements. Where it hits along the neck has to be very carefully considered because it can close him in when you least expect it.

Broadway dancers are used to having their figures pushed around and having their bosoms enhanced.

Occasionally I've had a female ballet dancer who likes to be padded up above, but by and large, they're just not used to it, and they don't understand why you're doing it.

I've had ballet bodices made several ways by different shops. The more flexibility you can build into even a classical tutu bodice, the happier the dancers are. Because they are now so used to dancing only in spandex, when you go into something else, they resist it. Even though fabric doesn't have to stretch, the weave does have to *give* if it is at all fitted. Occasionally when you use something that's a tight weave like a Thai silk, you just have to give it more room. I use as little boning as possible; they usually take it out as soon as the designer leaves. The size of the tutu plate can be a huge issue.

A Broadway man would be shocked if you put him in tights, because there's almost never a reason to. So the best thing to do is learn how to cut a man's suit, and get tailors who know how to cut the pants and the jacket so that dancers can move with as much freedom as they were used to when they were wearing their t-shirts. It's possible—it's never quite the same—but it's possible to get pretty close.

RC: How does dance collaboration differ from theater?

MP: Well, the thing that's sort of wonderful is—it's you, the choreographer, and maybe the lighting designer. It's generally a smaller thing. I find I get to talk a lot more with the lighting designer when I do a dance piece. One of the reasons I've gone so easily from form to form is that I don't separate them that much. I treat them all with a certain amount of open communication. They know they can come back to me and talk to me again. It's best to break down those barriers, because happily, there's more in common than there is different.

A lot of designing dance is just practicality. It's just listening to people and then watching how clothing is made, and keeping your mind incredibly open to go in any direction. Don't assume that you have to have the answers in your back pocket already.

RC: What should a designer avoid when designing dance costumes?

MP: It's very important that you do not make the clothing too heavy. When I did *The Pirate Queen,* a Broadway musical, it was a very tricky, long process for us to figure out how to make the dancers look like they were in Elizabe-

Figure IV.3   One of Martin Pakledinaz's Tony-award winning costumes for the Broadway production of *Thoroughly Modern Millie*—Amy Heggins.

than clothing, but still give them the freedom they were used to in their rubber-band [stretch] costumes.

RC: What advice do you have for a young designer interested in designing dance?

MP: My biggest advice is: *Do not get in the way of the dance.* Don't try to make your statement so big that we forget there are dancers and steps going on. I say that about almost any costume. There are times when I'm asked to do stupendous, spectacular costume and that's great, but actually our first job requirement is that we support the dancers and the choreographer in what they're trying to say. I actually think for a lot of my dance costumes *less is more.*

I think that you can't see enough; there is so much dance out there. If you are truly interested in dance, you should see as much as you can. Dancers love to go from a jazz style to a classical style to an extremely pared-down modernist style. So, the more you see, the more comfortable you'll be when all of a sudden you are presented with that dance form—you'll know what to do.

And always be aware that *every day we learn more.*

Chapter 7
Choosing Fabrics

Another piece of real slop-work. What a selvage! Here it's broad, there it's narrow; here it's drawn in by the wefts goodness knows how tight, and there it's torn out again by the temples. And hardly seventy threads weft to the inch. What's come of the rest? Do you call this honest work? I never saw anything like it.

The Weavers, Gerhart Hauptmann

Fabric Basics

Because fabric is the medium through which the designer develops the costume, more than just a casual knowledge of its properties is necessary. The characteristics of fiber, yarn, construction (weave), and finish all contribute to produce different effects of texture and movement in a fabric.

Fiber

A minute, hair-like tissue having a length of at least 100 times its diameter or width is called a *fiber*. Fibers are the basic components of textile fabrics. *Staple fibers* are short lengths measured in inches or fractions of an inch. *Filaments* are long continuous fibers, measured in yards or meters. Fibers fall into two basic categories: *natural fibers* and *synthetic fibers*. Natural fibers are derived from animal and plant sources. All natural fibers, except silk, are staple fibers; silk and synthetic fibers are filaments, but can be cut to staple lengths. Each fiber has its own characteristics and care requirements. (See box 7.A.)

Box 7.A   Natural and synthetic fibers

Natural Fibers

Fiber and Source	Characteristics	Typical Fabrics	Care
Cotton From seed pod of cotton plant	Strong, absorbent, tends to wrinkle, dyes well, shrinks unless treated	Corduroy, denim, poplin, velveteen, muslin	Most may be washed: colorfast in hot water, warm or cold for others; dryer safe, iron while damp, chlorine-bleach safe for white fabrics
Linen From flax plant	Strong, absorbent, difficult to dye, wrinkles unless treated, shrinks	Variety of fabrics with coarse texture and natural luster, very delicate to heavy weights	Dry clean to preserve crispness, wash for softness, iron while damp
Silk From cocoons of silkworms	Strong, absorbent, retains body heat, wrinkle-resistant, dye may bleed, weakened by sunlight and perspiration	Brocade, chiffon, satin, crepe, jersey, charmeuse	Usually dry cleaned, may be hand washed, no bleach, iron at low temperature
Wool From fleece of sheep	Less strong, highly absorbent, holds in body heat, wrinkles fall out, dyes well, needs mothproofing	Crepe, knits, flannel, tweed, gabardine, jersey	Usually dry cleaned, some knits are hand washable, do not use chlorine bleach, some wools are machine washable—follow instructions of manufacturer
Hemp From the stalk and seed of the industrial cannabis hemp plant	Strong, extremely durable, porous, naturally resistant to mold and UV light, absorbent, dyes and retains color well	Herringbone, muslin, twill, satin, jersey, knits, webbing, canvas, gauze	Machine or hand wash in warm water, rinse thoroughly, no bleach, unfinished edges fray significantly
Bamboo From the pulp of bamboo grass	Light, strong, excellent wicking properties, somewhat antibacterial, very soft, smooth, nonallergenic, water-absorbent, insulating, dyes well, drapes smoothly	Fleece, satin, terry cloth, velour, denim	Machine wash and dry, gentle cycle, warm or cool water, possibly in lingerie bag

Synthetic Fibers and Sources

Fiber and Trademarks	Characteristics	Typical Fabrics and Uses	Care
Acetate Acele, Avicolor, Avisco, Celanese, Celaperm, Celara, Chromspun, Estron	Relatively weak, moderately absorbent, holds in body heat, tends to wrinkle, dyes well but is subject to atmospheric fading, resists stretching, accumulates static electricity, luxurious and silklike, excellent draping qualities	Brocade, crepe, faille, satin, taffeta, jersey, tricot, lace	Usually dry cleaned, hand washable or gentle cycle, low heat drying cycle, iron at low temperature
Acrylic Acrilan, Creslan, Orlon, Zefkrome, Zefran	Strong, low absorbency, resists wrinkles, holds in body heat, accepts dye, accumulates static electricity, often blended with other fibers, heat sensitive, tends to pill	Fake fur, fleece, double knit, knits	Dry clean if recommended, can be machine washed and tumble dried, use fabric softeners for less static electricity, little or no ironing required
Glass Beta, Fiberglas	Strong, nonabsorbent, resists wrinkles, resists dyeing	Drapery fabrics from sheer to heavy *[Should NOT be used for clothing—may irritate skin]*	Hand wash, ironing not usually needed
Metallic	Weak, nonabsorbent, heat sensitive, may tarnish if uncoated	Glitter fabrics, lamé, eyelash cloth	Dry clean or hand launder in warm water, iron at low temperature
Modacrylic Dynel, Verel	Low absorbency, holds in body heat, resists wrinkles, very heat sensitive, dries quickly, nonallergenic, flame resistant, resists mildew and moths	Fake fur Wigs	Dry clean Hand wash, do not iron fabrics or use curling irons on wigs
Nylon Antron, Blue C, Caprolan, Cedilla, Celanese, Enkalure, Qiana, Touch	Strong, low absorbency, holds in body heat, tends to pill; resists wrinkling, moths, mildew, and dirt	Satin, jersey, fake fur, chiffon	Hand wash, gentle machine wash, use fabric softener to reduce static electricity, tumble or drip-dry, iron at low temperature

(continued)

Fiber and Trademarks	Characteristics	Typical Fabrics and Uses	Care
Olefin Durel, Herculon, Marvess	Nonabsorbent, holds in body heat, difficult to dye, heat sensitive, nonallergenic	Upholstery, insulating fillers for outer garments	Machine wash in lukewarm water, use fabric softener in final rinse, tumble dry at low setting, iron at lowest temperature
Polyester Avlin, Dacron, Encron, Fortrel, Kodel, Microfiber Quintess, Trevira, Vycron	Strong, low absorbency, holds in body heat, resists wrinkling, accumulates static electricity, retains heat-set pleats and creases, difficult to dye in piece	Crepe, knits, linings, blends	Wash by hand or machine using warm water, tumble or dripdry, use fabric softener to reduce static electricity, needs little or no ironing, low iron setting for touch-ups
Rayon Avril, Beaunit, Coloray, Englo, Fibro, Zantrel	Relatively weak, absorbent, holds in body heat, dyes well; wrinkles, shrinks, or stretches unless treated, dye unstable	Butcher linen, crepe, matte jersey	May require dry cleaning, may be washed by hand in warm water, chlorine bleach may be used on white, iron at moderate temperature
Spandex Lycra	Strong, nonabsorbent, great elasticity, lightweight	Knits, blends	Hand wash or gentle cycle, avoid chlorine bleach, drip or tumble dry, iron at low temperature
Triacetate Arnel	Relatively weak, resists wrinkling and shrinking, dyes well, retains heat-set pleats	Sharkskin, tricot	Hand or machine wash in warm water, dripdry pleated garments, tumble dry, iron at moderate temperature

The shape, length, chemical composition, and performance characteristics of fibers contribute greatly to the final characteristics of the fabrics in which they are used. Natural fibers are irregular and subtle, absorbent and porous. Short staple fibers give rougher, fuzzier, duller qualities to the texture of a fabric, whereas long filament fibers produce fabrics that are shinier, smoother, and cooler feeling. Staple fibers, because they are short, tend to make softer, less smooth yarns that reflect light off more minute surfaces, diffusing that reflection. Synthetics are highly resilient (thus wrinkle-resistant) and generally low in porosity and absorbency. Filaments, being long and smooth, tend to make harder-surfaced yarns that reflect more light in sharper highlights. The way a fiber reflects light is a factor in our perception of texture in the finished fabric, and therefore in the costume. (See box 4.D.)

Fiber *blends* are fabrics that combine two or more different fibers. The characteristics of the fiber present in the highest percentage dominates the fabric, but all fibers contribute to the final character of the fabric.

Yarn

Most fabrics are made of yarns. *Spun yarn* is made by twisting together staple fibers into a continuous piece of the desired length and thickness. *Filament yarn* is the fiber unwound from the cocoon (silk) or extruded from a chemical solution (synthetics). *Ply* yarn is made by twisting two or more single yarns together. The characteristics of the yarn determine many of the characteristics of the fabric in which it is used. In particular the surface texture and the hand (feel) of the fabric are related to the characteristics of the yarn. Yarns with tighter twist are used in smoother, sturdier fabrics; yarns with looser twist are used for rougher, fuzzier fabrics. Some yarns (bouclé, slub) are irregular and create interesting surface textures when woven.

Construction of Fabrics

The basic methods of constructing fabrics are weaving, braiding, knotting, knitting, crocheting, felting, and bonding.

Woven Fabrics

The most common method of making fabrics is *weaving*. Weaving is generally the sturdiest and the most stable type of fabric construction. Lengthwise (warp) yarns are stretched onto a loom in such a way that they can be alternately raised and lowered by movable frames (harnesses). Crosswise (filling or weft) yarns are then inserted at right angles to the lengthwise yarns by the use of shuttles. Weave structures can be varied by the rearrangement of the pattern in which lengthwise and crosswise yarns intersect.

The basic weaves are *plain weave, twill weave,* and *satin weave.* Most other weaves are variations of these three. Figure 7.1 shows these basic weaves and some of their variations.

Figure 7.1A
Samples of the three basic weaves. (i) A plain weave linen fabric. The diagram shows the plain weave structure. (ii) A wool twill. The diagram shows the twill weave structure. (iii) A silk charmeuse. The diagram shows the long floats of the satin weave. Photos by Hilary Sherred.

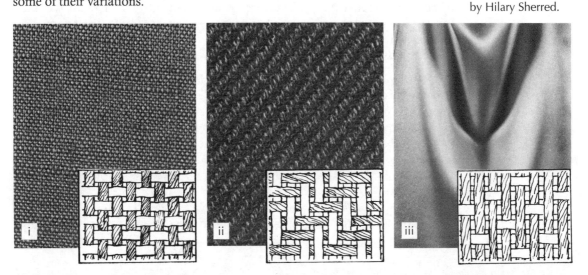

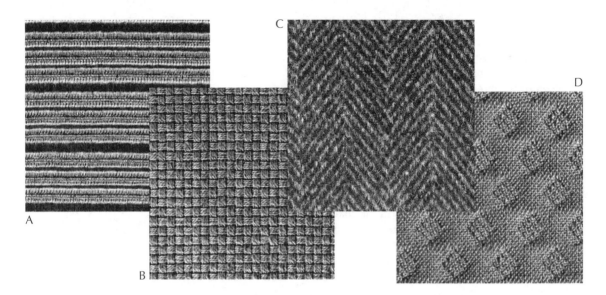

Plain Weave. The simplest weave is the *plain weave,* in which each crosswise yarn goes alternately over and under each lengthwise yarn. Examples are muslin, voile, challis, percale, buckram, crinoline, chintz, chiffon, crepe, georgette, organdy, and shantung.

Twill Weave. The *twill weave* is a basic weave in which crosswise yarns pass over at least two, but not more than four, lengthwise yarns; on each successive line, the crosswise weave moves one step to the right or left, forming a diagonal ridge. Twill weaves are generally sturdier, heavier, closer in texture, and more durable than plain weaves. Examples are cavalry twill, denim, foulard, gabardine, serge, sharkskin, silk surah, and whipcord.

Satin Weave. The *satin weave* is a basic weave in which a lengthwise yarn passes over four to eight crosswise yarns in a staggered pattern similar to the twill weave but spaced so as not to produce ridges. The yarns exposed on the surface, called *floats,* contribute substantially to the characteristic sheen of satins. The most reflective types of satin are made of filament yarns. Examples of satin weave are antique satin, crepe-back satin, charmeuse, and slipper satin. The *sateen weave* is a variation in which the floats are formed by the crosswise yarns. Sateen is usually made of cotton.

Variations of Basic Weaves. The interlocking of yarns in various weaves combined with the variety of fibers and types of yarn produce a wide variety of fabrics.

In the *rib weave,* a variation of the plain weave, a *rib* is produced by using heavy yarns as either the lengthwise or the crosswise yarns, by grouping yarns in specific areas of the length or cross, or by having more lengthwise yarns than crosswise. Examples are bengaline, faille, grosgrain, piqué, ottoman, rep (repp), and taffeta.

The *basket weave* is a variation of the plain weave in which two or more yarns are used in the alternating pattern. The yarns are not twisted together, but

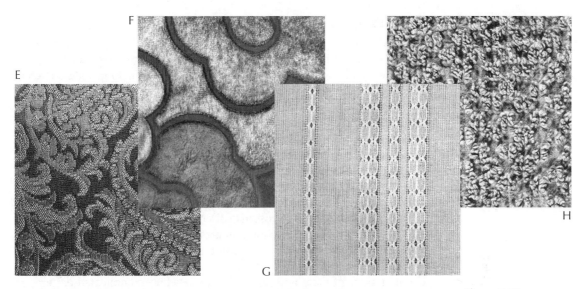

Figure 7.1B
Variations of the three basic weaves. The illustrated fabrics are a few of the variations on the basic fabric weaves. (i) Otto-man—example of the rib weave. (ii) Monk's cloth—example of the basket weave. (iii) Herringbone. (iv) Bird's eye piqué—an example of a dobby weave. (v) Brocade—an example of a jac-quard weave. (vi) Cut panne velvet—an example of a pile weave. (vii) Leno—a decorative leno weave combined with areas of plain weave. (viii) Che-nille—an example of a swivel weave. Pho-tos by Hilary Sherred.

laid side by side in the weave. If the fabric is made of a relatively low number of yarns to an inch, it will tend to stretch, shrink, and fray. Examples are hopsacking, monk's cloth, and oxford shirting.

In a *herringbone weave,* a variation of the twill weave, the ridges reverse directions, forming a zigzag pattern. This pattern is often emphasized by the use of different colored yarns in the cross and length.

Numerous small-patterned weaves are produced by attaching to the plain weave loom a "dobby," which raises and lowers certain sets of lengthwise yarns. The resulting *dobby weave* fabric has small all-over floral or geometric patterns. An example is bird's-eye piqué.

When a Jacquard attachment is added to the loom, cross and lengthwise yarns can be controlled individually to create elaborate woven patterns called *jacquards.* Examples are brocade, damask, and tapestry.

In *pile weave* fabrics, extra crosswise or lengthwise yarns are added to a plain or twill weave and are drawn into loops on the surface by thick wires. The loops can be cut, sheared, or left in loops. Examples are corduroy, fake fur, plush, terry cloth, velour, and velveteen.

Velvets are woven on double shuttle looms that weave two layers of fabric at once with the pile yarns stretched between the two layers. The layers are cut apart through the pile yarns with a blade, leaving half the pile yarn attached to each layer of cloth.

A leno attachment to the loom continually changes the position of the lengthwise yarns to twist them in a figure eight around the crosswise yarns. The *leno weave* is used to produce an open mesh structure. This weave may be combined with other weaves to create patterns. Examples are gauze and marquisette.

In *swivel weave* fabrics, extra crosswise yarns are added to the fabric to form small figures like dots on the surface of a basic weave fabric. Each swivel yarn is carried on the wrong side of the fabric from one design to the next but is usually cut after the fabric is woven. Examples are dotted Swiss, coin-dot chenille, and eyelash cloth.

Knitted Fabrics

Knitted fabrics are made by creating a series of interlocking loops with continuous yarns. Knitted fabrics come in a wide range of textures from fine and sheer (tricot), to heavy, bulky, novelty knits. All have some stretch. Some knits stretch in one direction, others in both directions. Generally, knits are not as durable as woven fabrics, but their soft, clinging properties and their interesting textures more than compensate for their weaknesses. Figure 7.2 illustrates knit construction.

The plain *jersey knit* is a single construction in which all loops are pulled to the back of the fabric, leaving the right side smooth. Plain knits stretch more in width than in length.

The *purl knit* is a single construction in which loops are pulled in alternating rows to the right and wrong side of the fabric. Purl knits have nearly the same stretch in both lengthwise and crosswise directions.

A *rib knit* is a single construction that arranges rows of purl and plain knit to form ribs on both sides of the fabric. Rib knits have exceptional stretch in the crosswise direction, making them useful for cuffs and waistbands.

Combinations of plain and purl knits can produce complicated patterns in the knitting process.

Double knits are produced with two yarn-and-needle sets working simultaneously. The resulting fabric has two layers of knit fabric that are connected. Double knits have limited stretch and substantial body.

Other Types of Fabric Construction

Braiding, knotting (netting), and *crocheting* all produce decorative fabrics or trim with interesting textures. The strength of these fabrics and trims varies but, in general, is a great deal less than that of woven fabrics. Figure 7.3 illustrates a few of the possibilities of novelty fabrics and trims.

Lace construction is varied and complex. Most laces have a netted ground with a pattern of other openwork construction. Laces come in all widths, many with borders or edgings. Handmade laces are produced by knotting or looping one or more yarns together in a decorative pattern. Machine-made lace is produced by machines that loop or twist threads into a pattern or by embroidering a

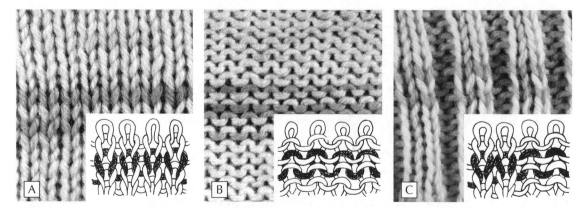

Figure 7.2   The basic knits. (A) A plain jersey knit. (B) A purl knit. (C) A rib knit construction. Photos by Hilary Sherred.

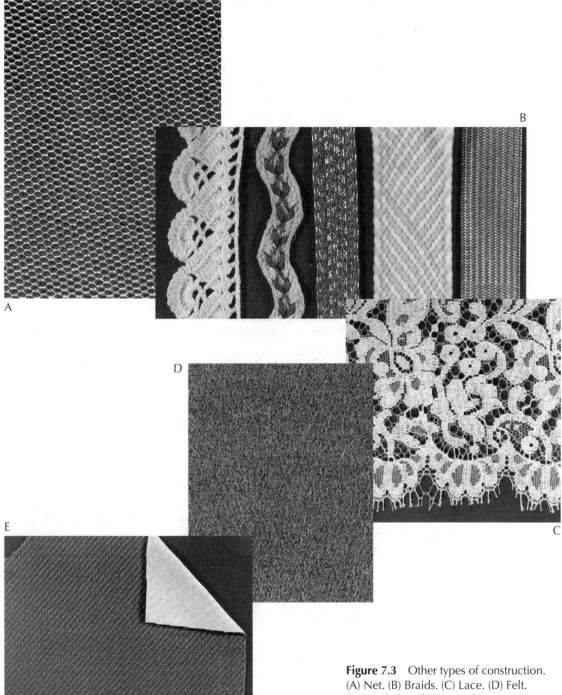

Figure 7.3 Other types of construction.
(A) Net. (B) Braids. (C) Lace. (D) Felt.
(E) Bonded. In this example, two woven
fabrics, wool twill and nylon tricot, have
been bonded together; over a long time the
bonding adhesive may deteriorate and the
fabrics separate. Photos by Hilary Sherred.

pattern to a foundation material that is then dissolved away (known as *burn out*) leaving only the embroidery stitches behind.

Felting produces a fabric (felt) that has bulk but not great strength. Moisture, compression, and heat are applied to short fibers, causing them to adhere to one another. The "no-raveling" properties and the soft, light absorbent surface of felt makes it a popular fabric for appliqué use.

Similar to felting, fusing or *bonding* uses an adhesive or bonding agent to cause fibers to adhere to one another. Fabrics made by this process are often used for interfacings.

Finishes

Processes applied to woven fabrics are known as *fabric finishes*. Most finishes are decorative: dyeing, bleaching, glazing, flocking, embossing, moiréing, and printing are examples. Some finishes are functional, such as permanent press finish, mildew resistance, waterproofing, and flameproofing. The type of finish applied to a fabric may alter its structural or visual texture and its hang.

Fabric Considerations

> . . . *It is useless for a producer to spend hundreds and thousands of francs in purchasing authentic costumes and real jewels, when a great designer will procure a far more sumptuous impression by focusing a ray of light on a doublet of coarse cloth studded with lumps of glass.* . . .

Remembrance of Things Past, Marcel Proust

Many designers begin to swatch fabrics during the "rough" or "thumbnail" stage. If decisions are made before the sketches are painted, fabrics can be suggested in the final rendering. If sketches are painted first, the designer or shopper should analyze the hang and look of the fabric suggested by the sketch and choose a suitable fabric for expressing it. Choice of costume fabric is determined by (1) the visual effects desired, (2) appropriate period fabric choices, (3) concept requirements, (4) stress requirements, (5) planned fabric treatments, and (6) budget limitations.

Visual Effects

The designer's first consideration is finding fabrics that will produce the desired visual effects of the costume. Most designers start looking for fabrics in suitable colors, but the way a fabric hangs and moves is often more important than the color, which can sometimes be modified. The designer may choose a fabric with an airy, floating quality to express the character's personality, even if that fabric is not historically accurate. A heavy fabric might be chosen to express a deep, moody character. If the decorative motif and texture are appropriate, but the fabric is too soft to hold the desired line, a lining may be used to give the correct hang. If the fabric is too stiff, sometimes washing it with fabric softeners can soften it. (Test the process on a small piece of fabric before treating all the fabric.) Cutting the garment on the bias softens the way it hangs, but bias cutting may not be appropriate for the period. In costume designs like the one in figure 7.4, suitable fabric choices are essential to effective interpretation. Much detail may be lost between the stage and the audience, but the flow and weight of a garment are visible over long distances.

The choice of a suitable fabric texture to express the character may be the next consideration. Even textures that are not clearly seen can add depth and richness to the overall feeling of the costume. The layering of sheer fabric over a base fabric gives variety in texture and a depth of color that is more interesting than a single layer of fabric. Fabrics with the appropriate patterns and qualities of light reflection must be sought for each character. (See chapter 4 for other considerations.)

Matching the colors of the sketch with suitable fabrics takes time and patience. Some flexibility may be necessary on the designer's part, but remember that color changes made for one character will surely affect the colors chosen for other characters. Dyeing or dipping to the desired tone may be required.

Choosing the appropriate scale of a desired pattern may be the most difficult problem for the novice designer to solve. The larger the house (theater), the larger the print or pattern must be in order to read, but very large-scale motifs begin to take on a comic or operatic feeling that may not be desirable. Finding a group of prints or brocades in related colors and compatible designs can be very time-consuming, but the effect can be rich and interesting. Sometimes over-dyeing or painting can bring a

Figure 7.4 *Electra*. Chorus. Effective interpretation of Michelle Ney's costume sketch for the Chorus required the use of soft rayon and soft cotton gauze in the skirt to permit the movement indicated. Designed for the University of Idaho.

print into the color range needed. In color plate 20, a sketch for *Falstaff,* the combination of the printed fabrics produces a costume of rich visual texture.

Period Fabrics

The research for a play should include information on the types of fabrics used within the period or culture. Reproducing in the costumes the same silhouette or feeling as that of the original garments may well depend on choosing the appropriate fabrics. Many older fabrics are no longer made or may now be called by different names. The study of antique garments familiarizes the designer with older fabrics and makes effective substitutes possible.

The more realistic the play, the more necessary the use of historically appropriate fabrics is. If a play is stylized, more liberties in the choice of fabric are possible. In a stylized production the designer may decide to select fabrics to carry out a concept rather than reproducing a period look. The smaller the theater, the more obvious the fabric effects are to the audience.

One thing that dates a costume design is the choice of fabrics. For example, in the 1920s designers used currently fashionable fabrics to build costumes rep-

A

resenting other periods. These costumes have the limpid look of fashionable 1920s clothes. In figure 7.5A the lady's gown for *The Three Musketeers* (1920s production) was made of soft panne velvet such as might have been used in a fashionable dress of the 1920s (figure 7.5B) instead of the heavier, stiffer, crisper fabric typical of the seventeenth century. However, the costume designer may choose to use fabrics different from those associated with a given period for special effects or when designing "fancy dress" in a production. For example, costumes designed for the Act III masquerade ball in *The Boyfriend* offer the designer an opportunity to create 1920s versions of period or fancy dress.

B

Figure 7.5 (A) *The Three Musketeers,* 1920s production. Billy Rose Theatre Collection, New York Public Library at Lincoln Center; Astor, Lenox and Tilden Foundations. (B) The soft fabric hang preferred in the 1920s is illustrated in this fashion plate. *Très Parisien,* 1926.

The use of modern fabrics also dates a contemporary production. The more authentic a designer desires to be, the more carefully the fabrics must be selected. However, in theater, authenticity is not the primary consideration. A new interpretation of a period play may require the use of modern materials and effects. A modern fabric may offer desirable characteristics that solve specific problems. For example, few occasions call for authentic cotton muslin petticoats, and their care is a great burden to the wardrobe crew. A permanent press cotton and polyester fabric is a welcome alternative.

The designer must deal with the difficulties presented by modern synthetic fibers. Until the twentieth century all fabrics were made of natural fibers, which are mellower and absorb light differently than most synthetic fibers. Synthetic fibers often reflect light in a harsh and vibrating manner. Many designers prefer to use only natural fibers on stage because of their subtler qualities of light reflection. Unfortunately, few costume budgets allow for 100-percent-natural-fiber fabrics. Blends of synthetic fibers with cotton, wool, or silk are more economical substitutes. Some proportion of natural fibers lessens the objectionable traits of the synthetic fibers while retaining the desirable properties of the natural ones. Unless a deliberate modernization is desired, the designer should attempt to choose synthetics or blends with the same hang and reflective qualities as the fabrics from the play's historical period.

Stress Requirements

If costumes are being built for long-running shows, for traveling productions, or for rental or reusable stock, the choice of a durable fabric is important. If built properly of suitable fabrics, costumes should not need frequent replacement. Costumes to be used for fight scenes, dance sequences, acrobatics, or other vigorous action should be planned with durable fabrics and linings. Stretch fabrics resembling suitable period fabrics may be needed to solve serious stress problems.

Other forms of stress to which costumes are subjected may include rough flooring, stage blood, food, stage makeup, heavy perspiration, frequent cleaning, and quick changes. Fabrics must be chosen that hold up under these stresses for the run of the show or at least for a reasonable length of time. Some delicate fabrics become satisfactory if suitably lined or backed. Taffeta, washed muslin, cotton twill, or poly/cotton broadcloth are reasonable linings, but others also are used depending on budget, surface fabric, desired effect, and availability. Linings must be laundry-compatible with outer fabrics.

Fabric Treatments

Sometimes a designer must choose between buying the wrong fabric in the right color and dyeing an appropriate fabric. Time and budget permitting, dyeing should be the choice.

The fiber content is important when paint, dye, or other such processes are being planned. Household or union dyes work best on natural or cellulosic fibers. Many modern fabrics designed for ready-to-wear or home sewing are made of all or part synthetic fibers; some of these fibers are difficult to dye and may require special types of dyes. If painting or dyeing is necessary, fabric should be selected very carefully. If the fabric is not labeled, a burn test may help the designer determine the fiber content. Box 7.B (on the following page) describes the result of burn tests on common fibers. Tests can be made on the swatches of fabrics under consideration. Burn tests *cannot* be done in the store, however. If a swatch cannot be acquired, it may be necessary to buy a yard of fabric for testing before purchasing large quantities to be treated.

Budget

The amount of money allotted to each costume is a major factor in making fabric choices. Designers must usually be reasonable about the price of the large yardages required, but may splurge where smaller quantities are needed. A larger share of the fabric budget should be allotted toward more important or higher ranking characters. More discussion on budget is found in chapter 8.

Sources and Swatching

The process of swatching for a show can be very time-consuming and tiring. The designer, assistant designer, or shopper may be sent to seek out suitable possibilities. Whoever shops, careful preparation and organization are necessary. A list of fabrics required (organized by type), approximate yardages, and appropriate price range should be prepared before the shopping trip. Copies of the sketches also are helpful. Without this information, the shopper may waste time looking at fabrics that are too expensive or at pieces with insufficient yardage.

General fabric categories for groups of characters should be determined. These categories should evolve from the design concept. For example, the women's dresses in a scene might all be planned in taffetas. The similarity of fabric would provide unity as well as simplify the shopping and fabric decisions.

The costume designer must take the time to cultivate local fabric sources. Most fabric stores are not in the habit of providing swatches of fabric. Ask to speak to the manager and explain the necessity for swatching the show. Be prepared to show some proof of the project (sketches). Being on friendly terms with the store owners and personnel can sometimes net the designer big bargains, help in locating difficult items, special orders, and even donations. Buying large amounts at one time in a store can sometimes earn large discounts. Negotiate for the best price.

Swatches should be cut along the cross grain of the fabric and should include three-quarters to one inch of the selvage and a few inches across the width of the fabric. If a swatch has already been taken from a fabric, start at the place where the first swatch was cut and continue across the fabric so that the store does not lose additional yardage. The manager may prefer that the store personnel cut the swatches. Mark each swatch with a tag giving the source, the price per yard, approximate available yardage, and the width of the fabric. Indicate fabric content if the bolt is labeled. Staple swatches to a card labeled with the name of the store, or put the swatches into an envelope marked with the store's name.

Box 7.B   Fiber reaction to burn tests

Fibers	Approaching Flame	In Flame	After Removal	Odor	Appearance of Ash
Natural Fibers					
Cotton	Does not fuse or shrink away from flame	Burns quickly without melting	Continues to burn without melting afterglow	Burning paper	Small, fluffy gray ash
Linen	Does not fuse or shrink away from flame	Burns quickly without melting	Continues to burn without melting afterglow	Burning paper	Small, fluffy gray ash
Natural Silk	Fuses and curls away from flame	Burns slowly with some melting	Burns very slowly; sometimes self-extinguishing	Burning feathers	Round black bead, brittle, pulverizes easily
Wool	Fuses and curls away from flame	Burns slowly with some melting	Burns very slowly; sometimes self-extinguishing	Burning hair	Lumpy, blistered ash, brittle, breaks easily
Hemp	Does not fuse or shrink from flame	Burns and chars	Not self-extinguishing	Burning grass	Soft gray ash
Synthetic Fibers (Cellulose)					
Acetate	Fuses away from flame	Burns with melting	Continues to burn with melting	Acetic acid or vinegar	Leaves brittle, black, irregular-shaped bead
Rayon	Does not shrink away from flame	Burns very rapidly	Leaves a creeping ember	Burning wood	Small or no ash
Synthetic Fibers (Chemical)					
Acrylic	Fuses away from flame	Burns rapidly with melting	Continues to burn with shreds melting	Acrid	Leaves brittle, hard, black, irregular-shaped bead
Nylon	Fuses and shrinks away from flame	Burns slowly with melting	Usually self-extinguishing	Boiling string beans	Leaves hard, gray, tough, round bead
Polyester	Fuses and shrinks away from flame	Burns slowly with melting	Usually self-extinguishing	Chemical	Leaves hard, black, tough, round bead
Spandex	Fuses but does not shrink away from flame	Burns with melting	Continues to burn with melting	Chemical	Leaves soft, fluffy, black ash

Unmarked swatches are useless. Do not expect to remember the price or where the fabric came from after shopping several stores. Etiquette demands that the shopper not refer to competitors' fabrics while swatching in a store.

Stores specializing in upholstery and drapery fabrics often have very useful fabrics for period costumes. These stores may also be more agreeable to giving swatches, since their customers are often trying to match fabrics to paint or furniture. The shopper must be creative about sources. Specialty houses (suppliers to specific businesses like tie and hat manufacturers), industrial suppliers, and craft supply houses should all be investigated. If costumes are being designed far enough in advance, fabrics can be ordered from sources specializing in theatrical fabrics.

Fabric Web sites offer other sources. Some Web sites offer samples of fabrics available online and make every effort to respond quickly to requests. Many vintage and specialty fabrics also can be found online. However, they may only be small yardage pieces. Since online purchases cannot be handled until received, some risk is attached, and extra time and shipping costs should be allowed for their purchase. A solid knowledge of fabric is helpful for successful online fabric purchases, and allowances for shipping time and costs should be made. The designer and the costume shop manager should develop a list of helpful online sources.

A costume shop should develop sources and maintain an up-to-date source file for fabrics and other often-used items. Each designer should also develop a personal file that indicates sources' specialties and idiosyncrasies and that helps the designer to keep track of vendors for unusual items. Figure 7.6 is a sample source-file sheet. This or a similar form reminds the designer what information may be needed for future reference. A source file can also be maintained electronically, in a spreadsheet or address book.

The designer will find it helpful to keep a collection of fabric swatches. These are useful when the designer is planning color schemes, deciding on fabrics, and discussing with the shop supervisor and shopper what types of fabrics are needed.

Linings, backings, and fabric trims must also be located and purchased. Some costume shops keep these items in stock and charge them off to each show, as they are needed. In other situations all necessary materials will need to be purchased for each garment.

| SOURCE FILE | Category __Fabric__ |
| Date __Sept. 4, 2008__ |

Vendor __Paron Fabrics__

Address __20 West 40th Street__   Phone 212-768-3266
   __(between 7th & 8th Aves.)__   Contact __Joe__
   __New York, NY__   Zip Code __10018__

Web Site __www.paronfabrics.com__

Email Address _____

Purchase Order ✔ Check ✔ Cash ✔ Discount ___
Credit Card: MC ✔VISA ✔ AMX ✔DISCOVER ✔ PAY PAL ___
Shipping: USPostal ✔ UPS ✔ FedEx ✔ Other ___

Item/Price Information:

Beautiful fabrics
   well organized -- helpful staff

Good prices, medium to high-end fabrics
   * 1/2 price annex in back

Deigner fabrics
Student discounts

   * They give swatches
has commercial patterns

will ship COD

Figure 7.6 A sample source file sheet that suggests the type of information needed for future reference.

Final fabric decisions should be made on large yardages first. Groups of identical costumes, and costumes that require complex cutting or special fitting, are usually dealt with first in a costume shop. Consult with the costumer about shop priorities and attempt to make the relevant fabric selections first.

Adapting Fabric

When the perfect fabric cannot be found, the designer must choose between second choices. Many aspects of a fabric can be changed. Color and pattern can be altered. The hang and reflective quality can sometimes be modified. Weave cannot be changed, but sometimes the wrong side of a fabric has the desired effect.

Dyeing

The most common method of adapting fabric is to alter the color by dyeing. If the appropriate fabric will respond, and the facilities are adequate, dyeing a suitable fabric is preferable to using a too-stiff, too-shiny, or otherwise inappropriate piece, even if it is the right color.

Most costume shops have some dye facilities. The designer should check on the capacity of these facilities before planning dyeing projects. When possible, dyeing should be done in the piece (before the garment is cut). This requires extra time at the beginning of the production period: the fabric must be washed, dyed, rinsed, dried, ironed, and rolled before the cutter can begin to cut the garment. This process can add ½ to 1½ days to the production calendar for each large fabric piece. Mixing and matching dyes to paint samples can be quite difficult, unpredictable, and time-consuming. The shop manager will evaluate the amount of fabric the shop facilities can successfully dye. Pieces over 25 yards should be sent out to professional dyers, if the budget allows.

In some shops the designer may be responsible for the dyeing. The guidelines in boxes 7.C and 7.D (on p. 202) will be helpful for the beginning dyer.

Applying Pattern

Painting designs and patterns on fabric is a relatively simple but time-consuming process. Many methods are available to the designer.

Stencil

This is a useful technique for applying repeat designs on fabrics. The standard technique is to cut the design from stencil paper or thin plastic and spray or paint the motif on the fabric with textile paints, permanent felt-tip markers, dyes, or leather sprays. Variations of this technique use sticky-back shelf paper to make the stencil and adhere it directly to the cloth. "Found" objects like plastic doilies can be used as masking devices or incorporated into a stencil to create interesting effects.

Box 7.C   Dyeing guidelines

1. Select fabrics and dyes that are compatible. (See the chart in box 7.D.) Read the directions carefully. Check for chemical assistants (mordants) required.

2. Wash the fabric to remove sizing and finishes. Permanent press finishes resist dye and are extremely difficult to remove. Fabrics with these finishes should be avoided for dyeing projects.

3. For even color, the fabric must be uniformly damp before entering the dye bath. This process of dampening is called "wet-out."

4. Mix the dye with a small quantity of hot water and stir to dissolve.

5. Stir the dye into the water for a dye bath, straining if any undissolved particles remain.

6. Always close the dye containers immediately and clean any spilled dye before proceeding. Keep damp fabrics out of the way until the area is clean. Dye particles settling on damp fabric will spot instantly.

7. Test a swatch for color accuracy before immersing the whole piece. Keep records of dye swatches and formulas.

8. The color is darker when fabric is wet, so samples should be dried to check the color. Rinse the swatch and iron it dry between paper towels. Do not place an iron directly on the sample, since direct heat may alter the color or scorch the fabric.

9. Saturation of color is determined by the quantity of dye to the weight of the fabric, fiber content of the fabric, temperature, and length of time in the dye bath, not by the amount of water in the dye bath.

10. Promote even dyeing by (a) allowing sufficient water for the fabric to move freely, (b) keeping the fabric moving at all times, and (c) heating the fabric slowly.

11. Use rubber gloves to protect the skin from chemicals in the dye. Wear a particle mask when mixing and handling large quantities of powdered dyes, to prevent inhaling of chemicals.

12. When the fabric has reached the desired shade (remember it will dry lighter), rinse it completely. Some dyers recommend a cold, "shocking" rinse followed by warm and then hot rinses. Check directions for the dye used. Do not skip or skimp on the rinse process. Dye that is not absorbed during the dyeing process will not *permanently* adhere to the fabric. This excess dye will come off in handling or wearing and can stain the skin of cutters, stitchers, and actors. Additional dye will come off poorly rinsed fabric during future washings and will stain other garments in the same wash. Hand-dyed fabrics are best washed separately or dry-cleaned. A sample of the fabric should be tested to determine the best cleaning procedure.

13. Do not delay the rinse process. Dye will settle in fabric folds and cause streaking.

14. When the fabric is dry, iron and roll it on a cardboard tube. Be careful to maintain proper grain alignment while ironing.

15. Dyeing before cutting is usually preferable to dyeing a completed garment. Careful cutting can avoid unevenly dyed areas. Dyeing after cutting, but before construction, can create some interesting effects but may distort the cut pieces. Garments dyed after construction may have less life than garments made from pre-dyed fabrics.

16. Clean dye area, containers, and washing machine immediately and thoroughly to prevent transfer of dye residue to other projects and personal items.

Box 7.D	Fiber–dye compatibility
Fiber	**Dyes**
Cotton	Fiber-reactive dye, direct dye, basic dye (with mordant), union (household) dye, vat dye
Linen	Fiber-reactive dye, direct dye, basic dye (with mordant), union (household) dye, vat dye
Wool	Fiber-reactive dye (less intense color), acid dye, some direct dye, basic dye, union (household) dye, disperse dye
Silk	Fiber-reactive dye (less intense color), acid dye, some direct dye, basic dye, union (household) dye, or disperse dye
Rayon	Direct dye, basic dye (with mordant), vat dye
Nylon	Some acid dyes, some direct dye, union dye, disperse dye
Polyester	Sometimes union dye, disperse dye
Acrylic	Sometimes basic dye

Stamping

A *stamp* made of rubber or foam can be used to transfer simple designs to cloth with textile paint. The layout of the design must be established on the fabric so that spacing can be more easily controlled.

Silk Screen and Block Printing

These techniques require more equipment and experience and add extra time to the production period. They are, however, useful for reproducing complex patterns. *Block printing* is the printing of a motif by pressing onto the fabric an inked block of wood or linoleum on which the design has been carved. *Silk-screening* is the printing of a motif by forcing thick ink through a piece of silk that is mounted on a frame. The areas through which the ink should *not* pass are blocked by attaching to the silk a lacquer film or paper stencil or by sealing the silk with a blackout liquid designed for this process. Silk-screening can perfectly reproduce a period fabric, creating an authentic note in just the right color combination.

Dye Sublimation

For this process the fabric or motif is developed by computer. A computer printer employs heat to transfer dye from a transparent color film to a medium such as paper, transfer paper, or fabric. The heat converts the dye particles into a gas that bonds with any polymers present in the product before changing back to a solid.

Freehand Painting

Designs that need not repeat precisely can sometimes be sketched on the fabric and painted by hand with textile paints or dyes. Printed fabrics can be enhanced with hand painting to add color or definition to the design. Color

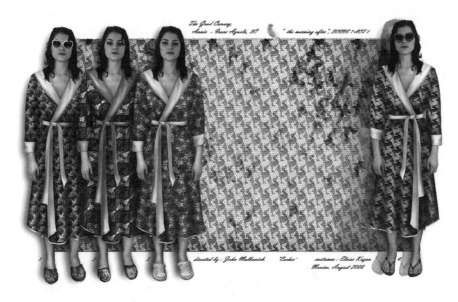

Figure 7.7 *El Buen Canario (The Good Canary)*. Anna. The fabric for Anna's robe is based on the art of M. C. Escher and was reproduced by dye sublimation. Designed by Eloise Kazan for the Teatro Insurgentes.

plate 16 shows an unbleached muslin cowgirl skirt and vest that has been hand-painted with textile paints in a broad decorative style. Color plate 22 shows a dress with a hand-painted ombré effect designed for *Burn This* by Laura Crow.

Many products are available for painting on fabrics—textile paints, inks, acrylics, leather dyes, and a variety of other media. Always check labels carefully for instructions, and especially make sure the fabrics are appropriate for the medium under consideration.

However, even apparently simple painting projects can sometimes become major time-consumers. The designer must consider the length of additional time hand painting will add to the construction time.

Skillful painting can enhance and add dimension to many stage costumes. When the intensity of stage lighting washes out details, the contours of the garment and figure may be emphasized with paint.

Aging and Distressing

Many plays require the costumes of certain characters to look old, dirty, or torn. These are referred to as "distressed costumes." The first step for the designer is to consider which type of fabric will distress well, yet hold up to stage use.

Aging is accomplished by dyeing, iron-in waxes, bleaching, painting, scraping with a grater, wire brushing, sandpapering, and numerous other aggressive techniques. Distressing for stage may be fairly broad and bold; whereas distressing for film is usually more realistic to allow for close-ups. See color plate 30 for examples of distressed costumes.

Because dyeing and painting often require special equipment and skill, the designer must be sure that time, facilities, staff, and budget permit these processes. On the other hand, skillful use of these crafts may prove to be an economical substitute or alternative for expensive trims and fabrics.

Appliqué

Fabric design can also be altered by the use of appliqué. Fabric choices for appliqué work should be considered carefully. Fabric too loosely woven may fray and sag when used as an appliqué. Appliqué work stiffens the effect of the garment and may alter the hang of the entire garment. Careful consideration should also be given to the effect of the combination of fabrics. A heavy fabric appliquéd to a lighter fabric may cause sagging and distortion of the garment. In figure 7.8 a bodice in pink spandex, a skirt in pink taffeta, and an apron in black and white satin serve as fabric backgrounds for colorful satin and spandex appliqués and hand-painted designs in this highly stylized 18th-century costume.

Fabric shopping and selection is time-consuming and tiring for the designer, but the final effect of a set of costume designs rests solidly on the fabric decisions

Figure 7.8 *The Game of Love and Chance.* Silvia (as Lisette). Colorful appliqués and hand painting decorate this highly stylized 18th-century costume. By the author for Brooklyn College.

made. Little can be done for a costume that does not hang correctly because of a poor choice of fabric. Much time and effort might be needed to overcome the disadvantages of a too-shiny, too-soft, or too-stiff fabric.

Sometimes a fabric cannot be found that answers the challenge posed by the designer's concept. All the creative energies of the costume design team must be applied to find a solution. In color plate 17 a fabric was created for the Goddess in *Tempest* using a Mod Podge appliqué technique to attach swatches and chards of color on the back side of thin plastic. The goal was to suggest that Prospero conjured up the wedding masque from debris that had washed up on the island.

Box 7.E is a designer checklist that will help the designer make appropriate fabric selections.

Box 7.E   Designer checklist V: Fabrics

1. Do the fabrics chosen help define the character?

2. Do the fabrics support the concept?

3. Are the fabrics suitable for the period and/or the hang of the garment? Are linings or extra stiffeners required?

4. What fabric treatments will be needed? Is there enough time and labor available to handle the required treatments?

5. Is the scale of each pattern compatible with the character and style of the production?

6. Will this fabric meet stress and maintenance requirements?

7. Does each fabric fit within the budget allotment? Can adjustments be made in other areas to allow for extra expenditures on certain fabrics?

8. Can the extra time and labor required to make a cheaper fabric work be balanced against dollar savings? Will the cost of extra linings, dyes, and paints override the savings?

Interview V.
Designing for Film.
A Conversation with
William Ivey Long.

*At the time of this interview with the author Broadway designer
William Ivey Long had received multiple design awards including
five Tony Awards, four Outer Critics Circle Awards, and
five Drama Desk Awards. (See bio, page 421, for career details.)*

RC: What differences do you find between designing for film, TV, and the theater?

WIL: Designing is becoming less and less different between film and stage. A primary reason is that designing clothes for characters is all about *truth* and character development: what you hide, what you expose. It's all about what reads for the audience member. For film, it is about character as expressed through small movements and gestures, as opposed to stage where it is about broader strokes.

RC: What role does script analysis play in your designs?

WIL: It is crucial for any medium. I read a script and have to analyze it for character development and storytelling. That part is exactly the same for film and stage. I ask the same questions. Who are these people? How do we want to perceive them, and what is the arc of their development? However, notating the script for a film is different than for the stage due to many factors, which I will discuss a bit later. There is a computer program called PlotPro that helps you break it down for film scripts.

RC: How does the level of detail differ between film and stage design?

WIL: I will start by saying that audiences are getting smarter. I think what we expect from the stage is also becoming more about truth. The people in the first ten rows see a very up-close-and-personal view, so the clothes cannot become a caricature. The design also has to read true for the people sitting in the back row. So that is another set of challenges: near and far at the same time, but nearer usually wins, both on stage and in film.

Of course, film is nothing if not near. The close-up cannot be too bold; you have to believe it. If you can see the face, it has to be a real collar; it has to be a real necktie. For the stage, the trick is to use contrast: color contrast, dark and light contrast—ways to find the face, ways to find the people from a distance, while staying real. So what I'm saying is that I think stage is becoming more like film, and I think the leader in this march is Ann Roth.

A comparison: For *The Producers*, I designed both the Broadway show and the film. One big difference between the two productions is the design for the production number, "I Want to be a Producer," which is a fantasy sequence in which Leo Bloom dreams of being a producer. On Broadway, I designed a set of "Gold Girls" (figures C-28 and C-29), which were chorus girls from the fifties, wearing gold coins and dollar bills. For the film, because we knew we wanted to *up* that number, and we had the gorgeous ladies, Mel Brooks said, "Well William, why don't you follow my lyrics for this number?" and I said, "Oh?" He said, "Yes, I wrote 'Beautiful girls, wearing nothing but pearls.'" . . . Well, yes, he did.

I thought, "Okay, it's for film, 'beautiful girls wearing nothing but pearls' means you want to see a lot of skin; you want to see that they're wearing nothing but pearls." So we made these completely see-through net leotards and covered them strategically with pearls (figure 9.4). For the days of shooting, we had a team of eight people maintaining those costumes. There were lots and lots of Pearl Girls. We could never have used those costumes on Broadway because they would never have lasted. The producers would have killed me! Mel Brooks himself would have killed me! But this was a different medium, so I was able to show the pearls in detail on those beautiful bodies, and I can tell you, it looks like they're completely naked, because I matched the skin tones of the leotards to the wearers' skin. There are *27 different shades*. I remember, because there were only like five on Broadway. It's very naughty! The hats are beautiful; the *details are finer;* the skin tone is matched more closely.

So there you have it!

Figure V.1　William Ivey Long's Tony-award winning costume design for Edna's "Pucci" dress from the Broadway production of *Hairspray*.

RC: How is your working procedure different designing for film as opposed to stage?

WIL: I do know that, after having designed only four feature films, working procedures are wildly different. I like to say that films have five opening nights a day. Once you've filmed that scene, you save everything, because you never know if you need to go back. Films are not necessarily shot in time [order], so the first dress is not necessarily made before the aged version. In the theater, the storytelling is usually in order, and there is little flashback.

The reasons for shooting out-of-order are many. Sometimes you have a rain day and a sun day, or an exterior that you have to shift and that throws everything off. Real film designers just know; they can smell it; they can tell it; they have the Farmer's Almanac under one arm, I don't know. I think you learn that through experience.

RC: Is there any difference in how you treat character development?

WIL: Character development is the same for all mediums. I gather information at the beginning of the process. I talk with the director and the actors.

Figure V.2 The Pick-a-Little Ladies in their costumes by William Ivey Long for the Broadway production of *The Music Man*.

Everyone is part of the process. So you really know where they are going; where their arc is.

The trick *onstage* is to always make it a total surprise, so you don't know what's going to happen. And of course in *film*, you actually can make six dresses and rip them in the same way to use for multiple takes.

RC: How is the collaboration process with producers and directors different?

WIL: Well, in films, the producers are in charge. On Broadway, the director's in charge. This shifts a lot of the emphasis. On Broadway, the leader of the pack, even when you have Mel Brooks, the great legendary powerful Oz himself, Susan Stroman is in charge. She's the director and choreographer. And when we're running it and giving notes and changing it, he tells her what he thinks, but she's the one who finalizes and balances it all out. It's very clear who the leader of the team is—very, very clear. This is the best way to work, because you know who you have to please. Of course, I also have to please Mel Brooks and the producers, and everyone else who comes in and has an opinion. That's the same. But in film, the producer gets very involved with every detail.

Television is very close to film, though in many cases the producer hires different directors for different episodes. In episodic television, you will probably have a different director for each episode, and that allows each director to focus on his or her particular episode. In the meantime, overlapping for another episode is the next director, who is generally using the same characters, but with a different story arc. Also, for television, it is very much about lighting and angles and close-ups. The plans tend to look like football diagrams; all planned for the movement of the actors and cameras. So with all that in mind you can understand how the producer of a television show is very, very important.

RC: What about the differences in design collaborations?

WIL: Onstage, the scenic designer comes first, because the set creates the world. The costume designer then comes in and populates the world, and thirdly, the lighting designer enters the process and tells the audience members where to look. But it happens sequentially; I love working that way.

For design in the film world, the director of photography rules over everyone. This is not an understatement. He's really a co-director. It's as the DP lights it. He's in charge of the lighting, and he's in charge of the angles, because remember *it's only as you see it*!

Chapter 8

Getting the Show Together

. . . a tailor called me in his shop
And showed me silks that he had bought for me,
And therewithal took measure of my body.

The Comedy of Errors, William Shakespeare

Organizing the Work

Once sketches are approved, the designer's focus shifts from designing appropriate costumes to supervising and participating in the translation of the sketches to the finished costumes. Efficient organization of this work requires the division of the various costume problems into an endless number of categories. Each designer has a personal approach to this organization, but the forms presented in this chapter are designed to simplify the process for the novice designer.

Costume Lists; Pull/Rent/Buy Lists

The designer can get an overall view of the total requirements of the play by listing all necessary items for each costume for all characters. The costume list in figure 8.1A is a form to assist this process. The pull/rent/buy form helps determine the probable source of each part of the costume and gives the designer an idea of the budget difficulties and the amount of work that may be required.

The designer should assemble all the sketches in the order of appearance in the play. A sketch or plate number consisting of the actor's number and the number of the costume for that actor should be assigned to each costume sketch. A form to correspond with each sketch should be filled out with the required information marked with the plate number.

Assuming that the actor is providing nothing but modern underwear, the designer should list each article of clothing, piece of jewelry, and costume accessory in each sketch (indicating plate number and act/scene numbers). If the character just stepped out of the shower, what would he or she need to wear? Dance belt? Tights? Corset? Petticoats? Each layer of clothing should be considered from the skin out. What is necessary to create the shape of the garment? Are the same undergarments suitable for all the costumes worn by one character? Will the character be seen dressing or undressing on stage? Will the undergarments need to be period designs? What personal underwear must the actor

Figure 8.1A The costume list in figure 8.1A is a form that assists the designer in determining the parts of each costume.

provide? How does this list compare with the original costume notes? Are there any additions or eliminations?

When each list is complete, the probable or preferred source of each item should be determined. Will it be bought, built, rented, or pulled from stock? Can it be borrowed or supplied by the actor? This information is then transferred to pull/rent/buy and to-build forms (see figures 8.1A, 8.1B, and 8.13A). All related items from the same source are grouped on the same form and sizes are added from the measurement sheets as soon as measurements are taken.

These lists serve as the basis for organizing and distributing the work of pulling from stock, shopping, and selecting rental costumes. Although this procedure may seem to take up valuable time, it ensures that nothing is overlooked. Variations of the system may be developed to meet the requirements of different shows. Reorganizing and grouping the items according to source and kind of garment makes it possible to divide up the work among several assistants. All skirts can be pulled at one time; all shoes, petticoats, and tights can be dealt with as a group rather than each piece individually. Even when only one person is working on a show, good organization ultimately saves time and duplication of

☑ PULL ☐ RENT ☐ BUY

Show _____ Marriage of Figero _____

Item _____ shirts _____ Crew _____ Millie _____

✔	Actor	Character	Description	Size
	J. Smith	Antonio	peasant—beige	15-1/2 – 34
	M. Romero	Padrillo	peasant—beige	15 – 33
	K. Leech	Figero	peasant—off white	15-1/2 – 33
✔	K. Kowikow	Bartholo	18th Century—white	15 – 32
✔	J. Holland	The Count	18th Century—white	16 – 34
✔	V. Blaine	Cherabino	18th Century—pale rose	14-1/2 – 31
✔	E. Felix	Basil	18th Century—White	15-1/2 – 34
✔	S. DeMasi	Goosegridle	18th Century—beige	15 – 34
✔	J. Classen	Bailiff	18th Century—grey	16 – 32
✔	M. Campo	Double-deal	18th Century—beige	15-1/2 – 34
	B. Briggs	Peasant #1	peasant—khaki—rags	large
	J. Smits	Peasant #2	peasant—brown	XXL
	R. Lenn	Peasant #3	peasant—brown	small
	H. Cruz	Peasant #4	peasant—grey—rags	medium
	J. Doe	Peasant #5	peasant—brown	medium

Figure 8.1B The pull/rent/buy form helps determining the pr0ource of each part of the costume.

effort. One of the most useful functions for a computer in the costume shop is developing spreadsheets to keep track of the details of assembling the costumes.

Beginning designers often resist making lists. Confident that they have excellent memories, they insist on keeping all the information in their heads. One problem with this method is that even if they manage not to forget anything important, no one else can be of much help, except for those gifted in mind reading. Working out ways to make clear notations frees the mind to do more important things and lessens the chances of truly disastrous lapses of memory. One of the most difficult problems for the costume designer is coping with the staggering number of details involved in even the simplest costume project. No aid to easing this burden should be scorned.

Rehearsal Costumes

The need for rehearsal garments varies with each production. Once the final sketches have been approved, the director and designer should draw up a list of rehearsal costumes with projected dates for introducing them into the rehearsal process.

What kinds of rehearsal garments are needed? The designer should look at the costume sketches and analyze the actors' needs. Handling costumes that are greatly different from currently worn garments requires practice. Long skirts, trains, capes, and shoes with appropriate heels are typically provided for period plays. In plays requiring unusual undergarments (bustles, crinolines, farthingales) the actor should be given rehearsal garments that at least suggest the size and movement of the finished costume. The actual undergarments should be put into work in the costume shop first, and as soon as they are no longer needed in the shop, the actors should use them with rehearsal garments. However, the designer and shop manager must remember to retrieve these undergarments for fittings.

Costume pieces that are frequently handled or needed for special stage business may have to be provided early or "mock-ups" made. Handbags, large hats, fans, and parasols or umbrellas are items that the designer and director may agree are needed for rehearsals. Sometimes an actor will request a specific rehearsal costume.

Not all rehearsal items are needed at the same time. Long skirts and shoes should be worn as soon as blocking begins, but items to be hand carried or taken off and on are not useful unless the actors are "off book" (no longer carrying the script).

A complete list is required for the person responsible for pulling together the rehearsal items. In some situations actors are asked to provide their own rehearsal garments. The properties person may provide some items. In producing organizations that have stock costumes available, rehearsal garments may be pulled from stock by the shop manager. The designer must be aware that doing this takes time and must be considered in the labor budget. Sometimes pulling rehearsal clothes is the designer's responsibility and must be coordinated with the shop manager. At other times an assistant designer may be assigned to assemble rehearsal costumes from stock or thrift stores.

Although rehearsal items are important to the actors and director, the designer must limit the amount of time spent on these items or the actual costumes may not get finished. For educational and repertory theaters a collection of items reserved for rehearsals is a practical solution.

The designer should be sure that a responsible person (usually the stage manager) has provided suitable storage and procedures for the use of rehearsal costumes. Keeping in contact with the stage manager concerning schedule changes, new stage business, and problems related to the rehearsal costumes helps the designer make adjustments as costume construction progresses and minimizes the confusion during dress rehearsals.

Designers are often called upon to provide costumes for a photo call for press photos weeks before dress rehearsals. The designer should be proactive about finding out the date and needs of this event in order to have enough time to assemble the needed costumes or suitable mock-ups.

Assessing Resources

Prepared with sketches, costume plot, and accurate lists, the designer confers with the costume shop manager. Although preliminary discussions may have been held when the designer was developing roughs, complete plans for execution of costumes must now be made. The shop manager is responsible for organizing and guiding the show through the costume shop, ordering supplies, and hiring and supervising costume staff. The shop manager must thoroughly understand the costume designs, budget, and designer's requirements. A complete discussion of the responsibilities each person undertakes is imperative. In order to divide the work efficiently, the designer and the shop manager must each have a clear picture of the whole project. The designer should not minimize the work or hold back information. While some additions and changes are inevitable, deliberately omitting or minimizing costume requirements is unprofessional and detrimental to the final product.

If the theater maintains a stock of costumes, the shop manager, costume supervisor, or stock person determines what might be available. Items like tights, petticoats, capes, hats, and men's shirts may be found in stock. If items on the pull list are not available from the stock, they should be added to the rent, buy, or to-build lists.

The designer and shop manager should discuss the stress requirements of costumes used in strenuous action and the durability of fragile garments. Back-up garments may be needed for garments that are at risk. Duplicates are usually required of costumes that are exposed to stage blood or water, particularly if more than one performance a day is scheduled. These duplicates must be figured into the cost and time schedule as separate costumes.

The shop manager distributes the work among the available personnel according to their skills and positions in the shop. Box 8.A (on the following page) lists the types of positions found in costume shops and provides a general job description of each. The number and types of positions in any given costume shop vary greatly according to the type of shop, the kind of projects usually undertaken, and the labor available. The job descriptions, responsibilities, and skills vary from shop to shop as well. While organizations vary in the size of their production staff, figure 8.2 (p. 218) illustrates the lines of authority generally found within theater costume personnel and their relationship to the other members of the producing organization.

Box 8.A   Costume construction personnel

There is much variation in the use and definition of terms for costume construction personnel. Many theater craftspersons and technicians are skilled in more than one area. The following definitions provide a general guideline.

Costume Designer: Theater artist employed to design, coordinate, and supervise the execution of costumes for stage, television, and film. Hired by the producer and/or director.

Assistant Costume Designer: Assistant hired by the designer to do research, swatch fabrics, shop, organize, take notes, or do any other job required by the designer.

Costume Shop Manager or *Costume Shop Foreman:* Highly skilled technician with experience in all areas of costume construction. Responsible for supervision of personnel, maintenance of shop equipment, purchase of supplies, scheduling the work through the shop, and some construction projects.

Costume Director or *Costume Supervisor:* Regional theater or academic theater position incorporating responsibilities of the costume designer, costume shop manager, and sometimes teacher.

Costumer: Person skilled in costume patternmaking, construction, and sometimes costume crafts and capable of seeing projects through from sketch to finished costume.

Patternmaker: Person skilled in making patterns, usually by flat-pattern or drafting methods. Responsible for making patterns, cutting all parts of the garment, and preparing the garment for stitching.

Draper: Person skilled in making patterns by the draping technique. Responsible for patterns, cutting all parts of the garment, and preparing the garment for stitching.

Cutter: Another term used for the person responsible for cutting garments after the patterns are made by the patternmaker. The term is also used for either the patternmaker or the draper.

First Hand/Draper's Assistant: Assistant to the patternmaker, costumer, draper, or cutter.

Tailor: Specialist in men's wear responsible for patternmaking and construction supervision of men's costumes and special women's costumes.

Project Manager: In large costume shops where several projects are worked on at the same time, a liaison person is hired by the costume shop to work with the designers and shop personnel and to guide each project through the shop.

Shopper: Person responsible for locating, pricing, and purchasing fabrics, trims, and accessories needed to assemble costumes. May be hired by the shop or directly by the designer.

Stitcher: Sewing machine operators employed by the costume shop to stitch costumes together.

Finisher: Personnel skilled in hand-stitching techniques used to finish costumes—hems, snaps, hooks and eyes, buttons, trim.

Stock Person: Person responsible for organizing, maintaining, pulling, and striking stock costumes in a rental house or educational or regional theater.

Craftsperson: A general term for a technician skilled in one or more of a variety of costume- and prop-related crafts: Vacu-form construction for masks or armor, latex and foam molding, fiberglass construction, jewelry making, and many others.

Milliner: A specialist in hat construction and decoration. Hired by the costume shop or freelance.

Dyer/Painter: A specialist in fabric dyeing, fabric painting, and aging or breakdown techniques for costumes or fabric.

Wardrobe Crew: Persons responsible for the maintenance of the costumes during the run of the show (laundry, dry cleaning, repairs), pre-show setup, and quick changes. Hired by the producer.

Wardrobe Supervisor: Person responsible for the supervision of the wardrobe crew.

Dresser: A member of the wardrobe crew assigned to assist actors with changing costumes, or a personal costume assistant hired by an actor to help with dressing and makeup.

The designer and the shop manager should have a clear understanding of the timetable for shopping for fabric, taking measurements, pulling from stock, fittings, and the arrival of rental costumes. On the basis of available personnel, the manager estimates the time required to produce the costumes, the time for fittings, and the time needed for alterations of bought and rented costumes. The designer may need to make adjustments in the planned costumes because of time and personnel limitations. Renting one or two more costumes instead of struggling to build them may make the difference between a good-quality production and an unfinished show with an exhausted, burned-out shop crew.

Copies of the sketches, costume plot, and all the lists should be given to the shop manager to be placed in the shop bible for easy reference.

Shop (Production) Calendar

At this point the designer and the shop manager must update and complete the shop calendar. Working backwards from the first dress rehearsal, they establish a set of dates and deadlines for the *dress parade* (a preliminary onstage presentation of actors in costumes under lights), final fittings, arrival of rental costumes, first fittings, patterning, arrival of fabrics in the shop, dyeing or painting (including ordering of painting materials), the dummy show, items required for rehearsal, measurements, production meetings, and any other important phase of the work.

Priorities should be established. Rehearsal items, garments to be distressed, fabrics or costumes to be painted, and foundation garments to be built should be scheduled into work first. Careful planning of the production schedule reduces traffic jams in the costume shop and helps the designer and shop manager pace the work. Good scheduling also prevents the designer or crew from straying off into trivial work while important priorities remain undone. Figure 8.3 (p. 219) shows a carefully planned work schedule. The designer and the shop manager have coordinated responsibilities, projects, deadlines, and rehearsal requirements.

The designer must be realistic about the time required for various projects. A given project will never take *less* time than anticipated; invariably it will take *more* time than expected. Box 8.B (p. 220) gives an approximation of the amount

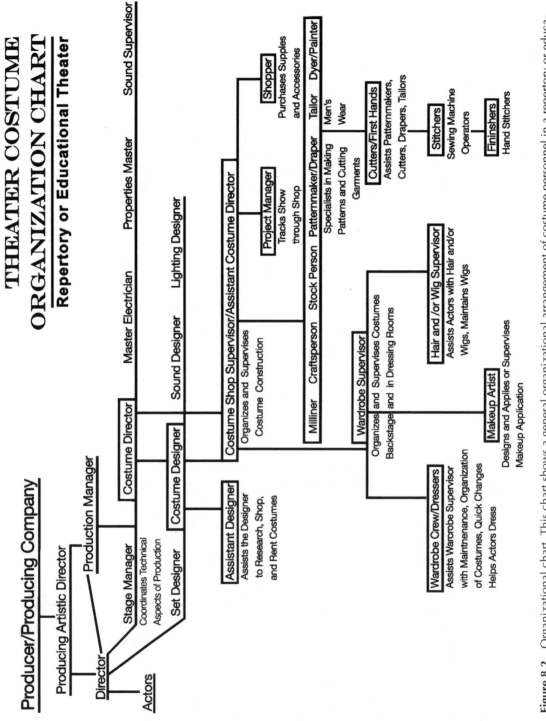

Figure 8.2 Organizational chart. This chart shows a general organizational arrangement of costume personnel in a repertory or educational theater.

SHOP SCHEDULE				*Twelfth Night*		
Sun	Mon	Tues	Wed	Thurs	Fri	Sat
October 15 *Off*	16 *NYC Shopping*	17 *First read-thru Sketch presentation *measurements*	18 *Full staff in*	19	20	21 *10-4 Local Shopping*
22 *Off*	23 *NYC Shopping Actors day off*	24 *All fabric due*	25 *First fittings muslins & stock*	26 *Dyer in* ←	27	28 → *10-4*
29 *Off*	30 *NYC rental Actors day off*	31 *Extra help in Haircuts* ←	November 1 →	2 *Painter in* ←	3	4 → *10-4*
5 *Final fittings*	6 *Rentals due in Actors day off*	7 ← *Final*	*Fittings* 8 →	9 *2:00 Dress 8:00 Run thru*	10 *2:30 Tech 8:00 Tech w/costume pieces*	11 *2:00 Dress tech *8:00 Full dress*
12 *2:00 Dress? 8:00 Full dress w/ photo call**	13	14 *2:00 Dress 8:00 Preview*	15 *2:00 Run thru 8:00 Preview*	16 *2:00 Run thru 8:00 Preview*	17 *2:00 Run thru? 8:00 OPEN*	18 *Off COLLAPSE!*

Figure 8.3 Shop schedule. Careful organization of the shop production schedule is needed to keep work flowing. (See also figure 2.10.)

of time that must be allowed for different types of costume activities. The actual time spent on each costume varies greatly depending on the complexity of the garment, quality of desired workmanship, skill of the crew, and availability of sources. The shop manager, familiar with these variables, should assist in estimating work time. Time studies suggest that the average constructed costume requires between forty and fifty work hours. Forty hours may be a week's work for one person or ten hours each for four people. There is, however, a point at which additional people may not speed the work. At certain stages of construction, shop space and equipment may limit the number of persons that can work at a time.

Projects also must be matched to the skills of available personnel. After conferences with costume shop personnel, necessary revisions should be made in designs, organization, schedules, and budget. If discussions were held with the shop in the early design stages (roughs), major revisions should not be necessary. However, the director must be informed if limited staff or funds require major changes in approach. Ideally, these discussions occur in production meetings in which all concerned parties participate.

Box 8.B   Estimating work hours per task for each costume

Actual time spent on each costume varies greatly. This chart is a guide for evaluating the workload of a production. The designer should confer with the shop manager when considering work time. (Work time does not include interruptions!)

Task	Time Allotment
Measurements (per actor)	15 to 25 minutes
Shopping (per costume)	1 to 8 hours
Patternmaking (per costume)	1 to 16 hours
Layout and cutting (per costume)	30 minutes to 16 hours
Pattern grading (per size, per costume)	15 minutes to 5 hours
Fabric preparation (per yardage piece): wash, iron or steam, roll	2 to 6 hours
Dyeing (in addition to above time)	30 minutes to 4 hours
Marking (per costume)	15 minutes to 2 hours
Serging or merrowing-finishing seams with overlock stitch (per costume)	10 minutes to 2 hours
Stitching (per costume)	1 to 24 hours
Finishing (per costume)	15 minutes to 8 hours
Painting (per costume)	1 to 16 hours
Pulling (per costume)	15 minutes to 4 hours
Fitting (per rented or pulled costume)	20 minutes to 1 hour
Fitting (per costume muslin)	30 minutes to 1 hour
Fitting (per constructed costume)	1 to 3 hours

Evaluating Budget Allotments

Each costume presents its own cost problems. For regional and educational theaters, the skill level of workers may be a large factor. Less skilled workers take longer and make more mistakes than professional costumers. The costume for Olivia in figure 8.4A was designed for a production of *Twelfth Night* at Brooklyn College using both student and professional labor. Figure 8.4B is an analysis of the factors involved in determining the cost of the garment. Other cost variables include the quality of the fabric and trim chosen and the acceptability of stock petticoats. (See the finished garment in figure 1.3.)

Once the pull/rent/buy lists are complete, an estimated budget can be worked out. Figure 8.5 (p. 222) shows a sample budget, excluding labor. (Labor costs in many producing organizations are figured as part of general running expenses. If permanent staff cannot handle the size show planned, extra personnel may be hired and that cost is assigned to the show budget.) Shoes, wigs, and hats must be accounted for in the budget; these items can gobble up large portions of time and money if they are not available in stock or owned by the actors.

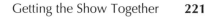

Figure 8.4A *Twelfth Night*. Olivia. A costume design by the author for Brooklyn College.

COST FACTORS

Character _____ *Oliva* _____ Plate #_*0802*_
Show _____ *Twelfth Night* _____

Work Hours		Materials
DRAPER ___ 12 ___ HOURS		*Dress – 1 yard cotton*
1ST HAND ___ 23 ___ HOURS		*twill lining*
STITCHER ___ 25 ___ HOURS		*4 yards pink crepe/satin*
FINISHER ___ 10 ___ HOURS		*4 yards off-white*
PAINTER ___ 0 ___ HOURS		*chiffon*
SHOPPER ___ 8 ___ HOURS		*7 yards point d'esprit*
MILLINER ___ 5 ___ HOURS		*4 yards 8 inch lace*
		10 yards 2 inch lace
		25 yards 1/2 inch
TOTAL ___ 83 ___ HOURS		*white satin ribbon*
		2 yards pink moire faille
OTHER: _____		*8 bunches pink and*
		peach flowers
petticoat from stock		*hooks and eyes*
purchase shoes,		*1 yard horsehair*
tights & new bra		*1 heavy duty zipper*
		Veil – 4 yards 1/2 inch
NOTES: _____		*peach satin ribbon*
		4 yards 1/2 inch pink
designer to set up		*ribbon*
basket motif		*1 yard all over white lace*
		5 yards lace edging
		comb

Figure 8.4B Cost factors. The analysis of the labor and materials for this costume took into consideration the fact that both student and professional labor was involved in its production. (See finished costume in figure 1.3.)

COSTUME BUDGET

Show _Twelfth Night_

Total Budget $7,500.00

Rentals	$450.00
Ready-to-Wear/Thrift	$750.00
Fabric	$2,250.00
Notions/Trim	$600.00
Millinery	$600.00
Shoes	$750.00
Accessories	$300.00
Wigs/Hair Goods	$300.00
Paints/Dyes	$300.00
Craft Supplies	$300.00
Laundry/Cleaning	$600.00
Miscellaneous	$300.00
Total	$7,500.00

Figure 8.5   Sample budget. The costume budget is estimated and analyzed to determine how to cover all necessary items.

(Equity actors must be paid a rental fee for personal clothing used in costumes.) Some pre-shopping may be necessary to get an idea of the current market value of required items. For producing organizations that maintain a costume stock, the value of an item may depend on its future use. If an item is a desirable addition to stock, buying better quality is more economical in the long run. The shop manager should assist by advising on stock items and estimating the fabric yardage required for the costumes being built. Dividing the total yardage figure into the overall allotment for fabric gives the shopper the approximate average price per yard for the fabrics to be purchased. (See also chapter 7.)

For a large professional production, several costume houses may bid on the job, giving estimates of the cost of building the costumes. The producer may take the lowest bid, or the designer may urge the use of the costume house whose work the designer prefers. Or the total number of costumes may be divided among several costume houses, spreading the work around.

Although the designer is sometimes asked for budget estimates, the amount of production money allotted to costumes is usually predetermined by the producing organization. This allotment may not be realistic for the style of the production, size of staff available, and the director's requirements. Obviously, adjustments are needed. A number of options are available: request additional funds, consider rented or borrowed items, seek volunteer help, seek sources of free items or items to use in exchange for program credit, simplify designs, develop a new concept, pull additional items from stock, negotiate director requests, compromise in all areas, withdraw from the project. Designers are often asked to work absolute miracles on shoestrings or less. In such a case the designer must decide whether the experience and credit for doing the show warrant the effort to overcome insurmountable odds. There is a tendency to view costumes as "clothes" and to fail to comprehend the complexity and cost of even the simplest costume projects. The designer should have realistic estimates of cost and time and be prepared to discuss these with the director and the producer. Costumes make a major contribution to the success of a production, and the designer should not allow that contribution or the work of the costume staff to be undervalued.

A commercial costume shop determines the cost (the price to the producer) of building a costume by estimating the number of work hours required for each phase of the work, multiplying each by the rate per hour for that type of labor, then adding the cost of materials, overhead, and, hopefully, profit for the shop. The costume for _The Daughter of the Regiment_ in figure 8.6A (p. 224) was

---

Box 8.C   Designer checklist VI: Organization

1. Does the director understand and approve the sketches?

2. Are rehearsal costumes needed? What kind? By when? Who is responsible for providing and caring for rehearsal items?

3. Are all pieces of the individual costumes listed on the costume lists and the pull/rent/buy lists?

4. What resources are available to assemble this show? Are they adequate to meet the design needs? What adjustments can be made with the least damage to the visual concept of the production? Hire more staff? More money? Rent or pull more costumes? Are there creative and imaginative solutions to these challenges?

5. Is the production calendar complete and reasonable? Is sufficient time allowed for each part of the project? Have arrangements been made for all required personnel and supplies?

6. Are appointments for measurements and fittings properly scheduled and conducted?

7. For what special projects should I assume responsibility? How can I see that work goes smoothly?

8. What staff is available? How should the work be assigned?

---

designed to have all buttons, patches, and trims painted onto the garment. That required not only patternmaking, cutting, stitching, and finishing, but also dyeing, painting, and steam setting. Figure 8.6B (p. 225) is an analysis of the cost factors involved in building the costume in a professional shop. If additional personnel are hired to meet the needs of the show, the cost of such additional labor is figured into the total cost.

Taking Measurements

Accurate measurements are crucial to the correct fit of the costume. The designer should know how to take measurements correctly and should be prepared to do so. In professional productions and many educational situations the costume shop staff take the measurements. Most tailors, patternmakers, and drapers prefer to take the measurements of actors for whom they will make patterns. In repertory companies measurement sheets from previous shows may be kept on file, but they should be updated when reused, since some actors gain and lose weight frequently. Many actors (particularly in very active roles) can fluctuate greatly in size from the beginning of rehearsals to opening night.

Taking measurements should be approached in a very professional manner. Comments or asides about the actor's size are inconsiderate and unprofessional. Appointments with the actor should be made in the costume shop. A complete set of measurements should take 15 to 25 minutes.

Figure 8.6A *Daughter of the Regiment.* Marie. Designed by Eduardo Sicongco for Texas Opera Theater.

Measurements must be taken carefully. Tailors and patternmakers may vary slightly from one another in their methods of measuring, but figure 8.7 and box 8.D (pp. 226–227) show a standard way to take basic measurements. The actor should provide the shoe size (including width), weight, and other statistics not easily measured.

Figure 8.8 (p. 228) shows an example of a measurement form for use in a costume shop. These measurements provide most of the information needed for building costumes, but additional measurements may be required for special projects. Figure 8.9 (p. 228) shows a short measurement form for shopping or renting costumes. Separate sheets should be used for men and women. The second form can be filled out from the first or may be the only form required if the show is completely rented or shopped.

Photocopies of the measurement sheets should be made for shoppers, patternmakers, and the designer.

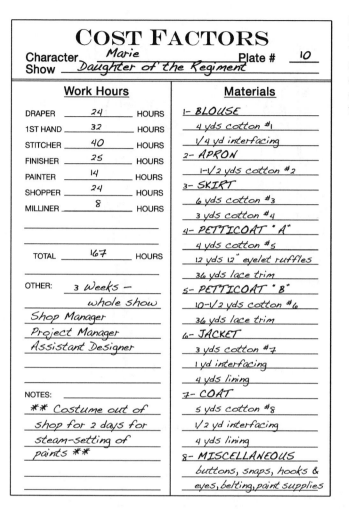

COST FACTORS

Character _Marie_   Plate # _10_
Show _Daughter of the Regiment_

Work Hours		Materials
DRAPER	24 HOURS	1- BLOUSE
1ST HAND	32 HOURS	4 yds cotton #1
STITCHER	40 HOURS	1/4 yd interfacing
FINISHER	25 HOURS	2- APRON
PAINTER	14 HOURS	1-1/2 yds cotton #2
SHOPPER	24 HOURS	3- SKIRT
MILLINER	8 HOURS	6 yds cotton #3
		3 yds cotton #4
		4- PETTICOAT "A"
		4 yds cotton #5
TOTAL	167 HOURS	12 yds 12" eyelet ruffles
		36 yds lace trim
OTHER: 3 weeks —		5- PETTICOAT "B"
whole show		10-1/2 yds cotton #6
Shop Manager		36 yds lace trim
Project Manager		6- JACKET
Assistant Designer		3 yds cotton #7
		1 yd interfacing
		4 yds lining
NOTES:		7- COAT
** Costume out of		5 yds cotton #8
shop for 2 days for		1/2 yd interfacing
steam-setting of		4 yds lining
paints **		8- MISCELLANEOUS
		buttons, snaps, hooks &
		eyes, belting, paint supplies

Figure 8.6B Cost factors. Labor is the major cost factor in a professional shop. The number of work hours are determined and multiplied by the rate per hour for each type of labor, and then is added the cost of materials, overhead, and profit for the shop.

The Shop Bible

Most costume shops assemble a book, referred to as the *bible*—one for each show in the shop or a master book of all the work in the shop. All pertinent information (copies of the costume sketches, measurement sheets, production schedules, ledgers, rehearsal schedules, costume lists, pull/rent/buy lists, to-build or swatch sheets) is kept in the bible, where everyone working on the show can find it. Appointments for measurements, fittings, and conferences are also kept in the bible or an appointment book. The designer also must maintain a personal book and calendar containing much of the same information plus any information necessary for designing, but not relevant to assembling the costumes.

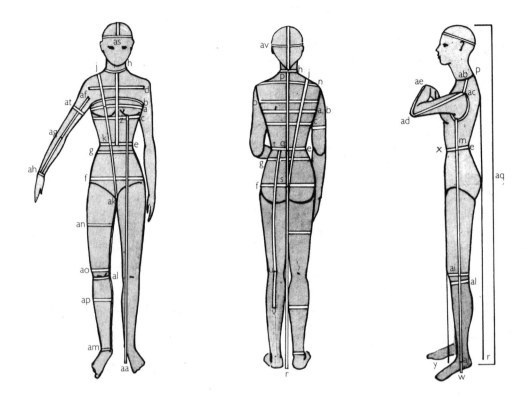

Figure 8.7   Taking measurements. The basic positions for the tape measure on the human form.

Box 8.D   Taking measurements (Compare to figure 8.7)

(a)   Chest or bust: over nipples, straight across back

(b)   Above bust: (not needed for men) above breasts, around back

(c)   Below bust: (not needed for men) under breasts, straight around back

(d)   Across front: across chest from arm to arm

(e)   Waist: around waist, level with small of back

(f)   Hips: around fullest part of buttocks

(g)   At bone: around at top of pelvic bone

(h)   Neck: around at base of neck, form ring with tape measure

(i)   Front neck to waist: down the front from pit of the neck to the waist

(j)   Shoulder to apex: from center of shoulder to tip of apex (nipple)

(j/k)   Shoulder to waist: from center of shoulder across apex to waist

(l/m)   Armpit to side waist: from bottom of armpit to waist at side

(n)   Across shoulders: across back on the top of the shoulders from bones at shoulder/arm joint

(o)   Across shoulder blades: across back from arm to arm over largest part of shoulder blades

(p/q)	Back neck to waist: down center back from top bone of spine to small of back
(p/r)	Back neck to floor: down back from top bone of spine to floor, skimming body
(q/s)	Waist to buttocks: down center back from waist to fullest part of buttocks
(t/u)	Waist to knee: from waist, over buttocks to back of knee
(t/v)	Waist to calf: from waist, over buttocks to fullest part of calf
(q/r)	Waist to floor at back: down center back from waist to floor
(m/w)	Waist to floor at side: down side from waist to floor, not following leg curves
(x/y)	Waist to floor at front: down center front from waist to floor
(z/aa)	Under bust to floor: down from under bust at side front to floor, skimming body

Outsleeve

(ab/ac)	Neck to shoulder: from neck along shoulder ridge to bone at shoulder
(ac/ad)	Shoulder to elbow: from bone at shoulder around to elbow with arm raised and bent
(ac/ae)	Shoulder to wrist: with arm raised and bent, from bone at shoulder around to elbow and to wrist bone

Insleeve

(af/ag)	Armhole to elbow: from where arm joins chest down inside arm to elbow
(af/ah)	Armhole to wrist: from where arm joins chest down inside arm to wrist
(ac)	Armhole: around arm from shoulder to bottom of armpit back up to shoulder
(at)	Upper arm: around the bicep
(ah)	Wrist: around the wrist at wrist bone

Outseam

(m/ai)	Outseam to knee: from waist at side to kneecap
(m/aj)	Outseam to ankle: from waist at side to anklebone. Outseam to pants length: based on costume sketch or period information

Inseam

(ak/al)	Inseam to knee: from crotch to knee on inside of leg
(ak/am)	Inseam to ankle: from crotch to ankle on inside of leg
(an)	Thigh: around upper leg
(ao)	Knee: around kneecap
(ap)	Calf: around fullest part of lower leg
(am)	Ankle: around ankle at anklebone
(al)	Below knee: around knee below kneecap
(j/ak/j)	Girth: around body from center of shoulder in front, through crotch, up the back to center of shoulder (for unitards/leotards)
(aq)	Height: measured without shoes
(av)	Head: around head, above ears on forehead and angling down in back
(as/p)	Forehead to nape: across top of head from hairline in front to nape in back

MEASUREMENTS

DATE: 10/89

ACTOR: _J. Doe_   HOME PHONE: _718-555-4321_
SHOW: _Marriage of Figero_   CELL PHONE: _317-555-1234_
CHARACTER: _Peasant #5_   EMAIL: _jdoe@aol.com_

MALE __X__ FEMALE _____	OUTSEAM _____
CHEST/BUST _____ 40	TO KNEE _22-1/2_ TO ANKLE _42_
ABOVE _39_ BELOW _37_	TO PANTS LENGTH _45_
ACROSS FRONT (CHEST) _15_	INSEAM _____
WAIST _32_	TO KNEE _18_ TO ANKLE _33_
HIPS _38_ AT BONE _36_	TO PANTS LENGHT _36_
NECK _15-1/2_	BELOW KNEE _12-1/2_ GIRTH _66_
FRONT NECK TO WAIST _16_	HEIGHT _6'4"_ WEIGHT _180_
SHOULDER TO APEX (FRONT) _—_	HEAD _23-1/2_ HAT _____
TO WAIST (FRONT) _18-1/2_	FOREHEAD TO NAPE (WIG) _14_
ARMPIT TO SIDE WAIST _9_	SHOES _12C_ TIGHTS _XLARGE_
ACROSS SHOULDERS (BACK) _16_	DRESS SIZE _—_ BRA SIZE _—_
ACROSS SHOULDER BLADES _15_	SHIRT _16/35_ BLOUSE _—_
BACK NECK TO WAIST _17-1/2_	SUIT _42 XL_ PANTS _32/36_
TO FLOOR _64_	PIERCED EARS _NO_ GLOVE _LARGE_
WAIST (BACK) TO BUTTOCKS _20_	EYES _BLUE_ HAIR _DK BROWN_
TO KNEE _23_ TO CALF _28_	COMPLEXION _OLIVE_
WAIST TO FRONT AT BACK _47_	
AT SIDE _46_ AT FRONT _45_	
UNDERBUST TO FLOOR _—_	ALLERGIES _NONE_
OUTSLEEVE: NECK TO SHOULDER _6_	
SHOULDER TO ELBOW _13_ TO WRIST _26_	CHARACTER OR FIGURE NOTATIONS
INSLEEVE:	_ACTIVE—GYMNAST_
ARMSEYE TO ELBOW _9_ TO WRIST _26_	_CHECK FOR GUSSETS_
ARMSEYE _22-1/2_	ITEMS PROVIDED BY ACTOR _____
UPPER ARM _13_ TO WRIST _6-1/2_	_SHOES, DANCE BELT_
THIGH _22_ KNEE _13_	OTHER NOTES _____
CALF _15_ ANKLE _10_	

Figure 8.8   Measurement sheet. This measurement sheet is designed for either male or female actors, omitting unnecessary measurements.

MEASUREMENTS

MALE [X]   FEMALE [ ]   SHOW _MARRIAGE OF FIGERO_

ACTOR	NECK	BUST/CHEST	WAIST	HIPS	ACROSS BACK	HEIGHT	WEIGHT	DRESS SIZE	SHIRT/BLOUSE	PANTS	SUIT	TIGHTS	HEAD	SHOES
T. SMITH	15 1/2	40	32	41	15 1/2	5'8"	150	—	15 1/2-32	38-32	40R	MED	23	10C
M. ROMERO	15	38	31	39	15	5'10"	135	—	15-33	30-34	40R	MED	22 1/4	9D
K. LEECH	15 1/2	39	30	40	15 1/4	5'11"	143	—	15 1/2-34	32-34	40R	MED	22 3/8	10D
K. KONIKOW	15	37	32	38	15 1/2	5'7"	129	—	15-31	34-35	38S	SM	23	8D
J. HOLLAND	16	42	34	44	15	6'3"	160	—	16 1/2-35	30-32	42L	LG	23 1/2	11D
V. GLADSTONE	14 1/2	36	29	37	16	5'9"	143	—	15-32	31-31	36R	LG	22 3/4	9C
E. FELIX	15 1/2	37	30	38	15	5'8"	152	—	15 1/2-33	34-34	32S	MED	23	9C
S. DeMASI	15	37	31	37	15	5'9"	155	—	16-34	32-34	38R	MED	24	10D
J. CLASSEN	16	44	36	49	15 1/2	5'5"	173	—	16-34	32-32	46L	MED	23 1/2	11D
B. BRIGGS	15 1/2	39	32	40	16 1/4	6'	180	—	15 1/2-33	30-31	40L	LG	23 1/4	10C
J. SMITS	15	38	34	39	14 3/4	5'8"	145	—	15-32	30-31	40S	MED	24	9D
H. CUNNINGHAM	15 1/2	43	30	37	15	5'11"	165	—	16-32	32-31	38R	LG	22 3/8	10C
J. DOE	15 1/2	36	32	39	16	6'4"	210	—	15 1/2-32	32-36	42XL	XLG	28 1/2	12C

Figure 8.9   This shortened form is more convenient for shopping, renting, or pulling costumes from stock.

Assembling the Costumes

Good-mornin', ladies and gentlemen! . . . Has the young mistress anything for me today? I've got beautiful ribbons in my cart, Miss Anna, an' tapes, an' garters, an' hooks an' eyes. An' all in exchange for a few rags.

The Weavers, Gerhart Hauptmann

The costumes for most productions are assembled by a combination of purchasing, pulling from stock, renting, and building garments. The proportion of costumes from each source depends on the size and quality of the stock, the size of the budget, and the size of the costume crew available.

Shopping

Shopping should be planned like a military offensive. Any expedition should have a clear set of priorities. Which fabrics are needed first? Are shoes more important than underwear? Which items are needed for rehearsal? Which items are needed for the first fittings? Will any items need to be ordered and shipped? Shopping trips should be planned so that vendors in the same area of the city are dealt with at one time, provided the highest priorities can be met with this approach. Basic materials are needed before trims, but if the trim store is in the same block as the fabric store, two trips should be unnecessary.

Thrift-store shopping is particularly unpredictable. Items come and go daily or even hourly. Thrift shopping requires the designer to make instant decisions, but few low-budget shows can do without this source of costumes.

Shopping online is a boon for costume designers and costume technologists provided the budget allows for the shipping expenses. Unique vintage items, fabrics, garments, and patterns can sometimes be found online, as well as specialty shoes, corsets, wigs, and makeup. Always keep in mind the additional time required for shipping online purchases.

Locating Sources

Costume shops develop a source file or vendor book for the items frequently needed for shows. Web sites of particular interest should be bookmarked or otherwise noted for future reference. Each designer should likewise develop a personal file of sources; it saves valuable time locating supplies. A sample page appears in chapter 7 (figure 7.6). Pertinent information on vendors and items available are entered on the form, which is kept in a ring binder. Some designers and costume shops prefer to keep their source information on index cards in a Rolodex or in a desktop file on a shop computer. The information should be dated to indicate how current the prices are. Each time the information is used, corrections should be made. Notes about service and billing procedures are helpful to the next person to use the file. The name of a contact person saves time on return calls and allows the designer to build up an understanding with the vendor about the special needs of the costume shop. The source file should be organized by category or subject with a table of contents or index of vendor names. Box 8.E lists some of the categories that might be found in a designer's source file.

To develop the source book or to find items not listed in it, online or print phone directories are the obvious choice. Time spent checking on supply sources by phone is time well spent. Calling ahead to make sure the item is in stock in desired colors and sizes saves time, frustration, money, and energy. The vendor may be asked to deliver or to hold the order for pickup. Of course, only items that can be specifically described over the phone can be dealt with this way. Unfortunately, some vendors do not give prices or other information over the phone. When this method is successful, however, the time saved is worth the effort. With access to the Internet, the designer/shopper is no longer limited to local source, but must remember to allow time and money for shipping online purchases.

Costumers and other theater technicians often need specialized materials. These materials are advertised in theater publications and listed in theater

---

Box 8.E   List of source file categories

Accessories (ties, suspenders, shirt fronts, collars)

Armor (weapons, military gear, costume armor)

Art supplies (adhesives, paints)

Books (catalogs, magazines, directories)

Corset supplies (bones, corset cloth, laces)

Costume and formal rental

Craft supplies (beads, hemp, fabric printing supplies, basket materials)

Dance wear (leotards, tights, dance shoes)

Dyes (dyes, fabric paints)

Equipment (sewing machines, steam irons, steamers, laundry equipment)

Fabrics (specialty and regular)

Feathers and flowers

Foam rubber

Labels

Laundry supplies (bulk detergent, bleach, fabric softener)

Leather goods (leather, leather tools, glues, findings)

Makeup

Millinery supplies (hat supplies and manufacturers)

Notions and trims (sewing supplies, closures, trims)

Novelties and magic tricks

Patternmaking supplies (paper, tools)

Plastics

Repair services

Shoes (special order, special sizes, slippers)

Theatrical supplies

Wigs and hair goods (rental, period, modern)

source directories. Membership in theater associations and subscriptions to theater magazines give the designer access to the directories they publish as well as much other valuable information.

Before going shopping, the designer should check that the lists are complete, the priority items are indicated, and suggested sources are listed. Good preplanning makes shopping less strenuous and less time-consuming.

Keeping Track of Expenditures

The designer needs to have a firm understanding with the producer concerning the procedures for purchasing. Some cash is necessary for small items, but the theater may have charge accounts with some merchants or may prefer to issue checks or purchase orders made out to the vendor. Some organizations provide debit cards or credit cards to costume personnel. Whatever the arrangement, the designer should be cautious about spending personal funds if the producer is slow to advance cash. Many designers have found themselves unwittingly subsidizing a production by purchasing supplies with personal funds for which reimbursement was slow or nonexistent.

Keeping careful records of expenditures is absolutely essential. All receipts should be immediately checked for correct totals and clear figures. The designer should initial the back of cash register receipts and write the item purchased, the date, and the store name (if not on the front). Carbon copies of receipts should be checked for legibility. Receipts should be kept separate from the purchases themselves to prevent loss in transit or during unpacking. As soon as possible, purchases should be entered in a spreadsheet or on a ledger sheet to provide a running account of expenditures. Receipts should be kept in a secure place until reimbursement. A record of purchases made by charge, check, or purchase orders must be kept to provide an overall total of expenditures. Figure 8.10 shows one method of keeping a record of expenditures and receipts. Note that entries are initialed if more than one member of the shop is entering items in the ledger. (Ledger paper can be purchased at stationery stores.)

COSTUME RECEIPTS

SHOW _TWELFTH NIGHT_   DESIGNER _R. CUNNINGHAM_

Receipt Number	Date	Vendor	Account	Payment Method	Amount	Petty Cash Balance	Show Balance 7,500.00	
	10/12	Petty Cash Received	—	Check		1,500.00	6,000.00	RC
1	10/14	Art Max Fabric	Fabric	P.O.	600.00	—	5,400.00	RC
2	18/16	Beckenstein	Fabric	Cash	388.50	1,100.50	—	EF
3	10/18	B & G Fabrics	Fabric	Check	960.00	—	4,440.00	RC
4	10/19	Capezio	Shoes	Check	600.00	—	3,840.00	RC
5	10/19	Selva Shoes	Shoes	Cash	45.00	1,066.50	—	RC
6	10/19	M & J Trim	Trim	Cash	90.00	976.50	—	EF
7	10/19	Putnam Dye Co.	Dye	Check	225.00	—	3,615.00	MR
8	10/23	Tinsel Trading Co.	Hats	P.O.	675.00	—	2,940.00	RC
9	10/23	Art Max Fabrics	Fabric	Cash	330.00	646.50	—	MR
10	10/24	Pearl Paint	Paint	Check	150.00	—	2,790.00	RC
11	10/30	Costume Collection	Rental	P.O.	525.00	—	2,265.00	RC
12	10/30	Ideal Wig Co.	Wigs	Check	300.00	—	1,965.00	RC
13	10/31	Salvation Army	Accessories	Cash	75.00	571.50	—	EF
14	10/31	Steinlauf & Stoller	Trim	Cash	267.00	304.50	—	EF
15	11/1	Tandy Leather	Craft	Check	330.00	—	1,635.00	CR
16	11/2	Macy's	R-T Wear	Check	568.50	—	1,066.50	CR
17	11/2	Salvation Army	Accessories	Cash	45.00	259.50	—	CR
18	11/2	Travel Expense	Misc.	Cash	54.00	205.50	—	CR

Figure 8.10 Costume receipts. This form simplifies the keeping of basic financial records for the designer or shopper.

Procedures for handling money vary among theater organizations. In order to be clear about the specifics for each project, the designer should meet with the business manager, bookkeeper, and/or accountant responsible for costume expenditures and follow their guidelines. Be creative with the costumes, but not with the handling of production funds!

When purchasing new articles of clothing, the designer must make sure that store policy allows for return of merchandise for *refund* if the garments do not fit. Some stores only allow return for exchange or store credit. If purchases are made on credit cards, refunds will be credited to the card, not made in cash. In thrift shops and discount houses returns are not usually possible. If the budget allows, several possibilities may be purchased and final decisions left until fittings. If care is taken not to soil the garments during fittings and if store policy permits, extras may be returned later.

Some garments are best purchased by the actor. Bras and shoes can present special fitting problems. The actor should purchase the correct style and present the receipt for reimbursement if the designer agrees to cover the item in the budget.

Rental Procedures

Ideally the designer should go to the rental house him- or herself to pick out the costumes. This allows decisions on necessary substitutions to be made more easily. A quick inventory of the period-appropriate racks gives the designer an idea of what is available and what catches his/her eye. If something is appealing, further scrutiny is warranted. The designer should measure costumes for size, since rental stock is frequently altered and cannot be permanently sized. Waist, across back, chest or bust, waist to floor, or inseam measurements can be measured on the garment. Seams and hems should be checked to see if alterations are possible. If the designer cannot travel to the rental house, photocopies of the sketches with complete color notations should be sent along with the measurement sheets and order blanks provided by the costume house. Careful note should be made of the time required for delivery and the fees charged for various types of shipping. Shipping costs must be provided for in the budget. The director should be alerted to the deadlines for rental orders to minimize cast changes after costumes are rented. The producer should be informed if a deposit is required and if there is a separate cleaning cost.

Some modifications can be made in rented costumes. Some trims may be removed or replaced. Fitting alterations are permitted. Layers of sheer fabric can be added over finished garments to modify color or texture. Anything that can be undone before the costume is returned is usually permitted. Rental costumes should *never* be cut, painted, or dyed without the written permission of the rental house. The rental contract should be read carefully, and the crew instructed on correct handling of the rented items.

Rental houses usually charge a flat fee per costume per week of use. This fee usually covers everything needed for the costume except shoes. This system makes estimating the budget much easier. However, a "miscellaneous" category still is necessary for additional trim, accessories, and last-minute items, even if *all* the costumes are rented. Careful attention should be paid to the inventory list sent

> **Box 8.F   Designer checklist VII: Thrift shopping and rental selection**
>
> 1. For rental: Was the appointment made well in advance for the preferred time? Is sufficient pull time allowed for the number of costumes desired?
> 2. Has the rental fee and method of payment been cleared with appropriate producing personnel?
> 3. For rental and thrift shopping: Has the designer or shop manager verified budget allotments and methods of payment for items sought in shops?
> 4. Is a folder prepared with all the necessary measurements, photocopies of the sketches (or roughs), and costume lists? Is a *measuring tape* included in the folder?
> 5. Is the shopper familiar with the period research so appropriate substitutes and quick decisions can be made?
> 6. Has a *list* been made, organized by garment type with priorities and budget limits indicated?
> 7. Has a plan been made of the order of shops to be visited according to location, usual items stocked, and price point?
> 8. Thrift shopping reminder: Items purchased in thrift shops *cannot* be returned.
> 9. To analyze a garment's period potential study its fabric, cut, and shape.
> 10. Always check the measurements of a garment: *do not* rely on label sizes in garments. Sizes of vintage clothing vary from contemporary garments, and even contemporary clothing from different price points vary in measurements. When in doubt, check the bust/chest, waist, hips, across the back, and, if relevant, sleeve-length measurements.
> 11. Check rental costumes for extra seam allowances in case alterations are required.
> 12. Keep receipts separate and secured in a special envelope or wallet. Initial and label each receipt with the name of the garment as soon as possible to prevent later confusion. If given cash for shopping, keep it separately from personal funds.
> 13. Consider taking a backpack, rolling suitcase, or tote bags for carrying purchases.

with rented costumes to be sure that all items were received. The inventory should be used to check garments as they are packed for return to prevent mistakes.

Because of the high cost of tailoring, men's costumes are often rented. For period shows it is often cheaper to rent a costume than to build it. Rental stock may be limited for modern dress, however. Much more variety is usually available in thrift shops, in department stores, or from personal wardrobes.

Adapting Stock and Thrift Shop Purchases

Whereas restraint is required with rental costumes, designers may be allowed to cut up, take apart, or otherwise change garments purchased or pulled from stock. Clearance for irreversible alterations should be received from the shop manager or costume director.

Permission may not be granted to alter antique garments from stock, since these may be more valuable as study pieces than as costumes. Actual period garments may be too small and too fragile to be of real use as costumes. They may also be too expensive to purchase and maintain for low-budget shows.

When pulling or shopping, the designer should keep in mind the basic construction of the desired garment, the type of fabrics that would be desirable, and the possible alterations that would make a garment over into a useful piece. Reshaping the neck, dyeing the garment, and shortening the sleeves or skirt are all relatively simple alterations to give the garment the right style.

With a complete understanding of the silhouette and fabric requirements of the desired period, a designer can often make "a silk purse from a sow's ear." In figure 8.11, two 1980s bridesmaid dresses (A, B) of suitable fabric (hang) and silhouette have been converted to a 1950s formal gown (C). The net and taffeta skirt of the pale dress has become the petticoat, the sleeves have been used to create the bosom effect and the flower, and the bow has been moved to emphasize the side drape.

When the stock, shopped, and rental costumes are collected, a "dummy show" or "rack review" may be presented for the director's approval. This can be arranged character-by-character or in the order of appearance, act-by-act or scene-by-scene. For missing items, sketches, mannequins draped with the fabric, or similar garments in other sizes or colors may represent costumes that are missing. Seeing the garments together gives the designer and the director a concrete idea of how they will look onstage together and reduces unpleasant surprises late in the production schedule. The designer will find it much easier to make changes or find whole new items early in the process than to replace or adapt costumes after dress parade or first dress.

Understanding Costume Construction

Here's snip and nip and cut and slish and slash,
Like to a censer in a barber's shop.
Why, what, a devil's name, tailor, call'st thou this?

Taming of the Shrew, William Shakespeare

The term *construction* or *building* is used for the cutting, sewing, and assembling of costumes because of the heavy-duty techniques so often required for costumes. Because the garments must withstand vigorous activity, perspiration, body heat, and heat from stage lights, costumes cannot be assembled delicately. Costumes also may include craft items of leather, wire, metal, plastics, and other materials that are not lightweight and may not be sewn.

Patternmaking and costume construction are major areas of study, requiring great skill and expertise. A complete study of these fields (costume technology) is beyond the scope of this book. However, this general discussion will help

Figure 8.11 Stock or thrift shop purchases (A, B) have been adapted to suggest a gown from the 1950s (C). Designed by the author for Retro Productions. Photographs by Jack H. Cunningham.

Figure 8.12 This dummy show for *God Sees Dog* allows the designer and the director to see the pulled and purchased garments together for a preview of how they will look. Costumes by Jeanette Aultz for Brooklyn College. Photo by Jack H. Cunningham.

the novice to understand the procedures involved and will give the designer a working vocabulary in these fields. A more thorough study is necessary for the professional designer. The more knowledge a designer has of cut and construction, the better able that designer will be to clearly explain the costume design, to supervise and collaborate with the costumer, and to produce a costume personally when the need arises.

Designer/Costumer Collaboration

The costume designer's sketch is a plan or blueprint for the costume. A good costumer can take a poor sketch and make a wonderful costume; a poor costumer can take a good sketch and interpret it clumsily. Just as the designer strives to interpret the director's concepts of the play into costumes, the costume technologist must work to interpret the designer's sketch into a finished costume that creates the desired effect, fits the actor playing the role, and meets budget and schedule requirements. *The skilled costumer is as much an artist as the designer.* The sensitive and knowledgeable interpretation of a sketch requires an aesthetic understanding of clothing, fabric, the human form and movement, and theatrical values. A practical understanding of patternmaking, cutting, construction techniques, and historical period also is required.

Translating the sketch into the finished costume is a critical aspect of the designer's work. Close collaboration between the designer and the costumer is required. Building a costume is a constant process of making choices. Many of these decisions can be made on the basis of the experience the designer or costumer has had with other garments. Other choices depend on the requirements of the current production or the designer's taste. The designer must be available to make decisions and answer questions during the entire construction process. The wise designer appreciates the skill and experience the costumer brings to the project and encourages the costumer's creative input. The designer should attempt to make the development of the costumes an exciting and creative process for everyone involved.

In a large costume shop the shop manager distributes the various costumes among the staff. The designer and/or shop manager then discusses with each costumer (patternmaker, draper, cutter, or tailor) the garments for which each is responsible, covering the specifics of garment cut (darts or princess seams? gores or half-circle?), fabrics, trims, and closures (front or back? zippers or lacing? Velcro?). The designer needs to explain any unusual aspects of stage business to be done in the costume and any special requirements of the director or actor.

The designer should provide any pertinent technical information or research material that would be helpful to the costume technologist. In color plate 12, a sketch by Robert Edmond Jones for *Central City Nights,* the designer has included a photo of the costume on which he based his design. (See also figure 1.8.)

For large constructed shows, keeping track of all the different stages of the work can be very difficult. Figure 8.13A shows a sample to-build chart. Each process or step for all costume items to be built is listed on the chart. Since many different people may be working on the different steps, checking off the various processes as they are completed helps the shop manager, costumer, and designer keep track of the progress of each garment piece. In professional shops every person working on the garment fills out an attached card, indicating the amount of time each spent on the costume. Tallying up the hours and multiplying each person's total by their rate of pay helps the manager keep track of the labor costs for each costume. This information is valuable for evaluating future projects as well as making budget adjustments on the current one.

As the work progresses, the designer should be available to approve each stage of the costume's development.

Figure 8.13A
To-build chart.

TO BUILD

SHOW _THE MARRIAGE OF FIGARO_
ACTOR _T. SMITH_   CHARACTER _ANTONIO_   PLATE # _1501_

COSTUME ITEM	FABRIC SWATCH	BUY	WASH	DYE YES	DYE DONE	IRON/ ROLL	CUT	PAINT YES	PAINT DONE	FITTING READY	FITTING DONE	FINISH	NOTES
SHIRT		✔	✔	BEIGE	✔	—	—	NO	—	✔			STOCK
VEST		✔	✔	NO	—	✔	✔	YES	✔	✔			AGED
BREECHES		✔	✔	NO	—	✔	✔	YES	✔	✔			AGED
JACKET		✔	NO	NO	—	STEAM ✔	✔	YES	✔				AGED
SCARF		✔	✔	ROSE	✔	✔	✔	NO	—				
SASH		✔	NO	NO	—	✔	—	NO	—				
SNOOD	STOCK	NO	NO	—				YES					

WORK TALLY SHEET

SHOW _A DOLL'S HOUSE_   PLATE _XI_
ACTOR _L. BEITCHMANN_ GARMENT _RED SKIRT_

DATE	NAME	JOB	TIME	TOTAL
9/1	JAL	pattern	9:15-10:30	1 hr – 15
9/1	KS	cut skirt	10:30-12:00	1 hr-30 min
9/2	MD	stitch ribbon	10:00-11:30	1 hr-30 min
9/2	KS	prep ruffle	1:00-2:30	1 hr-30 min
9/2	MD	stitch skirt	2:30-5:00	2hr-30
9/4	CR	fitting - 1st	1:30-2:00	30 min
9/5	KS	attached ruffle	9-10:00	1 hour
9/5	CL	hand finishing	10:00-12:00	2 hours
		TOTAL	11 HOURS – 45 MINS.	

Figure 8.13B Work tally sheet for keeping track of time spent on garments.

Interpreting the Sketch

How to begin? The designer and/or costumer must first analyze the sketch in terms of the *shapes* produced by the separate parts. Visualizing the costume without the trim should reveal its basic structure. Once the units are isolated, to what shapes do they relate? What type of pattern or garment cut would best reproduce the desired shapes? Decisions can then be made about the most efficient and appropriate method of patterning each unit. Box 8.G (p. 240) is a designer checklist for interpreting a sketch for patterning and construction.

Calculations for yardage, lists of materials, and decisions about cutting, stitching, and trim are easily forgotten. Most costumers keep a notebook in which the decisions and information about the garments can be kept. The notebook is a valuable reference when the designer is not available. Some costumers add this information to the shop or show bible. These bibles are kept in case a costume must be replaced for a new actor or touring production. The information provided allows a quick assessment of the replacement cost, sources, and build-time required.

Figure 8.14A shows a sketch for Nora's tarantella dress from *A Doll's House*. What must be done in this costume? How must it move? What undergarments are required to hold the shape? Although Nora does not actually dance in this dress, it must appear that she could. A small bustle and a full-bosom corset are needed to suggest the period. How is the dress cut? Of what shapes is it composed? The bodice is princess style and dips to a low "U" in the front. The neck is low, but not revealing. The skirt is assembled of straight panels. The lace trim at the neck appears to be straight and gathered. The skirt ruffle is a straight piece of even width, but is cut on the bias (note the diagonal stripes). Figure 8.14B shows a more complete analysis and notations on construction decisions for this costume. Figure 8.14C shows the finished costume on stage.

Figure 8.14A   *A Doll's House*. Nora. Designed by the author for Brooklyn College.

Developing Costume Patterns

There are times when the designer is expected to produce a pattern and cut and sew the costume. To prepare for this possibility, the prospective designer will want to collect useful patterns and study patternmaking techniques.

There are essentially five sources of costume patterns: (1) new or old

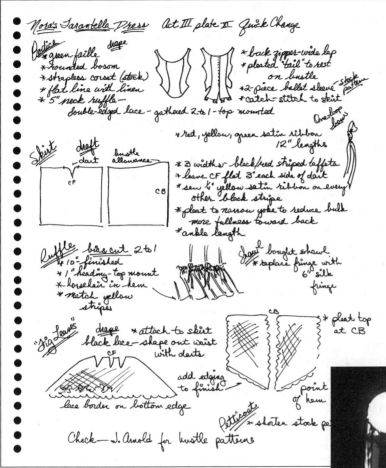

Figure 8.14B Costumer's notes. An analysis of the costume's shapes helps determine the type of pattern to be developed.

Figure 8.14C   Photo of tarantella dress for Nora.

commercial patterns, (2) enlargements of scale drawings in costume books, (3) drafting patterns from measurements, (4) flat-patterning from slopers, and (5) draping. The choice of pattern source depends on which option is available, the designer's or costumer's training and skill, the equipment and space available, time, the demands of authenticity, and personal preference.

**Box 8.G   Designer/costume technologist checklist VIII:
Interpreting a sketch**

1. What are the basic shapes of the garment?

2. Are the different units separate or connected? What patterns are required: Bodice? Skirt? Tunic? Sleeve? Pants?

3. How narrow or full are the different parts? How do the different sections relate to the body: Neckline depth? Sleeve length? Bodice length? Skirt length?

4. How do the different parts of the garment fit: Tight? Easy? Skimming? Loose? Baggy? Voluminous? How should the shape and fit be best achieved: Darts? Seams? Pleats? Gores? Insets? Gathers? Tucking?

5. What is the finished length desired: Calf-length? Ankle-length? Floor-length?

6. Are garment sections cut on the straight grain or the bias?

7. What type of pattern or garment cut would create the shapes desired? Is a similar pattern in stock or commercially available? Should this garment be an authentic period cut? Are there stock patterns available that could be adapted?

8. What is the best method by which to develop each pattern part: Drafting? Flat-patterning? Draping? Is this a garment that can be computer-drafted? Should a combination of patterning methods be used? Which method is fastest?

9. Where are the closures? What type is desired or required?

10. What type of fabric is being used? What inner structure will be required: Inner facings? Flat linings? Wires? Horsehair? Buckram? Other stiffening? What parts require linings?

11. Are any fabric treatments planned: Dyeing? Painting? Aging? At what stage of construction will these treatments be applied? Will the costume leave the shop for treatment?

12. What types of trim are to be used, and how are they to be applied: Mounted on top? Caught in seam? By machine? By hand? Bonded? Glued?

13. Are special undergarments required? Are they in stock? Can they be purchased? Are they to be built? At what stage of the costume development will they be needed?

14. What must the actor do while wearing the costume: Dance? Fence? Fight?

15. Where does this costume stand in order of priority: High priority? Medium priority? Low priority?

16. Is this costume to be built for short-term use? Long-term use? Stock?

17. What is the most efficient or economical way to produce this costume without sacrificing style and quality? Do the cost and level of priority justify the approach? Can any part be purchased or made to order more quickly or at a more reasonable cost than in-shop construction?

Commercial Patterns

Only a limited number of contemporary commercial patterns are useful for period shows. The majority of commercial patterns for masquerade or costume dress are oversimplified and overinfluenced by contemporary fashion. "Fancy dress" patterns frequently have darts for period styles that had no darts, and they are designed to be worn over currently fashionable underwear. There is rarely adequate fabric in the skirts of "period" styles. Men's costume patterns are cut along modern lines and have simplified patterning and construction. These patterns are rarely appropriate for stage costumes. Of course, commercial patterns are more useful for modern dress costumes.

If the designer is careful to analyze shapes, silhouette, and fit, however, some useful basic patterns can be found in commercial pattern books. Adjustments must be made for period fit and style. Adaptable patterns include pajama patterns, basic fitted bodices and skirts, gored skirts, princess-style dresses, and wedding-dress patterns (often loosely based on period garments).

Some authentic patterns for peasant and period dress are available through small specialty shops and mail-order sources, many of which can be found online. These patterns may include transfer designs for embroidery and other special decoration.

Authentic period patterns can sometimes be purchased in thrift shops, flea markets, and antique stores. Although these patterns are usually too fragile to use, they can be copied onto heavier paper or muslin.

The advantages of using commercial patterns are (1) they save time, (2) they usually require less knowledge and skill, (3) they cost less than the cost of the labor needed to develop a pattern, and (4) they may be available in a large range of sizes. The disadvantages are (1) many are seriously lacking in period feeling and detail, (2) a limited number of appropriate styles are available, (3) they must be located and purchased, (4) they have inadequate seam allowances, and (5) they have contemporary fit and modern consciousness.

Reduced Scale Patterns

Many of the books listed in the bibliography show period patterns in reduced scale. Ladies' magazines of the nineteenth and twentieth centuries often included patterns for ladies' clothes. These can be enlarged to full scale by using the technique illustrated in figure 8.15 (on the following page) and explained in box 8.H (p. 243).

The scale of the published drawing varies depending on its source and should be indicated on the pattern. The patternmaker must remember that the pattern is not necessarily represented in the size required for the costume. In some examples a standard size is printed; in others, the pattern is taken from an authentic garment that was sized for a specific person. After scaling up to full size, the costumer needs to adjust the pattern to fit the actor's measurements and then test it in muslin over appropriate undergarments.

The advantages of using patterns from these diagrams are (1) if they are based on authentic garments, they will represent very accurate period looks, and (2) more variety is available than in commercial patterns. The disadvantages are (1) diagrams in some books do not adequately credit the source of the

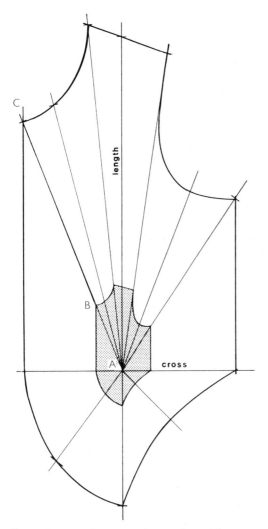

Figure 8.15   Enlarging scale patterns. After the pattern is copied from the source, lines are extended from one chosen point A through all pertinent points of the pattern. The length of the lines depends on the scale of the pattern: for 1/8-inch scale the distance from point A to B is multiplied by eight to find point C. When all lines are extended, the new points are connected for the enlarged pattern.

pattern, (2) some patterns do not fit well and must be extensively reworked, (3) the scale of some patterns is unclear, (4) some diagrams look authentic, but are based on reinterpretations of period dress, and (5) authentic patterns may require adjustments to account for differences in modern body development. (The contemporary human form is taller, broader in the shoulders, and longer in the arms and legs than previous generations. Women of many previous generations began wearing corsets as children, altering the development of the bone structure in the torso.)

Drafting from Measurements

Drafting is a method of creating patterns from measurements using one of the systems developed for this technique. The costumer follows a series of instructions using the measurements of the actor or the standard size desired and creates the pattern shape on paper. The pattern is then cut out of muslin and checked for fit and hang. Many simple garments and garment pieces can be patterned in this way. There are systems for men's tailored patterns, and many women's styles can also be developed by this approach. Figure 8.16 (p. 244) and box 8.I (p. 245) illustrate a sample project for a drafted pattern.

The advantages of this method are (1) little special equipment is needed, (2) patterns can be developed to size, and (3) patterns can be crisp, clean, and accurate. The disadvantages of this method are (1) a set of instructions for the pattern project must be available, (2) extensive skill and training are required for complex garments, (3) visualizing the three-dimensional garment on flat paper can be very challenging, and (4) in the hands of a novice, garments made from drafted patterns may look stiff and fail to relate properly to the body.

Flat-Patterning with Slopers

The *flat-patterning* technique uses *slopers* to develop a variety of more complicated patterns. Slopers are basic pattern shapes (bodice front, bodice back, sleeve, straight skirt front, etc.) that are cut of oaktag or cardboard and have no seam allowances. Slopers can be developed from commercial patterns, drafted from measurements, or copied from draped garments. The designer/costumer will find a set of basic *slopers* in small, medium, and large sizes very useful.

Box 8.H   Enlarging scale patterns

1. Trace the pattern carefully from the source using tracing paper. Transfer the copy to pattern paper, using carbon paper.

2. Establish a lengthwise line and a crosswise line intersecting at right angles (point A in figure 8.15) to each other and relating to the pattern at important points (waist, bottom edge, center front or back).

3. Draw lines from intersection A to each point of the pattern that represents a corner or the depth of a curve.

4. Measure the distance from intersection point A to the outline of the pattern on each line and multiply that measurement by the scale ratio. The scale is indicated in the pattern diagram source. (For example, if the diagram is marked 1/16-inch scale, each 1/16 inch on the diagram represents 1 inch on the finished pattern, and the scale ratio is 16 to 1; 1/8-inch scale = 8 to 1; 1/4-inch scale = 4 to 1. If scale ratio is 4 to 1, a 1-inch line on the traced pattern will be 4 × 1 inch, or 4 inches on the enlarged pattern.)

5. Measure the calculated distance along the line from intersection A and cross-mark.

6. Using a ruler and a French curve, connect the cross marks to produce the pattern in the enlarged size.

The two basic techniques for manipulating slopers are *slash and spread* and *pivot*. Figures 8.17 (p. 246) and 8.18 (p. 248) illustrate the two techniques applied to the development of a sleeve pattern. (See also boxes 8.J [p. 247] and 8.K [p. 249].)

Books on flat-pattern techniques are listed in the bibliography. After learning the basic methods of sloper manipulation, the patternmaker learns to adapt the techniques to the requirement of a specific costume.

The advantages of flat-patterning are (1) precise measurements can be made of parts being manipulated, (2) patterns can be very accurate, (3) it is more economical to use paper than muslin for the early stages of pattern development, and (4) the work can be put away or transported in an unfinished state with little risk. The disadvantages are (1) visualizing the three-dimensional garment on flat paper can be difficult, (2) the finished garment has a tendency to look stiff and awkward if it is not properly refined in muslin, (3) it requires skill and training, and (4) instructions are needed for developing many patterns. Some costumers refer to all forms of patternmaking done on paper as "drafting."

Computer applications for pattern drafting are available. These applications are based on the same principles as those used in hand drafting. Once an understanding of pattern drafting has been developed, computer patternmaking can increase the speed and accuracy with which the patterns can be developed. *Grading* (developing the same pattern in two or more sizes) is much easier with computer patternmaking. However, the initial cost of the software and an appropriate printer may make this approach too costly for individuals and many shops.

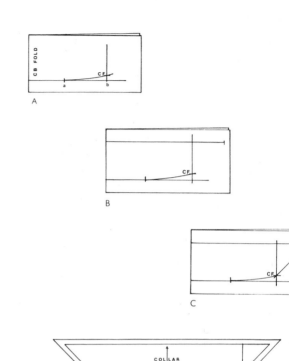

Figure 8.16 Drafting. The project is a simple drafted collar developed from measurements. Compare to box 8.I.

Draping

Draping is a method of patternmaking in which fabric (usually unbleached muslin) is smoothed over and pinned to a dressmaker's form in the shape of the desired style. The resulting seams are marked and *trued* (corrected) to produce a pattern. The muslin pieces may then be used for cutting the costume or may be traced to paper for a more stable pattern. Once on paper, they can be manipulated, as a drafted pattern would be. Adjustments to the specific measurements of the actor may be made in the muslin or in the paper pattern. The draping technique is used frequently for women's costumes because this approach allows for easier visualization of the garment. Figure 8.19 (pp. 250–251) and box 8.L (p. 250) show the bodice pattern for Nora's tarantella dress (figure 8.14) being developed by the draping technique. Note that the bustle has been added and the dress form is padded for period shape.

The advantages of draping a pattern are (1) it is easier for the patternmaker and the designer to visualize the garment, (2) it is possible to experiment with the hang and fall of the fabric, (3) subtle refinements can be built into the pattern as it is being developed, because muslin behaves like fabric whereas paper behaves like paper. The disadvantages of draping are (1) more expensive equipment is required (dress forms), (2) muslin is easily distorted in manipulation and

---

Box 8.1   Drafted convertible shirt collar

1. Measurements required: (a) neckline from center back (CB) to shoulder and (b) neckline from center back to center front (CF) (See figure 8.16.)

2. Cut a rectangle of paper 2 × (b) + 6 inches by 2 × desired width of collar.

3. Fold paper as illustrated in A. Label the fold, "CB fold."

4. Draw a base line the length of the paper and perpendicular to the CB fold.

5. Measure off the distance (a) and cross-mark. This mark becomes the shoulder notch.

6. Measure off measurement (b) and cross-mark. Draw a line perpendicular to the base line at this mark.

7. Measure 1/2 inch up from the base line on this perpendicular line. Mark. Label "CF."

8. Use a metal curve to connect the shoulder notch and CF mark. Measure from CB along the base line and following the curve the distance (b) and adjust the distance if required.

9. Measure the desired width of the collar along the perpendicular line from the CF mark (B). Mark.

10. Draw a line through this mark, perpendicular to the CB fold. This line represents the outside edge of the collar. Extend the line to the desired length of the point.

11. Connect the CF mark to the collar edge to form point C.

12. With layers of paper pinned together, trace lines and notches to the second layer and add seam allowances.

13. Trim along the seam allowance lines and unfold D.

14. Establish the CB notch and grain line on the CB fold. (Collars may also be cut on lengthwise grain or the bias.)

15. Cut the collar out of muslin and test the pattern on the garment.

---

the resulting pattern may be distorted, (3) the piece cannot be removed and transported without risking distortion, (4) many students find the techniques difficult to learn.

The Fitting Muslin

The first fitting for constructed costumes is usually done with *fitting muslin.* This is a full garment of muslin that is tried on and adjusted to the actor's body. It enables the costumer to check the pattern and adjust the fit, style, and proportion. This garment should be sewn together with large machine stitches for easy adjustment. If the pattern has been adjusted to the actor's measurements in the paper stage, the lining or backing fabric may be used for the first fitting.

All fittings should be made over appropriate undergarments. The actor should provide modern underwear, but the designer or costume shop must provide period or special undergarments. If body padding is to be used, it must be constructed and fitted first in order to properly fit costumes to be worn over it. Hoops, bustles, paniers, and other special shapers must be constructed before the outer garments can be fitted. Rehearsal items and stock pieces may be fitted either at this time or later, depending on schedule.

The designer should be present at all fittings to make a number of decisions: Should this be prepped for quick change? How short should the skirt be? (If the audience seating is below stage level, skirts tend to look shorter than they are.) Is it full enough? How low should the neck be? What kind and where should the closure be?

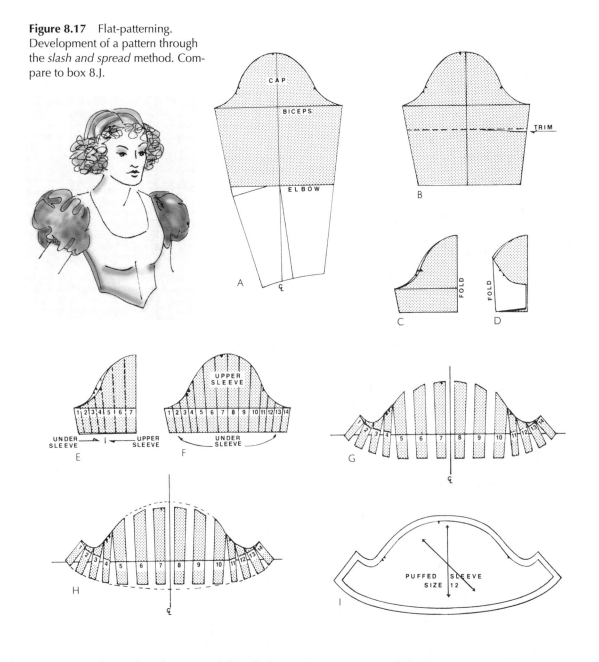

Figure 8.17 Flat-patterning. Development of a pattern through the *slash and spread* method. Compare to box 8.J.

The sketch should always be available for reference. The designer should show the sketch to the actor in order to help the actor visualize the finished costume. The actor should demonstrate any action or stage business that may affect the fit or use of the costumes. Notes should be made on required adjustments (extra ease, lower neckline, reinforcements, double stitching, gussets, stretch fabric, elastic sections).

Careful notes should be made concerning changes in the pattern, and the muslin should be marked clearly. Safety pins should be used where possible for fitting and marking so that the corrections will not be lost. Depending on the complexity of the costume, 30 to 45 minutes should be allowed per muslin fitting *per costume.* If possible, several of an actor's costumes should be ready for fittings at one time, to save the actor trips to the shop, and to save shop time for setting up accessories and undergarments. Extensive and time-consuming fittings require short breaks for both actor and shop personnel.

Box 8.J   Flat-patterning puffed sleeve by slash and spread method

1. Copy the sleeve sloper from cap to elbow line including biceps line, centerline (CL), and notches (A). (See figure 8.17.)

2. Trim the sloper to the desired length of sleeve (B).

3. Fold on the centerline (C). Match the outside edges to the center fold (D), dividing the sleeve into under and upper sections.

4. Divide the folded undersleeve into four sections and the upper sleeve into three sections (E). Unfold the sleeve and number each section *before* cutting them apart (F). Cut sections apart.

5. On pattern paper, draw lengthwise and crosswise grain lines intersecting at right angles (G).

6. Matching the biceps line on each pattern piece to the cross grain line on the pattern paper, arrange the upper sleeve sections in numerical order with half of the pieces on each side of the center line. The spaces between the pieces should be equal. (The size of the spaces depends on the size of sleeve desired and the weight of the fabric to be used.)

7. Arrange the undersleeve sections (1–4 and 11–16) on each side of the upper sleeve sections so that the tops (sleeve cap edge) are touching and the bottoms are spread about one-half the space between the upper sleeve sections.

8. Mark the top and bottom edges and underarm seams. Transfer the notches for the shoulder and for front and back of the sleeve cap. Remove the paper pieces.

9. Add 1/2 inch to the top and bottom at the center line (H).

10. Using a French curve, blend a line along the top and bottom from underarm seam to underarm seam as illustrated.

11. Establish a grain line on CL or at a 45-degree angle for bias (I).

12. Add seam allowances.

13. Cut out the sleeve pattern. Label.

14. Cut a muslin copy to test the pattern.

Fittings should be conducted in a courteous and businesslike manner, efficiently but without rushing. Major problems should not be discussed in front of the actor, but rather discussed with the costumer privately. After solutions are found, a new fitting can be scheduled.

Cutting and Stitching

The costumer should make careful, clear corrections of the pattern before cutting the costume, to prevent mistakes when stitching the garment. The cutting must be done with great care because mistakes in cutting may be impossible

Figure 8.18   Flat-patterning. Development of a pattern through the *pivot* method. Compare to box 8.K.

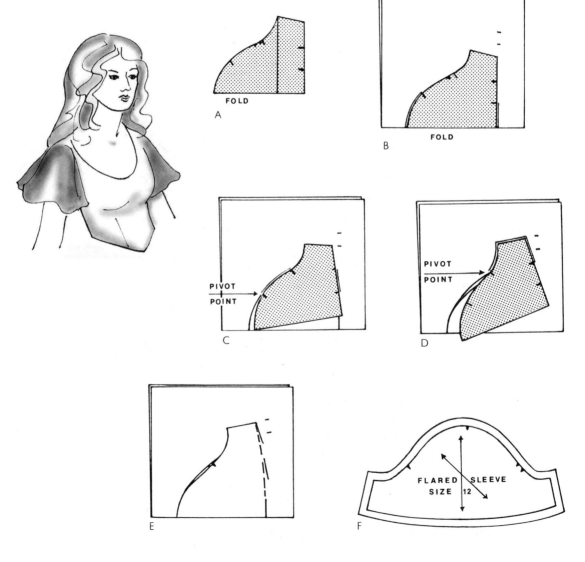

to correct. The patternmaker or cutter lays out the fabric and places the pattern according to the planned use of the fabric. Patterns, stripes, and plaids must be matched or placed strategically on the garment. Costumes made of one-way prints or napped fabrics must be cut with the top of all pattern pieces going in the same direction.

In addition to the main garment pieces, linings, interfacings, ruffles, facings, cording, pockets, and other extra pieces must be planned and cut. Special padding, boning, closures, or quick-change rigging must be worked out before the garment is stitched. All pieces of a costume should be bundled together to prevent lost parts, and the bundle should be labeled with the actor's name and the costume plate number or the act and scene number.

Stitchers then sew the major pieces of the garment together to prepare it for the second fitting. This may be done with a large stitch so that it can be easily ripped out for changes.

Box 8.K   Flat-patterning flared sleeve by the pivot method

1. Copy the sleeve sloper and adjust the copy to the desired length. (See figure 8.18.)

2. Fold along the centerline and place the sleeve front down (A).

3. Divide the cap into three equal sections and mark.

4. Divide the bottom edge into three equal sections and mark.

5. Cut the pattern paper 6 inches longer and 10 inches wider than the sleeve sloper. Fold in half as illustrated. (B).

6. Match the folded edge of the sloper copy and the folded edge of the paper.

7. Divide the distance between the edge of the sleeve and the desired width of the finished sleeve into two equal parts and mark it on pattern paper.

8. Copy the cap to the first cap mark and the bottom edge to the first bottom mark.

9. Holding the sloper at the first pivot point, pivot the sleeve to the first width mark (C). Copy the second section of the cap to the second cap mark, and the second section of the bottom to the second bottom mark. Fold back the top layer of the sloper copy to draw in the front cap line.

10. Holding the sloper copy at the second pivot point, pivot the sleeve to the second width mark (D). Copy the third section of cap, the third section of the bottom, and the underarm seam. Fold back the top layer of the sloper copy to draw in the front cap line. Copy the notches.

11. Using a French curve or metal patternmakers curve, draw in the bottom line and true (correct) the cap shape, eliminating small dips (E).

12. Pin the paper together. Trace the bottom line through to the other side of the folded paper.

13. Unfold the paper and correct the front cap line (F). Add seam allowances and indicate the desired grain line. Cut out the pattern.

14. Cut a muslin copy to test the pattern.

A

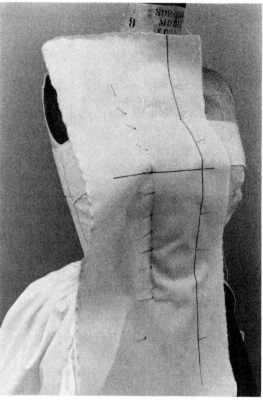

B

Box 8.L   Draping a bodice

1. The dress form is padded for period shape and dressed with a bustle pad and a petticoat. The new neckline is marked with seam tape. Note the seam lines marked on the padding. (See figure 8.19A.)

2. Muslin is pinned to the dress form along the neck, center front, and princess seams. The cross grain line is centered on the apex. (B)

3. The side front was developed and is pinned to the center front panel. Large seam allowances have been left to permit adjustments. (C)

4. The bodice pattern has been pinned together to check the fit of the seams and the shape of the bodice. (D)

5. The muslin pieces have been pressed and are being transferred to paper. (E)

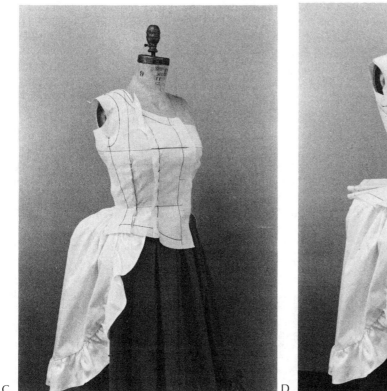

C

D

Figure 8.19 Draping. The bodice for the costume in figure 8.14 being draped. Photos by Melissa A. Wentworth. Compare to box 8.L.

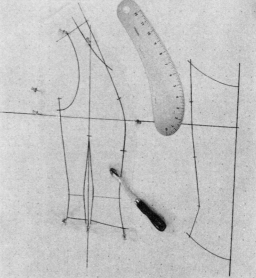

E

Trim may be applied by machine or by hand, depending on the skill of the stitcher, the stress on the costume, the effect desired, and the costume's reuse potential for stock. In figure 8.20 yellow satin ribbon is being applied by machine to enhance the striped taffeta for Nora's skirt.

The basic sewing skills required for sewing costumes are the same as for home sewing, and several good sewing books are available. Special techniques for sewing costumes may be found in *The Costumer's Handbook* by Ingham and Covey, *Basic Sewing for Costume Construction* by this author, and other books listed in the bibliography. (See sections on Developing the Costume and Getting the Show Together.)

The designer should expect, even insist upon, quality construction. Seams should be carefully matched, stitched with firm stitches (8 to 10 stitches to the inch), and pressed smooth and pucker-free. A few extra minutes of care can make a big difference in the finished garment. On the other hand, responsible judgments regarding the amount of time to spend on a particular garment must be made. Is the garment for stock? A long run? A few days? Does it have high stress requirements? Is it on stage for the whole play or only a few moments? Can it be reused? The designer and costumer can easily get side-tracked into construction details and lose sight of the onstage product and the overall production schedule.

Second and Final Fittings

Ideally, all the pieces of the costume should be ready for the second fitting. The undergarments must be complete so the garment can be correctly fitted. The shoes must be available so the hem can be marked. The wig must be available so the hat can be fitted. (Trim may not be important if it is to be applied to the finished garment instead of stitched on before the garment is constructed.) All pieces of the costume should be labeled with the actor's name.

If the costume is very complicated, both a second fitting and a final fitting may be required. In the final fitting, the actor should move

Figure 8.20   Stitching. Satin ribbon is being applied to striped taffeta to add definition to a too-subtle stripe. Photo by Melissa A. Wentworth.

around in and get the feel of the costume. The actor should attempt any business he or she feels might be affected by the costume. The designer should suggest or demonstrate ways to use the costume to best advantage.

All aspects of the costume should be checked. Depending on the complexity of the costume, the second fitting may take 45 minutes to an hour or more.

Box 8.M   Costume industry standards

While there are many ways to construct costumes and the situation and preferences of the designer may dictate the methods used, it is still possible to suggest overall industry standards for work in costume shops. (The following list is partly based on information from Deborah Weber, Costume Shop Manager at San Jose State University.)

1. Patterns are made *without seam allowances*. Notations are sometimes made on the pattern edges to indicate the amount of seam allowances to be added when cutting.

2. Seam allowances generally used are:

    Side seams and shoulders—1½"

    Necks, armholes, and princess seams—3/4"

    CB and closures—2"

    Hems—3" to 4"

3. Seam lines (stitching lines) are marked unless the garment is very loose-fitting and absolute accuracy in stitching is not important.

4. Stitchers are instructed to match the seam lines, line-to-line.

5. Stitchers are expected to have knowledge of and a reasonable level of skills in the following basics:

    Use of industrial sewing machines

    Use of overlock and blind hemmer machines

    Knowledge of basic seams—basic, flat fell, French

    Knowledge of sewing facings, including understitching

    Ability to mount zippers—lapped, centered, fly type

    Flat lining garments

    Making and inserting binding and piping

    Pleating—knife, cartridge, and box types

    Boning a corset

6. Finishers are expected to have knowledge of sewing the following:

    Buttons

    Snaps

    Hooks and eyes

    Hems and facings

    Linings

    Trimmings

Fittings should never be set for more than one actor at a time or scheduled too close together. Also allow time at the end of the fitting to label, mark, and write detailed notes about the work still to be done. Poor fitting notes can cause confusion about remaining work, result in poor quality finishing, or create the necessity for an extra fitting. Box 8.N is a designer checklist for fittings.

Finishing

The term *finishing* refers to the final touches required to complete the costume. Mostly handwork, finishing includes hems, facings, hooks and eyes, snaps, buttons, and trim. The quality of the finishing often makes the difference between a well-made costume and one that lacks finesse and does not hold up well.

Assembling Accessories

In addition to garment construction, a designer needs to know something about millinery, hair styling, and costume crafts. In educational and repertory theaters the costume shop may handle all of these areas. For professional productions different specialists work in each area.

Box 8.N   Designer checklist IX: Fittings

1. Are the chosen undergarments appropriate and well-fitted?

2. Does the garment fit neatly across the bust/chest area? Are the darts or princess seams in the correct position? Is there enough room across the back? The front? Do the center front and center back line up properly with the body?

3. Is the waist at the correct place for the period or desired style? Is it snug, yet reasonably comfortable?

4. Are the armholes correctly shaped and low enough? Does the sleeve allow for enough movement to meet the needs of the blocking? Is a gusset required for movement? How long should the sleeve be?

5. Does the neck fit smoothly across the back, comfortably in the front? Is it the right shape and depth? How much chest/bust is to be shown?

6. Does the skirt hang properly? Is the shape correct? Are the petticoats sufficient to maintain the proper shape? What is the desired length? Should it be even all around or longer in the back?

7. Are the closures appropriate? Do they work properly? How will the quick change work?

8. Do the accessories work well with the costume?

9. Can the actor perform the action required in the costume? Does the action create undue stress on the costume? Does the action distort the look of the costume in undesirable ways? Is the action appropriate to the character and period? Can the action be performed in other more appropriate ways?

10. What guidance can be given the actor for effective use of the costume?

11. Will another fitting be necessary?

Hats, wigs, shoes, and jewelry can be major consumers of time and money. A great deal of shopping time may be required to find appropriate shoes of the correct size, affordable hats, jewelry of the right type, suitable wigs, and hair accessories.

Constructing a hat may require as much time as making a garment. Hat-making requires some special supplies and equipment that may not be available in a small shop. A milliner may need to be hired for a show with many important hats. Men's hats and women's hat shapes of the correct type may sometimes be purchased from costume specialty houses and trimmed in the costume shop.

Hats that are not removed on stage should be attached securely to hair or wig. Straps of ¼-inch elastic for under the chin or the back of the head should be added where needed. (Straps should be dyed to match skin tone or hair color.) Small combs can be sewn into a hat to help secure it. Horsehair loops through which hairpins can be pinned are also helpful. Hat pins can be used on hats that must be removed onstage, provided there is sufficient hair through which to pin.

Some modification of stock shoes (change of color, addition of decoration or gaiters) is possible. The correct style of toe and heel should be sought for the period. The type of shoe required by the actor for the character's walk and posture should be found. However, fit is crucial. The actor cannot be expected to hobble around in ill-fitting shoes, no matter how period-perfect they are.

Shoes for dancers should be constructed specifically for dancing and purchased through a dance supply house. The addition of heel braces and dance rubber to the heel and/or sole may be required for safety and comfort. Non-dancers may also need these modifications if they run or fight on stage, or if the stage floor is *raked* (built on a sharp slant).

Wigs can be purchased or rented. Special costume wigs are available through costume supply houses, or some commercial styles can be adapted for period use. A sketch should be provided for the wig rental house, and the wig will be dressed accordingly. For shows using many wigs, a wig supervisor should be available for wig maintenance and to assist actors with attaching wigs.

Craft items like masks, armor, and jewelry may require long periods of time for sculpting, making molds, and casting. Large work areas away from garment construction are needed for craft work, which may involve paint, glue, chemical solvents, and other messy materials. Some items can be built on basic shapes purchased from theatrical supply houses, but unusual masks, armor, or jewelry will need to be built. Knowledge of many materials and craft techniques is necessary for the designer to choose the one that produces the most appropriate effect. Research into new materials and experiments with new techniques are part of the designer experience. Theater publications offer articles on solutions to specific craft problems as costumers and designers share discoveries and experiences with new and old materials.

Whatever technique is chosen, accessories should be begun early in the production schedule to ensure their on-time completion. An assistant or crew person assigned specifically to accessory problems helps to keep the work moving.

Preparing for Performance

. . . Go, and make thee ready straight,
In all thy best attire, thy choicest jewells,
Put them all on, and, with them, thy best lookes. . . .

Volpone, Ben Jonson

Organizing the Costumes

As the pieces of each costume are assembled and finished, they should be labeled and put together on a "done rack" or in a cabinet, where they will not be mixed up with items still "in work." Small articles like tights, handkerchiefs, and gloves can be kept in a plastic zip-lock or muslin drawstring bag on a hanger with the larger costume pieces. Very small items like jewelry and crushable accessories like fans are safer in a small box inside the bag. Rack markers with the actors' names help the wardrobe crew and the actors to locate the correct costumes easily. Traveling companies need large trunks, hampers, or wardrobes on wheels designed to keep the costumes organized.

Wardrobe Crew

The wardrobe crew is the staff responsible for the orderly maintenance and use of the costumes during the run of the show. Often this crew begins a few days or a week before first dress rehearsal to help with the organization and finishing of the costumes. In some theaters, some shop personnel may switch over to wardrobe responsibilities as first dress approaches. The designer and shop manager should discuss the maintenance and special requirements of the costumes with the wardrobe supervisor. The designer should instruct the wardrobe crew on the proper sequence of costumes in the show and give them copies of the final costume plot, sketches, and costume lists. A discussion of quick-change problems and special costume situations will help the wardrobe crew prepare and set up the costumes for the dress parade and the first dress. The wardrobe supervisor should attend several run-throughs (rehearsals of the entire play) before the first dress rehearsal for a clear understanding of the onstage action.

The designer and the wardrobe crew organize the backstage changing areas and work out the logistics with the stage manager and properties crew. Pre-planning for backstage costume changes saves a great deal of time and minimizes confusion when dress rehearsals begin. The wardrobe supervisor should make specific requests for the kind of racks, tables, lights, mirrors, and screens that are needed. The setup and organization of the dressing rooms is also the responsibility of the wardrobe crew.

Once the show opens, the wardrobe crew is responsible for the repair, cleaning, and pressing of the costumes. The designer and shop manager should instruct the crew on any special costume care required. For long-running shows the wardrobe supervisor should notify the stage manager or producer if replacement costumes or major repairs are needed.

Dress Parade

Many designers and directors like to schedule a *dress parade,* a time specifically for the director and designer to see each actor on stage in costume and to look carefully at the total effect. The costumes should be seen against the scenery and under appropriate lighting for their effect to be accurately evaluated. Characters who play together in certain scenes should be studied together so the combined effect can be assessed. While in complete costume, actors should try stairways and doors to check for problems. If the schedule permits, a walk-through in costume with time to work trick costumes and quick changes will alleviate many problems before the first dress rehearsal.

Unfortunately, time is often not available for a dress parade. In the professional theater actors and required crews must be paid for their time, and the producer may not wish to incur this extra expense. The dummy show or a quick walk-on before first dress can give the designer and director some of the information provided by the dress parade.

Dress Rehearsals

Dress rehearsals are the time to integrate costumes into the performance. The designer must attend the dress rehearsals to evaluate and assist with adjustments to the costumes. Designer assistance may be necessary to work out quick changes and blocking of special costume effects. The visual balance of the costumes in each scene should be analyzed. Costumes that are too bright may need to be sprayed, dipped, or dyed down. Costumes that fade out or seem too dark may need more colorful trim or accessories. Adjustments may need to be made for any unexpected effects of the lighting. Changes in lighting levels or gel colors may be a faster, better solution than changing the costume. The director, lighting designer, and costume designer should discuss the problems and work out the most expedient and esthetically valid solutions.

The designer may need to work with individual actors to solve movement problems presented by the style or fit of the costume. The goal is to make the actor look and feel at home in the costume and to create the desired visual effect. Period costumes are usually more confining than modern clothes and may alter the posture and movement of the actor. The actor will need time to become accustomed to the feel of such costumes. Practice will be required to handle capes and trains. Some actors will have difficulty with high-heeled boots or shoes.

Costume is part of *performance.* The visual effect of the costumes and the drama of the costumes in motion should be a major contribution to the total effect of the play. Actors should be encouraged to use their costumes for dramatic effect. Many inexperienced actors are overwhelmed by and resist using their costumes. The designer should point out how the costume was designed to enhance the actor's portrayal of the character and offer whatever assistance the actor may need to use the costume effectively. If time was allowed at the final fitting for the actor to work with the costume, there should be less difficulty at the first dress rehearsal.

Actors should be asked not to smoke, drink, eat, or leave the theater in their costumes. Costume items furnished by the actor are to be considered property of the theater while being used in a production. They should be kept with other costume items and cared for by the wardrobe crew. Care should be taken that all costume items are kept safe from damage or theft between performances. The wardrobe crew should be given full instructions on the use of back-up garments.

The wardrobe crew and the designer should make clear notes on adjustments, corrections, and misuse of costumes during dress rehearsals. Notes should include the actor's name, specific costume, act and scene, and the specific problem. Figure 8.21A shows some sample notes from a dress rehearsal. The actor should also be asked to give personal costume notes to the wardrobe crew in writing whenever possible. In the confusion of the dressing rooms, verbal communications may be forgotten or misunderstood. Notes should include the actor's name, the specific costume, and a brief description of the specific problem, as in the example in figure 8.21B.

Some designers take notes on a notebook computer and e-mail the list to the costume shop or wardrobe crew. Actor notes can be given verbally in person, printed out and handed to the actor, or posted on the show's Web site.

Figure 8.21A Dress rehearsal notes. Careful observation at dress rehearsal helps the designer refine the costumes and foresee difficulties.

Making Adjustments

The dress rehearsal period is a hectic time. Changes are made daily based on the notes taken at the previous dress rehearsal. The designer must keep the priorities clearly in mind. The first things to deal with are fitting corrections and solving problems with items with which the actor needs to work. Trim and visual problems can be solved later. The director's notes to the designer must be given careful consideration. Discussion of the director's priorities and the timetable for dealing with notes should follow each rehearsal.

The designer should supervise revisions or corrections and check that all pieces are in usable condition for the next rehearsal. Box 8.O is a designer checklist for dress parades and dress rehearsals.

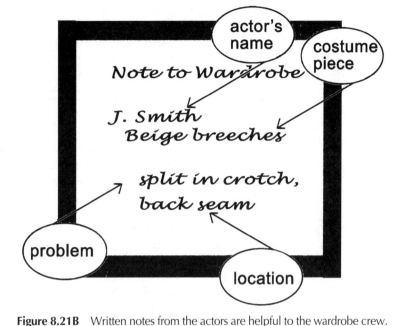

Figure 8.21B   Written notes from the actors are helpful to the wardrobe crew.

Box 8.O   Designer checklist X: Dress parade and dress rehearsals

1. Is everything organized for orderly distribution to the actors? Is the wardrobe crew well briefed?

2. How does each actor look in his or her costume? Does each costume help the actor project character and presence?

3. Do the costumes look good together? Do the appropriate characters stand out? Are adjustments needed?

4. Are all the costumes in the same scale?

5. Do the costumes look complete?

6. Do all costumes function well for the action?

7. How do the lights affect the costumes? Is any costume "glowing" (reflecting too much light) or vibrating?

8. Are there areas of the set that might catch or snag the costumes? Are there problems with using doorways or stairs?

9. Are quick changes smooth? Can improvements be made?

10. Can actors be assisted to use the costumes better?

11. Are the pants and skirt hems the correct length and even? Do petticoats show?

12. What corrections must be made before the next dress rehearsal?

Opening Night

*Brains I have beyond question, with good taste sufficient to pass judgement
and give an opinion on everything without need of study, to sit on the stage
and play the expert at first nights (occasions I dote on) and give a rousing lead
to the audience at all the fine passages that deserve their applause. . . .*

The Misanthrope, Molière

The excitement of rehearsals and preparations culminate with the performance on opening night. The designer must then turn the show over to the wardrobe crew. Running the show becomes their responsibility when the curtain goes up.

On opening night many designers write thank-you notes and/or extend tokens of gratitude to the costume crews and others with whom they have worked on a show. Successful collaboration deserves recognition. This practice creates good will among all parties, but may not erase any serious working problems that existed between designer and staff.

During long-running shows conscientious designers return periodically to check the overall look of the costumes. If the show has begun to look shabby, duplicates of the costumes may be needed. Sometimes the actors become creative with their costumes and alter the way they are worn. The stage manager and wardrobe supervisor should be consulted and corrections made. Diplomatic negotiations may be necessary.

Strike

In some situations the designer is expected to help with the *strike* (closing and putting away) of the show. In repertory, stock, small professional, or educational theater the designer may be responsible for assisting with the final cleaning, storing, return, or disposal of the costumes. Rental costumes should be returned promptly or a late fee may be charged. Added trim must be removed; items removed from the original costume must be returned in the same box. The rental contract should be consulted to determine if the costumes should be cleaned before return. Delay in striking a show may interfere with the schedule of the next show in the costume shop.

Avoiding Hysteria

With all the variables involved in assembling the costumes for a production, there are frequent opportunities for hysteria, flaring tempers, and chaos. The primary reasons for confusion and hysteria are:

1. Poor organization of work.

2. Overdesigning of the show resulting from a lack of consideration or understanding of the limitations of the budget, staff, or time.

3. Failure to meet deadlines.

4. Poor communication between costume designer and director, producer, or shop manager.

5. Lack of experience, self-confidence, or decisiveness on the part of the designer or other staff members.

The designer should work to keep the project well organized and communication open and meaningful. When the designer has a clear vision for the show and has designed the costumes with reasonable consideration of the circumstances of the production, then decisions can be made with relative ease and authority.

The art of the costume designer lies in the ability to create costumes that engage the audience and serve the actor and the production. Beginning with the research and planning the designer does before the sketch, through the supervision and collaboration with the costume shop and the adjustments deemed necessary in rehearsals, the designer's ability is challenged at each level. These enormous challenges make costume design an exciting, stimulating, ever-changing, never boring, rewarding artistic endeavor.

Interview VI.
How to Design for an Elephant.
A Conversation with Gregg Barnes.

At the time of this interview with the author Broadway designer Gregg Barnes had received multiple design awards including a Tony Award, an Outer Critics Circle Award, a Drama Desk Award, an L.A. Drama Critics Award, and other award nominations. (See bio, page 421, for career details.)

RC: How do you approach design for the circus and other large-venue performances?

GB: The circus develops a new show every year for one of its two companies, alternating between the Red Unit and the Blue Unit. Designing for the circus is a long process. I met with the circus representatives once a month for nine months. We started with no concepts. They were just beginning to book the acts when I was invited to participate. The order of the acts kept shifting as new ones were booked. In addition to the acts, there are three parades—*opening, spec, and finale*—where the garments need to be spectacular. Everyone else at the meeting had a circus background with a lot of knowledge and information. It turned out there is a lot to know.

For example, animals are very sensitive to the costumes their trainers wear. Lions and tigers must be acclimated to the costume—the trainer puts on the costume and introduces it to the animals—the lions and tigers must give their approval. You don't want them eating the trainers! And you don't want three-dimensional items on garments worn near the elephants because elephants will eat anything!

Fittings for performers are very important—where does it rub? Does it stretch in the right places? Is there anything to catch on the wires or nets?

Most of the performers in the acts can wear nothing on their heads, and their shoes are determined by the requirements of the act. The performers tend to be small and muscular, so there is a limited amount of "real estate" on which to apply color or decoration—it can't be too fussy and there are new issues all the way up to opening night.

For large-venue costumes, I learned to stand far away and judge things from a distance—as the audience will see them—and to determine the special needs of each type of production. For example, beads falling off the costume on the Broadway stage are annoying, but in the ice show they are actually very hazardous. Also, silk will not hold up to the damp atmosphere of the ice rink. The costumes should look unique, special, and justify the expense.

I learned to be an incredible listener—to the things they were saying and the things they were *not* saying. I learned to be very careful not to overdo, but *to focus on reinforcing the storytelling.*

RC: So, you've got your bag of tricks and you have become known for certain things—how does that influence the other things you do?

GB: It's great to have a niche, but I long to do *Hamlet.* I take other things to keep my hand in. Ultimately it is *a business* and we all have to make a living and cover the cost of our studios. Often the monies for the assistant runs a little short, and you may have to kick in to cover the parts of the job that you are not so keen on doing.

It's hard to even get an interview on a show if the director and the producer don't think of you in the context of that kind of work. I think they look for somebody they are confident in to do the work. Sometimes, when you look through what you are going to bring to the interview, you may not even have something similar.

RC: This brings us to advice for young designers—how do they get started?

GB: When you are young, especially, I think you have to go to the theater as much as you can; you have to expose yourself to as much as you can, not just theater, but dance and opera, and crazy things downtown. Learning through theater experiences as a spectator is a very, very important part of what we do. It is expensive.

Figure VI.1 and VI.2   Two of the Tony-award winning costumes, Kitty and Gangster #1, designed by Gregg Barnes for Broadway's *The Drowsey Chaperone.*

Figure VI.3   A dancer designed by Gregg Barnes for the Broadway production of *The Rhythm Club*.

Figure VI.4   Performer #131designed by Gregg Barnes for The Ringling Bros. Circus.

When you are not sure where your next meal is coming from that seems impossible to do, but there is always a way. You have to be a good networker. You need friends. Make a company manager as your best friend, and you will find yourself with a lot of free tickets. They paper the house when the thing is in preview. Go stand in front of the theater; just get to the theater and—go.

Don't get too locked into your own work. If you are doing sixty-five showcases at the same time, you are only going to learn what sixty-five showcases can teach you. That's a great way to begin, but I think you have to keep your eye on the prize. Ultimately, you have to figure out how to make a living.

It is hard to give advice on this because you can work so many different ways. I had opportunities to assist, but I really didn't want to assist. I had a job I didn't want to lose, a little bit of job security even though it wasn't a big paycheck each month. So I did every single thing that I could manage. Often they were showcases with no fee, not even subway tokens, and I knew that it was costing me money to do them. But my learning curve was enriched by those experiences. Actually, I got to do a lot of Shakespeare, which I haven't gotten to do working as a designer all the time. I don't get that call. But I got to do it; I got to work in a lot of different ways that became part of my destiny, and I am so glad that I have them in my back pocket. I feel like I bring the intelligence of that experience to whatever I am currently asked to be a part of.

I would also say to students, you have to be *healthy*. If you tend to be someone who gets sick easily, you can't do this. You've got to be hearty. That's one thing.

Another thing is people have *to want to spend time with you*. So you can be a brilliant artist, have a brilliant mind, but if you are inner-focused, you will never get to use those talents, because *people have to want to spend time with you*. That's part of it. When you check the back of the playbill, you see that people work together all the time. You can connect the dots on how they got from "a" to "b" to "c" by seeing who they worked with. Obviously, people have relationships that last their entire careers—so that's crucial.

I also think it is really good to be a person who is not afraid to be generous. I know that sounds a little bit crazy, but I find that we are in a very competitive business, and we are sometimes slow to say "thank you" or "job well done." When you are young, even if you don't know the person, and you genuinely admire something you have seen, take the time to get their address and write them a note. Not just because you want a job with them, just do it because you have a generous heart. I think those things come back to you tenfold. I'm not saying I am so good at it myself, but I just feel that you should want to be part of the community. If there's a lecture, or if they are asking you to donate work for Broadway Cares, Equity Fights AIDS, a flea market—donate, go be part of the event. Be a part of the community. It is a *very small* community, and sure enough you will have done something, a kindness here or there, and someone is going to say next week I need somebody to do this task. I am looking for this kind of person, and your name is going to be on their mind. Your talent is sort of taken for granted—if you don't have that, then forget it—but you need so many other things.

Once you actually do get your career going, that nature will then come into the fitting room, into your meetings with producers, and into your relationships with vendors. You know in this business you need a lot of favors to keep yourself afloat. I am always calling up a fabric store, a costume shop, a friend who is a fabric painter and saying, "I'm in a pickle, can you help me out? And if you can, this is what I will do," and they usually won't want anything in return.

You just want to have good relationships with your fellow artisans, I think.

Figure VI.5   The costume for Joy designed by Gregg Barnes for *Cinderella* at The New York City Opera.

Chapter 9

Designing for Film
by Holly Cole

All right, Mr. DeMille, I'm ready for my close-up.

Sunset Boulevard. Paramount Pictures.
Directed by Billy Wilder; written by Billy Wilder,
Charles Brackett, and D.M. Marshman.
Costumes by Edith Head.

Designing costumes for film and television is often associated with the excitement of working with movie stars, exotic locations, and blockbuster budgets. Those elements can be part of the experience, but designers find that compared to working in the theater, the stakes are very high and the pressures are much more intense. Switching from theater to film is not unlike moving from a small town to a big city: the designer has to *think and move faster*.

Learning to See Like a Camera

At every level film work is driven by what can actually be seen through the camera and what "reads" on screen (the details that can really be seen in the finished film). In a film script *POV* notation (film terminology for the camera's "point of view") is vital information for a designer in planning how the costume will be seen on the screen.

The movements and different positions of the camera force the audience to focus on the actor and his/her clothing through a series of different frame sizes. Designers must look closely at what the character's costume design communicates within each frame size, remembering that very often the shooting or editing process will not show the audience the full costume. The standard shots used are: the full face *close-up*, the mid-chest and head *waist-up*, the three-quarter body *loose cowboy*, the full-length *tight shot*, and the full-length distant *wide shot*.

Figure 9.1 *Sunset Boulevard.* Norma Desmond, played by Gloria Swanson. Norma Desmond's scene announcing her readiness for her close-up has become a film classic. Costumes by Edith Head.

| **Scene 2   Int. A Tent Field Hospital Near Forest.** | **Day 1** |

The camera tracks and pans past a series of cots filled with wounded soldiers. Sisters of Mercy nurses hurry past the camera ahead of 2 orderlies bearing a stretcher with a blinded soldier. The camera pans to the opening of the tent.

Long shot. Through the tent flap at the end of the room we can see triage and hear the sound of helicopters arriving with more wounded. We see a cluster of officers rushing the wounded King Duncan toward the hospital tent.

Figure 9.2   POV script notations for a film adaptation of *Macbeth*. Holly Cole.

Design Priorities Must Focus on What Shows in the Shot

The large scale of productions and the overall speed of the prep process in filmmaking force costume personnel to be pragmatic about what needs to be beautifully detailed and what corners can be cut. Fit and surface details become obsessively important in close-ups. Collars must be perfect. Insignia must be right. The jewelry, the quality of the tie, and the "surface truth" (or feel) of the garment's aging all require careful attention. For distant shots, like the background "blur" of extras or the quick pass of a stunt man, the designer may apply a different set of standards: quickly taped hems, imperfect fit, and non-period styles may all be forgiven.

All costume designers learn to identify the most powerful costume details that can be used to reveal a character and the world in which he or she lives. As in theater, some characters appear on the screen for a long time, and some do not. The film designer learns to take into account the length of a character's screen time when designing his or her costumes. The longer the audience sees an actor, the more information the costume designer can express about that character's mood, status, eccentricity, sexuality, and overall personality.

Film and television designers learn to vary the subtlety of their character delineation according to the production format for which they are designing: two-hour feature films, one-hour or half-hour episodic series on TV, 15-minute music videos, or one-minute commercials. Wide-screen images demand exquisite detailing because everything is ten times life-size; television's small-screen images are less demanding. All formats dictate different design solutions for the creation of character arcs and character detailing. A half-hour episodic series may demand very clear and easy-to-read character statements while allowing subtleties to be explored over many episodes. A feature film delineates a character's growth and change in the same way a stage play does—in one continuous sitting. A commercial dictates the same kind of simple and quick delineation of a character that is usually given to the extras in a film.

Just as in the theater, principal characters in film usually get the greatest amount of detailing. However, even extras may require detailed accessories and good fit if they may be caught in short, featured close-ups in the final cut. Because screen time for an extra may be short and sweet, the designer needs to define that character in a glance. Extras should make enough of a statement to be recognized

A

B

C

quickly as a character type, and then they should visually "go away" so the audience can concentrate on the principal players. Like in theater, color-palette control for the extras and color contrast with the lead characters helps designers achieve the desired focus on the leads.

The camera adds a sensual element to the image; the audience emotionally *feels* the camera's viewpoint. Camera movement and close-up views heighten our tactile sense (*sense of visual texture*) of the visual details (e.g., the creamy-smooth skin of the leading lady, the supple softness of a designer jacket). The intensity of this experience empowers the film's visual details and amplifies their impact on the audience—which is why the color of an actor's eyes can be so startling, the strength of a red shirt (as opposed to green) so commanding, or the sensual softness of a fine wool suit or an angora sweater so moving. The viewer almost feels the visual texture on their skin. The camera makes the visual harmony of the film world so palpable that any flaw is magnified on the screen.

To use this tactile power, the designer has to develop the art of knowing what the camera loves. A film designer may ask: Why are some people more photogenic than others? What is it about their bone structure, their skin's texture, or their coloring that makes them look so good on the screen? Every designer at some time will ask: Why did the dress look great in the fitting and fall flat on the screen? Some of the answers lie in how the image is lit,

Figure 9.3   The multiple camera points of view. (A) Full-length tight shot, (B) waist-up, and (C) close-up. Photos by Kristen Vaughan.

some in the color and textural harmonies of the atmosphere around the character. Other answers may be found in how well the garment is fitted, how gracefully it moves on the actor, and how well the texture reads on the camera. Designers must focus both on the *context* of the character's image within the scene, and on the *costume details* that dominate when the camera zooms in or

out. Designers can lose the audience's perspective if they only look at the costume up close; some distance is necessary to see what dominates the whole image.

Lighting, POV framing, and the camera's manipulation of depth of field have an enormous impact on how beautifully a form is sculpted and how accurately textures and colors are revealed. Because cinematographers control these aspects of filmmaking, they are very powerful in the film industry. They even have the authority to dictate the color palette of a film. Films generally take more care with their lighting and camera set-ups than television programs. This care creates a stronger mood and a richer, more detailed, more luxurious look to the images.

Since costume designers cannot control how their garments are lit, they must aim to present their costumes as camera-worthy as possible; however, making a costume look really good on the screen is a very complex art. Designers should plan carefully for their color palette to work well with the set and with the film stock and film processing being used. (Different brands of film and different kinds of film processing can distort colors.) They should look at the costume as if through a

Figure 9.4 *The Producers.* Pearl Girl. See Interview V (pp. 206–209) for the designer's comments. Compare this film costume with the costumes for the Broadway production of *Gold Girls* (color plate 28 and color plate 29). Photo property of William Ivey Long Studios, Inc.

series of frames to check how the fit and textural details read. They can ask the actor to move during the fitting to see how the fabric flows with the body's movement. Broadway and film designers have learned that workrooms that use couture-quality finishing techniques (interfacings, beautiful linings, hand-stitched detailing) improve the way garments lay on the body; high-quality fabrics and custom fit help the garments move better on the actor.

Custom-made goods can adjust the proportions of a design to perfectly fit any actor's body and hand tailoring or proper understructures can mold the garment to the form, producing that glamorous "looks-just-right" garment on the actor. This is vital if the actor has difficult proportions (like a bodybuilder) or serious body flaws (like stooped shoulders, spinal scoliosis, or a dowager's hump). Period tailoring, compared to modern tailoring, also demands subtly different proportions and construction techniques to get the look as authentic as possible. Period women's wear requires perfect period underpinnings to get the correct proportions and line of the garment.

The heightened tactile sense that the camera creates makes the viewer especially sensitive to the feel and depth of texture and color. Beautiful fabrics are one of the reasons that designer-label goods work well on camera. A rayon crepe moves better than a polyester crepe. The supple wools used in some designer suits just seem to mold to the body. Beautiful silks have a more luxurious luster and movement than any other type of fabric. Great film designers develop an eye for materials that work beautifully on the body *and* look good on camera.

Film designers also study what looks "real"—the glamorous fit and feel of couture clothing is not right for all characters. Designers study how people really wear clothing, and what colors are seen repeated in a mass of people. They look at how garments really age and break down; how colors and textures change as garments are repeatedly worn and washed. Compared to theater, film productions need more subtly detailed realistic images. Instead of the bold painting techniques used for theatrical aging, film requires finely detailed surfaces. Film *distressers* (or *agers*) prefer to use bleach and heavy washing effects to get garments to soften, and to use dye and ironed-in colored waxes to get color into the fibers, so that the surfaces will read as authentically aged as possible. (See examples of distressed garments for film in color plate 30.)

Understanding the Costume Process for Film

To work in the film industry, the designer must become oriented to the standard working conditions found there.

Perpetually Evolving Productions are the Norm

Scripts evolve. Much like working on a new play in the theater, new scripts and a constant flow of script changes are common in the film industry. *Staffing evolves.* Casting is ongoing throughout the production's development and *very*

C-17 *Peter Pan*. Pirate. This sketch by Gregg Barnes demonstrates a complex layering of watercolor wash with some resist techniques, overlaid with touches of opaque paint that suggest sparkle. Designed for the Paper Mill Playhouse.

C-18 *La Levedad de las Enaquas (The Lightness of Crinolines)*. The Blue Girl. This sketch is an example of computer-assisted design. Designed by Eloise Kazan for the Humanicorp Dance Company. (See box 6.A for description of technique.)

C-19 *Love's Labour's Lost.* Dumoine and Berowne (A). Princess (B). These sketches by Catherine Zuber were developed on a computer from hand-drawn figures that were scanned and enhanced in an art program. Designed for the Shakespeare Theatre.

Dumoine 4.1   Berowne 2.1

C-20 *The Merry Wives of Windsor.* Falstaff. A profusion of printed fabrics in subtle colors is combined in this costume to suggest the "crazy quilt," patchwork quality of the town. Designed by Michelle Ney for the Illinois Shakespeare Festival.

C-21 *Bella Rosa Polka.* Bella Rosa. This sketch shows a cowgirl skirt and vest hand-painted with textile paints in a broad decorative style. Designed by the author for Brooklyn College.

C-22 *Burn This.* Anna in Flame Dress. This sketch shows a dress with a hand-painted ombré effect—one color blending into another. Designed by Laura Crow for Broadway, the Plymouth Theatre.

C-23 *Tempest.* Goddess. Appliquéing fabric swatches and bits of color on the backside of thin plastic created the fabric for this costume. The goal was to suggest that Prospero conjured up the wedding masque from debris that had washed up on his island. Designed by Bill Brewer for the British Resident International Theatre at the University of South Florida. Photo by Bill Brewer.

THE TEMPEST   WEDDING MASQUE x2

C-24 *Swan Lake.* Spanish Dancers. Ethnic detail creates the Spanish look of these traditionally cut ballet costumes designed by Paul Tazewell for the Pacific Northwest Ballet.

C-25 *Thoroughly Modern Millie.* Millie at the Speakeasy. This flapper dress designed by Tony-award winner Martin Pakledinaz has retained its twenties glitz and glamour, but has been cut to allow for complex dance movements. Broadway.

C-26 *The Hard Nut.* Dancer. For this quirky re-choreographing of *The Nutcracker,* Martin Pakledinaz drew on mid-twentieth-century fashion sources for these witty snowflakes. Designed for the Mark Morris Dance Group. Photo by Peter DaSilva.

RINGLING BROS. AND BARNUM AND BAILEY CIRCUS

C-27 Circus Stilt Walker. Gregg Barnes incorporated and disguised the stilts in the boots of this colorful and glittery costume for the Circus SPEC (spectacular) parade. Designed for Ringling Bros. and Barnum & Bailey Circus.

C-28 *The Producers.* Gold Girls (sketch, bottom left). William Ivey Long designed the costume for this production number on stage to read from some distance and to hold up to rigorous use and daily wear. Designed for Broadway.

C-29 *The Producers.* Gold Girls (photo). Mathew Broderick and Showgirls. Designed by William Ivey Long for Broadway. Photo © Paul Kolnik.

C-30 Film distressing. Costumes for film require subtle, careful distressing because the camera may come in very close and catch obvious or clumsy aging attempts. Photos by Holly Cole.

SCENE 2 INT. A TENT FIELD HOSPITAL NEAR FORREST   DAY 1
The camera tracks and pans past a series of cots filled with wounded soldiers. Sisters of Mercy nurses hurry past the camera ahead of 2 orderlies bearing a stretcher with a blinded soldier. The camera pans from the soldier's face to the opening of the tent.

*Helicopter pilot
Doctors
Nurses
Wounded orderlies*

Long shot. *Through the tent flap at the end of the room we can see triage and hear the sound of helicopters arriving with more wounded. We see a cluster of officers rushing the wounded King Duncan towards the hospital tent.*

*Duncan #10
Malcolm #10
Donalbain #1
Lennox #1
Bloody Srgt #1*

Medium close-up. *A bleeding King DUNCAN hobbles in supported by a doctor, MALCOLM, DONALBAIN, LENNOX, and Attendants. Nurses and officers rush to him with bandages, supplies, and messages from the field.*

Close-up *on Duncan's face as he looks back towards the battle*
DUNCAN: What bloody man is that?

Pants torn for bandaging?

Over Duncan's shoulder *we see a badly wounded sergeant yelling for the King who runs and stumbles towards the tent opening.*
DUNCAN Voice Over: He can report, as seemeth by his plight, of the revolt.

Blood doubles for nurses, doctor?

Stunt rig - squirting blood

Medium close-up *on the bloody sergeant, supported by MALCOLM*
MALCOLM: This is the sergeant who like a good and hardy soldier fought 'gainst my captivity. Hail, brave friend! Say to the king the knowledge of the broil as thou didst leave it.

Close-up. BLOODY SERGEANT: Doubtful it stood;
The merciless Macdonwald-- from the western isles of kerns and gallowglasses is supplied; and fortune, on his damned quarrel smiling.
But brave Macbeth--well he deserves that name--disdaining fortune, with his brandish'd steel . . . *he looks towards the battle outside and the scene shifts to*

SCENE 2a EXT. THE BATTLE   **Flashback**
Macbeth, with a machine gun mowing down his enemies as he fights his way toward Macdonwald in the battlefield

*Macbeth #1, lxs
Macdonwald #1
Stunts?
Norwegian soldiers?
Scottish soldiers?*

SERGEANT V.O. . . . which smoked with bloody execution carved out his passage till he faced the slave. He unseam'd him from the nave to the chaps,

Close-up. *Macbeth looks down at Macdonwald's corpse and fires a burst across the corpse's neck, severing the head.*
Macbeth picks the head up and strides toward the tank that is coming up behind him, his men cheering. He jumps onto the tank, the head held high, and hooks the head onto the gun turret.

*Tank crew?
Stunt Man?
Stunt double 1x*

C-31 Film notations. Careful study of and notations on the script are the first steps to preparing costumes for a film shoot. Holly Cole.

KEY		
Featured men — blue highlight	Stunt Doubling — green underlining	
Featured women — pink highlight	Blood Doubling — red underlining	
Extras — gray highlight	Costume Notes/Questions — gray underlining or circle	
With Change numbers — "x" indicates state of distress, "d" indicates a doubled change		

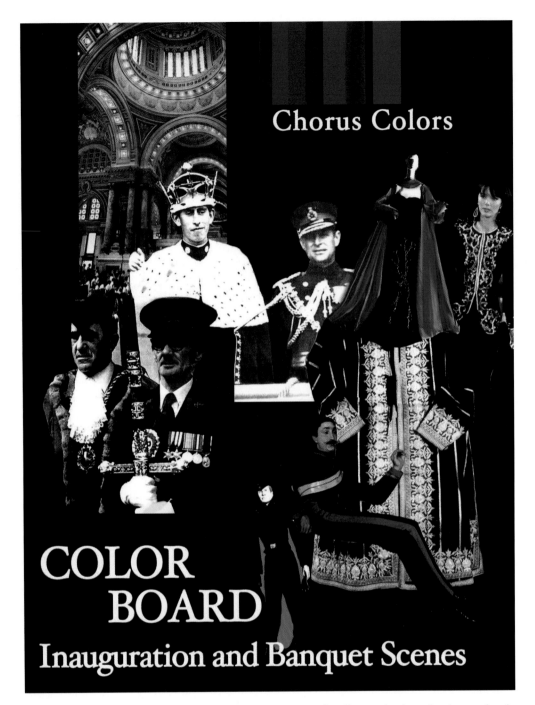

C-32 Color boards of research and concept images are used in film work where the time to sketch is severely limited. Holly Cole.

late casting is the norm. Many actors work only a few days of the film shoot. A few of the production's design and tech staff work the entire preparation and shooting periods, but most are brought in for limited periods of time. *Performances evolve.* Rehearsals for films are kept to a minimum, and very few are rehearsed in advance of shooting. Acting evolves on the set as scenes are shot multiple times to capture the best performance. The performance is then shaped in the cutting and editing process. Unlike in the theater, a film costume designer never sees the whole production while designing the film.

Short Preparation Periods are the Norm

Costumes may be planned from two years to two days to two minutes before the cameras start to roll. The industry assumes that until a costume is *established* (recorded on film during the shoot), the design is not finalized; many costume details can shift at the last minute to improve the look on camera or to enhance the actor's performance. Like the costume adjustments that happen during dress rehearsals in the theater, the film costume is fine-tuned on the set just minutes before the camera captures the performance.

Figure 9.5 Film costume designers need to observe the fit and detailing of garments on real people. Photos by KristenVaughan.

Higher budgets tend to imply longer prep and shooting periods, but production companies are increasingly cutting back on how much time is allotted to make a movie or television show. Even complicated period films commonly have only about four weeks of *prep* (pre-production preparation period), and television episodes may have only two or three days. Costume personnel have to know how to "hustle," and careers can be built based on how quickly designers can put costume stocks and wardrobe teams together. Experienced personnel can adapt to every kind of situation by knowing the nitty-gritty of where to shop, rent, build, and borrow what they need and who to call when they need help.

Working Conditions Are Expected to Vary in Film

Films and television programs may be shot (1) on a *sound stage* (like a theater, a sound stage is a warehouse equipped and designed to support filming and recording sound within a carefully controlled environment) or (2) *on location* (a site converted to support filming by trucking in equipment, personnel, and scenic elements). Location shooting demands nomadic work strategies for all the production departments. Wardrobe departments go mobile using *dressing room trailers* for the principal actors and special *wardrobe trailers* for costume storage. When a Broadway show tours, it also must plan to bring equipment, stock, and supplies, but the company also knows that each tour site has at least a stage and dressing rooms. On a film location costume construction work, fittings, and extras dressing rooms are improvised at the shooting site—a tent, a gas station bathroom, or the sidewalk—may all be appropriated.

Figure 9.6
When shooting on location, all equipment and personnel must be transported and set up at the site. Photograph by Jack H. Cunningham.

Working on exterior locations means coping with changes in the weather, problems with the terrain, or long hikes to the set—to name only a few of the headaches that can cause production delays and difficulties. Filmmaking personnel are expected to plan for and cope with difficult shooting conditions regularly; these demands are part of the film adventure and part of the reason the pay scale is significantly higher for film than for the theater.

Figure 9.7 Wardrobe trailers. Large trailers outfitted with (A) racks, storage drawers, washers and dryers, ironing and steaming equipment. (B) Worktables and supplies are required for shooting on location. Photos by Jack H. Cunningham.

A

B

Films Are Rarely Shot in Continuity

Unlike a theater performance, a film is usually not developed scene by scene from the beginning to the end of the story (*in continuity*). Some television situation comedies, soap operas, game shows, and news programs may be shot in continuity, but any production that shoots on locations faces the need to shoot scenes out of sequence. Because moving production personnel and equipment from place to place is costly and each shooting location can involve logistics, contracts, permits, and permissions to prepare and adjust the site for shooting, standard policy in the film industry is that all shooting schedules take maximum advantage of each location. Scenes are shot according to what takes place at each specific location. Therefore, all the scenes requiring the same location are shot one after another, no matter what their original script order (shooting *out of continuity*).

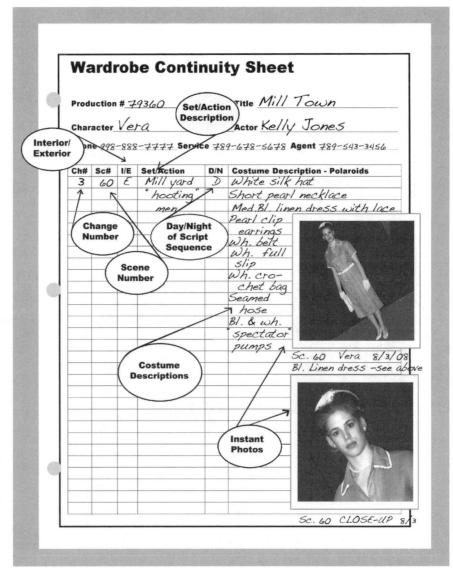

Figure 9.8 A wardrobe continuity sheet is prepared with pictures of each principle actor as he or she leaves the set. This record of the costume details is necessary in case a reshoot of the scene is required. Photos by Kristen Vaughan.

For film wardrobe departments this means carefully taking note of the way characters wear their clothes from scene to scene to make sure that their looks match in a continuous film sequence. This is called *tracking costume continuity*. The wardrobe staff takes pictures of each of the costumed characters after they have been filmed to record the exact details of the costume as caught on film. The jewelry that was worn, the position of a scarf, the number of buttons that were unbuttoned, the angle of the hat—all are important details to record.

Developing the Design for the Production

The costumes for a film are put together in two phases: the *prep* phase in which the design is planned and most of the costume stock is gathered, organized, and prepared; and the *shoot* phase, during which some costume personnel dress the actors *on-set* while others prepare for future scenes.

The Prep Process

Although the job titles, language, and responsibilities of filmmaking are a bit different, the overall development of the costume stock for a film has much in common with costuming for the theater.

Collaborating on the Design: A Variation on Theater's Approach. Preparing for a film requires the costume designer to collaborate with a director and a team of designers, which includes the *art director* or *production designer* (the film equivalent of theater's set designer), the *cinematographer* or *director of photography* (who replaces the theater's lighting designer by heading both the camera *and* lighting departments), and the hair and make-up designers.

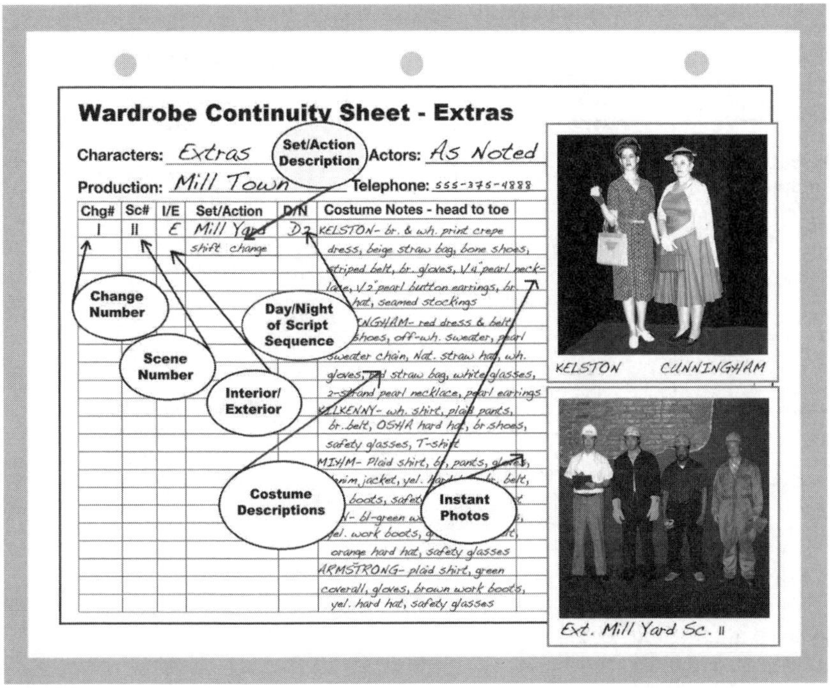

Figure 9.9 Even the details of extras costumes must be tracked for retakes on continuity sheets. Photos by Kristen Vaughan.

Film and television directors come from many different backgrounds—writing, performing, camera work, and theater. Theatrically trained film directors usually have formal education in design areas, but other film directors may not. Some directors are acutely uncomfortable talking about clothes or responding to costume sketches. Many need to see the actor *in* the garment to know if they like it. Particularly for these directors, conferencing with *photo boards* and *photo collage sketches* can be very useful. (See figures 9.11A and 9.12B [p. 280], and color plate 32.)

Film designers face many of the same challenges that theater designers face when designing for a very busy director or with a very busy design team. For film directors and producers design presentations need to be uncluttered and visually compelling. The director wants to see the *character*, not the costume. Quaint fashion drawings or dull research details that do not create a "life" for the director are detrimental to the collaboration process. Well-edited *tear sheets* (photo research collages) that clearly communicate the taste and condition of the characters and a well-prepared rack of clothes for the director and design team to review are good ways to establish a quick rapport and understanding.

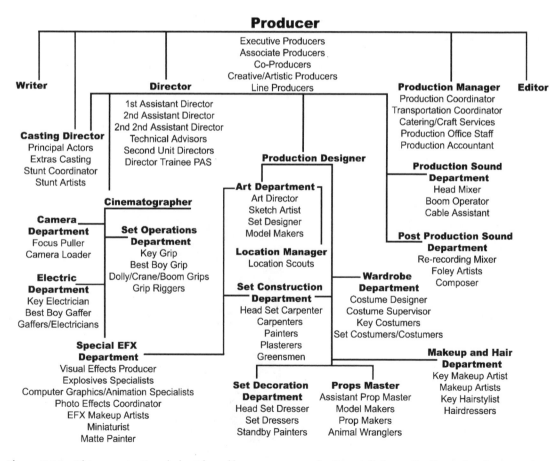

Figure 9.10   This organizational chart for a film company production staff shows the lines of authority and responsibility of personnel working on a film.

Macbeth
changes 1 & 2

Figure 9.11   The photo board of a series of costumed characters (A) was prepared to help the designer and the director discuss the "look" for the extras. The collage sketch (B) illustrates clearly the costume changes planned for *Macbeth*. These could be created with scanned images on the computer or by pasting up magazine cutouts. Holly Cole.

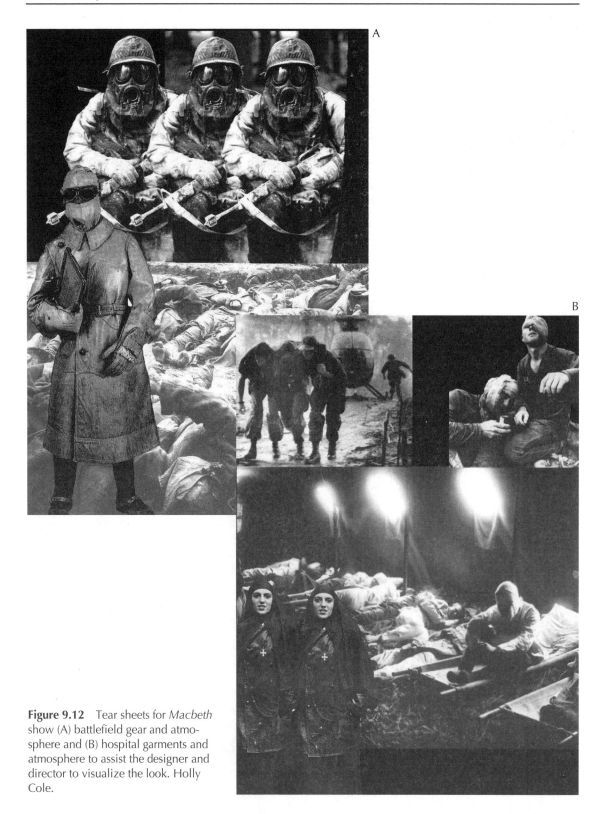

Figure 9.12 Tear sheets for *Macbeth* show (A) battlefield gear and atmosphere and (B) hospital garments and atmosphere to assist the designer and director to visualize the look. Holly Cole.

Color boards are particularly useful for working with the cinematographer and the production designer, both of whom will be particularly interested in the color palette and the tonal range within the palette for each scene.

Collaborating within the Costume Area.   The costume designer also collaborates with the film's *wardrobe department* and any costume shops that build or alter costumes for the film. Unlike a theater's wardrobe crew, who are exclusively focused on *maintaining* the look of the costumes delivered to the theater, a film's wardrobe department focuses on *acquiring* the costuming stock, *fitting* and *styling* the characters (with the help of construction and alteration services from costume shops), and *maintaining* the look of the production. Figure 9.14 (on the following page) shows how a wardrobe department for film is organized.

Figure 9.13   Preparing a rack review (A) or a dummy show (B) of proposed costumes are other ways to help the director visualize the costume look. Holly Cole.

Figure 9.14 An organizational chart for a film wardrobe department indicates how costume personnel relate to each other and to the costume work.

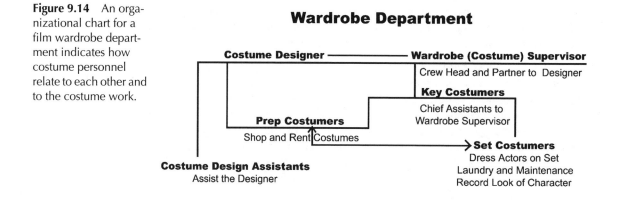

Breaking down the script and setting budget strategies: A variation on the theater approach.   During the prep period, the film costume designer works with the wardrobe supervisor to set strategies for gathering and preparing clothing for the characters. A wardrobe supervisor performs many of the functions that belong to a costume design assistant in the theater, in addition to supervising the wardrobe crew. (Many productions do not hire design assistants for this reason.) Together, the designer and the wardrobe supervisor share responsibilities for research, *script breakdown* (script analysis focusing on the size of the costume load), and *budget breakdown* (the development of a budget estimating all the clothing, accessories, services, supplies and equipment needed for the run of the shoot). After the initial breakdowns determine the workload and budget priorities, the designer and wardrobe supervisor generate additional character and scene "breakouts" to refine the workload and prepare for the shopping, fitting, and the run of the costumes. (See color plate 31 for an example of *Macbeth* script notation and analysis.) Because filmmaking almost always involves working on a new, developing script, the costume budgets and the costume load are readjusted as the script and production evolve, as happens in the theater when a new play is being produced.

Like script analysis for the theater, formulating the film breakdown requires a carefully detailed analysis of the script's action, atmospheres, and events, and the passage of time in order to determine the number of changes that each character will need. Location shooting, stunt and special effects work, and the evolving nature of film productions place increased demands on the costume team's ability to anticipate all the needs and costs of the production. In general, the costume designer focuses on the artistic needs of the design; the wardrobe supervisor focuses on the practical requirements of the shoot.

Stunts require special planning, whether they are as simple as pushing actors into a swimming pool or as complex as dragging them under a truck or setting them on fire. Stunts require a wide variety of padding and protective gear (generally provided by the stuntpeople themselves). For example, costumes that use *squibs* (small, radio-controlled explosives for bullet effects) require protective padding under each squib for the explosion to work safely. Fire can require both fireproofing the costume and a full fireproof bodysuit worn next to the skin. Immersion in water can require flesh-colored diving suits under the clothing to protect the actors during long hours of shooting. Any of the protective gear used will impact the fit and look of the costume worn over it, so *costume duplicates* may be needed to maintain the look of the design.

Costume duplicates also are required for a *stunt double* (a specialist who replaces or doubles for an actor in a stunt) or for characters involved in action that gets their clothing dirty. These *distress doubles* are used to *restore* the original look of a character for reshooting a scene quickly or to *preserve* different phases of distress for scenes that are filmed out of sequence. For example, a character getting stabbed and gushing blood may be filmed from several different angles; each new camera POV requires reshooting the scene from scratch with a clean set of clothes. Or the hero's stabbing might be filmed *before* the scene where he is first seen in the clean outfit (requiring a minimum of two duplicates: one clean and one bloody); and later in the shooting schedule the bloody outfit is seen again (necessitating the bloody outfit be preserved for later in the shoot). Costume designers and wardrobe supervisors must gamble on the number of copies

Figure 9.15 This *Macbeth* scene breakout sheet lists scene-by-scene the costumes needed for each principle character and the condition and stress that is required of each.

SCENE COSTUME BREAKOUT   **MACBETH FILM PROJECT**

Sc #	D/N	Set/Action	I/E	Character	Change	Costume	Notes	
1	D1	Fringe of Battlefield, witches in storm	E	Witch 1	1D	Bag lady refugee	Rain and mud	BL
				Witch 2	1D	Bag lady refugee		BL
				Witch 3	1D	Bag lady refugee		BL
				Dead soldiers	1	Both armies	Bloody and torn	
2	D1	Tent, field hospital	I	Duncan, wounded	1D	General's field dress	Left leg wound, pants ripped for bandaging	RD
				Malcolm	1D	Officer field dress	Gets bloody	RD
				Donalbain	1	Officer field dress		
				Lennox	1	Officer field dress		
				Bloody sergeant	1S	Sergeant field dress	Spurting blood rigging	RD
				Ross	1	Officer field dress		
				Four Sisters of Mercy	1D	Nun nurses	2 bloodied	RD
				2 soldier orderlies	1	Orderly field dress	Hospital unit patches	
				Wounded soldiers	1	Mix of uniform parts, bandages and underwear	On stretchers & cots	
				Battle dress couriers	1	Battle dress	Courier pouches and walkie-talkies	
				Triage army doctors	1D	Field dress doctors and surgeons		RD
2a	flshbk	Muddy battlefield w/ tank Macbeth kills Macdonwald	E	Macdonwald	1S	Battle dress enemy officer	Beheaded during fighting	RD
				Macbeth	1S	Battle dress officer	w/ machine gun	RD
				Banquo	1D	Battle dress officer	Bloodied and war torn	BR
				Enemy foot soldiers	1	Enemy battle dress	Bloodied and war torn, mix of stunts	BR
				Scottish foot soldiers	1	Battle dress	Bloodied and war torn, mix of stunts	BR

KEY	S – indicates a *stunt*		
	E – indicates *exterior*	BLUE indicates *water*	BL
	D – indicates a *destructive action* requiring costume multiples	BROWN indicates *dirt*	BR
	I – indicates *interior*	RED indicates *blood*	RD
	FLSHBK – indicates *flashback*		

Figure 9.16 The *Macbeth* extras summary breakdown sheet organizes the costumes for the extras that will be used in various scenes.

MACBETH Extras Summary Breakdown

Sc#	D/N	I/E	Set/Action	Costume types	Notes	Quantity
1, 3	D1	E	Battlefield,			
24	D7	I	Macbeth's castle call to arms		Muddy, bloody	
26, 27	N7	E	Final battle	Scottish battle dress	soldiers & dead	100
1, 2, 3	D1/N1				Rigging for	
26, 27	N1	E/I	Battlefield and hospital scenes	Scottish wounded soldiers	gushing wounds	50
1, 2, 3	D1	E	Opening battles	Norwegian battle dress		70
4,	N1	I	Duncan's field office,			
6,11	D2/D3	E	Arrival & departure from Macbeth's,			
7, 8, 9	N2	I	Macbeth's home party,		Add traveling	
18	D5	I	Macduff's home attack,		coats for scenes	
24	D7	I	Castle gossip and watch	Scottish BDU field uniform	6,11,18	75
5, 6, 7,	D2			Macbeth's house servant		
8, 9, 11	D2/N2	I	Macbeth household & party scenes	dress		15
7, 8, 9	N2	I	Macbeth's house party	Whores & entertainers		35
12, 14	D4/N4	I	Macbeth's Coronation & banquet	Scottish dress mess formal uniform		100
12	D4/N4	E/I	Macbeth's Coronation	Diplomatic day wear		50
				Court lady day wear		50
12	D4/N4	E/I	Banquet party	Diplomatic evening wear		50
				Court lady evening wear		100

KEY	Sc # - scene number	D - day	N - night	I – interior	E - exterior

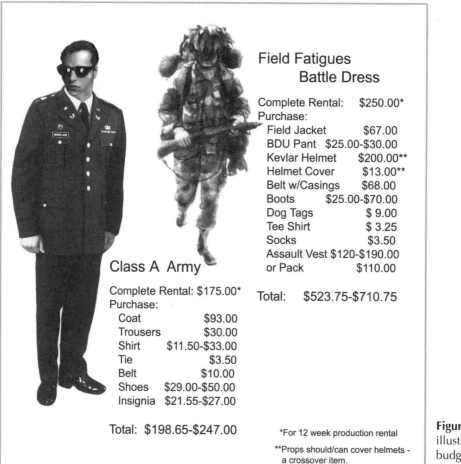

Field Fatigues
Battle Dress

Complete Rental: $250.00*

Purchase:
Field Jacket $67.00
BDU Pant $25.00-$30.00
Kevlar Helmet $200.00**
Helmet Cover $13.00**
Belt w/Casings $68.00
Boots $25.00-$70.00
Dog Tags $ 9.00
Tee Shirt $ 3.25
Socks $3.50
Assault Vest $120-$190.00
or Pack $110.00

Total: $523.75-$710.75

Class A Army

Complete Rental: $175.00*

Purchase:
Coat $93.00
Trousers $30.00
Shirt $11.50-$33.00
Tie $3.50
Belt $10.00
Shoes $29.00-$50.00
Insignia $21.55-$27.00

Total: $198.65-$247.00

*For 12 week production rental

**Props should/can cover helmets - a crossover item.

Figure 9.17 This illustration shows a budget breakdown for a uniformed character.

A

Fabric:
  Chiffon (3 layers) 10 - 15 yds
    Lame chiffon
    Metallic chiffon
    Beaded chiffon
      $14 to $28 a yd.
  Underdress Silk 5 yds.
    $15 a yd

Built-in Foundation

Labor Costs:
  $3,000 low-end
  $8,000 - $9,000 norm
  $14,000 high-end

B

Fabric:
  Velvet 7-9 yds.

    $23 a yd. for rayon, or
    $45 a yd. for silk

Built-in Foundation

Labor Costs:

  $3,000 low-end
  $5,000 norm
  $7,500 high-end

Figure 9.18   Sketches A and B illustrate two MTO costume designs and their estimated costs with variants in fabric prices and labor. Holly Cole.

of a garment that may be needed because action often evolves on the set and may become more messy and violent than anticipated.

Gathering and Developing the Costume Stock: A Variation on Theater's Approach. Based on the breakdown of the script, the costume designer and the wardrobe supervisor share the responsibilities for picking and directing the crew, directing the purchasing and organization of the costume stock, supervising fittings, and delivering the costumes on time and on budget. Work priorities are set by the *shooting schedule* (the production's calendar for what will be shot each day). The shooting schedule drives all the priorities for the prep and shoot phases of the production for all production departments.

Just like in the theater, film wardrobe may be rented, built by costume shops, or bought from clothing stores. Broadway companies and most film production companies do not own shops like regional theaters and university theaters do; any costumes that must be constructed must be contracted out to workrooms that specialize in the construction of custom-made (*made-to-order* or *MTO*) garments. Film studios from the Hollywood glory days of the 1930s (such as Warner Brothers, MGM, and Disney) can provide workrooms and costume rental collections to their productions, but many more film production companies rely on buying or creating these services.

Because films often require hundreds of costumes and often have a surprisingly small costume staff, their costume stocks must be kept beautifully organized to keep personnel working at maximum efficiency. Special emphasis is placed on the tagging and organization of the stock so that each character's garments can be found very quickly.

By using many costume sources, the costumes for a production can become physically spread out. The bigger the production, the more problematic it becomes for the wardrobe department to make sure everything works together and can be delivered to the shoot when needed. To ease this situation film designers and wardrobe supervisors sometimes rent office and storage space to create a *home base* where they can gather their wardrobe stock and prepare for the shoot. The home base may be as simple as a lockable storage area with a desk and phone or as elaborate as a warehouse with an office area, mini costume shop and fitting area,

---

General Storage Organization

Principal player rack stock:

Male characters	A	B	C	D	Female characters A	B	C
Change #	1,2,3,4	1,2,3,4	1,2,3,4	1,2,3,4	1,2,3,4	1,2,3,4,5,6	1,2,3,4,5,6

Boxed accessories tucked under the different changes.

Menswear general rack stock:

Shirts	Vests	Sweaters	Sport coats	Pants	Suits	Jackets	Overcoats	Belts	Suspenders
Hats: felt	Hats: straw	Jewelry	Underwear	Sox: light	Sox: dark	Tennis shoes	Dress shoes		

Menswear boxed stock tucked under the rack.

Women's wear general rack stock:

Blouses	Vests	Sweaters	Jackets	Skirts	Pants	Suits	Dresses	Overcoats	Scarves	Belts
Hats	Jewelry	Bras	Panties	Slips	Sox: light	Sox: dark	Hose	Flat shoes	Heels	Purses

Women's wear boxed stock tucked under the rack.

Children's wear rack storage: *Uniform rack storage:*   *Stunt rack storage:*

Infants	Boys	Girls	Cops	Army	Medical	Stunt doubles	Nomex
Hats	Sox	Shoes		Hats	Belts	Shoes	Pads

Figure 9.19 An organizational chart for film wardrobe stock. Garments are hung in logical groups following head-to-toe guidelines and in size sequence small to large to simplify and speed their retrieval.

and laundry and dye facilities. On very, very low-budget films the home base may be the back of the designer's car, and the fittings may be done in the actors' homes or at the shooting site.

Fittings are done for *principal players* (the lead actors) and *featured day players* (actors who are featured in some scenes) as they are available during the prep period. *Extras* are fit in advance of the shoot only if fitting them at the shooting site is impractical. For example, extras that wear sci-fi stormtrooper or monster suits may require trickier-than-usual fittings or time-consuming alterations not easily done on location. Period and sci-fi films usually pre-fit a good percentage of their extras.

Films almost universally costume extras in mass calls where many characters are each "styled" in 15 minutes or less. Film wardrobe departments try to accumulate stocks that can accommodate a broad range of sizes because most films must provide *walk-in styling* for the extras to keep the alteration workload reasonable and to provide instant clothing options for the director's approval.

After an actor's fitting, costume personnel carefully photograph, tag, and hang together costume pieces to specific *costume units* or *costume changes*.

Figure 9.20   All pieces of each costume are hung together in a garment bag and tagged with the actor's name and/or number to reduce lost pieces and confusion. Photo by Jack H. Cunningham.

This provides both a photographic and a written record of all of the details of each character's costume change for refiling and reshooting purposes. As the film is shot and costumes are adjusted, a continuity sheet is kept for each change and additional photos are taken to keep accurate records of the character's look on camera.

As the prep period draws to a close the set costumers arrive to help with final preparations for shooting. If location shooting is involved, wardrobe trailers are prepared and the costume stock is divided so that any garments, supplies, or equipment needed on the set will be available in the trailers. Once shooting begins, the set becomes the new *home base* for wardrobe operations. The wardrobe set-up area that was the base of operations for the prep may continue as a storage facility and prep area for future shooting, but the heart and soul of the wardrobe department shifts to the set with the shooting.

The Shooting Process: Developing the Performance

I make this look good. . . .

Men In Black. Directed by Barry Sonnenfeld;
written by Lowell Cunningham,
Robert Gordon, and Bobby Fanaro.
Costumes by Mary E. Vogt.

For theater designers the filmmaking process fundamentally changes their understanding of the development of a performance. Every day of a film shoot is an "opening night." The clothing must be perfect every time the camera rolls, but unlike theater, each day's performance is different. The entire story of a film is not seen until each scene is shot, the film processed, and the processed film stock cut and edited together to create one complete story. There are no dress rehearsals where designers can adjust the costumes before the audience comes in; once the camera rolls the costume is *set* (established).

"Rehearsing" is redefined in the filmmaking process. In theater rehearsing is the "organic" part of the process—things grow and change as the actors rehearse. When the show opens, the performance "freezes" so that the viewer who sees the show next month will be as happy as the viewer who sees the show today.

Most films do not have significant pre-shoot rehearsal periods; the "organic" part of the process happens while the camera is rolling for *take* (filmed performance of a scene) after take. To prepare a shot the actors will go through a *camera blocking rehearsal* to choreograph how the camera needs to move to clearly capture the actors' action. Then, each scene is shot repeatedly to explore the actors' performances, to get the best, most "alive" performance, and to cover a variety of viewpoints to keep things visually interesting and to provide options for the editing process. Text, acting, and design all evolve in response to the immediate shooting circumstances. Anything can change on the set—and regularly does.

Shooting scenes over and over again means that working on the set involves a lot of "hurry up and wait" for the costume staff—hurry to get the characters in costume before shooting begins, then wait while the scene is shot numerous times. Every day that new costumes are established, the costume designer comes to the set and works with the set costumers to style and/or tweak the look of the characters. Scenes with large numbers of extras require rapid styling by all the members of the wardrobe staff under the guidance of the designer. Mass calls require the wardrobe crew to take one look at each extra; analyze his/her size, body strengths, and weaknesses; and instantly commit to the design look for that actor's image. To survive this pressure, film designers must create both a *design process* for themselves and a *very well prepared wardrobe stock*. As an actor finds the moment or a cinematographer adjusts a shot based on an instant of inspiration, the designer, when meeting an extra for the first time, must respond instantly to the "character" that he or she can become. Supported by a selection of both "neutral" stock (garments that provide basic coverage) and "character" stock (garments that create specific, unique, or eccentric images), a designer can quickly and playfully improvise garments for all characters.

After the actors are dressed, the designer follows the characters to the set to make final adjustments to the costumes and to get the director's approval. The designer then focuses on prep for future shooting, while the set costumers take up their wardrobe duties on the set, preserving and recording the look of the characters.

The camera department sets the shooting pace because each shot demands different camera set-ups and lighting adjustments—a time-consuming process involving camera tracks, dollies, and much other equipment. In film, the better lit the shot is, the better it will look on the screen, but lighting a scene well can be very time-consuming and, therefore, expensive. The budget ultimately determines the pace of the shooting schedule. The average pace of the shooting schedule for high-budget feature films is forty to sixty days, shooting two to three pages of the script per day; the pace for very-low-budget feature films is as little as twenty days, shooting eight pages of the script per day.

As tedious as the shooting process may sound, the pace is actually a great gift to the wardrobe department, because it provides time to work on the wardrobe for future scenes. Designs for a film are delivered *throughout the shooting period*, prioritized according to the shooting schedule's daily deadlines.

Location work creates many challenges for the film designer. Because films shoot in many locations and focus on action, a wardrobe crew must be prepared for almost anything: bullets, blood, and car chases; fire or flood; a snowy mountaintop or a steamy jungle. Wardrobe crews may be asked to work on their home turf or far, far, far away; they have to be flexible, adapt to new conditions quickly, and learn to both plan and improvise. Experienced film personnel know how to outfit and set up a costume shop and a costume stock from scratch wherever they need to be.

To keep crises to a minimum designers and wardrobe supervisors learn to plan very carefully for all the wardrobe needs of the production and routinely provide options and backups for emergencies. Designers must plan for shooting in different weather conditions and are expected to provide foul-weather gear (rain gear, layers for warmth, sun shades) for the crew as well as the cast to support the production and to keep the cameras rolling during the twelve- to sixteen-hour workdays.

To help the crew heads cope with the difficulties and expense of outfitting a wardrobe department, each member of the wardrobe crew on set is expected to come with his or her own *set kit* of tools, supplies, and equipment that may be needed to fit and repair costumes on location.

During the shoot the film's wardrobe department is responsible for dressing the actors for the scenes to be shot each day, recording costume continuity, gathering and fitting costume stock for scenes to be shot later in the shooting schedule, and *wrapping* the costume stock that is finished for the day (cleaning

Figure 9.21   The set kit, sometimes known as a "bucket buddy," provides portable waterproof storage for items frequently needed on set and a handy seat during takes. Photo by Holly Cole.

and storing the costumes in *principal character* units for the leads or by *scene stock* for the extras).

Filmmaking's Final Wrap

Unlike in the theater where a strike follows immediately after the production's last performance, a film production must hold costumes from the film until the shoot (or *principal photography*) is processed and the editing is developed to be certain that no scenes need to be reshot. *Reshoots* may be required for a variety of reasons; perhaps the film stock was ruined in the processing or the producer wants the ending changed.

A film production holds the costume stock for several weeks before *final wrap,* after which the costume stock is returned to its rental sources or sold. The result of this prolonged wrap policy is that costume rental for a film is usually contracted for a *production rental period* (sixteen weeks).

Accepting the Film Industry's Priorities

Maintaining a positive attitude throughout the film process is a fundamental requirement for success in the film and television industries. The fast pace and high demands of filmmaking can make costuming a film very challenging for beginners. Once designers have gained enough experience to tap the many resources that support the fever-pitch pace of filmmaking, they can rise to the challenge. The better a designer understands the business and its resources, the more marketable he or she becomes.

Understanding and accepting the film industry's priorities as a part of the wild ride of filmmaking are fundamentally important to a career in film. Would-be film designers are advised to take film production classes to learn what directors, editors, cinematographers, art directors, and producers experience as they work. With some film classes under their belts, young designers can focus on understanding the scale and cost of film and television productions, working in sync with the filmmaking process, and understanding how the industry is geared to support the speed of filmmaking.

Adjusting to the Scale and Cost of Film Production

The process of filming a production is inherently more expensive than mounting its theatrical equivalent because of the high cost of cameras, film stock, film processing, and the additional staff required by the camera department. Stunts, special effects, and location shooting create more casting and logistical complications, resulting in the need for more personnel and an increased budget.

Multimillion-dollar star salaries and production budgets make filmmaking costs seem astronomical, but considering the worldwide audience a film or television show can reach one can easily understand why film-production companies may choose to risk millions. Compared to theater, films have a far greater potential to reap huge profits.

Because producers recognize their box-office value, stars command enormous salaries. In fact, "star power" is a palpable force in the industry because a commitment from a star can get a production the *green light* (started)—and millions will be invested based on the star's appeal. Producers recognize that the filmmaking process is very demanding and a film staff generally earns more than an equivalent theater staff because they are expected to work longer hours and to cope with more pressure, discomfort, and process complications.

Producers negotiate and re-negotiate salaries and delay contract dates to save money. On most films personnel are contracted for as little time as the production can safely afford. For example, some characters may be cast very, very late in the prep period and costume designers may be dismissed several weeks before the end of filming if all the characters' *looks* (changes) have been established. In extreme cases productions may opt to do without a costume designer altogether, assigning the costuming of the characters to the wardrobe crew to save money.

Sample costume budgets of $250,000 for a $20 million dollar film, $8,000 for each episode of a TV series, or $150,000 for a commercial can make designing for film or television seem very attractive, but those budgets have to stretch surprisingly far to meet the needs of the production. Compared to theater, films have more crowd scenes, and the crowds are larger. While costume designers may be encouraged to lavish funds on the stars, they can face real battles with the producers to get sufficient costume stock for the hundreds, sometimes thousands of extras cast in a film. A designer must learn to budget very carefully to cover *all* of the costumes required for filming.

Working in Sync with the Other Members of the Film Production Team

The financial pressures on producers are so extreme that many are happy to trade a "costume design" screen credit to a fashion designer or clothing manufacturer who is willing to give clothes to the production for free (*product placement*). While some film designers are offended by the loss of credit, others are happy to work with free goods, carefully determining where product placement best supports their designs. By developing and maintaining good relationships with product placement sources designers become more desirable to producers.

Designers must prove to a producer that they are both talented and *practical*. They must be prepared to justify expenses and services and to develop cost-cutting design strategies. Producers understand that schedule and load changes can incur new costs; they simply expect to be advised of the cost to enable them to prioritize their options. To work well with film producers, costume designers must be highly skilled at estimating costume and service costs.

Producers often equate *stylists* (fashion-oriented personnel who focus on dressing the actors for events) with designers (who focus on interpreting a story and creating characters). Film designers must be willing to "style" characters from available clothing like a stylist would when the cost for made-to-order goods is too much to spend on certain characters. But they must also know when a made-to-order garment will work better for the actor or the story, even though similar ready-made garments are available.

Working with Directors

Directors are often so overloaded and the demands on them are so great that their very *last* priority may be reviewing the wardrobe. Often they want only minimal contact with the costume designer, so film designers get used to working from their own instincts. Designers learn to prioritize the information they need from the director for the short conferences they may be given. Every film designer should be prepared to quickly adjust designs to satisfy the requests of the director. The film designer must be strong in his or her vision for a character, but flexible on the character's details.

Working with the Cinematographer and the Art Director

Like in theater, the designer must design the characters in the context of the set and lighting that will surround them. Color and value contrast are key issues for both the cinematographer and the art director, the design team members responsible for the set and lighting. Costume designers actively pursue approval from the cinematographer and the art director because they have the right to request color-palette changes. Costume designers try different strategies to insure successful collaboration with these personnel: conferences with color boards or rack reviews, requests for location photos, and visits to the scene shop or art director's studio for key set color information all are helpful. As a last resort, the designer can back up costume stock with a varied palette and tonal range to help get the costumes approved.

Favorite costumes may not make it into the final cut. A cinematographer always shoots by the director's dictates and always with an interest in achieving the maximum emotional value from the moment. Different close-ups, different kinds of camera movements, and different angles and points of view all are explored in addition to letting the actors try new line readings or stage business with every take. The many versions of the scene are then cut and edited together to make the most compelling version of the story. If a favorite costume gets lost in the process, the designer has to take it in stride for the good of the whole production.

Working with the Actors

Like in theater, the designer must design costumes to *enhance* the actor's performance. His or her performance is magnified on the screen and any discomfort with the costume will be magnified as well. Stars' lives are very complex and very public. Their comfort and cooperation are essential on a film. The costume designer must be willing to accommodate their wishes and their complex schedules.

Working in Sync with the Shooting Schedule

Most importantly, the designer must design the wardrobe to facilitate the needs of the shooting schedule. Schedules change, characters are added with regularity, and designs must adapt to meet the new demands. The designer's mantra should be: "The production should never wait for the wardrobe."

Every aspect of a production unit is focused on getting the camera rolling. The efforts of so many people are required to set up a shot—grips, gaffers, electricians, camera crew, set dressers, prop men, actors, stunt players, sound techs, costumers, and more—that an army of people stands waiting to get the shot.

Time is money—major amounts of money—on the set. Everyone is under great pressure to move as quickly and efficiently as possible. Film-production units are equipped to be as self-sufficient as possible to keep the cameras rolling. Causing production to slow down is impractical, irresponsible, and risky.

This time pressure impacts the wardrobe department in two key ways. First, when the actors go to the set, they must be dressed correctly or redressed correctly with the costume stock on hand within fifteen minutes.

Secondly, duplicate costumes must be provided for stunts or actions that may stain or soil the clothing, so that shooting can continue. In some cases an action sequence may require an extraordinary investment by the wardrobe department to make sure that filming does not slow down. For example, for a chase sequence in the movie *Dressed to Kill* a lead character needed fourteen custom-made, white wool coats and two sleeves (for close ups). This number was needed to support retakes and preserve the different stages of distress that the coat suffered as the character endured a long and bloody run through dirty city streets. Fourteen copies of a custom-made coat at thousands of dollars each may be very expensive—but they are still cheaper than the cost of stopping the shoot to clean up one coat between takes.

The Film and Television Industries Are Geared to Support Speed

Film demands a highly streamlined process from a designer. Costume designers must research quickly, sketch quickly, budget quickly, shop quickly, and dress characters quickly or they will never keep pace with the production. In television work the designer regularly gets a script on Wednesday, fits the actors on Friday, and shoots on Sunday—a marathon of designing that requires the most streamlined process.

Labor unions trade on the flexibility and expertise of their members, justifying the larger salaries earned. The Motion Picture Costumer's Union and the Costume Designers Guild require their members to pass entry exams that test quick script breakdown, budgeting, and research skills and their detailed knowledge of the industry's labor, craft, and garment resources.

In the two strongest film centers in the country, Los Angeles and New York, films are supported by a network of costume services that can speedily provide production companies with high-end and low-end costume offices, workrooms, wardrobe trucks, rental collections, costume storage areas, cleaning delivery, fireproofing, dyeing, distressing, and shopping. Costume craft companies can provide made-to-order buttons, buttonholes, custom-made shoes, pleating, embroidery, knitting, beading, millinery, and trims. Both cities have shopping guides developed by industry personnel that list resources and personnel that can be tapped: *The Entertainment Sourcebook* covers New York, and *Shopping L.A.* covers Los Angeles.

Los Angeles is more focused on the unique needs and processes of the movie and television industry and supports the fastest rental, styling, and costume construction practices. From Hollywood rental collections the designer can obtain dozens of costumes delivered to the set overnight and *camera-ready* (correctly altered and with all the right patches and accessories). Hollywood workrooms are accustomed to only getting the actor for one fitting, so they provide rush and super-rush services as needed. All of it is available—for a price.

In an industry where every minute counts, these special services, and the support of experienced wardrobe teams, make it possible for designers to cope with the pressures and emergencies that regularly come up on the job. As a standard practice, key personnel develop teams that they work with over and over again to simplify communication and to keep work moving with maximum efficiency. To earn a place on a team, newcomers must prove that they can adapt to each team's way of working and each new challenge.

Chapter 10
Preparing for a Costume Design Career

. . . Oh, wait—are Ragnar's drawings in there?
Yes, I don't think he took them along.
See if you can locate them for me. I could give them a look maybe, after all!

The Master Builder, Henrik Ibsen
(translated by Rolf Fjelde)

To develop a career, costume design students need to simultaneously study and work. Bachelor's degrees in theater build a strong basis for design careers. Many universities offer Bachelor of Fine Arts degrees in theater design. For students who continue their education, graduate programs are available providing two- or three-year programs leading to Master of Fine Arts degrees in theater design, costume design, and/or costume technology. Schools generally require a *resume* and a *portfolio* as part of the application for entrance into these programs.

A resume is a list of a person's work experiences submitted with an application for entrance to an educational program or for a job opportunity. A portfolio is a collection of visual materials provided to the school admissions officer or to a job interviewer as examples of the applicant's skills and experience. A systematic approach to collecting these materials is necessary for managing one's costume design career.

The Resume

Resumes for College or Graduate School Applications

The resume accompanying undergraduate applications should include all theater experience—participation in high school productions, musical events, art classes or exhibits, theater camps, community theater productions, school or church choral programs or similar events—that might indicate to the college admissions officer the extent of a student's interest and skill with focus on the most important areas of that experience.

A resume also is required when applying to graduate school. In addition to theater work done as an undergraduate student, applicants for graduate schools are often expected to demonstrate professional experience outside of educational programs. The prospective designer should use summers to build his or her resume. Students should plan for the long term and choose, whenever possible, to enhance their future careers. Paid or volunteer work in summer stock theaters, professional costume shops, regional theaters, or university theaters all prove beneficial. Community theater experience varies greatly in the type and quality of experience and may not carry equal weight in the evaluation process. High-school experience diminishes in importance for graduate applicants and may be limited to a single statement or eliminated depending on its strength. Some graduate programs also prefer mature students who have worked in the field a few years and are returning to complete their education.

When developing a resume for a graduate application, the student should also list any relevant non-theater experience or classes such as fashion design, literature, history, and art classes. Even though a transcript is required with every application, an evaluator will find a separate listing on the resume useful for quick reference.

Resume for Job Applications

The job resume is similar to that prepared for school applications, but directed at a potential employer. All recent experience is of interest to an employer as an indication of the depth of the candidate's knowledge and skill. The resume should be tailored to the position being sought and the organization to which it is being sent.

Collecting Material for the Resume and Portfolio

Designers should develop the habit of collecting certain items from each production on which they work. For the resume, each job or position, the name of the play or project, the name of the producing organization or theater, the year, and the director should be listed for each production. An easy way to accumulate this information is to keep a file with playbills or programs from each project.

Some items that may be useful in a design portfolio are: research for a project, design concept statements, rough sketches, finished sketches, in-process and fitting photos, costume and wardrobe plots, photos of finished costumes, production shots, thank-you notes or letters of appreciation, programs, and posters. A designer should collect these items in an envelope labeled with the name of the show and sort the material after each production for possible inclusion in his or her portfolio. Request "to whom it may concern" letters of recommendation from the directors and producers of a production soon after opening.

The Parts of the Resume

As a designer's career develops, the resume may take different forms. However, it will usually include the following sections: (1) *heading*, (2) *statement of*

Figure 10.1 Portfolio/resume materials. A designer should collect certain items from each production on which he/she works. An easy way to accumulate this information is to keep a file with sketches, photos, and playbills or programs from each project. Photo Jack H. Cunningham.

goals, (3) *experience/job list,* (4) *related experience or interests,* (5) *list of special skills,* (6) *awards,* (7) *education,* and (8) *references.*

Letterhead or Heading

The resume should have a *heading* that states the applicant's name, the area of interest or the job title the applicant is seeking, and his or her contact information, including an e-mail address. This information, in a large, bold typeface, may be centered or aligned left or right at the top of the page. Many designers create an eye-catching decorative heading that underscores the creativity of the person presenting the resume. Word-processing programs can be used to create simple graphics for resumes and business cards, or a heading can be designed in an art application and pasted into the resume file. While it is usually wise to keep these decorative headings simple and businesslike, they can still reflect the designer's personality and aesthetic style. This heading can also be adapted as the designer's masthead on a design Web site or as a motif on the pages of a digital portfolio. Some designers include their union affiliation in their heading.

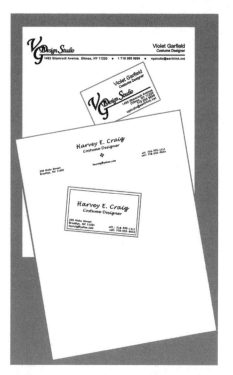

Figure 10.2 Heading samples. Some designers create a decorative heading for their stationery and business cards that reflects the designer's personality and aesthetic style.

Statement of Goals or Summary Statement

Some designers state simply the area of design in which they are seeking employment; others place a brief *statement of goals* immediately following the heading. The statement should explain the designer's choice for his or her next experience. A statement like, "Seeking a position as costume designer or assistant costume designer for an Off-Broadway or regional theater production" helps the reviewer determine immediately if the available position is likely to be appropriate. Other designers make a more general statement like "Seeking work in costume design or costume construction." This statement widens the prospects for the applicant. The statement of goals should relate to the open position when applying for a specific job.

Another approach is to compose a brief *summary statement* describing each of the designer's qualifications, skills, or proficiencies. Follow either statement with a list of specific projects.

Costume Experience or Project Categories

Sort the information regarding experience into sections, such as costume design, costume technology, wardrobe experience, masks and/or crafts, education, teaching, and related interests. Costumers may need to rearrange experience sections so that the experience that relates to the job being sought is presented first. Within each section, list experiences in reverse chronological order with the most recent first. When applying for a job as a costume designer, put the costume design section first and other information in descending order of relevance to the job. The rough order of importance is: costume designer, assistant designer, shop manager, project manager, draper/patternmaker or cutter, shopper, stitcher, finisher, wardrobe supervisor, wardrobe crew. Under the section title, list each project entry with the title of the play, the theater, the producing organization or university, the director, and the date of each project. Be careful to list all parts accurately and spell everything correctly. Arrange the entries for easy reading and double-space between each.

As a designer develops additional experiences, the list may be subdivided and regrouped into additional sections under film, television, and theater, or in other meaningful categories. Material may be divided into several resumes, each targeted to specific job opportunities.

The purpose of each section is to give the reviewer the most relevant information in the shortest possible time.

Related Experience or Interests

Separate related items should be grouped into a general category until there are enough jobs to subdivide the category. For example: one construction, one wardrobe, and one craft experience could be combined into a category of "related costume experience." Pertinent interests like art exhibitions, foreign travel, professional conferences, and panel participation may be listed under "related activities."

List of Special Skills

Some designers list separately special skills such as puppetry construction, costume craft skills, industrial sewing machine experience, draping, tailoring, millinery, dyeing and painting, and specific computer applications. This makes a quick reference for the interviewer who is looking for a specific skill.

Education

In the education section, list first the highest degree earned and other degrees in descending order. Include the school or university, the degree, and the dates each was earned. After the bachelor's degree is earned, the high-school notation may be dropped unless the school is known as a high school of performing arts. Unfinished degrees may be listed as "in progress," "all but thesis or dissertation" or "expected graduation: (year)"

Courses in related or specialized fields can be listed under "education," "special skills," or "related experience," even if they did not lead to a degree. Candidates should always represent their work honestly. Credentials may be checked. Applicants who are found to have exaggerated or falsified their resumes are not likely to be hired, and their professional futures are jeopardized.

Awards

A list of academic or theater awards the student has earned should be placed at the end of the resume in reverse chronological order. If the award was related to a specific production, it also could be noted in the project listing. If union affiliation was not listed in the heading, it may appear at the head of the awards section or at the head of the references.

Box 10.A Samples of project or experience entries for resumes.

(A) Resume for college entrance. If a resume is requested with a college application, the student may group costume experiences together and list them in reverse chronological order—most recent first. Other experiences can be grouped together, also in reverse chronological order. Headings may be at left margin, centered, or indented, but should be consistent throughout the resume.

COSTUME EXPERIENCE

Once Upon A Mattress, Costume Design Assistant, Wilson School of Performing Arts, Spring, 2008.

Thoroughly Modern Millie, Costume Crew, Green Mountain Performing Arts Camp, Summer 2007

Grease, Wardrobe Supervisor, Wilson School of Performing Arts, Spring 2007

The Lion the Witch and the Wardrobe, Wardrobe Crew, Larchmont Community Theater, Fall 2007

OTHER EXPERIENCE

Chorus, Wilson School of Performing Arts, 2006–08

Technical Staff, Green Mountain Performing Arts Camp, 2006–08

Actor, Green Mountain Performing Arts Camp, 2002–05

(B) Resume entries for graduate school. If a separate resume is requested with a graduate school application, a similar format may be followed.

COSTUME EXPERIENCE

The Apple Tree, Costume Designer, Central State University, Spring 2008

Blood Wedding, Shopper for Women's Costumes, Central State University, Fall 2007

Blue Lake Renaissance Fair, Costume Shop Crew, Summer 2007

Romeo and Juliet, Costume Designer, Central State University, Spring 2007

The Littlewoods, Assistant Costume Designer, Central State University, Fall 2006

Annie, Wardrobe Supervisor, Green Mountain Performing Arts Camp, Summer 2006

The Mouse Trap, Costume Shop Crew, Central State University, Spring 2006

(C) When applying for a job, items might be separated and listed with the experience *pertinent to the job* listed first.

WARDROBE AND COSTUME CONSTRUCTION

Annie, Wardrobe Supervisor, Green Mountain Performing Arts Camp, Summer 2006

Blue Lake Renaissance Fair, Costume Shop Crew, Summer 2007

The Mouse Trap, Costume Shop Crew, Central State University, Spring 2006

Blood Wedding, Shopper for Women's Costumes, Central State University, Fall 2007

COSTUME DESIGN

The Apple Tree, Costume Designer, Central State University, Spring 2008

Romeo and Juliet, Costume Designer, Central State University, Spring 2007

The Littlewoods, Assistant Costume Designer, Central State University, Fall 2006

References

References should be listed at the end of the resume. Never list anyone as a reference without his or her permission. Asking for a letter of recommendation or reference is not only acceptable but recommended to designers at all stages, as it is desirable to have these letters as up-to-date as possible.

Reference letters should be from individuals who know the candidate well in specific situations and can honestly describe the candidate's work in a positive way. Letters of reference from directors, designers, or the supervisors of a project who can describe the candidate's work ethic, talents, skills, and dedication to the project are more impressive than letters of general support. The designer or student should ask for references soon after a project is complete, while the work is fresh in the supervisor's mind.

Although a designer might keep a file of letters to use, the most effective letters are from colleagues in recent projects. Some applications require new letters, and some universities or potential employers may require that letters be sent directly from the reference writer.

The applicant should supply the reference writers with a list of specific aspects of the project for which he or she was responsible. Referring to the list, the letter writer will be reminded of the applicant's skills and contributions to the project, making a more specific and detailed letter possible. The applicant should indicate the letter's intended use, but should not dictate its contents.

Resumes may state "references upon request." Copies of "to whom it may concern" letters may be sent with the resume or in response to requests. Reference letters are separate from the resume, but may be attached to it or the application letter. The applicant should ask reference writers how they wish their personal contact information to be handled. Prospective employers or school admissions officers may need to contact reference writers to verify the information given in the letters.

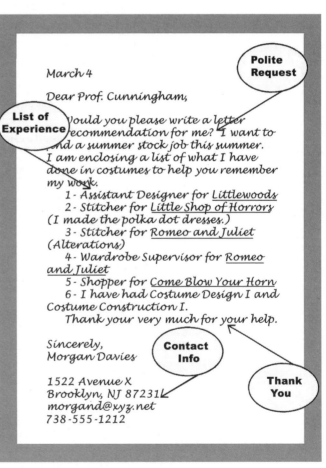

Figure 10.3 "Dear Prof" note. The applicant should write a note or letter when requesting a reference, giving a description of the project(s) for which he/she was responsible, making it easy for the reference writer to provide a specific and detailed letter.

Figure 10.4 Sample resumes. These two resumes illustrate two possible formats. As experience increases, more than one resume may be developed to separate projects into different categories with each resume focused on a specific type of experience.

RESUME

Marianne Holliday   300 W. 34th Street   New York, NY 10063
mholliday@email.net

COSTUME DESIGN & CONSTRUCTION
- *The Power of Ten,* The Theater Project, NY. Design and construction.
- *Singapore Mikado*-Theater Tonight, NY. Design.
- *Sight Unseen,* Brooklyn College, NY. Design and construction. Project included draping and construction of 2-piece woman's knit ensemble.
- *Mother Courage,* Brecht Repertory, NY. Design and construction. Project included dyeing and use of many distressing techniques.
- *A Little of What You Fancy,* Theater Tonight, NY. Design.
- *Pygmalion,* The Hole in the Wall Theater, NY. Design, construction and millinery.
- *Kenneth-What is the Frequency,* 90th St. Theater. Edinburgh Fringe Festival. Design, construction and fabric painting.
- *The Water Engine,* 90th St. Theater. Edinburgh Fringe Festival. Design.
- *True West,* White Horse Theater Company, NY.
- *Blood Wedding,* Brooklyn College, NY. Design and construction. Project included draping and construction of 1930s gown, embroidery, dyeing and fabric painting.
- *Mark of Cain,* 90 St. Theater, NYC. Co-design and construction. Built reversible 2-piece woman's suit.
- *The Glass Menagerie,* Brooklyn College, NY. Design and construction. Project included draping and construction of 1910s gown.
- *As it is in Heaven,* Brooklyn College, NY. Patterned and constructed 9 bodices.
- *He Who Gets Slapped,* Brooklyn College, NY. Design (costumes and makeup).
- *Romeo & Juliet,* Brooklyn College, Brooklyn, NY. Co-design and construction, costumes and masks.

TECHNICAL EXPERIENCE
- Costume Shop Internship (4 semesters), Brooklyn College, under Rebecca Cunningham. Duties included draping & pattern making, fittings, alterations, dyeing, millenary, crafts and construction.
- Costumer/Stitcher under Jim Harrington, Haydon Theatre, E. Haddam, NY. Season included seven main stage shows and four children's shows. Projects included design and construction of several hats, and construction of hoop frame for Anna's gown, *The King and I.*
- Costumer/Stitcher for Virginia Historical Pageant. Researched and designed Native American Indian makeup and wigs.

EDUCATION
- MFA, Design & Technical Theater, CUNY Brooklyn College, NY. Sept. 2004.
- BA, Speech Communications & Theatre Arts, University of Richmond, VA. May 1988.
- Semester abroad, Richmond College, London, England.

HONORS/AFFILIATIONS
- Member USITT.
- Member Alpha Psi Omega.
- Artist-in-residence, Columbia College, Columbia, SC.
- Dean's List, University of Richmond.

SPECIAL SKILLS
Draping, Flat Patterning, Marrow machine, Blindstitch machine. Computer skills: Mac and PC User. Microsoft Word, Excel, Powerpoint, Access, SharePoint. Photoshop, Quark, Vectorworks

Resume Style

Format

A resume should be arranged for easy reading and quick reference. Many reviewers recommend that a resume be kept to one or two pages. Sections should be divided with extra space, bold lettering, or lines. The applicant should think of developing the resume as a design project, choosing font style and size, spacing, paper, and layout to support the aesthetic quality of the designer's work.

Resume

ʚ *Annette Schultz* Costume Designer ʚ

1881 East 37th St.   (646) 123-5554   aschultz@gmail.com
Brooklyn, NY 11255   http://costumesbyannette.com

Original Costume Design
Theater since 2004

Date	Play	Director	Theatre/Company
2008	Jimi and Mr. B	Darrin Beltzer	The Barn Theater, Albany, NY
2007	The Miracle Plays	Christopher Moore	The Workshop Theater, Brooklyn, NY
2007	Poetry in Space	Opal Erwin	Manhattan Theater Lab
2006	The Beauty Queen of Leenane	David Crane	Center Stage, Brooklyn
2006	Twelfth Night	Greg Grossberg	Lake Frances Theater Lab
2005	A Month in the Country	Scott Davies	The New Adventure Theater
2004	Two Sisters and a Piano	Beverly Beasley	Harold Prince Theater, Brooklyn, NY
2004	Knives in Hens	Susan Harrison	The Workshop Theater, Brooklyn, NY

Dance since 2004

Date	Ballet	Choreographer	Theater/Company
2008	The Storm Howls	Andrew Mano	Marissa Long Theatre, Manhattan College
2007	Minutes	Andrew Mano	Merce Cunningham Studios
2006	3 Times 3	Greggory Doneger	Marissa Long Theatre, Manhattan College
2006	Vinyl Symphony	Donna Dale	Marissa Long Theatre, Manhattan College
2005	Insomnia	Karren Langston	Marissa Long Theatre, Manhattan College
2005	Reaching for Water	Charlene Green	Marissa Long Theatre, Manhattan College
2005	Forced Entry	Andrew Mano	Marissa Long Theatre, Manhattan College
2005	Over the Moon	Donna Dale	Marissa Long Theatre, Manhattan College

Film since 2004

Date	Title	Director	Production Company
2007	The Love of Art	Charlene Spanner	New Square Pictures

Assistant Costume Design since 2004

Date	Play	Designer	Theater/Company and Director
2007	The Power of Dark Eyess	Polly Duncan	Peppermint Theater, Dir. Morgen Proust
2006	On the Verge	Kitty Graham	Gershwin Theatre, Brooklyn, NY
2005	Bailey/Ford BFA Dance Concert	Irina Komene	Bailley University Theater
2004	Traces Dance Company	Irina Komene	New Jersey University

Education
2003-2006 **MFA in Design and Technical Production, Concentration in Costume Design, Brooklyn College of the City University of New York.**
1996-2000 **BFA Dance, cum laude, Manhattan College**

Publications/Other Projects
2008   Fashion History 2000-2008 for *The Magic Garment*, by Rebecca Cunningham Costume Design Texbook.
May, 2005 Exhibit "*A Fierce Determination*" – Brooklyn College Library
          Mounted a portion of the exhibit, antique clothing from the 1930s to 1950s, for Brooklyn College's 75th Anniversary.

Professional Organizations
United States Institute for Theater Technology National and New York Chapters, Member since 2004

Editing

The resume need not be written in complete sentences, as it is essentially a list, but careful editing is absolutely necessary. The applicant should use the software's spell-check and grammar-check features. However, if the wrong word has been used, though spelled correctly, the computer will not catch the mistake. Because theater has its own vocabulary and usage, the grammar-check may not always recognize errors, or the recommended changes may be incorrect. Check and double-check the spelling of names and theaters and the complete, correct titles of the plays listed in the resume. The applicant should have at least one other person proofread any document being sent out for school or work applications.

The applicant should remember that the resume is his or her personal representative, and poor grammar and misspelled words do not make a good impression. Cross-throughs and handwritten notes on the resume detract from the desired professional quality. Arrange the margins and spacing so that either all the material fits on one page, or with at least two complete sections on a second page. A page with only a few lines on it may be lost or overlooked. A resume of more than one page should be stapled or paper clipped together.

A resume file should be updated frequently. A basic resume file can be kept on a disk or hard drive ready to be updated or customized when new resumes are required.

Duplication

The resume can be printed out as interviews are scheduled. If many interviews are anticipated, a group of resumes can be prepared ahead of time. Choose a quality paper (20# bond) and consider a soft color, like beige or pale gray, to catch the eye. Strong colors are not advisable since some people find reading difficult on intensely colored paper. Personal preferences play a part in the color selection of paper and ink, but the applicant should remember that the resume is an ambassador to the interviewer. Rarely would someone be looking to hire frivolous or silly personnel. The applicant should consider the nature of the school or job venue when preparing a resume. When in doubt, err on the side of simplicity.

Resumes are sent with job applications and presented to interviewers. A few extra copies should be kept in the portfolio. Many photocopy and printing stores assist in preparing resumes and making duplicate copies for distribution. Editing and checking spelling and grammar are always the responsibilities of the designer.

The Portfolio

There are two basic categories of portfolio based on their function—*storage* or *archival* and *presentation* portfolios. A *storage portfolio* or *archival portfolio* is a file of materials that have not yet been incorporated, are no longer needed, or may be inappropriate for current presentations. A *presentation portfolio* contains a group of specially chosen items from the designer's body of work selected to best illustrate the designer's skills and experience. A presentation portfolio should demonstrate that the applicant is a designer who can read a script, analyze the needs and style of a play, and conceptualize the presentation. To do this, a series of steps should be illustrated, including research, concept statement, roughs, sketches, paperwork, construction and fitting photos, and production photos.

As each new design experience adds to the designer's development, it should be considered for the updated presentation portfolio.

Types of Portfolio Formats

The type of portfolio organization should be chosen based on the designer's needs and skill set and may vary at different stages of the designer's educational and professional careers.

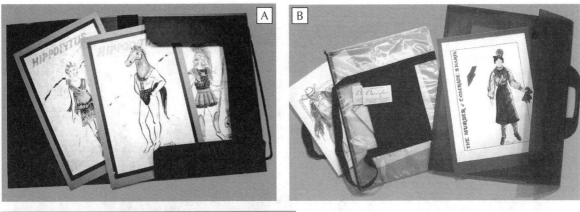

Figure 10.5 Three types of portfolio cases. (A) A cardboard folder with flaps to hold sketches and an elastic band to hold it closed can be used for archival or loose-sketch presentation. (B) Plastic envelope-style portfolio cases with carrying handles hold sketches, business cards, and small items like disks or notebooks and pencils. (C) A leather multi-ring binder with carrying handles can be arranged with acetate sheets to hold and protect original sketches and photos. Sketches by author. Photos by Jack H. Cunningham.

Archival or Storage Portfolios

For basic storage the portfolio materials can be organized in string-tied portfolios, manila envelopes, file folders, or file boxes. For long-term storage of archival artwork and other paper documents, acid-free boxes and tissue help protect items from deterioration from the off-gassing of chemicals in the paper. Items from each project should be stored together to facilitate developing new sections in an active portfolio.

Presentation Portfolio Formats

The simplest and easiest form of portfolio, *loose-page presentation,* is collected in a large string-tied envelope or folder. Each sketch or photo is placed loose in the portfolio. However, because items of different sizes can get shuffled around and sometimes lost, the loose-page format is difficult to keep organized. Mounting each item on a standard-size backing board of a project-specific color helps to keep projects organized. Sets of material can be easily switched in and out of the portfolio to address the individual job interview. This style of presentation is effective, but soon produces a heavy portfolio.

Many designers choose to prepare a *presentation portfolio book* in a large ringbinder portfolio case. The ring binder allows the designer to arrange and maintain materials, including original artwork, in the specific order desired.

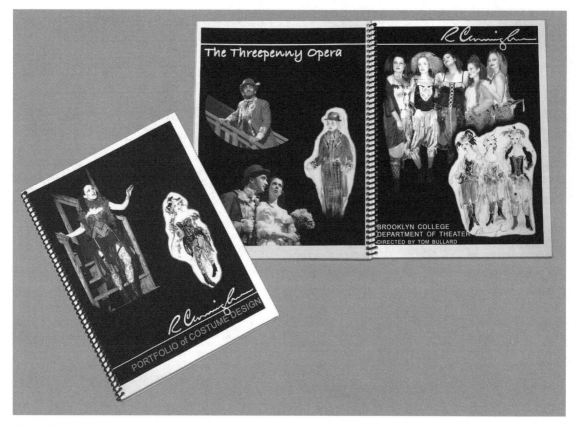

Figure 10.6 Reproduction portfolios. A portfolio of sketch reproductions and photos of costumes designed can be put together by computer, reproduced, and spiral bound. This type of portfolio can be easily copied and carried for interviews, or mailed for long-distance review. Portfolio photo by Jack H. Cunningham. *The Threepenny Opera* photos by John Ricasoli.

Other designers develop *reproduction portfolios* in smaller, more manageable sizes with reproductions of their sketches and photos. An introduction, a resume, and a table of contents should be added to assist the reviewer. These are computer-printed or photocopied and spiral-bound at office supply stores. They can be produced and easily distributed in larger numbers, but are less flexible as they cannot be changed once they are bound. This choice can become expensive, as the booklet may not be returned to the designer. If the portfolio is large, providing return postage may cost more than a new booklet. Another disadvantage is that the designer may be tempted to include too much material and may reduce the photos and sketches too much for proper reviewing.

Design material collected and organized for a paper portfolio can be translated into a *digital portfolio* by scanning or photographing artwork and burning it to CD or DVD, importing it into a software application like PowerPoint, or using it to create a portfolio Web site. These portfolios are easily updated, very effective, and can be viewed by a wide audience.

The designer's choice of portfolio presentation style depends on the cost of development for each, the individual's skill set, how the portfolio is to be shown, and the sizes and quantity of material to be included. A student with highly developed computer skills will ultimately find a digital portfolio very attractive and useful, but the student's first portfolio should probably be an art folder or zipper case purchased in an art store. This style of portfolio is very effective for personal presentations. As the designer's career and the corresponding portfolio expands, several different presentation styles might be developed.

The Parts of a Portfolio

Although each designer's portfolio is ultimately different because of different experiences and personalities, the basic organization of portfolios is similar for all. The possible parts of the portfolio include: (1) *introduction*, (2) *costume design section*, (3) *costume technology section*, (4) *unproduced work section*, (5) *related artwork section*, (6) *archival section*, and (7) *resumes*.

Introduction

A book-style portfolio should begin with a title page that includes the name, picture, and contact information of the designer. In loose-page portfolios the title page may not be necessary, but the designer's name and contact information should be affixed to the inside of the portfolio in case it is accidentally mislaid. On Web sites and in digital portfolios a home page with masthead would include this basic information, or it can be split between the home page and a contact page.

Costume Design and/or Technology Section

While resumes are usually arranged chronologically, portfolios may be arranged either chronologically, by job title, or by artistic choice. Since the purpose of the portfolio is to show off the designer's skills and experience, the most effective work in the available portfolio materials should be chosen, and then the best order of presentation determined. The arrangement of different projects may depend on which is the most eye-catching. Some designers believe that while the first design project presented should be attractive and demonstrate a series of elements, the central group of projects should present more dramatic and creative designs, with less interesting and more straightforward examples presented last. Other designers like to end with the most dramatic project, leaving the reviewer with the best impression. The portfolio may begin with the work most related to the job being sought.

Since most interviews have a time limit, the designer is wise to limit the number of projects in the basic portfolio in order to focus the attention of the reviewer. A portfolio need not include everything a designer has ever done, but a selection of the best, most recent, most pertinent, most interesting, and/or most effective work. Additional work may be placed in an archival section to be made available if the reviewer wishes to see more. Each section can be identified with a tab or divider page for easy reference.

Unproduced Work Section

This section is for class projects and sample projects. If the student has only a few actually produced costume-design examples, he or she could choose a play

and develop a series of costume designs to suggest aspects of work not represented in the produced work. For example: If a designer has only modern dress
productions in his or her produced work, a project showing period dress or fantasy costume would be an excellent addition to the portfolio. As the designer's
experience increases, this section can be reduced and finally eliminated.

Related Artwork Section

Particularly for school applications, portfolio reviewers are interested in
work from art classes, studio work, and personal artwork. For other portfolios,
only the best or most relevant of this material should be included.

Archival Section

As the number of production designs increases, good editing will suggest
removal of some work from the main portion of the portfolio. The archival section can hold the extra work where it can be accessed, if needed. For personal
presentation portfolios, this section may need to be reduced or packaged separately as the portfolio becomes too heavy to carry or ship. The use of digital
portfolios makes the archival section more manageable, since size and weight
are no longer an issue.

Resumes

A current resume should be included at the end of the portfolio and a group
of resumes and business cards should be kept handy in a pocket of the presentation portfolio to distribute at the beginning or end of the interview.

Selecting Portfolio Material

The designer must select the materials from each production that help "tell
the story" of his or her participation in that project. A series of items for one
aspect of each production gives a more complete picture of the student's abilities
to carry out different responsibilities. Collecting a range of items from each
project provides options that allow the most interesting, varied, and pertinent
final selections. Possible series are:

1. inspirational research, period research, rough sketches, finished sketches,
   costume photos,

2. program, costume sketches, patterns in progress, fitting, finished garment on actor,

3. poster, program, costume sketches, construction in progress, photos of
   the performance, thank-you notes from supervisor, designer, producer,
   or director.

The designer should spread out the materials for each project and eliminate
inappropriate or inadequate photos, sketches, or other materials. Edit the selection with an eye to the drama of the portfolio presentation. From the chosen
material the designer then determines the order that best shows the work, holds
the reviewers' interest, and demonstrates design skills. The portfolio should
illustrate the story of the designer's work, and the presentation of each project
should demonstrate its contribution to his or her experience.

The selection of material should indicate the designer's versatility and strength and be chosen to make the most impact. The designer should ask whether each item says something important about his or her work, talent, or skills.

Inspirational and Specific Research

A few pieces of the research that inspired the designer on a project helps the reviewer understand the candidate's design process. One page of selected period research or character-specific research can introduce a series of pages including rough and finished sketches and photos to give a complete picture of the designer's process.

Sketches

A designer should choose the best artwork to represent each project in the portfolio. Some touch-up work is acceptable to improve sketches. Whenever possible, display sketches with available photos to show the development of the costume from thought to stage. Prospective employers are interested in knowing that a designer can carry a project through from idea to reality. All sketches should be labeled, signed, and dated. If the originals are oversized, they can be photocopied or scanned, and reduced to fit the portfolio. Compare the resulting copy to the original for clarity and color accuracy. Photocopying also reduces the weight of the presentation portfolio.

Photos

The designer must take responsibility for making certain that his or her costumes are photographed. The designer should ask the stage manager or director for permission to take portfolio photos with a flash at the scheduled photo call or during the final dress rehearsal. If the actors in the production are members of Actor Equity, they must be given advanced notice of photo sessions and they must give permission for their photos to be taken. Flash photos should *never* be taken during a *performance*, as the light is distracting to the actors and the audience. Most theaters forbid taking any pictures during performances. If the designer engages an independent photographer to take costume pictures, he or she should get permission from the stage manager and/or the director or producer. A clear explanation of the restrictions of costume photography and the types of photo desired should be made to the photographer. A list based on the scenes in the play or the costume plot is helpful for the photo shoot.

The best costume photos show one or two characters, full figure, onstage in the stage set with bright light and some sort of action. Photos should be taken from a position at eye level to the actor's head and shoulders and close enough for details to read. The use of a digital camera makes the process much easier and eliminates extra steps in developing the digital portfolio.

A bad picture should never be used in a portfolio. Poor photos can be scanned, cropped, and enhanced in *Photoshop* or a similar computer photography/art program. Taking the photos with a digital camera simplifies the process of assimilating them into the portfolio and Web sites. The designer can remove red-eye, strange reflections, partial figures on the edges, and odd bits of scenery that detract from the photo. These programs allow sharpening and improve-

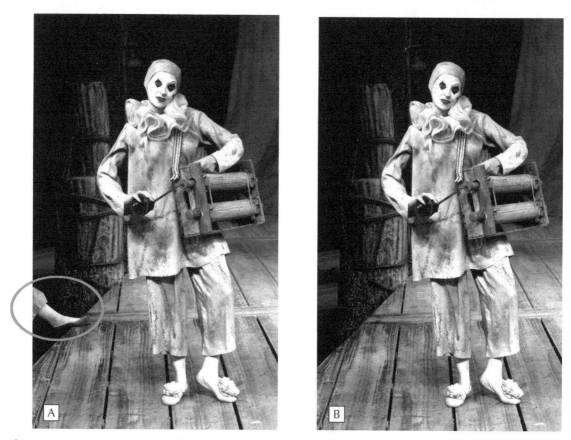

Figure 10.7   Improving photo in Photoshop. (A) An otherwise charming photo is slightly spoiled by a stray foot entering the left side of the photo. (B) Careful correction in Photoshop or with other photography software improved the photo's impact. Photo by Richard Grossberg.

ments of the photo's contrast and color. However, it is unwise to overwork the photos to the point that they no longer represent the production honestly.

One or two full-stage photos for the overall feeling of the production may be useful, but the majority of the photos should feature the costume designer's work on the show. If the producer arranged for a professional photographer to take production shots, the designer should try to get at least one or two photos that show off the costume designs to good advantage. The focus of the portfolio should always be on the skills of the presenter.

Posters, Flyers, and Programs

A few posters or flyers can add an attractive and interesting element to the portfolio. Use only the best examples and only when they support the design concept and the designer's work. Using a poster, flyer, or program validates the experience and gives the viewer a more complete picture of the production's quality and how the applicant fit into the production process. The applicant's name and position can be highlighted or underlined in the program. However, only a small percentage of the overall portfolio space should be given to work not done by the designer to avoid it looking like "filler." As the quality and quantity of the portfolio materials improves, the number of posters and programs should be reduced or relegated to the archival section.

Planning the Order of Portfolio Materials

A portfolio should demonstrate that the applicant is a designer who can read a script, analyze the needs and style of the play, collaborate with the director, and conceptualize a design. Illustrating a series of steps for one or two projects such as research, concept statement, roughs, sketches, paperwork, construction and fitting photos, and production photos helps a reviewer judge the designer's abilities.

When planning the order of the presentation, placing the most important, pertinent, or artistically impressive design jobs first may be more effective than a chronological arrangement. (See the section on resumes in this chapter for the order of importance of various experiences.) When applying for a job, try to arrange the portfolio so that the experience that relates to the job being sought is presented first.

One of the most important parts of developing a portfolio is editing out excessive, unsupportive, or old material. The series of projects presented in the portfolio should offer costume design for different types of drama, in different periods, and in different sketching styles. Demonstrating the breadth and scope of the designer's skills is an important aspect of the portfolio.

Assembling the Portfolio

For loose page portfolios, items can be mounted on stiff backing board, like illustration or mat board. Several small items can be arranged artistically, mounted on the same board, and covered with acetate or plastic to protect the artwork. This protects the work from damage if it is handed around in the interview. Using coordinated colored mat board will help the presenter keep the items related to each show together.

For book-style portfolios with acetate pages, arrange each project page to display the material in an attractive and artistic manner, generally without mixing projects on the pages. All pages for the book portfolio should be arranged with the same orientation so that the book does not have to be turned around to view the next page. For the most flexibility, sketches, photos, and other items should be mounted on backing sheets of black construction paper. Use one side only of backing sheets so that material can easily be rearranged in the portfolio book or removed for mounting in a display. To use the portfolio to maximum efficiency, two backing sheets back-to-back can be placed into each acetate sleeve.

Page Layout

Although page layout is an expression of an individual's personal aesthetic, as a general guideline, photos and sketches should be arranged in an artistic grouping without crowding the page. Images may overlap or be arranged at angles for more interesting compositions provided the focus of the page is clear. Sketches and photos may be presented in several sizes, creating variety. Borders,

Figure 10.8
Page arrangements. When arranging material in book-style portfolios, the designer should be consistent with facing page orientation. Turning the book around to display first horizontal pages then vertical ones looks disorganized and wastes valuable interview time. Photos by Jack H. Cunningham, Richard Grossberg, and author. Sketches by author.

A

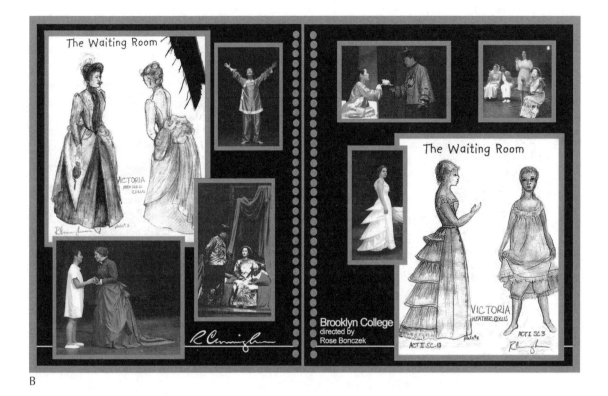

B

lines, motifs, and other decorative elements may be added for emphasis, but should not detract from the main focus or make the pages look too cluttered. Swatches of fabric or trim add textural interest and indicate the designer's knowledge and taste in these items.

A brief written description accompanying the sketches makes the presentation easier and clearer. The designer should use correct costume terms when labeling and describing the sketches presented in the portfolio. Adhesive-backed labels printed from a computer or neatly written by hand can be added to the presentation portfolio. All labels should be carefully checked for correct spelling and grammar.

For reproduction portfolios and digital portfolios, scan or digitally photograph sketches and other material, resize as needed, and arrange material attractively on pages in Photoshop or any suitable computer software. The designer can print out the portfolio and place it in a binder or have it reproduced at an office supply or printing store, where it can be spiral bound. If the file is not too large, it can be e-mailed. Copies of the file can be burned to CD or DVD and sent by post to prospective employers. The same material can be developed for a Web site that is made available to any interested party. The disadvantage of reproduction portfolios is the smaller size of photos and sketches. The disadvantages of digital portfolios are the possible technical limitations of the designer or the reviewer.

The designer should plan the layout of each page carefully, whether paper or digital portfolio, to help the reviewer understand its "story." Some decorative embellishments may be added, but an overly decorative presentation may detract from the work, and a flashy presentation does not improve the content.

Materials and Tools

The first item needed is a cardboard folder or envelope to hold all the materials being gathered. A string-tied envelope or cardboard portfolio serves this purpose well. After determining the type of presentation portfolio desired, the designer should purchase the folder or binder needed to contain the material and a selection of the good-quality art materials to use for enhancing the layout. Refer to box 10.B for a list of supplies.

Box 10.B   List of portfolio supplies

Binders or folders—cardboard, plastic, or leather—string- or elastic-tied or zippered ring binders	Computer
	Color printer
Acetate sleeve pages	Photoshop or similar computer art software
Adhesive-backed labels	Scanner
Adhesive dots	Digital camera
Mat knife	Right-angle triangle
Paper cutter	Clear plastic ruler
White paper glue and small flat brush	T-square
Colored papers (construction paper or mat board)	

Labeling

Sketches, plots, and photos should always be labeled with the name of the show and the producing organization. If pages are set up with items from different productions, labels should indicate for which aspect of the production the designer was responsible—e.g., wardrobe supervision, costume construction, quick changes. The reviewer should not have to refer to the resume to understand the relevance of the portfolio entry.

Adhesive-backed labels printed on a computer make labeling quick, easy, and neat. Poor labeling can detract from an otherwise neat presentation. Use good-quality acetate pages and backing sheets in the ring-binder portfolio. To mount work on backing boards use double-faced tape, adhesive dots, or other reversible paper adhesive for best results. *Do not use adhesive on the face of sketches or photos.*

For costume construction photos, the applicant should indicate in what capacity he or she worked—draper, tailor, patternmaker, machine stitcher, finisher, designer, or assistant designer. If the responsibility is not specified, the reviewer may assume the lowest level of participation.

The designer should remember that the neatness and organization of the portfolio reflects on the presenter, and may be taken as an example of the designer's work habits.

> **Box 10.C   Designer checklist X: The portfolio**
>
> 1. How is this portfolio to be used? College entrance? Graduate school entrance? Job application?
> 2. How will the material be collected and stored?
> 3. What type of presentation portfolio is most useful now? Will it be mailed, e-mailed, or presented in person?
> 4. How should the material be organized? What categories or sections of similar experiences should be used?
> 5. In what order should the material be arranged?
> 6. Is the layout attractive? Does it reflect my aesthetic sense?
> 7. Are the labels neat, clear, adequate?
> 8. Does this portfolio plan show my design work honestly and to good advantage?

Portfolio Specifics for College or Graduate School Applications

The student's first encounter with the need to provide a portfolio and resume is usually for school applications. The *college* applicant must fulfill the requirements of and follow the directions provided by the college or university. Portfolios for school applications may contain all or some of the following: (1) an introductory section with a bio and photo of the student and a brief personal statement or statement of goals, (2) a table of contents, (3) a design section with materials from realized productions, (4) in-class designs or paper projects, (5) a construction and/or craft section with photos, patterns and samples from projects in patternmaking, stitching, costume crafts production, makeup or wig making/dressing, (6) sketches and paintings from art classes and/or photos of sculpture, (7) a resume, and (8) copies of letters of recommendation.

A portfolio for undergraduate school applications is likely to be more general than specific. A collection of programs from high-school productions on which the student has worked is a good start. A label or highlight mark in each program identifying the student's participation is important. A few photos from the production might be included and should be labeled explaining the relevance of the photo to the student's participation in the production. All labels and materials should be neat and clear.

A student with no actual costume-design experience could prepare some sample designs based on the information in this text. The designs should be for a specific play and labeled as "projects." The play should be one that the student has experience with and has read carefully. The student should include photocopies of research and rough sketches and should be prepared to discuss the project with an interviewer.

Include work from art classes, such as figures, landscapes, or abstract designs. If the accumulated work seems inadequate, additional material should be developed. Students should only put their best work in the portfolio. A poor piece of artwork can unmake a good impression built on other items. Student applicants should get good advice from a teacher or professional in the field when developing the portfolio.

Experiences rarely come in neat and specific order. Placing the most important jobs first may be more effective than a chronological listing.

In addition to the suggestions above, the *graduate school* applicant must present material collected from undergraduate theater experiences to further develop a portfolio for graduate school applications. These materials should be more focused in the area of desired specialization, but should also indicate the student's breadth of theater experience. Again, placing the most important and pertinent experiences first may be the more effective presentation strategy.

Graduate school reviewers are particularly interested in students that have already developed skills in drawing and painting. Photos of sculpture work also are relevant as they demonstrate an understanding of working in three dimensions.

Although not everyone evaluating a resume or portfolio is looking for the same things, here are some questions the reviewer may consider. What related skills, experience, or background does this applicant bring to the graduate school experience? Does the applicant have a background in theatrical performance, dramatic literature, art, or fashion? Can this applicant express ideas in dramatic and visual terms? Has this applicant worked in theater outside of the educational environment? What special skills does this applicant demonstrate? Does this applicant demonstrate some ability to draw and paint?

If the portfolio is not being presented in person, original art material should be photographed or scanned and printed for the portfolio, so as not to risk damage or loss in shipping. If a student is submitting multiple applications, the whole portfolio may need to be duplicated. A spiral-bound portfolio booklet that can be sent without requiring return is a good choice for school applications and long-distance job applications. Extra time and expense must be allowed for color photocopying or scanning, printing, and binding the materials. Digital portfolios and designer Web sites are also effective and efficient for long-distance portfolio review.

Portfolio Specifics for Job Applications

Many costume designers work *freelance*, or on a job-by-job basis. A freelance designer must constantly be prepared to provide a portfolio and resume for prospective employers. When applying for a job, arrange the resume and portfolio so that the production experience that relates to the job being sought is presented first. A designer applying for a position of designer or assistant designer should place design examples first in the portfolio and technology examples second. Having the portfolio pages in a ring binder with only one production represented on a page makes rearrangement quick and easy. Digital portfolios and Web sites can also be expanded with relative ease and labeled so that the reviewer can determine the viewing order.

Digital Portfolios and Web Sites

When designing a digital portfolio to be distributed on disk or posted on the Internet, much the same consideration should be given to material choice and arrangement as when developing a book portfolio. The possible parts of the digital portfolio include: (1) home page, (2) bio/resume, (3) costume design section, (4) costume technology section, (5) unproduced work section, (6) related artwork section, (7) archival section, and (8) contact information.

Visual materials for digital portfolios and Web sites must be scanned or digitally photographed and saved as PDF or JPG files at the largest possible resolution (the maximum *dpi*). Smaller files are less flexible and save less detail.

When a digital portfolio is sent to reviewers on CD or DVD, design material can be set up as a slide show in a presentation program like *PowerPoint*. The arrangement of the digital portfolio on PowerPoint follows an order similar to the paper portfolio. The designer generally has more control over the order in which the reviewer sees the presentation with a PowerPoint portfolio than on a Web site. One disadvantage of providing a CD or DVD is that the person receiving the disk must have compatible software applications to view the files.

Advance planning of the overall artistic look of the Web site is perhaps even more important than for a paper portfolio. Because the presenter cannot control the order in which the material is viewed, unity of visual design helps present a focused portfolio story. The designer should choose Web design software or another Web development method with which he or she is proficient. Web sites are most successful when they are updated frequently.

Consideration should be given to the different areas to be listed and the relationship of these areas to one another. Mapping out the organization of the Web site in a flowchart assists the designer to develop a logical presentation of the available elements.

Home Page

The first page that a visitor to a Web site sees is called the *home page*. Similar to the letterhead on stationery, the home page should include a *masthead* with the designer's name, titles, e-mail address, and perhaps a decorative motif or logo. A photo and bio may appear on the home page or on a separate page. Design awards may be listed on the home page or mentioned in the bio and/or resume. A series of buttons or links can be arranged horizontally or vertically. The buttons indicate the pages within the Web site available to the viewer and make travel to these pages possible.

The home page is the designer's first opportunity to express an aesthetic point of view. The choice of colors, decorative style, and organization of materials all convey something to the viewer about the designer's artistic attitude. The masthead should be bold and easy to read. The button design should be simple and attractive. A sketch or photo may be used with the button for each section. Heading buttons are repeated on each page, with a "home" button added.

Resume

The *resume* should be available as a distinct Web page. As the costumer's experience grows, separate resume pages may be posted for costume design, costume technology, and other specialties. The basic resume should be kept as a Word file, updated as needed, and saved as a PDF before uploading onto the Web site.

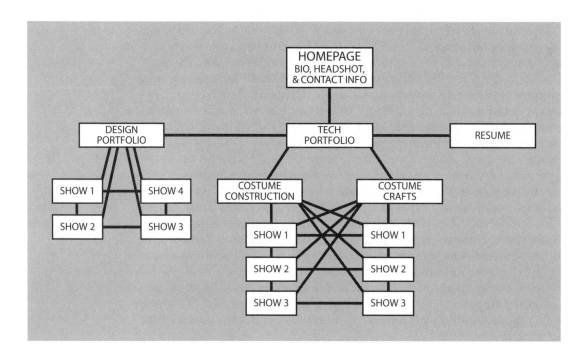

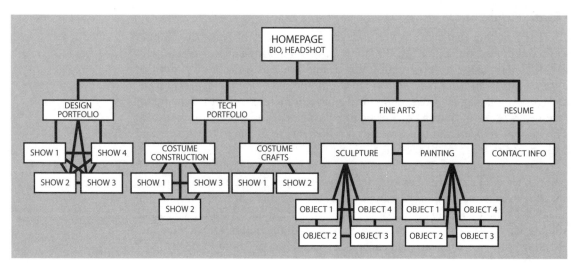

Figure 10.9   Sample methods of organizing portfolio Web site elements (flowcharts). The two charts are suggestions for arranging material for Web sites for beginning designers. Adaptations can be made based on material available.

Costume Designs or Projects

The main section of the portfolio lists each production experience as a separate page with photos, sketches, and other materials accessed through the title of the production. A decorative button specific to the production can be made or the productions accessed by title. If both costume design and costume technology experience are represented, separate pages for each, linked to the individual show section, may be provided. Pages can be adjusted to accommodate drafting, artwork, or other paperwork.

A section of *unproduced work* may be included under a "projects" link, but only if the amount of produced work is small. Unproduced work should be eliminated or stored in archives and replaced with actual production designs as soon as material is available.

Archival Section

This section is useful when the designer has more production examples than can be reasonably included in the main design section, but he or she wishes to keep the older work available for perusal.

Contact Information

Some portfolio Web sites present a separate page with contact information. Some designers choose to include their e-mail or other contact information as part of the masthead so that it is easy to find on every page of the portfolio. However, the designer should consider carefully before providing personal information such as addresses or personal phone numbers. Once personal contact information is posted on the Web, it is available to everyone and open to misuse.

Choosing a Web Host

After the Web site is developed, a host service is chosen and the portfolio is uploaded to the site. The designer should pick a unique domain name and matching e-mail address for professional use, even if he or she already has personal e-mail and Web addresses.

Many e-mail and Internet service providers offer free Web hosting as part of the benefits of subscription; however, advertising usually appears on such pages. Other hosting services are available for small monthly fees. Be sure that the service selected provides some level of customer support. The lowest price may not be the best deal if problems occur and no customer support system is available. The size of the hosting space needed is proscribed by the size of the Web site. Additional space may be added for an additional fee as the Web site grows.

Other places to put forth your qualifications as a designer are professional networking Web sites provided by unions and professional organizations.

Beyond the Classroom

Expanding Costuming Experience

When developing a resume and portfolio, the designer may discover weaknesses in his or her preparation for the next career step. The designer should seek ways to develop skills, expand experience, and add to the quality and quantity of productions included in the resume and portfolio. Some ways are:

1. Seek a job or internship with a local theater or costume shop.

2. Take additional classes in theater, art, design, or related areas. These need not be taken for credit since the goal is to improve and develop artistic skills.

3. Volunteer to work in a costume shop, local theater, or for a working designer for free. Almost everyone in theater accepts free labor. A volunteer should be specific about his or her available time. The volunteer should offer to solve problems, run errands, or work in specific areas. If the work schedule allows, ask questions. Almost everyone is willing to take the time to answer reasonable questions. The volunteer should ask permission to photograph and document work for his or her portfolio. Being observant provides valuable insight into shop procedures, work etiquette, and special construction techniques. Sometimes the most valuable lesson is what *not* to do. Proving that one is a useful addition to the team may result in a letter of recommendation or even a job offer for the volunteer.

Box 10.D   Software applications useful to costume designers

As computer technology develops so quickly, this list is only a suggestion of the types of software with which the costume designer or technologist will need to be familiar. The designer's operating system should be kept updated to current levels.

Word processing:
Microsoft Word
WordPad
simple text editors
Corel WordPerfect
Adobe Buzzword

Web site design:
Dreamweaver
iWeb
Site Masher
Site Builder

Internet browsers:
Safari
Firefox
Microsoft Internet Explorer
Opera

Spreadsheets:
Microsoft Excel
Numbers

Photo editing/art:
Adobe Photoshop
Adobe Illustrator
Corel Paint Shop Pro
Picasa
Corel Painter
Expression
Sketchbook Pro
Corel PhotoPaint

Drafting:
AutoCAD
Vectorworks

Garment/pattern drafting:
Wild Ginger Pattern Drafting
PatternMaker

Making Contacts and Networking

Applicants for undergraduate and graduate school programs and jobs need contacts with professional knowledge and reputations to write letters of recommendation and to help make contacts. The student's initial peer group in school is often the strongest network base for his or her entire career. Keeping in touch, exchanging professional invitations with classmates, and supporting and congratulating their efforts lays a strong basis for a network. Each job in and after school widens the circle of professionals that forms the designer's network. In addition, joining professional organizations and unions gives the beginning designer the opportunity to meet more experienced designers in the field and other members of the business. These groups offer job listings and workplace protection.

Young designers must learn to put themselves forward and introduce themselves to others in professional situations. In organization meetings, the young

---

Box 10.E   Designer checklist XI: Networking and interviewing to-do's

At Interviews:

1. Prepare your introduction: who you are, what you do, where you are from.
2. Smile and maintain eye contact.
3. Practice introducing yourself in front of a mirror until you are comfortable.
4. Mind your manners; be polite and sincere. Etiquette is important.
5. If possible, know something about the organization, the interviewer, and the project before arriving.
6. Know when to *stop* talking.
7. Dress appropriately.

At Professional (Networking) Events:

1. Make a plan before attending meetings or other networking occasions.
2. Make a list of people you would like to meet at events, do some research on them, seek them out, and introduce yourself.
3. Focus on each person when you are talking to them; get their business card, or write down their information.
4. Carry a notebook and pen.
5. Conduct yourself professionally at all times. Never drink too much alcohol.

Maintaining Contacts:

1. Keep a spreadsheet or index-card file of business contacts.
2. From the larger group of contacts, develop a smaller, closer group of business friends in the same or related fields to help each other by sharing contacts and making referrals for future work.
3. Write thank-you notes or e-mails for favors and assistance received.
4. Honestly praise the accomplishments of others.
5. Write notes or e-mails of congratulations to members of your network on their accomplishments.

designer should greet many new people and renew previous acquaintances. At forums or panels the designer should ask pertinent questions and introduce him or herself to speakers. The designer should always carry a notebook for taking down names and addresses, notes of interest, and questions for future encounters.

Young designers need to learn to be outgoing and friendly without dominating a discussion. A good way to relax in these situations is to first listen to the other person and then follow with questions relevant to the topic of discussion. The young designer should not present him- or herself as an expert, but as an eager student of the topic. Working to make other new people feel comfortable by introducing everyone to each other makes the young designer feel more comfortable as well.

Organizations are always looking for people to volunteer to assist or participate in projects, forums, and other activities. Volunteers get a chance to meet many people and to get a look "backstage" at the workings of the organization. Organizations and unions have newsletters, job postings and e-mail lists to keep their members informed of available positions, new materials, and new techniques.

Business Cards and Postcards

Another tool a designer needs is a business card to hand out to new contacts, to include in portfolios and letters, and to give out at conferences, lectures, and job interviews. A business card efficiently presents the name and contact information of the designer and the theater or university with which the designer is connected. The design of the business card, postcard, letterhead, portfolio, and Web site should all be related.

Business cards can be printed by professional printers in large numbers or by the designer on a computer. If the affiliation or contact information of the designer is likely to change soon or frequently, printing his or her own business cards can keep them up-to-date without waste or handwritten updates. A designer should never be reluctant to hand out business cards when meeting new contacts.

Professional Notes

A business letter thanking an interviewer for his or her time and consideration is absolutely essential following a job interview. As a network of contacts is developed, the designer should make an earnest effort to keep in touch with the members of that network. A short phone call or an e-mail offering congratulations, a thank you, a holiday greeting, or some other brief sentiment will keep the connection fresh. Designers should let everyone in their network know when they are job hunting in case their contacts know of positions available.

A professional thank you is also necessary following a favor, no matter how small, from a member of the designer's network. A brief, specific, and personal message recognizing a reference letter, a referral, a speech, or a fulfilling work experience is always appreciated, marks the designer as a person of good manners, and suggests a pleasant working partner.

While e-mail is acceptable, a handwritten or typed letter can be more memorable. Keep e-mail messages short and pertinent so that they will be read; do not clutter everyone's inboxes with frivolous communication.

Figure 10.10   Sample postcard. Freelance designers sometimes develop postcards to use for maintaining contacts and displaying their work.

Applying for a Position

The applicant can send a cover letter and resume to designers, producers, theaters, or shops in which he or she is interested in working. These "cold contacts" have a low rate of return but are still a possible avenue for first contact.

Available positions are advertised in professional journals and newsletters and on professional Web sites, but many theater positions are advertised by "word of mouth." Advertisements give the name of the opening, the skills required, any restrictions or guidelines, and the person to whom inquiries regarding the position are to be addressed. A *cover letter* and resume should be sent promptly to the potential employer.

Cover Letters

A business cover letter should be brief and to the point. The purpose of this letter is to request an interview. The resume should be attached to give the interviewer an idea if the applicant's experience meshes with the needs of the open position.

The interview gives the applicant the opportunity to present his or her portfolio and give the interviewer a sense of the designer's talents, skills, and personality.

Job Interviews and Portfolio Presentation

Design applicants should treat every portfolio presentation and interview as extremely important. Applicants should always dress in a neat and professional manner and present themselves with good grooming, good posture, and good manners.

Preparing for an Interview

Just as an actor prepares for an audition, a designer should prepare for an interview by reviewing his or her portfolio and gathering information about the person and organization granting the interview. The designer should show enthusiasm for the potential project and the position for which he or she is applying. Prepare a list of pertinent questions to ask the interviewer. No one wants to hire someone who shows no real interest in the project.

An air of confidence is a strong recommendation in itself. This confidence comes to the designer in part from experience and in part from knowing the portfolio material and its arrangement thoroughly. The designer should practice the presentation before a mirror or arrange with a friend or fellow student to practice presentations to each other.

If possible, arrange a "cold review," one given on the contents of the portfolio but not relative to a specific position. Some teachers and professional organizations give such reviews and advise students about the contents and the

---

Box 10.F   Designer checklist XII: Interview/portfolio presentations

1. Did you arrive 10–15 minutes early with all documents in hand? (Portfolio, resume, business cards, letter of reference?)
2. Did you introduce yourself and shake hands?
3. Did you address the interviewer by name at least twice?
4. Were you able to state your career goals succinctly?
5. Were you able to answer the questions addressed to you?
6. Did you solicit questions from the interviewer?
7. Did you present the material in your portfolio in a straightforward, evenly paced manner?
8. Did you ask appropriate questions of the interviewer?
9. Did you remember to leave a resume and business card?
10. Did you smile and maintain eye contact with the interviewer?
11. At the end of the interview did you shake hands and thank the interviewer for his or her time and consideration?
12. Were you able to pack up your portfolio and exit the interview in a speedy, friendly, and graceful manner?
13. Did you present a well-groomed, professional, and confident appearance?
14. Did you get a business card or the full name and mailing address of the interviewer so that you can write a thank-you note?

presentation quality of their portfolios. Even some professionals will take the time to give a student an opinion on the portfolio.

Job interviewers are looking for someone who has experience in the specific areas required in the available position. The resume and design portfolio should be arranged to show the applicant's strength in the area of the open position first and then, if time allows, material in related areas might be shown. The applicant should *not* apologize for his or her work, but be positive without bragging about or overpraising the work. The designer should remember that although he or she has seen the portfolio many, many times, the reviewer has not seen it before. Do not make excuses for the portfolio, but present it with enthusiasm and confidence, explaining simply and clearly what the viewer is seeing.

The applicant should have an exit strategy that may involve preparing a closing comment thanking the interviewer by name for his or her time and consideration, leaving a resume and a business card, and maintaining a cheerful, positive, and confident attitude.

Box 10.G   Designer checklist XIII: Questions to ask an interviewer

Try to ask questions that are not simply answered by "yes" or "no."

1. What is the length of the design period?
2. What is the approximate number of costumes required?
3. When will the show be cast?
4. What is the budget for the costumes?
5. What is the proposed designer salary or fee?
6. What is the name and contact information for the director and stage manager?
7. What experience or skills are expected?
8. What on-site hours are required?

Follow-Up

A thank-you letter to the interviewer should follow the interview within three or four days, even if no definite action has been taken regarding the position.

The designer should keep in mind that all reviewers bring their own experiences and personal tastes to the portfolio review, and should not be surprised if the portfolio elicits conflicting comments from different reviewers. These comments should be analyzed and considered by the designer without undue distress and should be used to make reasonable changes and adjustments to the portfolio.

When a designer is hired, a thank-you note or letter of appreciation to the new boss, the interviewer, the references, or anyone else who was of assistance is an important way of preparing for a new position and maintaining good will in the network.

Managing a Design Career

Keeping Track

A spreadsheet of contacts and their relevant information is a helpful tool for managing a freelance career. Names, addresses, dates of contact, notes or e-mail communication, positions held, portfolios and resumes sent, and any other useful information of which the designer needs to keep track can be entered and dated. Be sure to record correct spellings and information at the time of contact. If a business card is not available, write down the information in a notebook. An e-mail group can be developed from the networking list that makes keeping contacts up-to-date an easy e-mail. Many e-mail programs and platforms include address books that can easily be imported and exported.

Another spreadsheet is required if a designer is working freelance, as he or she must take responsibility for keeping track of receipts for all expenditures and pay earned in order to properly report income for tax evaluation.

Job Decisions

Deciding to take a specific job requires consideration of several factors: (1) What does the position offer the designer; (2) Will this position fill in a missing aspect to the resume; (3) Will the position provide new experience or contacts; and (4) Will the position pay well? No job offers everything at once. While money is important, in the early stages of a career there may be other aspects of a position or project that are more beneficial.

Joining a Union

As a designer works in theater, he or she should analyze progress being made and consider the direction that he or she would like the career to take. To earn a living most designers must join a union. To work in theaters that are union houses for actors and stage crew, designers must be union members. Even in universities, designers with union membership often are preferred. Union membership provides another mark of qualification.

Unions are organized to protect the standards, working conditions, and wages of the performing artist and to insure artistic, technical, and safety standards in the industry. Unions usually have entrance requirements: an apprenticeship or exam, initiation fees, and membership dues. The union negotiates contracts; provides a grievance process, insurance, and retirement benefits; and protects designers' rights, including creative property rights.

As a designer progresses in a design career he or she will need to investigate the requirements for entrance into one of the design unions based on where the designer works and the types of design that he or she would like to do. Box 10.H identifies the costume unions and provides contact information.

A career in costume design can be exciting, challenging, and artistically fulfilling. However, the designer must work hard at developing the opportunities to do design work and be prepared for the challenges that come with those opportunities. Designing costumes can mean long hours of hard work and low pay for the beginner. A costume designer must be prepared for the lifestyle that comes along with working in the theater and really want to participate in the both the excitement and the exhaustion of it.

Box 10.H   Theatrical costume unions and professional organizations

Various regions of the country have locals to represent their workers. Contact the national offices for information or the prospective employer for information.

United Scenic Artists (USA), New York—Local 829

A labor union and professional association of *designers, artists, and craftspeople* organized to protect craft standards, working conditions, and wages for the entertainment and decorative arts industries. Members of Local USA are *artists* and *designers* who work for theater, film, opera, ballet, television, industrial shows, commercials, and exhibitions.

Categories or classifications of membership are: scenic designer, costume designer, lighting designer, sound designer, projection designer, scenic artist, art department coordinator, computer artist, graphic artist, allied crafts, and industrial members.

For further information—**http://www.usa829.org**

Costume Designers Guild (CDG), California—International Alliance of Theatrical and Stage Employees (I.A.T.S.E.) Local 892

A labor union and professional association of *costume designers, assistant costume designers, and costume illustrators* organized to protect the standards, working conditions, and wages for members working in motion pictures, television and commercials.

For further information—**http://www.costumedesignersguild.com/cdg-home.asp**

Theatrical Wardrobe Union, New York—International Alliance of Theatrical and Stage Employees (I.A.T.S.E.) Local 764

A labor union and professional association of *wardrobe supervisors (costumers) and assistants of feature films, pilots, soap operas, commercials, and a variety of television programs.* The union jurisdiction is defined as within a 50-mile radius of Columbus Circle for film, and New York City, Long Island, and Westchester County for theater.

For further information—**http://ia764.com/**

Unite Here (formerly UNITE, the Union of Needletrades, Industrial and Textile Employees and HERE, Hotel Employees and Restaurant Employees International Union)

A labor union that represents workers of apparel and textile manufacturing, apparel distribution centers, and apparel retail and industrial laundries, hotels, casinos, food service, airport concessions, and restaurants. The union negotiates wages and benefits. (Some costume-shop workers are members of this union.)

For further information—**http://www.unitehere.org/about/**

Association of Theatrical Artists and Craftspeople (ATAC)

A professional trade association for artists and craftspeople in theatre, film, television advertising, display, and education. Works to promote high artistic standards, better wages and safe working conditions for those working with props, costumes, millinery, puppetry, display, and special effects.

For further information—**ATACBiz@aol.com**

Publications: *Entertainment Sourcebook, The ATAC Quarterly*

United States Institute of Theatre Technology (USITT)

An association of design, production, and technology professionals in the performing arts and entertainment industry. Provides conferences, trade shows, symposia for furthering the members' education and knowledge of new technologies, listservs, and networking.

For further information—**http://usitt.org/**

Publications: *Sightlines,* Theatre Design & Technology: Journal of USITT

Appendix I

Historical Research Sources

The following chronological list of suggested research topics for the costume designer includes sources for costume detail and visual style. Though it is by no means exhaustive, a wide variety of references has been included. Note there is some overlap between periods, with a particular artist sometimes appearing more than once (second listing followed by an asterisk).

Egyptian, 4000 BC–30 BC

Statues   Wall paintings   Architecture
Mummy cases

Greek, 600 BC–100 BC

Sculpture   Architecture   Vase painting

Roman, 753 BC–AD 330

Sculpture   Architecture   Coins
Mosaics   Wall Painting

Byzantine, 400–1100; Romanesque, 900–1200

Mosaics   Frescos   Tapestries
Manuscript illumination   Sculpture   Architecture (especially churches)

Gothic: Early Gothic, 1200–1350; Late Gothic, 1350–1450

Sculpture   Paintings   Manuscript illumination
Stained glass   Brasses   Tapestries

ARTISTS

Italian

Cimabue   1240–c. 1302
Ducchio   c. 1255–1318
Giotto   c. 1266–1337
Simone Martini   1284–1344
Andrea Orcagna   1308–1368
Pietro Lorenzetti   active 1320–1345
Ambrogio Lorenzetti   active 1319–1347
Francesco Traini   c. 1321–mid-1300s
Fra Angelico   1387–1455
Antonio Pisanello   c. 1395–1455
Paolo Uccello   c. 1396–1475
Massaccio   1401–1428
Fra Filippo Lippi   c. 1406–1469

Flemish

Roger van der Weyden   c. 1400–1464
Dirck Bouts   c. 1415–1475
Jan van Eyck   active 1422–1441

Early Renaissance, 1450–1550

Woodcuts   Engravings   Manuscript illumination
Tapestries   Sculpture   Brasses

ARTISTS

Italian

Piero della Francesco   c. 1410/20–1492
Benozzo Gozzoli   1421–1497
Alesso Baldovinetti   1426–1499
Gentile Bellini   1429–1507
Cosimo Tura   c. 1430–1495
Andrea Mantegna   1431–1506
Giovanni Bellini   1431–1516
Andrea Verrochio   1435–1488
Antonio Pollaiuoli   1432–1498
Cosimo Rosselli   1437–1507
Piero Pollaiuoli   1441–1496
Luca Signorelli   c. 1445–1523
Perugino   c. 1445–1523
Sandro Botticelli   1447–1510
Domenico Ghirlandaio   1449–1494
Ercoli Roberti   c. 1450–1496

Leonardo da Vinci   1452–1519
Bernardino Pinturicchio   c. 1454–1513
Filippino Lippi   1457–1504
Lorenzo di Credi   c. 1458–1537
Michelangelo Buonarroti   1475–c. 1564
Giorgione   1476–1510
Raphael Santi   1483–1520
Sebastiano del Piombo   1485–1547
Andrea del Sarto   1486–1531
Titian   1487–c. 1576
Vittore Carpaccio   active 1490–c. 1526
Giovanni Baptista Rosso   1494–1540
Jacopo Pontormo   1494–1556
Paris Bordone   1500–1571
Francesco Parmigianino   1503–1540
Agnolo Bronzino   1503–1572
Francesco Primiticcio   c. 1504–1570
Georgio Vasari   1511–1574

French

Jean Fouquet   c. 1420–1480
Jean Clouet   c. 1485–1540
François Clouet   c. 1510–1572

Flemish/Dutch

Hans Memling   c. 1430–1495
Hieronymus Bosch   1450–1516
Quentin Matsys   c. 1464–1530
Gerard David   d. 1523
Anthonis Mor   c. 1517–1576
Pieter Brueghel   c. 1525–1569
Guillim Stretes   active 1530s–1550s

German

Matthias Grünewald   c. 1470/80–1528
Albrecht Dürer   1471–1528
Lucas Cranach   1472–1553
Hans Baldung   c. 1484–1545
Barthel Bruyn   c. 1492–1555
Hans Holbein the Younger (worked in England)   c. 1497–1543
Christoph Amberger   c. 1500–1561

Late Renaissance (Elizabethan), 1550–1625

Portraits	Miniatures	Authentic garments
Tapestries	Engravings	Sculpture

ARTISTS

Italian

>Francesco Primiticcio*   d. 1570
>Paris Bordone*   d. 1571
>Agnolo Bronzino*   d. 1572
>Georgio Vasari*   d. 1574
>Titian*   d. 1576
>Jacopo Tintoretto   1518–1594
>Giovanni Battista Moroni   1525–1578
>Paolo Veronese   1528–1588
>Michelangelo Merise de Caravaggio   1573–1610
>Guido Reni   1575–1642
>Artemisia Gentileschi   1593–1651

English

>Federigo Zuccari   c. 1540–1609
>Hans Eworth   active c. 1545–1574
>Nicholas Hilliard   1547–1619
>Marcus Gheeraerts   1561–1636
>Inigo Jones   1573–1652
>Isaac Oliver   active 1590–1617

Flemish

>Pieter Pourbus   1523–1584
>Peter Paul Rubens   1577–1640

Spanish

>Alonzo Sanches-Coello   c. 1531–1588
>El Greco (born Greek)   1548–1614

French

>François Clouet*   d. 1572

Seventeenth Century: Cavalier, 1625–1660; Restoration, 1660–1715

>Authentic garments   Woodcuts   Engravings
>Paintings

ARTISTS

Italian

>Guido Reni*   d. 1642
>Carlo Dolci   1616–1686

Flemish/Dutch

>Peter Paul Rubens*   d. 1640
>Franz Hals   1580–1666
>David Teniers, Elder   1582–1649
>David Teniers, Younger   1610–1690

Cornelis de Vos   1584–1651
Nicholaes Elias   c. 1590–1654
Jacob Jordaens   1593–1678
Anthony van Dyck   1599–1641
Adriaen Brouwer   c. 1605–1638
Rembrandt van Rijn   1606–1669
Jan Miensz Molenaer   c. 1609–1668
Adriaen Ostade   1610–1684
Bartholomeus van der Helst   1613–1670
Gerard Terborch   1617–1681
Jan Steen   1626–1679
Gabriel Metsu   1629–1667
Pieter de Hooch   1630–1677
Jan Vermeer   1632–1674

French

Antoine Le Nain   1588–1648
Jacques Callot   c. 1592–1635
Louis Le Nain   1593–1648
Simon Vouet   1590–1649
George de La Tour   1593–1652
Philippe de Champaigne   1602–1674
Abraham Bosse   1602–1676
Mathiew Le Nain   1607–1677
Pierre Mignard   1612–1695
Charles le Brun   1619–1690
Nicolas de Largillière   1656–1746
Hyacinthe Rigaud   1659–1743
Nicholas Lancret   1660–1743
Antoine Coypel   1661–1722
Jean François de Troy   1679–1752
Antoine Watteau   1684–1721
Jean Baptiste van Loo   1684–1745
John Baptiste Joseph Pater   1695–1736

English

Inigo Jones*   d. 1652
Daniel Mytens   c. 1590–c. 1647
Gerard S. van Honthorst   1590–1656
Cornelius Johnson   1593–1661
Wenceslaus Hollar   1607–1677
Sir Peter Lely   1618–1680
Jacob Huysmans   1633–1696
Sir Godfrey Kneller   c. 1646–1723

Spanish

Jusepe de Ribera   1588–1652
Franciso Zurbarán   1598–1664
Diego Velázquez   1599–1660
Bartolome Esteban Murillo   1617–1682

Eighteenth Century:
Early Georgian, 1715–1750; Late Georgian, 1750–1790;
Directoire and First Empire (Regency), 1790–1815

Antique garments	Engravings	Paintings
Book illustrations	Fashion plates (end of century)	

ARTISTS

Italian

Giovanni Battisti Tiepolo   1696–1770
Antonio Canaletto   1697–1768
Pietro Longhi   1702–1785
Francesco Guardi   1712–1793

French

Antoine Watteau*   d. 1721
Antoine Coypel*   d. 1722
John Baptiste Joseph Pater*   d. 1736
Nicholas Lancret*   d. 1743
Hyacinthe Rigaud*   d. 1743
Jean Baptiste van Loo   d. 1745
Nicholas de Largillière*   d. 1746
Jean-Marc Nattier   1685–1766
Louis Toque   1696–1772
Jean Baptiste Simeon Chardin   1699–1779
J. E. Liotard   1702–1789
François Boucher   1703–1770
Quentin La Tour   1704–1788
Carle van Loo   1705–1765
Louis-Michel van Loo   1707–1771
Jean-Baptiste Perroneau   c. 1715–1783
Jean Baptiste Greuze   1725–1805
François Hubert Drouais   1727–1775
Jean Honoré Fragonard   1732–1806
Antoine Vestier   1740–1824
Jean Michel Moreau (le Jeune)   1741–1814
Jacques-Louis David   1748–1825
Louise Elizabeth Vigée-Lebrun   1755–1842
Paul-Pierre Prud'hon   1758–1823
Louis Boilly   1761–c. 1830
J. B. Isabey   1767–1855
François Gerard   1770–1837
Antoine Jean Gros   1771–1835
Jean-Auguste-Dominique Ingres   1780–1867
Theodore Géricault   1791–1824

Spanish

Francisco de Goya   1746–1828

English

Sir Godfrey Kneller*   d. 1723
Joseph Highmore   1692–1780
William Hogarth   1697–1764
Arthur Devis   c. 1711–1787
Allan Ramsey   1713–1784
Joshua Reynolds   1723–1792
Francis Cotes   1725–1770
Thomas Gainsborough   1727–1788
Johann Zoffany   1733–1810
George Romney   1734–1802
Samuel Cotes   1734–1818
Francis Wheatley   1747–1801
Joseph R. Smith   1752–1812
Robert Dighton   1752–1812
William Beechey   1753–1839
W. R. Bigg   1755–1828
Thomas Rowlandson   1756–1827
Isaac Cruikshank   c. 1756–c. 1811
James Gilray   1757–1815
John Hoppner   1758–1810
Adam Buck (Irish)   1759–1833
John Opie   1761–1807
George Morland   1764–1804
Thomas Lawrence   1769–1830

American

Joseph Blackburn   1700–1765
Robert Feke   1705–1750
Joseph Badger   1708–1765
John Hesslius   1728–1778
John Singleton Copley   1737–1815
Benjamin West   1738–1820
Charles W. Peale   1741–1827
Ralph Earle   1751–1801
Gilbert Stuart   1755–1828
John Trumbull   1756–1843
Edward Savage   1761–1817

Scottish

Henry Raeburn   1756–1823

Nineteenth Century:
Romantic, 1815–1830; Crinoline, 1840–1865;
Bustle, 1865–1890; The Gay Nineties, 1890–1900

Authentic garments	Book illustrations	Engravings
Paintings	Fashion plates	Illustrated magazines
Daguerreotypes (1839–1851)		Photographs (after 1850)

ARTISTS

French

Antoine Jean Gros*   d. 1835
François Gerard*   d. 1837
Louise Elizabeth Vigée-Lebrun*   d. 1842
J. B. Isabey*   d. 1855
Jean-Auguste-Dominique Ingres*   d. 1867
Horace Vernet   1789–1863
Eugène Delacroix   1798–1863
Garvarni   1804–1866
Constantin Guys   1805–1883
Honoré Daumier   1808–1879
Jean-François Millet   1814–1875
Theodore Chassériau   1819–1856
Gustave Courbet   1819–1877
Edouard Manet   1832–1883
Edgar Dégas   1834–1917
James Tissot (worked in England after 1870)   1836–1902
Claude Monet   1840–1926
Berthe Morisot   1841–1895
Pierre-Auguste Renoir   1841–1919
Henri Rousseau   1844–1910
Paul Gauguin   1848–1903
Jean Béraud   1849–1935
Vincent van Gogh   1853–1890
Georges Seurat   1859–1891
Henri-Marie-Raymond de Toulouse-Lautrec   1864–1901
Pierre Bonnard   1867–1947
Joseph Marius Avy   1871–c. 1941

Italian

Pier Celestino Gilardi   1837–1905
Mariano Fortuny y de Mandraso   1871–1949
Amedeo Modigliani   1884–1920

Prussian

Franz Winterhalter (worked in England and France)   1806–1873

Belgian

Alfred Stevens   1828–1906

Swedish

Carl Larsson   1853–1919

English

W. R. Bigg*   d. 1828
Adam Buck*   d. 1833
Henry Alken 1784–1851
Robert Cruikshank   1789–1856

George Cruikshank   1792–1878
H. K. Browne (Phiz)   1815–1882
John Leech   1817–1864
Ford Madox Brown   1821–1893
Holman Hunt   1827–1910
Dante Gabriel Rossetti   1828–1882
John Millais   1829–1896
Edward Burne-Jones   1833–1898
William Morris   1834–1896
Aubrey Beardsley   1872–1898

American

Samuel Waldo   1783–1861
Thomas Sully   1783–1872
Samuel Morse   1791–1872
William Jewett   1795–1873
Winslow Homer   1836–1910
Thomas Nast   1840–1902
Thomas Eakins   1844–1916
Mary Cassatt   1845–1926
William Merritt Chase   1849–1916
Howard Pyle   1853–1911
James McNeil Whistler   1854–1903
Edwin Austin Abbey   1852–1911
John Singer Sargent   1856–1925
Joseph Pennell   1860–1926
Charles Dana Gibson   1867–1944

Twentieth Century

Authentic garments	College yearbooks	Paintings
Mail-order catalogs	Photographs	Men's magazines
Fashion magazines	Newspapers	Ladies' magazines
Movies	Book illustrations	Photo journals

ARTISTS

French

Alphonse Mucha   1860–1939
Henri Matisse   1869–1954
Raoul Dufy   1877–1953
Fernand Léger   1881–1955
Erté   1893–1990

Norwegian

Edvard Munch   1863–1944

Belgian

James Ensor   1860–1949

Russian

Marc Chagall   1887–1985

Italian

Giorgio de Chirico   1888–1978

Mexican

Diego Rivera   1886–1957
Frida Kahlo   1907–1954

Spanish

Pablo Picasso   1881–1973
Joan Miró   1893–1983
Salvador Dali   1904–1987

German

Max Ernst   1891–1976

Belgian

René Magritte   1898–1967

Swiss

Paul Klee   1879–1940

UK

Frances Bacon (English/Australian/Irish)   1909–1992
David Hockney (English)   1937–

American

Maxfield Parrish   1870–1966
Edward Hopper   1882–1967
Georgia O'Keeffe   1887–1986
Thomas Hart Benton   1889–1975
Grant Wood   1892–1942
Norman Rockwell   1894–1980
Reginald Marsh   1898–1954
Ben Shahn   1898–1969
Jackson Pollock   1912–1958
Andrew Wyeth   1917–2009
Roy Lichtenstein   1923–1997
Frank Frazetta   1928–
Andy Warhol   1928–1987
Jasper Johns   1930–
R. C. Gorman (Native American)   1931–2005
Red Grooms   1937–
Peter Max (German American)   1937–

Appendix II
Historical Costume Outline

The following historical outline is designed to give the student an overview of the history of occidental dress. The periods and cultures discussed are those most commonly required in Western European and American drama.

Fashion is evolutionary; major changes occur slowly. In every period there are holdover fashions. New features appear before major silhouette changes are made. Older people, conservatives, and the poor retain familiar or simpler styles; the young, the elite and wealthy, and counterculture groups seek new, different, and sometimes shocking fashions. The costume periods represented here fall into generally accepted divisions. The fashion emphasis can be seen to shift from vertical to horizontal, stiff to soft, and "natural" to "contrived" silhouettes.

Wars, powerful figures, exploration, new sources of trade, revolution, political viewpoints, economics, sexual mores, and archaeological discoveries have long been major influences on dress. More recently, improved communication, ethnic dress, popular music and dance, the discovery of new synthetic materials, and space exploration have all had their impact. This outline represents primarily major trends and influences. Idiosyncratic fashions are not generally addressed. Since the history of costume is not as episodic as such an outline suggests, it is offered only as a springboard for further study and diligent research.

Egyptian (4000 BC–30 BC)

GENERAL CHARACTERISTICS

Egyptian dress was simple in construction and depended on the graceful arrangement of fabric into folds and pleats for its effect. The silhouette for both men and women was essentially vertical and placed emphasis on the head by the use of wigs, makeup, and elaborate collars. Garments were made of linen in fabrics ranging from very fine to coarse.

Dress for Men

Egyptian men wore a simple loincloth (*schenti*), alone or topped by a wrapped skirt or a T-shaped tunic (*kalisiris*). The men's tunic or skirt length might be above the knees, calf length, or ankle length. Some men's skirts were stiffly starched, while others were softly draped. The tunic was often of sheer fabric and could be either very close-fitting or full and flowing. The excess fullness in all these garments was concentrated in the front with drapery or pleats held by a girdle or belt. The cloth or leather girdle could have a decorated tab.

A variety of shawls were draped to please the wearer. The royal *haik*, worn by pharaohs and their queens, was a large, sheer, shawl-type garment that when wrapped and tied around the figure, gave the impression of a skirt, a tunic with capelike sleeves, and sometimes a cloak.

Hair for men might be long or cut in a round bob or in "shingled" layers. Hair could be dressed in corkscrew curls or braids and was often arranged to expose the ears. Hair was usually parted in the middle and held by a *fillet* of leather, ribbon, or metal. The Egyptians' natural hair was black and abundant, but during some periods of Egyptian history heads were shaved and elaborate wigs were worn. Some wigs were dyed in fantastic colors such as red or blue. The hair or wig was sometimes covered with a cloth of plain or striped fabric. The characteristic shape of the Egyptian head and hair was broad at the temples and somewhat large in relationship to the body.

Very elaborate headdresses or crowns were worn by the pharaoh, his queen, and other members of the royal family. These headdresses incorporated the symbols of the *uraeus* (hooded cobra), the solar disk (symbol of eternity), the vulture, and the royal feather or plumes. Upper Egypt and Lower Egypt each had a characteristic crown. When the two portions of the country were united under the same ruler (around 1450 BC), the two crowns were combined into one.

The most recognizable Egyptian accessory is the collar. Made of enameled shapes or colorful beads strung together in rows both horizontally and vertically, the collar was worn by both sexes. Other jewelry included wide bracelets, armbands and anklets, simple necklaces, rings, and the decorated girdle. The *pectoral*, a semi-official ornament worn by members of court, was a necklace consisting of a large gold and enamel medallion hanging from a chain and resting on the chest below the collar.

Men were generally clean-shaven and used *kohl*, a black makeup, to create a black line around their eyes and extending outward toward the hairline. The *postiche*, the only beard represented in Egyptian art, appears to have been false and ceremonial in nature.

Simple sandals consisted of a pointed sole of leather or woven grass with a decorated strap through the toes and across the instep.

Dress for Women

The three basic garments for women were a skirt, a T-shaped tunic, and a shawl. The high-waisted skirt, supported by one or two straps, was wrapped or gathered on a string under the breasts, leaving them exposed. Covering some of these garments was a mesh of beads or cut leather worked in petal or feather motifs. The straps and girdles were often embroidered with geometric or organic designs.

Two versions of the tunic were worn by women: (1) a full tunic or robe of pleated or draped fabric, and (2) a plain, close-fitting version of the T-shaped tunic, loose or girded. Shawls were used by women to protect themselves from cool evening air and hot sun. Royal women might also wear the royal *haik*. A woman's garments might be draped in a wide variety of ways. Belts of leather, cord, and woven ribbons held them in place. Garments are represented in most Egyptian art as tight-fitting, but many were actually loose and flowing.

Collars, necklaces, armbands, and anklets all were worn.

Women also wore wigs, but in most periods they were worn over their own hair. Most styles for women were long, but there are examples of the short, shingled style for women. Women's wigs were dressed with fillets, diadems, cloth coverings, and crowns for queens. A cone-shaped ornament containing scented ointment was sometimes worn on the top of the head.

Women wore kohl eyeliner and eye shadow and painted their lips, fingertips, and toenails with henna.

Greek (600 BC–100 BC)

GENERAL CHARACTERISTICS

Greek dress was the result of the artful draping of rectangular pieces of soft, wool cloth. Fabrics were woven to size for their intended use and were edged with borders. Small, all-over designs were embroidered, woven, worked like tapestry, or painted. Fabrics were dyed in bright colors, and some were pleated.

The silhouette was vertical with a natural relationship between the head and body.

Dress for Men

Dress for Greek men consisted of a *chiton* and a *himation* or a *chlamys*.

There were basically two types of chitons: the *Doric* and the *Ionic*. The older Doric chiton (also called *peplos*) consisted of a large rectangle of cloth (usually wool) measuring the wearer's height plus one foot by twice the width from either fingertip-to-fingertip or elbow-to-elbow. The top edge was folded down, and the whole piece was wrapped end to end around the body leaving the right side open. With the back pulled over the front, the garment was pinned together on each shoulder with *fibulae* (decorative pins). The fabric was drawn taut across the back of the neck with a drape formed in the front by allowing extra fabric between the pins. A thin girdle was tied at the waist, and the excess fabric was bloused up over it.

The Ionic chiton was similar to the Doric but did not have an overfold. The Ionic was usually fuller and more often of cotton or linen. The ends of the rectangle might be sewn together. The garment was then pinned at the shoulders and girded in the same manner as the Doric. A distinguishing characteristic of the Ionic chiton was sleeves, created by pinning the top edges of the rectangle together with fibulae.

The himation, a large rectangular cloak, was usually worn like a shawl. First draped over the left arm and shoulder, it was then pulled across the back, under or over the right arm and shoulder, then again thrown over the left arm. The edge of the himation that rested across the back could be drawn up over the head for protection from the weather. Many variations of this arrangement were possible. The himation was often the only garment worn by men.

The chlamys was a smaller rectangle of cloth used as a cape by soldiers, horsemen, travelers, and sometimes women. It too might be worn by men as their only garment. The chlamys was wrapped around the neck and tied or pinned with a fibula.

Old men wore their garments to the floor, while young men often wore their chitons well above the knees. Occasional examples of the Asiatic tunic are found represented in Greek dress, usually as an undergarment for a chiton.

The Greek men wore rings but did not wear armbands or anklets. For festivals wreaths of leaves were worn, and kings might wear a gold diadem.

From the fifth century most Greek men wore their hair short and curly, held in place with a fillet. Older men wore short beards and moustaches.

The *petasus*, a large brim hat of felt or straw, was worn by Greeks when traveling. Other small caps were sometimes used.

Although men frequently went barefoot, sandals or soft, calf-length boots of leather also were worn.

Dress for Women

Greek women wore both the Doric and the Ionic chiton, often together. A wide variety of girding was used by women, creating high-waisted, natural-waisted, and low-waisted effects. The Doric overfold varied in length from just below the bosom to about knee-length. The side of the chiton might be open or stitched, and some were stitched across the shoulders.

Women wore both the himation and the chlamys, draped in a variety of ways. A fold might be brought over the head, or a separate veil might be worn.

Women's hair was dressed in a knot at the back of the head on a line designed to balance the nose. A variety of diadems, fillets, bag caps, and scarves were used around the head to hold the hair. Women also wore the petasus.

Women were often barefoot, but might also wear sandals similar to those worn by men.

Roman (753 BC–AD 330)

GENERAL CHARACTERISTICS

The Romans were influenced by the Greeks in art, culture, and dress. Roman dress tended to have more bulk than Greek dress. This was achieved by layering several garments or by wrapping the voluminous *toga* many times around the body. Roman art and dress expressed a taste for solid forms, bold colors, and strong contrasts.

In Republican and Imperial Rome the primary fabrics were linen and wool. Later, silk was imported from China. Fabrics were used in the natural off-white or were bleached for men's togas and other garments. Women's fabrics were dyed with borders embroidered or woven at the edges. In Imperial Rome increasing use was made of gold embroidery.

Dress for Men

The basic dress for Roman men consisted of a loincloth, tunic (*tunica*), and a large, wrapped *toga* or a cloak. Workmen wore a tunic and loincloth; upper-class men might wear a tunic and toga or a toga alone.

The Roman tunica consisted of two rectangles of cloth sewn together at the top and sides to form a knee-length shirt. The openings for the arms were allowed along the sides of the rectangle, rather than from the top as in the Greek chiton. Most tunics had sleeves to the elbow or just covering the upper shoulder. The long-sleeved tunic (*manicata*) was common by the time of the Empire. The long tunic with long sleeves (*talaris*) was worn by older men and dignitaries. A fuller, T-shaped tunic with wide sleeves (*dalmatic*) was developed about the second century. More than one tunic might be worn at a time. The tunic was often white or off-white wool and could be decorated with bands of embroidery or woven stripes at the neck, sleeves, and hem. The *clavi* (decorative bands about 1½ inches wide) were placed down each side of the tunica, front and back. Until the third century these decorations carried class distinctions.

For centuries the toga was the garment that distinguished Roman citizens from "foreigners." The earliest distinct version was a piece of woolen cloth shaped like a segment of a circle, approximately 16 feet along the straight edge by 6 feet at the widest point. The toga was sometimes trimmed along one edge with a colored band. The wrapping and arranging of the toga was varied and complex. A simple wrapping started with one point at the left foot, the fabric over the left shoulder with the straight edge along the neck and down the back, under or over the right arm, one or more wraps around the body, and up over the left shoulder or draped across the left arm.

The color and decoration of the toga identified its wearer by class and occasion. The *toga pura* or *virilis*, an untrimmed cream-white wool, was the ordinary dress of the Roman citizen. The *toga praetexta* was a toga trimmed with purple bands and reserved for public officials, priests, magistrates, consuls, and others. Candidates for public office donned a bleached white toga called the *toga candida*. For mourning, the *toga pulla*, a dark gray, brown, or black toga, was worn. The triumphal *toga picta* was worn by victorious generals and was the official dress of emperors. It is believed to have been of purple fabric embroidered with gold thread.

When not wearing the toga, the Roman men wore cloaks and capes. The *paenula*, a semicircular cloak with or without a hood, was made of heavy cloth or leather and was used as outerwear by poorer folk, travelers, and sometimes soldiers. Similar to the Greek himation, the *pallium* was associated with philosophers and teachers. The *palludamentum* was a square of fine wool—white, scarlet, or purple—that was worn by Roman military officers.

Men's hair was cut short, curled, and dressed forward over the forehead. Most men were clean-shaven, except while in mourning. In about AD 50 neatly clipped beards and mustaches came into vogue.

Few hats were worn, but the petasus was used for traveling, and small caps were worn by workers. The back fold of the toga was pulled up over the head for warmth or protection. Wreaths of laurel leaves were given as prizes, to celebrate victories, and, reproduced in gold, to denote divinity. Later emperors, declaring their divinity, claimed the gold wreath as their crown.

The *femoralia*, a kind of short pants adopted from the barbarians, was sometimes worn under the toga by soldiers. Otherwise, legs were bare. Feet were shod in sandals, soft leather shoes, or calf-high boots.

Men wore fibulae and signet rings that were used as seals. Young boys wore an amulet called the *bulla*.

Dress for Women

Roman women wore a variety of tunics, chitons, and shawls. They tended to wear more layers than Greek women.

A loincloth and a snug band that supported the breasts were worn as undergarments. The *tunica intima*, a version of the Greek chiton in fine linen, was worn as an undergarment and as a house-dress. The *stola* was sometimes a version of the Ionic chiton, at other times a tunica talaris. A variety of girdings were possible. The Roman woman wore her stola instep-length and sometimes added a train by inserting a piece of fabric (*institia*) into the back of the girdle.

Over the stola was worn a shawl, a draped *palla*, or, for travel, the paenula. An ungirded dalmatic gradually took the place of the palla in the later part of the period. Frequently trimmed with *clavi*, this garment is prominent among the representations of the early Christian saints.

Greek hairstyles were also worn by Roman women, but in the later periods hairdressing became much more elaborate. False hair-pieces were used. Roman styles featured height in front achieved by frizzing or curling the hair or wearing a coronet or false hairpiece. Back hair was arranged either high or low on the head in braids, buns, or curls. Women sometimes covered their head with a veil or a fold of the palla.

Sandals and soft leather shoes for women could be brightly col-ored—red, green, pale yellow, or white.

The Roman woman had bracelets, earrings, rings, fibulae, hair-pins, and coronets. Jewelry was worked in gold, inlaid with colors, or set with uncut stones or *cameos* (profiles carved in relief into pre-cious or semiprecious stones).

Byzantine (400–1100)
Romanesque (900–1200)

GENERAL CHARACTERISTICS

Garments in both the Eastern and Western Roman Empires developed from the garments of Imperial Rome. In Byzantium, dress reflected the Asian influence of the countries to the east and the wealth of the Eastern Empire. Garments in the Western Empire began to incorporate influences from the "barbarians." Modesty in dress was required of both men and women: no bare arms or legs for persons of status.

Byzantine fabrics were extraordinarily rich. Linen, wool, cot-ton, and silk were used. Borders and medallions of embroidery were enriched with gold, gems, and pearls. Western European fabrics were coarse, heavy, and usually unadorned. Wool was woven into stripes, plaids, and simple patterns. Various weights of linen and cotton were also available in solids, plaids, and stripes and were sometimes creped or pleated. Silk was rare and expensive in the

countries farthest from the east. Velvet was also available by the end of this period.

Dress for Men

For undergarments men wore a *chemise* (loose-fitting tunic with long sleeves) and *braccae* or *braies* (loose-fitting breeches). Hose cut of woven cloth were gartered or tied to the breeches. A tunic cut like the tunica manicata or talaris was then added. The neckline was high and round with a small slit to admit the head. The neck, wrists, and hem might be trimmed with a band of embroidery or braid. The length varied from slightly below the knee to the floor. A loose-sleeved overtunic (*dalmatica*) might be worn. This combination became associated with liturgical dress and royalty.

The Romanesque tunic (*bliaut* or *bliaud*) was a semifitted garment with sleeves; it was laced or sewn up under the arms each time it was worn. The sleeves of the bliaut were either close-fitting or wide at the wrist. Tunic lengths varied from above the knee to the calf or floor. Slits in the front and back or sides allowed for freedom of movement. Gores were sometimes added from the hip down for extra fullness. A girdle of leather or fabric might be worn at the waist or hip.

A rectangular or semicircular cape or cloak was then added for both indoor and outdoor wear. The *cope* was a half-circular cape that was worn draped over the left shoulder and fastened on the right shoulder with a large brooch. A distinctly Byzantine decoration consisted of a large square or diamond-shaped patch, the *tablion*, positioned to rest on the breast of the wearer. The *chausable* was a large circle or oval with a hole for the head. This garment later became part of church vestments.

The toga was reduced to a stiff and elaborately embroidered band used as a symbol of official office and became part of the church vestments of the Eastern Orthodox Church.

Hair for men could be a short (ear-length) or a long (chin-length) bob or "pageboy" style. Men either were clean-shaven or had small pointed beards and thin mustaches.

Byzantine men wore few head coverings, but Western European men wore a small skullcap, a *coif* (a cloth cap that tied under the chin), or a hood. Fillets (bands of material) were still common, and chaplets or wreaths of flowers were worn for festivals and celebrations. Soft, felt caps and the Greek petasus were worn. The Byzantine emperor's crown was a wide, gold band flaring outward and was set with jewels and strings of hanging pearls. Western European kings wore a variety of crowns, many of them with foliated tops.

Jewelry for men included collars, rings, brooches, elaborate girdles, and belts set with pearls and uncut stones. Byzantine jewels were more elaborate than those of Western Europe and boasted a profusion of pearls.

Men's shoes were slightly pointed and made of cloth or soft leather elaborately decorated.

Dress for Women

Women wore an ankle-length chemise of off-white linen with long sleeves and a high neck as an undergarment. A T-shaped tunic was worn over the chemise, usually covering it completely. A shorter tunic (dalmatic) might be worn on top. Byzantine and early Romanesque tunics were still decorated with the Roman clavi. The neck of the upper tunics might be high with a slash opening or a shallow scoop revealing the chemise or undertunic. The edges of sleeves, necklines, and hems were often trimmed with bands of embroidery or woven stripes. The position of the girdle varied from high to natural-waist to hipbone level.

The women's bliaut was the formal court costume in Western Europe during the eleventh and twelfth centuries. A gown with a tight-fitting torso, the bliaut was very full in the skirt and had hanging sleeves.

Romanesque women also wore the *cote*, another version of a T-shaped tunic. The cote was fitted in the body, usually had fitted sleeves, and flared from the hip to a very full hem. The neckline sometimes dipped in a wide, shallow curve. The sleeves and the body were laced up or stitched with each wearing. For ladies of status the length of garments began to exceed the wearer's height and dribbled luxuriously on the floor. The *surcote* was a loose, sleeveless overgown with large armholes.

A variety of rectangular and semicircular cloaks or mantles were worn over other garments, both indoors and out. Byzantine women wore a chausable or cope clasped with a brooch on the left shoulder (the empress on the right). Romanesque women wore a chausable or fur-lined mantle that opened in the front.

Byzantine women dressed their hair in the fashion of Imperial Rome. The empress added an elaborate crown set with uncut stones and decorated with hanging pearls. Other women wore turbans or veils. Byzantine hair fashions persisted in Western Europe until about AD 1000. Romanesque women parted their hair in the center and dressed it in long braids worn down the back. A fillet, a small crown, or a *chaplet* of flowers (real or of metal) might be worn around the head. Braids were sometimes pinned up and the veil wrapped around or draped over the head and pinned to the braids.

Jewelry for women included rings, belt buckles, brooches, and crowns made of gold and uncut stones. Byzantine women wore large earrings and elaborate collars of jewels and gold that covered the neckline of the garment underneath. Pearls were particularly abundant in Byzantine jewelry.

Shoes for women were embroidered cloth or soft leather and shaped to the foot. Knee-length stockings, cut of woven cloth, were worn.

Early Gothic (1200–1350)

GENERAL CHARACTERISTICS

A silhouette resembling a narrow-based triangle evolved. Garments were generally long, and finer fabrics made garments more fluid and graceful. Though not revealing bare arms, legs, or chest, clothing began to express a less serious nature through a variety of whimsical touches. *Parti-coloring*, the practice of making garments half one color and half another, was popular. Heraldry developed from the identification worn by the Crusaders.

Wool, linen, and cotton in various weights were used for garments and veils. Silk was more common than in previous periods and was woven into brocades, satins, velvets, and thin tissues for veils. Furs were used to line cloaks for sumptuousness and extra warmth.

Dress for Men

The man's chemise was shortened to mid-thigh and slit up front and back to facilitate movement. The cote might be knee, calf, ankle, or instep length. The sleeves of the cote were wide at the shoulder and narrow at the wrist. Buttons, a recent innovation, fastened the sleeve from the elbow down. Below the hip belt the cote flared slightly for easy movement.

The sleeveless surcote was added over the cote. The length of the surcote was also varied. Slits in the front and back of the skirt section were needed for horsemen. The surcote might be parti-colored and elaborately decorated around the neck. Many displayed heraldic designs. Later surcotes began to have sleeves or decorative hanging pieces at the armhole.

A new garment (about 1300) was the *cotehardie.* A tailored garment with a fitted body and slightly flared skirt, the cotehardie was often buttoned down the front. The length varied from the upper leg to the floor and it, too, might be parti-colored. The sleeves might end above the elbow with a *tippet* (narrow hanging strip of fabric) or be long and fitted (also buttoned from elbow down). For extra warmth a quilted or fur-lined *doublet* or *jupe* might be worn between the chemise and the cotehardie.

With the exposure of the legs, hose became better fitting and perhaps were made of knitted cloth. The wool hose were separate (not tights) and tied to a belt at the waist or to the underpants. As tunic skirts grew shorter, underpants grew shorter and hose became longer. Hose were often parti-colored.

Hair was cut jaw-length or a little longer, often with bangs, and set in waves. After 1300, small neatly clipped beards and mustaches appeared.

Jeweled circlets of metal worn on the head continued in fashion. Felt caps, some with brims, were worn, but the most common head covering after 1300 was the *coif.* A small, close-fitting cloth bonnet, the coif had strings that tied under the chin. Made of white linen or black silk, the coif was used for centuries, both alone and under other hats.

The *chaperon*, a hood with a shoulder-length cape attached, was a very popular head covering. Usually seen with the cotehardie, it was also worn with other tunics or robes. Combined with a long, loose-fitting tunic, it became part of the monks' habit. The point on the back of the hood was called the *liripipe* and grew to exaggerated lengths. The hood often was worn off the head, hanging down the back. The cape was frequently trimmed along the bottom edge with *dagging* (scallops or other shapes cut along garment edges).

Other capes and mantles also had an attached hood or shoulder-length cape (*pelerine*). The circular or semicircular cape or mantle continued to be worn both indoors and out.

Brooches were used as clasps on tunics and cloaks and to decorate hats. Elaborate belts were sometimes worn, either set the full length with jewels or adorned with decorative buckles and tips. Rings and ornate jeweled "collars" (c. 1350) might incorporate the insignia of a man's house or overlord.

Shoes, slippers, and close-fitting boots of soft leather were worn by men. Sometimes decorated, they were often black and had a more exaggerated point than those of the previous period.

Dress for Women

The women's cote (also called *kirtle*) was a simple, round-neck tunic with a slit down the front. The tight sleeves might now be fastened with buttons from elbow to wrist. Some versions had long hanging sleeves or tippets. The torso of the cote was snugly fitted to the hip where the skirt began to flare to a wide hem that dribbled several inches on the ground. Worn at the hip, the belt was tied or buckled, allowing a length of belt to hang to the knees. After 1300, cotes began to have lower necklines, scooped out in a wide shallow curve or square (particularly popular in Italy).

The woman's surcote might have large or small armholes and might even have sleeves tied into the openings. About 1300, a fashion for scooping out the garment under the arms, providing a glimpse of the tight-fitting cote underneath, earned it the name "windows of Hell." The surcote provided women with a way of displaying armorial bearings. It might be parti-colored and highly decorated with embroidery. A mantle lined in fur completed the costume of a lady.

The hair of married women was braided, wrapped into a bun, and covered with a veil or headdress. Gold nets sometimes held the hair. Free-flowing locks were reserved for queens and unmarried girls.

Headdresses might incorporate a chinstrap, stiffened band or small hat, a *gorget* (a draped neck covering), and a *wimple* (veil). The wimple and gorget were worn primarily by widows, older women, and pious recluses. Later this combination was adopted as part of the nuns' habit. Many brimmed hats were also worn by women, over either a coif or chaperon.

Jewelry for women consisted of brooches, crowns, hair ornaments, rings, elaborate belts, and decorative collars or necklaces. Few bracelets or earrings date from this period. Shoes were the same as in the Romanesque period.

Men and women hung purses from the belt of the cote (often concealed under the surcote). Other useful objects (shears, knife, keys) might also be hung from a hip belt or a *bandolier* (belt worn diagonally across the chest from one shoulder to the opposite hip). Gloves were more common than in previous periods.

Late Gothic (1350–1450)

GENERAL CHARACTERISTICS

Between 1350 and 1400 many earlier styles continued and a feeling of soft, flowing draperies prevailed; after 1400 the fashionable silhouette became stiffer and more restrictive. Many silhouettes suggested a wide-based triangle as hanging sleeves added to the width of the lower torso and tall headdresses extended the silhouette upward. Other styles featured width at the shoulders, foreshadowing the square silhouette of the Renaissance. Whimsical and charming details were added to dress and accessories.

Silk, linen, cotton, and wool were used to produce a wide variety of fabrics, including rich brocades and taffetas, many domestically reproduced from Asian samples. Velvet became increasingly available and popular. Furs were highly prized.

Dress for Men

Over the thigh-length chemise was worn the *jupe, pourpoint, corset,* or *doublet*—a short garment developed from the cotehardie. The doublet was tight-fitting, buttoned or laced up the front or back, and with or without sleeves. A second doublet with long, tight sleeves might be worn over the sleeveless one. While the inner doublet might be waist-length, the outer one had a short skirt. After 1400 this garment might be padded.

After 1400 a full gown or robe (knee-, calf-, or full-length) with moderate sleeves might be worn over the doublet. The fullness in this gown was arranged in pleats and was held into the body with a belt at or below the waist. This garment became associated with more sober and intellectual persons and eventually scholars.

A robe called the *houppelande* was developed near the end of the fourteenth century. The distinct characteristics of this robe include (1) a high standing collar, (2) long, wide hanging sleeves, and (3) a long, full skirt. This garment was used as an outdoor wrap, but it was also worn indoors. The top fitted the body neatly, and the full skirt section was usually held to the body at the waist or slightly above with an ornate belt. The stiffened collar of the houppelande might be a high, closed neckband or a flared collar, open at the front to reveal the neck. Collars soon began to appear on doublets and other garments.

Sleeves of earlier doublets were usually tight-fitting, but the fuller sleeves of the houppelande and gown were added to later doublets. These sleeves include a *leg-o'-mutton* (large at the shoulder and tapered from elbow to wrist) and a *bag* sleeve (a full sleeve caught into a wrist-size cuff, usually with a long vertical slit).

Hose were long and tied to the doublet, the waistband of underpants, or the bottom edge of the underpants with *points* (strings tipped in metal). For use with shorter garments, hose were made with a crotch like modern tights. Although they were primarily tailored of woven cloth, some may have been knitted. Some hose were made with feet, others with stirrups, still others with soles to be worn without shoes.

The bobbed hairstyle of the Early Gothic period continued to be worn, but some men cut their hair in a short, close-cropped style. Also common was the *bowl cut* (shaved partway up the back and cut straight around the head). Beards were more common than in the previous period.

The fillet might still be found in this period, but more and more hats and headdresses are found, many of them elaborate and whimsical. The coif in white linen or black velvet continued to be worn alone or under other hats. The chaperon was still found in its previous form. The liripipe grew to such length that it had to be tucked in the belt, draped over the shoulder, or wrapped around the neck. Toward the end of the fourteenth century the face opening of the chaperon was set on the head or over the crown of a hat, the cape section was arranged to the side, and the liripipe was wrapped around the head to keep the whole concoction on the head. Eventually, this arrangement was imitated in constructed headdresses of separate pieces sewn together for a turban-like appearance. A large variety of brimmed felt hats and soft caps were also worn by men.

Jewelry for men included rings, belts, crowns, S-chain collars or necklaces, jeweled daggers, pendants, buttons, and brooches, now set with faceted stones. A *baldric* or bandolier decorated with a foliated edge, jewels, or gold bells was worn as an accessory. Gloves of varying quality were worn by both elegant men and laborers.

Poulaines, shoes with long-pointed toes, were worn by fashionable gentlemen. Some extreme examples had points so long that they had to be tied up to the knee. Soft calf-length and knee-length boots were worn for hunting and riding. The *patten* (a slip-on shoe with a thick wooden sole) was worn by peasants and gentry to protect shoes from the mud. Shoes might have thick soles, but no heels.

Dress for Women

Women wore one or more gowns layered over a chemise. The *corset* was a "princess-line" gown essentially the same as the cote and kirtle, which fit snug in the torso and flared at the hip to a wide skirt. The corset laced up the back or the front. In Italy it was worn alone, but in northern countries it was usually covered by a surcote, gown, or houppelande.

The "Windows of Hell" surcote continued into the second half of the fifteenth century. Extra length was a prominent feature of all overgowns, many of them extending into a train.

The woman's houppelande was similar to the man's: close-fitting in the shoulders, flaring to a full skirt, arranged in pleats held with a belt at the waist or just under the breast. The sleeves flared into long trumpet shapes and were lined in fur or contrasting fabric. The collar might be the flared or standing style, a round turndown, or a large "sailor collar." The houppelande was often trimmed or lined in fur.

After 1400 the most fashionable gown had a high-waisted, snugly fitted bodice with a long, extremely full skirt set to the bodice in pleats. The excessive length required the lady to lift or tuck up the skirt when walking. A wide belt emphasized the high waistline. This gown had long, fitted sleeves with cuffs that could be worn over the hands or turned back to reveal a contrasting lining. The neckline was a deep V, plunging to the belt and revealing the corset underneath. A shawl collar of fur or contrasting fabric was added to the neckline.

Women wore hose to the knee and shoes similar to those of men, but with less exaggerated toes.

Unmarried girls still wore their hair loose, controlled by a chaplet or circlet (fillet), or topped by a turban or headdress. Unmarried older women wore gorgets and wimples. A variety of fanciful headdresses appeared in this period. In Italy a large headdress resembling a smocked cushion was worn on the back of the head, either enclosing the hair or on top of flowing locks. Turbans and *rondels* (a large stuffed ring worn around the head) were combined with veils and coifs.

After 1400 exaggerated headdresses began to sweep back and up from milady's face. The *hennin* was a conical-shaped hat with a veil of sheer fabric floating from the point. Variations of the hennin had two or three points or were cut off several inches short of the point. The veil could be supported by wires out from the hennin that made it appear to float. Women plucked their eyebrows and hairlines to create a high forehead. The frontlet (a black velvet strip across the front of the headdress) hung to the shoulders on each side of the face. Chaperons were worn combined with rondels and brimmed hats.

Jewelry consisted of crowns, jeweled collars or necklaces, pendants, buttons, and rings, sometimes set with faceted stones. Outerwear continued to consist of a mantle or cloak.

Renaissance (1450–1550)

GENERAL CHARACTERISTICS

National differences in dress became stronger. A broadening at the shoulders suggested either a square or wide trapezoidal silhouette. Padding and stiffening added bulk to the figure. Parti-coloring continued, but dagging was replaced by *slashing* (incisions that allowed a lining or undergarment to be seen).

Elegant garments were made of silk brocades, velvets, satins, taffetas, and metallic cloths. Silk mesh, gauze, crepe, and chiffon were used for hairnets, veilings, and scarves. Woolens were available in many qualities. Linen and cotton were less common and used for chemises and head coverings. Furs were used for collars and cuffs.

Dress for Men

The chemise developed into a shirt with full sleeves. The full body was gathered into a neckband or ruffle. The wrist and neck were often decorated with embroidery of black, red, and gold.

A *doublet*, with or without sleeves, was worn over the shirt. This garment had either a high, square neck or a deep V-neck and was laced or buttoned in the front or back. *Slashes* in the doublet allowed the shirt or doublet lining to be pulled through to create a "puff." The doublet was not usually worn alone.

The *jerkin* was worn over the doublet. The body of the jerkin was fitted to the waist, and a flared or pleated skirt was added. Its skirt varied from hip length to knee length. The square or V-shaped neckline sometimes cut away most of the jerkin front, revealing the doublet or shirt underneath.

Jerkin sleeves were often made of sections tied together and tied into the jerkin with strings or "points." The shirt was pulled through the spaces and arranged in puffs at the shoulder and elbow. While the doublet sleeve was close-fitting, the jerkin sleeve was large at the shoulder, full and stiff to the elbow or wrist. The armhole might be concealed at the shoulder by a *wing*, a crescent shape stitched to the shoulder of the doublet.

The legs were covered with hose to the waist or with *upper* and *nether stocks*. *Upper stocks* were either close-fitting trunks or full, bloomer-like pants. The *nether stocks* covered the lower part of the legs and were usually knitted. The *codpiece*, a triangle or pouch of cloth, was laced or buckled to the front of the hose to cover the opening.

Over the jerkin was worn a full, loose gown. Younger men preferred a short version; older men wore a longer style, the forerunner of the modern academic gown. A wide collar of fur or brocade decorated the front opening. A circular cape or other cloak might be added for outerwear.

Hair was worn "bobbed" at almost any length. Young Italian men wore long, loose styles; northern men wore shorter styles. Beards and mustaches, when worn, were neatly clipped.

The coif was still worn, often of black velvet and topped with a brimmed hat or soft cap. The cap and coif combination became associated with scholars. Brimmed hats might be decorated with slashes, feathers, or jeweled pins. Hats were worn flat on the head or tilted to the side with feathers drooping downward.

Jeweled brooches were used on hats, on sleeves, and as pendants. S-chains, belts, swords, sheaths, and dagger hilts all were jeweled. Men wore earrings and many finger rings.

Shoes widened at the toe to a broad duck-foot shape. Shoes were flat and many had ankle straps. Embroidery, slashes and puffs, jeweled ornaments, and buckles decorated the tops.

Dress for Women

The V-neck gown of the late Gothic period continued into the early part of the Renaissance. A number of new gowns appeared as transitional garments. Bodices were stiffened and pressed the bosom flat. Most featured a wide, square neckline (open or filled with the chemise), sleeves tied into the armhole revealing puffs of chemise, and voluminous skirts attached at the natural waist or above. Later gowns were open down the center front of the skirt to reveal the undergown. The characteristic square neckline developed a definite upward bow in the center.

After 1510, wider, fuller sleeves appeared on women's dress, especially in Italy. Northern European gowns had a natural shoulder with the sleeves widening at the elbow into a large fur or brocade cuff, or a balloon or hanging sleeve. Some gowns had short sleeves below which the sleeves of the chemise or undergown were seen. Bare arms were not revealed by women of status. Skirts were always long, sometimes with trains. The full silhouette was achieved by layering voluminous skirts one upon another.

Hairdressing and headdresses varied according to locale. Italian women displayed more hair than northern women. Small caps, hairnets, or large turbans might be worn. German women developed elaborate headdresses of starched white linen.

Popular headdresses included the *gable* headdress (also called *kennel* or *pedimental*). The jeweled front of this headdress resembled the roof of a house and the back of the head was covered with a velvet veil or a bag-like cap. The *crescent* or *horseshoe* headdress was a stiffened curve of velvet or brocade adorned with jewels and attached to a cap or veil. The crescent sat back from the forehead and revealed the hair, parted in the center and pulled down smoothly to the ears. The back hair was dressed in the cap or hidden by the veil. Another headdress, associated with Mary of Scotland, consisted of a heart-shaped brim attached to a bag or veil.

Women wore earrings, rings, pendants on hats or necklaces, jeweled belts or girdles, and jeweled headdresses. Pearls were increasingly popular. Small objects like scissors, rosaries, or keys were hung from milady's girdle.

Women wore soft slippers. Cloaks with hoods were used for outerwear.

Late Renaissance Elizabethan (1550–1625)

GENERAL CHARACTERISTICS

National preferences were evident in dress of both men and women. Northern and Spanish styles were generally stiff, dark, and extremely artificial in silhouette; Italian styles were softer and more graceful. The silhouette for men was somewhat narrower than previous styles. For women a square, rectangular, or trapezoidal silhouette created the feeling of great bulk. The torso gradually lengthened to a long point in the front, creating the illusion of a figure with a long torso and short legs.

Jewels, embroidery, slashes, and puffs decorated clothing in abundance. Lace appeared on ruffs, coifs, and cuffs. Padding and hoops were required to create the artificial silhouette. Bare arms were not seen, but décolletage was sometimes extravagant and some dresses were shortened for dancing or walking.

Elaborate fabrics like brocade, taffeta, metallic cloth, satin, and velvet were used in court dress. More modest garments were made of wool, linen, and cotton. Embroidery was used on caps, jackets, aprons, stomachers, and shoes.

Dress for Men

The full, soft shirt of linen or silk was finished with a plain neckband or turndown collar. Over the shirt was worn the *waistcoat*, an unstiffened jacket with or without sleeves. This garment was not visible when the gentleman was fully dressed.

Over the waistcoat a doublet with a standing collar was worn. The waist of the doublet dropped to a point in the front. A peplum or skirt was usually attached at the waistline. A wing or roll of cloth was attached at the shoulder to hide the armhole. Matching or contrasting sleeves were sewn in or tied in with *points*. Italian doublets were less stiff and followed the body shape. Northern and Spanish styles were often heavily padded with *bombast* (wool or cotton fibers). The doublet with the *peascod belly* was an extreme example of the padded doublet: in profile the shape of the doublet swooped out from the chest, expanded the belly, and hooked downward, sometimes to the crotch. Doublets usually opened in the front but might lace up the back.

Tied around the neck of the fashionable gentleman was the stiffly starched *ruff* (a plain or lace-edged ruffle mounted on a band). Ruffs varied in width and depth according to the taste and status of the wearer. An *underpropper* (wire structure) was used to support the back of the ruff and tilt it upward to frame the face. The *whisk* collar was a fan-shaped collar wired to stand up and away from the neck.

Sleeves varied from a moderate shape to an exaggerated *leg-o'-mutton* shape (large at shoulder, tapering to wrist). Long vertical slashes were found on some sleeves; others were decorated with braid, a series of short slashes, or fabric puffs.

Upper stocks developed into a wide variety of "breeches" ranging from very short to below the knee. *Pumpkin* or *melon hose* were short, round, usually padded breeches. They were worn over long hose or over a pair of *canions* (tight-fitting, knee-length breeches). Pumpkin hose might have *panes*, a layer of narrow panels caught at the waist and at the bottom of the hose, through which the lining might be seen. Sometimes the soft, full lining was pulled out between the panes and hung in soft puffs. *Venetians* were padded or unpadded breeches, full at the top and tapering to below the knee. *Galligaskins*, a favorite with sailors, were wide, calf-length breeches unbanded at the bottom. These and other full, unpadded breeches were also called *slops*.

Over the doublet and hose was worn a jerkin, gown, or cape as outerwear. These garments were fastened under the ruff or collar. The popular *Spanish cape* was hip length and very stiff.

Hair was cut short and brushed off the forehead. Small, pointed beards and mustaches were popular, but some men preferred to be clean-shaven.

Earlier, caps and coifs were worn by merchants, scholars, and clergy. The fashionable gentleman wore a hat with a narrow brim and tall crown with a jeweled band and feather. As the period progressed, larger brims were increasingly popular. Hats were made of leather, beaver, felt, velvet, or other fabric. The hat was worn indoors.

Men wore rings, earrings (usually only one), chains, brooches, and pendants.

After 1600 heels (sometimes red) were added to men's shoes. The sole was thick and the shoe was slightly tapered with a squared-off toe. The ankle strap was decorated with a rosette. Boots were of soft leather and were tight-fitting, often pulled high over the knee.

Dress for Women

The white chemise, sometimes with a low neck, was still worn as an undergarment. The *farthingale* was any one of a number of structures used to support the skirt in exaggerated shapes. The *Spanish farthingale* was a petticoat with graduated hoops (smaller at the top and larger at the bottom) that created a smooth bell shape. The *French farthingale* was wider on the hips and somewhat narrower in the back and front. The *cartwheel hoop*, popular in England, created a drum-shape skirt that was often ankle or instep length. The *bolster*, a stuffed roll that could be tied just below the waist, was also used. Some skirts were open down the front, revealing an undergown.

The sleeves of the undergown might extend below the sleeves of the *bodice* (a close-fitting garment covering the upper torso). The bodice developed a long point in the front. *Stays* (flat strips of metal, bone, or wood) were used to stiffen the bodice, which was flat across the breasts and laced very tightly to produce a small waist. The long bodice point was often accented by a *stomacher* (a triangle of cloth, elaborately decorated with embroidery and jewels). Later in the period, the undergown was worn less often, and the skirt and bodice became more elaborate. A round or square-shaped neckline was popular, but modest gowns had a high neck finished with a collar or ruff.

Ruffs were worn by women, as was the fan-shaped whisk collar set around the back and sides of the bodice neckline. An open-neck gown might be filled in with a *guimpe* (a shaped cloth placed around the neck and under the bodice).

Sleeves could be (1) large at the shoulder and tapering to the wrist or (2) short puffs worn over tighter undersleeves or combined with hanging sleeves. Sleeves often were finished with lace-trimmed cuffs.

A short, loosely-fitted jacket or loose uppergown was sometimes worn, either open or closed.

Hair was combed off the forehead and dressed over rolls to create a halo or heart-shaped effect, then adorned with pearls or feathers. A lace-trimmed cap or coif might be worn. Women wore mannish styles for riding and hunting.

Shoes for women were made of brocade or leather and often had high heels.

Ropes of pearls, chains, earrings, pendants, brooches, and rings were worn in abundance. Small rigid fans became a popular accessory for ladies. Makeup was used at court.

Cavalier (1625–1660)

GENERAL CHARACTERISTICS

Padding and starch disappeared from dress. Waistlines rose and artificial skirt supports disappeared. Excess ornamentation was reduced. Women's sleeves for the first time in centuries revealed part of the lower arm. Rounded shoulders combined with full, soft skirts to create a bell-shaped silhouette for women. The silhouette for men resembled an inverted triangle. Garments were trimmed with lace, ribbon, and braid.

Patterned brocades and cut velvets were still used, but plain satins and velvets were more prevalent. Lace and linen continued to be important for caps, collars, and cuffs. Wool, cotton, and linen in solid colors were used for modest dress.

Dress for Men

The full, white shirt had large sleeves and either a neckband or turndown collar. The doublet was no longer padded but might be stiffened. The high waistline was often decorated with a row of *points* (metal-tipped ribbons that held the breeches to the doublet). The hip-length skirt or peplum of the doublet was cut into tabs. The body and skirt of some doublets were cut together with long vertical seams for shaping. Long vertical slashes decorated the doublet front and back.

The sleeves of the doublet were moderate shapes, fuller at the armhole than at the wrist. Long, vertical slashes revealed the shirt or lining. The wrist was finished with linen or lace cuffs.

Older folk still wore the stiff ruff of the previous period, but the unstarched *falling ruff* was more fashionable. A square lace or linen collar appeared as a new accessory.

New tubular-shaped pants were upper-calf length and loose at the bottom. Unpadded knee breeches and slops were still worn. Most breeches were fuller at the top and tapered toward the bottom.

Men grew their hair long and wore it loose and wavy. Mustaches could be worn alone or with a small beard tuft in the center of the chin. The small, neatly trimmed mustache and beard (Vandyke) was popular.

The fashionable hat was a large-brimmed, low-crowned felt trimmed with a jeweled band and ostrich plumes.

Certain religious and political groups chose shorter hairstyles and more austere garments to express their religious beliefs or in opposition to the extravagance of the fashionable court practices.

Ankle-strap shoes with square or round toes and long vamps were trimmed with buckles or rosettes. The moderate heels (two inches) were often red. Boots were frequently substituted for shoes, and spurs were worn even when one was not riding. The tops of the boots could be extended over the knees but were usually worn turned down and back up to form a cup-shaped cuff. Inside the cuff could be seen the lace top of the *boot hose.* Shorter boots were turned down once to form a cuff.

The jerkin became a kind of jacket, frequently of leather, popular with soldiers, sailors, and hunters. Semicircular capes of varied lengths were the usual outerwear for men. The unstiffened cape was draped around the body in a variety of ways. The collar or ruff was always worn on the outside of the cape or jerkin. Long gowns were still worn by scholars, some clergy, and statesmen.

Gloves with large embroidered *gauntlets* (wide cuffs) were worn. A purse was tucked into the belt under the doublet or jerkin.

Dress for Women

The chemise was rarely visible. Except in Spain, petticoats replaced the farthingale structures that were previously used to support the skirt.

The boned bodice became shorter and was often finished with a set of tabs like a man's doublet. The stomacher was worn with its point resting on the skirt, and the overgown was laced over it. A split-front skirt might reveal an elaborate undergown or petticoat. Skirts were extremely long and were often held up or bunched through a belt for walking.

The square neckline shared popularity with a wide, slightly scooped neckline finished with a *Bertha collar:* a wide, round collar covering the shoulders. A variety of lace and linen collars were used on women's dress.

Three-quarter-length sleeves revealed the lower arm. Sleeves were one large puff or were divided into two or three puffs with ribbons and finished with a lace or linen turned-back cuff. Long gloves were worn with the shorter sleeves.

Widows, peasants, and older women continued to wear caps. Fashionable ladies dressed their hair with a center part, curled or frizzed the sides, and dressed the back in a high knot or bun. A fringe of curls or frizz was arranged across the forehead. Loops of pearls, feathers, and ribbons were used to adorn the head. Hoods or men's hats were worn outdoors.

Cloaks with sleeves or large circular capes were worn for outerwear. Hoods might be attached or separate.

Modest women wore long-sleeved, simple garments of current cut. A folded kerchief, pinned at the neck, might take the place of a collar. A white linen apron was a common accessory.

Bracelets, chokers, long strings of pearls, and small drop-pearl earrings were popular. Jeweled rings, buttons, pendants, and hair ornaments were worn.

Ladies' shoes were similar to men's styles and often had high, red heels. Other accessories for women included a muff, fan (rigid or folding), purse, and mask (in public).

Restoration (1660–1715)

GENERAL CHARACTERISTICS

A frivolous abundance of ribbons and curls and an exposed shirt or chemise was popular. The waistline returned first to the natural position and later to a lower line. Small shoulders, narrow torsos, coats, and skirts widening at the bottom created a narrow, triangular silhouette. The early frivolity gradually stiffened into a rigid, ornate, and dignified style.

In addition to the brocades, velvets, satins, and wools previously available, linen and cotton prints began to be produced in Europe. Lace was used for trimming sleeves, collars, caps, aprons, cravats, stomachers, petticoats, and handkerchiefs.

Dress for Men

The white shirt was made of fine fabric and was extremely full in body and sleeves. The neck was finished with a drawstring or collar. Over the shirt was sometimes worn a waistcoat.

Two types of coat were popular. One was very short (rib-cage-length) and allowed the shirt to show around the waist. The second, the *cassock* coat, was fitted in the body, above-the-knee length, and flared from the hip to the hem. This coat was collarless and buttoned down the front from neck to hem. It was often worn open from the chest down to reveal a puff of shirt and a bunch of ribbons at the waist. Both coats had short sleeves that exposed the shirt. The sleeves of the shirt might be caught into puffs with ribbons. Later coats had three-quarter-length sleeves with large turned-back cuffs. As the period progressed, waistcoats became more important. Cut along the lines of the coat, the waistcoat also had buttons from neck to hem, often had long fitted sleeves, and could match or contrast with the coat.

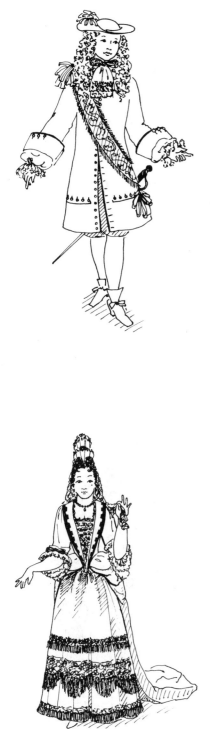

With the short jacket were worn either the tubular pants of the Cavalier period or the new *petticoat breeches* (a full, open-bottomed pant like modern culottes). The latter was often profusely decorated with ribbon loops at the bottom edge and on the sides. With the longer coat, full knee breeches were more common. By the end of the period, breeches were closer fitting and buttoned or buckled neatly below the knee.

Hose (above-the-knee length) were worn under or over breeches. Although boots were no longer worn for dress occasions, boot hose were sometimes still worn gartered to allow the lace ruffle to flutter at the knee. Shoes continued to have high heels, often red.

A lace collar with a front pleat might be tied at the neck. A pair of plain tabs set on a band might be substituted by conservative folk. As the period progressed, the *cravat* came into fashion. A long strip of fine white cloth with lace ends, the cravat was wrapped around the neck (over the shirt collar) and tied in the front with a bow or half-knot. A ribbon tied in a bow was sometimes added under the cravat.

Long wigs of luxurious curls were fashionable for men. Parted in the middle, the hair was dressed to rest on the chest and down the back. The gentleman's own hair was clipped short. A cap was worn for warmth when the wig was removed at home.

Steeple-crown hats developed with high crowns and stiff, narrow bands. By 1690 men were wearing wider hats and turning up the brims on three sides, and the resulting *tricorn* hat became the most popular style for the next century. The brim edges were trimmed with braid or ostrich.

Capes were still worn as outerwear.

Dress for Women

The bodice might have short sleeves or be sleeveless. The puffed chemise sleeves tied with ribbons showed below the bodice sleeves. Later, bodice sleeves were close-fitting to just below the elbow and finished with a flounce of lace or a puff of chemise. The waist of the bodice dropped to the natural waist or lower. The long, stiffened point in front was sometimes duplicated in the back. The neckline might have the wide Bertha collar of the previous period. The combining of an underbodice and an overgown created a square neckline. A kerchief or scarf was sometimes draped to fill the neckline, or the chemise might be visible. A wide, deep collar was worn by many modest women.

The overgown revealed part of the bodice front and the decorated petticoat. It might have a train and was often draped back, revealing the lining and creating a back drape. Horizontal trim emphasized the hem.

The *Dutch jacket* was a short, loose garment lined or trimmed in fur and worn indoors. The *night-rail* was a muslin and lace cape, originally a boudoir jacket and later worn as a light wrap over a gown.

Decorative aprons of lace or linen were worn by women of all classes. Knee-length hose gartered at the knee and shoes much like those of men were worn.

Hair was dressed with a center part or combed straight back from the forehead with loose curls around the face. Toward the end of the period a more formal style developed in which the hair was dressed in high mounds on the top of the head. The *fontage*, a cap featuring a tall arrangement of lace ruffles and ribbons, brought caps back into fashion for aristocratic ladies.

Drop earrings, rings, brooches, watches on chains, and necklaces of pearls or other stones were popular, as were fans and muffs as accessories.

Eighteenth Century: Early Georgian (1715–1750)

GENERAL CHARACTERISTICS

A shift to lighter, more delicate fabrics and colors began with the reign of Louis XIV in 1715. Powdered wigs, delicate trim, and a more feminine silhouette (soft shoulders, small waists, and full skirts on gown or coat) developed for both men and women. Decoration was applied to garments with embroidery, quilting, appliqués, ruching, ruffles, ribbons, and festoons.

Brocades, damasks, satins, taffetas, and printed cottons in pastels and floral tones were popular. Black velvet was much used for men's breeches. Wools were used for modest dress and outerwear. Silk gauze was used for scarves and fichus. Linen, lace, and cotton lawn were used for trim, caps, aprons, and undergarments.

Dress for Men

The full shirt was finished at the neck with a band or turndown collar. A *jabot* (ruffle) trimmed the front opening. The sleeves were finished in a ruffle of plain fabric or lace. Around the neck was worn the *cravat* (neck cloth) or the newer *stock* (a strip of crushed muslin tied or buckled in the back).

The waistcoat or vest reached just above the knee and buttoned from neck to hem. Some vests had sleeves. The vest might match or contrast with the rest of the ensemble. Many vests were elaborately trimmed with braid or embroidery.

The coat developed from the previous style. The skirts were flared and stiffened. The pockets moved up from the hemline. The collarless coat retained the row of buttons from neck to hem but was rarely worn completely closed. The coat sleeve was just short of the wrist (allowing the shirt ruffle to show) and was trimmed with a wide cuff buttoned back to the sleeve. The coat might be ornately trimmed with braid or embroidery.

Knee breeches were full at the top, neat fitting, and buttoned or buckled at the knee. Frequently of black velvet, breeches could also

be of light-colored satin, in matching or contrasting colors to the coat or vest. Knee-length hose were worn over or under the breeches. Dress hose were of silk, everyday hose of wool.

Shoes had heels, tongues, and buckles. For riding, men wore gaiters or boots fitted over the knee in front and cut out in back.

Although retained by judges and older men, by 1730 the full-bottom wigs of the previous period were generally replaced with tied-back wigs. The front of the wig was combed away from the face and dressed in rolls over the ears. The back hair was tied into a queue with a ribbon or caught in a black silk bag. Since most wigs were powdered to look white or gray, the silk bag protected the back of the coat. Conservative or unpretentious men wore their own hair tied back with the sides rolled or frizzed or in a chin-length pageboy style.

The tricorn was the most commonly worn hat. Quakers, clergymen, and country folk might still wear the steeple-crown hat from earlier periods. Tricorns were decorated with braid, ostrich, ribbons, cockades, and lace. Caps were worn at home after the wig was removed.

Jewelry for men was reduced to rings, fancy buttons, decorated swords, and watches on chains. Watches were worn under the vest and were not often visible when the gentleman was fully dressed.

Dress for Women

The bodices of the eighteenth century were slim, tight, flat-front, heavily boned, and long-waisted. The bodice usually dipped to a center front point that was emphasized by trimming, often a series of graduated ribbon bows. A square neck formed by the combination of corset or bodice and overgown was frequently seen, but a low, round neck also was popular. The neckline might be trimmed with a lace ruffle or collar, or filled with a fichu. Most bodices were laced up the back. A corsage of real or artificial flowers might be worn on the bodice. A small ruff of lace or ribbon was sometimes tied around the neck.

A slim, elbow-length sleeve finished with a lace flounce became popular, though modest women wore long, fitted sleeves.

The skirt could be trimmed in the front or split to reveal a decorative petticoat. Quilted petticoats were popular among middle-class women. Most skirts were floor-length or instep-length, some with trains. However, dance dresses and street frocks were sometimes shortened almost to ankle-length. Early in the period, hoops returned to fashion. Although many women relied on stiffened petticoats to extend their skirts, whalebone hoops created the bell shape under more fashionable gowns. Toward the middle of the century the *panier* (a series of hoops, wider on the sides than in front and back) was developed. As the panier became wider (some over three feet), the skirt was constructed with a seam along the top of the panier that allowed the skirt to fall evenly at the bottom.

The *sack-back* gown, an overgown with a loose back, was worn over a corset and petticoat. This gown was also known as the *robe à la française* in England and later as the *Watteau-back* gown because it appeared frequently in Watteau's paintings. The variations of this garment included a loose, sleeveless gown, and a sleeved gown with tight-fitting front (which could be worn without an undergown). The full back was pleated into a narrow yoke and fell freely from neck to floor. Garments in this style were worn as dressing gowns, for day-wear, and as formal wear.

Hair was dressed away from the face in the style now known as pompadour after Madame de Pompadour, mistress to Louis XV. The back was arranged in twists or curls, and loose tendrils or long ring-lets often were allowed to hang down the back or over the shoulder. Frequently powdered, the hair was also decorated with delicate ornaments of ribbon, flowers, lace, and pearls.

Caps were not worn for formal wear but were popular for day-wear. The *mobcap*, the most popular style for peasant and gentry alike, was a circle of fine cloth gathered to fit the head and trimmed around the edge with a plain or lace ruffle. The *shepherdess hat* (a large brimmed straw hat tied on with a wide ribbon) was often worn over the mobcap. A hood might be worn for warmth, either separate or attached to a cloak.

The tricorn hat was worn by women mainly as part of the riding habit, except in Venice, where it was combined with a black lace mantilla and accompanied by a half-mask to disguise the wearer.

Jewelry was simple and used with restraint. Pearl drop earrings, rings, jeweled buttons and hair ornaments, watches worn at the waist on chains, and small chokers or necklaces were among the possibilities.

Shoes had high, *spool* heels (wide top, narrow middle, wide base) and pointed toes. *Mules* (backless shoes with heels) were also worn.

Gloves and mitts were worn with shorter-sleeve gowns. Muffs were used for warmth. Folding fans made of silk were a necessary accessory for formal wear. Women carried parasols when walking outdoors.

Eighteenth Century: Late Georgian (1750–1790)

GENERAL CHARACTERISTICS

Fashion made a quick change of silhouette toward the end of this period. The first thirty years (1750 to 1780) saw two movements in women's dress. The first, an exaggeration of early eighteenth-century styles, included paniers of incredible widths and coiffures of incredible heights. The second trend was a romantic adaptation of peasant dress. Clothing for men gradually and steadily became slim-mer and neater.

Between 1780 and 1790 new styles rapidly appeared. For women the further development of peasant styles created elegant yet simple garments that omitted the artificial shape of the panier. For men a slim, vertical silhouette was developed with tight-fitting knee

breeches, short vest, and coat whose skirt was reduced to slim tails. Extremes of ornament disappeared after 1780.

Before 1780 elaborate brocades, damasks, satins, taffetas, embroideries, wools, plaids, stripes, and printed cottons were fashionable. After 1780 simple fabrics were more frequently used. Except for court dress, woolen broadcloth took the place of satins and brocades in men's wear, and cotton muslin was extensively used in women's dress. Velvet returned to favor for overgowns and turbans. Before 1780 light colors continued to be fashionable. After 1780 muslin in white or light tones was often teamed with heavier fabrics in dark, rich colors.

Dress for Men

The full shirt was rarely worn open at the neck. The stock and jabot (ruffle) were the usual neckwear, although cravats were still worn for more casual dress.

Vests gradually became shorter until they reached the waist. They were usually single-breasted and cut straight or with two points at the bottom. Late in the period double-breasted vests with lapels and standing collars appeared.

Men's coats began to lose skirt fullness, and by 1770 the *cutaway* style was predominant. This coat retained the vent in the back but sloped away sharply from the center front waist to the back hem. The front edge was decorated with buttons, buttonholes, braid, and embroidery. The sleeves were wrist-length, slim, and finished with cuffs, embroidery, or a buttoned slit on the outside of the arm. The shirt ruffle of lace or linen was seen at the wrist. Pocket flaps moved up toward the waist and farther to the back. After 1780 there appeared a short-waisted coat with high collar and sloping tails that started from the side front and dropped to knee- or calf-length. Workmen and country folk wore a short, informal coat called the *bobtail.*

As coats and waistcoats shortened, knee breeches became more neatly fitted. A buckled band finished the breeches just below the knee, and a row of buttons up the outside of the leg held the opening closed. Breeches were made of black velvet, light-colored satins, wools, and doeskin.

Pale knitted stockings of heavy silk, sometimes *clocked* (decorated with designs on the ankle), were worn by elegant gentlemen. Others made do with wool.

Shoes had low heels and medium-high tongues and were closed with buckles or strings. Top boots and gaiters were worn by civilians and military men.

Powdered wigs were dressed away from the face with a queue or pigtail down the back. Exaggerated versions had a very high roll in the front. After 1780 a fuller, bushy style of wig came into fashion, and more men began to wear their own hair, powdered or unpowdered. At home turbans were worn to cover shaven or clipped heads. Almost all men were clean-shaven.

The tricorn hat remained fashionable, but after 1780 three new hats appeared: (1) a low-crowned beaver hat with medium brim, (2) a hat cocked in two places (*bicorne*), and (3) a steeple-crown hat with a stiff brim and tall, tapering crown similar to the older "pilgrim" style.

Men's jewelry consisted of rings, watches, fancy shoe buckles, knee buckles, and snuff boxes.

For outerwear men wore capes and the *great coat*, a large overcoat shaped like the dress coat.

Dress for Women

Bodices continued to be tight, flat-front, and heavily boned. The earlier garments still featured the elbow-length sleeve with flounce popular in the first part of the century; later gowns often had wrist-length sleeves. The square neck was still predominant. Until 1780 bodices continued to be long waisted with a long front point.

Formal gowns were extended to amazing widths with paniers, but day dresses were less extreme. The sack-back overgown continued to be worn, sometimes with the skirts draped up in the back in the style known as *polonaise*. A short version of the sack-back gown was called the *sacque*. Petticoats and skirts were often elaborately decorated with quilting, ruffles, ruching, flowers, festoons, lace, or other trims. Overgowns matched or contrasted with petticoats and underbodices. Simple gowns with plain, fitted bodices and full skirts also were common. Dresses for walking or dancing were sometimes shortened to the ankle.

Coiffures for formal occasions were elaborately constructed of false hair piled high on the head, decorated with flowers, birds, jewels, plumes, birds in cages, miniature ships in full sail, and countless other novelties. Even a fairly modest style was swept up over a roll, with the back dressed in curls, held in place with pomade, and powdered.

Caps also returned to fashion, and their size increased with the increased size of the coiffure. Turbans and mobcaps were common. The *shepherdess hat* (large-brim straw) was still popular. Other hats were devised to wear on the large hairstyles, usually perched at a slant on the front of the head. The *calash*, a large hood held away from the hair by hoops, was devised to wear over the large hairstyles.

After 1780 many gowns had round, sashed waists and round necklines, sometimes filled with a fichu or scarf. By that time paniers were definitely out of fashion, and skirts were supported by heavy petticoats with extra fullness at the back. The *levite*, an undraped overgown with fitted back, became popular. After 1780 the height of hairstyles decreased, and their width increased. This style was less often powdered, and natural-colored hair gradually returned to fashion. Low-crowned, wide-brimmed hats and a feminine version of the steeple-crown hat were worn.

Cloaks and capes, sometimes with hoods or sleeves, were the usual outerwear. A shaped shawl called a *mantelette* was sometimes worn when only a light wrap was needed. A caped overcoat called the *redingote* was developed from the riding habit and was worn over a shirt, waistcoat, and skirt.

Rings, brooches, watches, bracelets, shoe buckles, jeweled drop earrings, necklaces, and hair ornaments were among the jeweled treasures of the eighteenth-century woman. Cameos, necklaces of gold beads, and diamonds were popular. Even a modest housewife might have a silver *chatelaine*, a hook to be attached to the bodice or waistband from which to suspend a key chain or other useful items.

Women carried parasols, fans, gloves, muffs, and walking sticks.

Directoire and First Empire/Regency (1790–1815)

GENERAL CHARACTERISTICS

A slim, vertical, high-waisted silhouette dominated the fashion scene for both men and women in this period. Simple fabrics, especially wool and cotton muslin, were extremely popular for most of the period. Later more lavish fabric and trim returned to fashion. Women's fashion featured "classical" drapery. Emphasis in men's fashion shifted from the use of elaborate trim and ornate fabrics to fine tailoring, sober colors, and impeccable grooming.

Dress for Men

A white shirt with jabot and standing collar was typical for the gentleman of the period. A black or white cravat wound around the collar or a white stock with a black ribbon over it finished the neck. The shirt sleeve was finished with a narrow ruffle or cuff.

Vests were waist-length or a little longer, square or cut with two points in the front. Often double-breasted, the vest was worn with the top buttons left undone and the lapels turned back. Stripes were popular for vests, and embroidery was used on formal wear.

Coats had high, standing collars, lapels, and tails. The front might be cut away starting just above the waist and sloping down to the knee in the back. A square-cut front with the tail starting over the hipbone was especially popular. Both styles revealed the vest at the front.

Knee breeches continued to be worn by older men, by peasant folk, and for formal or court dress. The newer look was a *pantaloon* like those worn by boys and sailors. The fashionable version was tight-fitting and was often made of knitted cloth. Originally calf-length, pantaloons by 1800 became ankle-length and a little looser.

White or neutral hose were worn with knee breeches and pantaloons. "Dandies" were fond of striped hose in bright color combinations. Flat pumps were worn for dress, and boots ranged from calf to knee height.

Hair at the beginning of the period was full on the top and sides with the back caught in a queue. Soon the hair was cut to the shape of the head with the top curled in imitation of Roman styles. Sideburns began to reappear. Powdered hair disappeared among fashionable men.

The bicorne and the *top hat* (stiff, tall-crowned hat with narrow brim) were the two types of hat for fashionable men.

Several short capes were added to the great coat in the style now known as the *coachman's* coat. Capes were still worn by men as outerwear.

Dress for Women

Simple, high-waisted, muslin frocks became the fashionable dress in the years following the French Revolution. Inspired by classical garments, early dresses of this period were often made of sheer fabrics trimmed with Greek and Roman motifs. Some ladies wore their dresses over pink tights without petticoats, and some went as far as wearing them wet to imitate the look of classical statuary.

For a time fashionable women abandoned corsets (stays). Within a short time, however, tight bodices with corsets returned. However, because the waistline remained high under the bosom, corsets did not cinch in the waist.

Sleeves were either short and puffed, long and fitted, or a combination of a long sleeve with a small puff at the top. The neckline was often square and quite low. A fishu might be tied around the shoulders. A muslin gown with a *surplice* neck (diagonally wrapped) also was popular. High-necked gowns were often finished with a ruffle at the neck.

Over the dress a knee-length tunic might be worn "in the Greek manner." A very short, fitted jacket called the *spencer* was worn for warmth. Long, rectangular shawls were extremely fashionable.

As the period progressed, heavier fabrics were used. To accommodate these fabrics, skirts were cut with a slight flare and less fullness at the waist. The flared hem was accentuated by horizontal trim near the bottom edge. Court dresses were furnished with the *court mantle*, an elaborate train of contrasting fabric falling from the high waistline and supported by straps over the shoulders.

Greek hairstyles were revived. Bonnets, turbans, and plumed headdresses added a modern note.

Shoes were flat and tied on with ribbons. Ladies carried small purses, muffs, parasols, and fans. Gloves were very important. With the short puffed sleeves, very long gloves were worn.

For outerwear women wore a *pelisse*, a coat-type garment open down the front and cut with similar lines to the dress. The *redingote*, a caped coat, was still popular. A *pelerine* was a small, shoulder-length cape.

Jewelry for women included bracelets, earrings, tiaras, brooches, necklaces, and hair ornaments. Often three or more of these were of a matching set.

Romantic (1815–1830)

GENERAL CHARACTERISTICS

The silhouette for women widened at top and bottom until it resembled two triangles balancing point to point. Frivolous bonnets and trims, enormous sleeves, tiny waists, ankle-length skirts, and flat slippers combined to give fashionable women a doll-like look. The silhouette for men echoed the wide, sloping shoulders, narrow waists, and full hips of the women's silhouette.

Men's wear favored sturdy fabrics of wool or cotton. White linen or cotton was used for warm climates. Women's daywear was made of lightweight cottons, such as chintz, muslin, and calico, or lightweight wool or cashmere. Evening gowns were made of taffeta, gauze, satin, silks, or velvet.

Dress for Men

The white shirt had a tall, stiff collar whose points sometimes rose high onto the cheek. Wrapped around the collar was a neck cloth. A bit of pleated shirt front or ruffle might be visible above the vest. Artistic types wore their collars unstarched and open or held together with a loosely tied scarf in the manner of Lord Byron. A great variety of shapes and arrangements of cravat or neck cloth was available to a fashionable gent.

Vests had collars and were cut to the natural waist. To help produce the small-waisted look, many men's vests were boned and laced in the back, much like women's corsets. Waistcoats were no longer visible at the waist when the tail or frock coat was buttoned, but a sliver of color could be seen at the neck, and men often left their coats partially open to reveal more.

The *frock coat* was worn for morning occasions and for sportswear. The *tailcoat* took over for formal occasions. The *bobtail coat* was worn by boys, men of low status, and occasionally by gentlemen for country or sportswear. Coat collars stood high on the back of the neck, and the shoulders sloped downward to a modified leg-o'-mutton sleeve.

The fashionable gent reserved knee britches for court dress, although these continued to be worn by country folk and older men. *Riding smalls*, britches made of doeskin, drill, or finely napped fabric, were full at the top and tapered to meet the calf-high riding boots.

Fine hose in neutral tones were worn. Black evening pumps were finished with a small bow or buckle. For day gentlemen wore short boots with blunt toes, narrow vamps, and a moderate heel.

Hair was full and brushed forward or back according to taste. Sideburns began to extend downward and slightly forward onto the check. The back of the hair was trimmed to the shape of the head. Small mustaches began to appear toward the end of the period.

Top hats, the most popular headwear, were made of beaver in gray, black, white, and fawn. A flat-crowned, broad-brimmed hat was favored for sportswear, by country folk, and in the American South and West. Caps were worn by boys and by men for sportswear or traveling.

A fitted overcoat was worn for day, and capes with contrasting linings and velvet collars were worn with evening dress. The caped coat worn by travelers and coachmen eventually became known as the *coachman's coat*.

Accessories for men included gloves, rings, watches, and canes.

Dress for Women

Corsets with small waists returned by 1825. The bodice worn over the corset had dropped shoulders and a slightly high waist. A wide-open neck—either round, square, or slightly V-shaped—was favored for evening and sometimes for daywear. The low-necked day dress might be filled in by a *tucker* or *guimpe*. The wide V-neck was often trimmed with a fabric drape, a feature fashionable through much of the nineteenth century.

By 1825 most bodices featured exaggerated sleeves. Extreme fullness was introduced into the sleeve at the dropped shoulder line or at the elbow. The sleeve then tapered to the wrist, where a snug fit was favored. Some sleeves extended to the knuckles.

Skirts expanded to about 2½ yards, and extra fullness at the waist was concentrated largely in the back. Almost all skirts were instep- or ankle-length, a few calf-length. The court mantle was added for court presentations. Skirt trim in horizontal bands was placed near the lower edge to accent the width.

Slippers with flat heels and ankle ribbons or small, dainty ankle boots were worn by ladies. Stockings were white or light colors.

For outdoors a lady added a spencer jacket, a *pelerine* (short cape), *mantelette* (shaped stole), or *pelisse* (long cloth coat cut and fitted like a dress).

Sets of elaborate jewelry were worn by women of means. Cameos cut of shell were set into brooches, producing an inexpensive ornament. Chains and ropes of beads circled the neck, and drop earrings were popular. Bracelets, rings, and hair ornaments were frequently worn.

Hair was arranged smoothly over the brow with a center part. Side hair was dressed in ringlets or loops, and the back hair was drawn up to a knot high on the head. Large bonnets with wide flaring brims were worn, and a variety of caps returned to fashion. Ribbons, plumes, and flowers adorned hats and bonnets.

A fan and gloves were necessary parts of a lady's wardrobe. Muffs, parasols, and *reticules* (small hanging purses) also were much evident.

Crinoline (1840–1865)

GENERAL CHARACTERISTICS

Though this style was less restrictive than the previous one, the male silhouette continued to be somewhat feminine, with sloping shoulders, padded chest, small waist, and full hips. A variety of garments were developed for special occasions. In women's fashion, a small head, sloping shoulders, and small, natural waist were poised over an ever-widening bell-shaped skirt. As skirts increased in width at the hem, hoops returned to fashion.

Wool, cotton, silk, and taffeta in solids and stripes were popular for women's dress. Except for the bold plaids that were popular for trousers, most fabrics for men's wear were sturdy, plain, and subdued in color.

Dress for Men

The white shirt had either a stiffened or pleated front. The starched stand-up collar was more formal, but the turndown style was worn in both starched and unstarched versions. A wrapped neck cloth, stock, bow tie, or string tie was worn over the collar. Day vests were cut high at the neck and included single- and double-breasted styles. Vest necklines varied from high (with and without collars) to a deep U-shape for evening.

The *sack coat*, which had been primarily a jacket for boys and men of low station, developed into a garment for sportswear, informal occasions, and sometimes business. The *tailcoat* and *frock coat* were the more fashionable styles, and variations suitable for many occasions were available. Evening wear generally included a black tailcoat and a black or white vest. Frequently part of the wardrobe of the upper classes, the black frock coat was also an important part of the average man's wardrobe, worn for special occasions from marriages to funerals. The *cutaway coat* was deemed suitable for daytime visits and gradually became known as a "morning coat." All styles of coat gradually became less fitted in the waist, and collars gradually decreased in height. Sleeves were straight and set in without extra top fullness.

Most trousers were tubular and had stirrups to keep them neat. Pants were worn without cuffs or creases. Plaid and striped pants were popular. In general, men's wear became more sober.

Men's hairstyles were full, but shaped to the head. Whether brushed straight back or parted on the side or in the center, men's hair was generously slathered with macassar oil to hold it in place. Long, full sideburns blossomed on cheeks and beards on chins, though not always accompanied by mustaches.

The top hat in one of its many variations was the appropriate hat for most occasions. A number of wide-brimmed straw or felt hats with low crowns were worn for the country, and the *bowler* (or *derby*) appeared.

Men wore short elastic-sided boots under their trousers and pumps or thin shoes for evening. Shoes with canvas tops buttoned up over the ankle also were worn.

Capes with velvet collars were worn with evening clothes. Topcoats and the plaid *Inverness cape* (coat with a shoulder cape added) were popular for outerwear.

Dress for Women

A lady's bodice was tight fitting and allowed for a rounded bosom shape. The front waist frequently dipped to a point, and the neckline and armhole contrived to create a drooping shoulder line. The wide V-shape was popular for evening. A small collar of lace or embroidery was often added to a high-neck day bodice; a lace *tucker* might fill in a low-neck gown. Bell-shaped sleeves were set into the dropped armhole. A sheer undersleeve was gathered into a band at the wrist or midarm.

Skirts were instep- or floor-length and gathered or pleated into the small waist. The bottom edge of skirts from the 1850s and 1860s measured from 10 to 25 yards depending on the thickness of the fabric. Horizontal rows of trim, particularly ruffles, accented the width of the hem. The voluminous *crinoline* (petticoat of horsehair or starched cotton) was replaced after 1855 by a hoop petticoat consisting of a series of graduated steel rings hung from the waist by tapes. This lightweight structure encouraged even further exaggeration of the skirt size. Toward the 1860s the skirt shape became elongated toward the back.

Hair was parted in the center with soft ringlets or braids arranged over the ears. The back hair was curled or braided and arranged in a bun on the back of the head. Caps were worn for day by widows and many modest women. Older women might wear them with evening dress. Younger women adorned their evening coiffures with feathers, lace, flowers, and pearls. Large- and small-brimmed hats or bonnets were worn for day.

Flat-soled, tight-fitting boots of soft leather were worn outdoors, and heelless slippers were worn indoors. Small parasols, folding fans, *reticules* (drawstring purses), and gloves or mitts were frequent accessories. Working women added large aprons.

Sets of matched jewelry were much prized. Small dangling earrings, necklaces, brooches, bracelets, rings, and hair ornaments were made of gold or silver and set with precious or semiprecious stones, pearls, and cameos. Black jet jewelry was considered appropriate for mourning; coral, turquoise, and garnets were popular.

Shawls, mantelettes (semi-fitted, triangular shawls), and capes (with and without armholes) were used for outerwear.

Bustle (1865–1890)

GENERAL CHARACTERISTICS

Men's dress developed soberly along previously established lines. The cutaway, frock, and sack coats varied little from previous styles. A slim, vertical silhouette with less padding in the chest and a natural fit in the waist was fashionable. An ever-increasing interest in sports required development of specific new garments for both participants and spectators.

The backward thrust of the women's skirts in the late Crinoline period led the development of the bustle skirt. When viewed from the front, the silhouette was narrow and vertical. In profile, however, the lower half of the figure extended backward dramatically. Heavy drapery and carefully controlled ruffles adorned most versions of the bustle dress, and trains were common. Eighteenth-century costume details enjoyed a revival.

Wool fabrics dominated men's wear, although cotton, linen, and some silk were also used. Women's fashions took advantage of a wide variety of fabrics, most of them with substantial body.

Dress for Men

The all-important white shirt was usually furnished with a starched front. The stiff collar and cuffs were often detachable and might be made of celluloid, white rubber, or heavy paper. Collars were of medium height and might be *wing-tip*, straight band, or turn-down style with points or rounded front edges. Separate collars were attached with collar buttons. A string tie, *Windsor* tie (soft silk), *ascot* tie, or *four-in-hand* tie provided a flash of color at the neck.

Vests were cut rather high with a collar and might match or contrast with the coat and pants. A knitted cardigan appeared in the 1880s and was sometimes worn in place of a vest.

Tailcoats were gradually relegated to evening dress, and their cut was changed little for decades. The frock coat and cutaway were equally popular for formal daytime functions—social, political, and business. The sack coat gradually began to appear in more situations. Striped *blazers* and *Norfolk* jackets (jackets with pleated body held in with a belt) appeared for sports and casual wear. Except for the tailcoat, most coats were cut high at the neck revealing a minimum of shirt and vest. All types of coats and vests might be trimmed in braid.

Pants might still be of plaid or stripes worn with plain coats. Suits consisting of matching sack coat, vest, and pants were popular, but combining contrasting pieces was also acceptable. Pants were long and uncreased. Casual pants might have cuffs, and *knickers* (full knee breeches) were revived for a variety of sporting activities.

Hairstyles for men were close to the head and featured a center or side part held in place with macassar oil. A wide variety of sideburns, beards, mustaches, and combinations were worn.

The top hat was still favored for most formal occasions, but the derby became increasingly popular. The *straw boater* was a popular summer hat, and a variety of other hats and caps appeared for sportswear.

Shoes with elastic insets on the sides, and high-buttoned shoes with canvas or kid tops became popular in the 1880s. Low-cut oxfords appeared for summer, and a canvas and rubber shoe was developed for tennis.

A variety of overcoats and topcoats were worn including the Inverness cape of plaid wool. A knitted cardigan sweater appeared in the 1880s.

Dress for Women

The bodice was smooth and tightly fitted, allowing for rounded bosoms. There were three variations of silhouette. The first bodice shape retained the sloping shoulders and the natural or slightly shortened waistline of the crinoline period. A round or slightly pointed waistline, a narrow V-neck, and three-quarter-length sleeves were typical of this bodice. The *basque* waist appeared in about 1874. This bodice was fitted in a smooth, tight line from shoulder to hip or below. (The basque was later extended into a *princess dress*, whose skirt fullness began at the knee.) The third bustle bodice extended just to the hip with its waist somewhat low. The shoulders were less sloping, the sleeves were full length, and in most day versions the neck was finished with a high-standing collar. Necklines in this period included a narrow square and a heart-shaped neckline. Evening bodices were often extremely décolleté, with small sleeves or bands across the shoulders. The back of most bodices was elongated and furnished with pleats that spread out over the bustle.

To create the bustle silhouette, a crescent-shaped pad was added at the back waist, or a half-hoop structure was worn, extending from the back waist to the floor. Early bustle dresses echoed the eighteenth-century polonaise dress, flat in front, with overdrapes and swags accenting the bustle. The skirt accompanying the basque waist was extremely tight and furnished with a flounce and train at the bottom. Toward the end of the period, when the bodice shortened again, the fuller skirt returned and garment trimming was reduced and simplified.

Skirts were usually floor- or instep-length, but some garments for walking or sports were shortened two or three inches from the ground. Floor-length gowns often had trains.

Hair was dressed high and to the back in braids, buns, and curls. A fringe of curls might soften the forehead. The early look echoed the eighteenth century, but as the period progressed, many women chose simpler styles, and the back hair was often worn low on the neck. Toward the end of the period hair was once again drawn upward, this time to the top of the head. Hats were worn at a tilt over the forehead at the beginning of the period, and later they were placed more squarely on the head. Some bonnets were worn on the

back of the head. Caps were worn indoors by older women, and evening coiffures were elaborately trimmed with ribbons, flowers, feathers, and jewels.

High-top shoes, buttoned or laced up the front, were popular. High-cut pumps were also worn. Both types of shoe had *French* (spool) heels.

Earrings and brooches continued in popularity; bracelets, lockets, and hair ornaments also were common.

Shaped capes and mantles, coats cut to fit over the bustle, and simple jackets were worn as outerwear.

The Gay Nineties (1890–1900)

GENERAL CHARACTERISTICS

Men's clothing developed gradually along previously established lines. The silhouette was somewhat straighter with square shoulders and less-fitted waists. Sack suits continued to take over the places formerly held by frock coats and cutaways. The latter were primarily found on professional men and at very formal daytime occasions. Wool flannels and tweeds became increasingly popular along with traditional broadcloths. Linen, cotton duck, and seersucker were used for summer wear.

Once again the fashionable silhouette for women resembled two triangles balanced point-to-point. Enormous sleeves created width at the shoulders, corsets reduced the waist to the smallest possible size, and gored skirts skimmed the hips and swept to a wide hem. Tailored combinations of jacket, *shirtwaist,* and skirt were worn by women for sport, work, and travel.

Stiff or sturdy fabrics were required for most women's dress, and solids, plaids, and stripes were prominent. Horsehair was used to support the sleeves and the bottom of the skirt.

Dress for Men

The stiff front, neckband shirt (with back opening) was still predominant for formal day and evening wear. The detachable collars worn on these shirts were stiff and extremely high, whether standing band, wing-tip, or rounded turndown style. The *shirtwaist,* a front-buttoned shirt, was popular for casual and sportswear. Farmers and workmen wore unstarched shirtwaists with attached collars, or collarless neckband shirts.

White bow ties accompanied evening dress; black bow ties were appropriate with tuxedos. Ascots, four-in-hand ties, or bow ties were worn with the sack suit, frock coat, and cutaway. Soft silk ties were worn for casual or sportswear and by men of "artistic" tastes.

Vests were high cut with collars. Conservative men wore plain vests, matching or contrasting with coat and trousers. More adventurous dressers might wear bright-colored vests. A watch chain was frequently draped across the vest front between the pockets. The vest was omitted from many summer and sports costumes. Pullover and cardigan sweaters worn under the jacket became a permanent part of the male wardrobe.

Sack suits were high cut and had straight fronts, squared at the bottom edge. The *tuxedo*, a dinner jacket based on the sack coat, was introduced for all-male evening functions and informal dinners at home. Frock, cutaway, and tailcoats had a less fitted look than in previous periods. Coat sleeves were straight and neatly fitted at the shoulder.

Dress pants were straight and narrow; casual pants were somewhat fuller. Informal suits might have cuffs and creases in the pants. Cuffed trousers were shorter and revealed a bit of hose. Knickers continued to be worn for active sports. Belts were sometimes substituted for suspenders on knickers.

Hair was close to the head and parted in the center or slightly to the side. Beards and extravagant sideburns were found only on older men; mustaches were cultivated in a variety of styles.

The top hat was still the appropriate headwear for important occasions, but the *boater* (stiff, flat-crown, medium-brim straw hat), *bowler* (hard, round-crown, medium-brim felt hat), *fedora* (creased-crown, medium-brim felt hat), and *slouch hat* (made of soft felt) were all popular. Caps were worn for many sporting occasions.

High-top shoes in black or brown were worn in winter. Low-cut, string-tied shoes (sometimes white) were worn in summer. Patent leather shoes and spats were appropriate for formal dress.

Overcoats of dark wool were worn in winter; gray or tan top-coats were worn in spring and summer. Overcoats varied from knee to calf length.

Dress for Women

The firm corset produced the fashionable S-curve figure that had a high, full, *mono-bosom* (no definition between breasts), a *wasp waist* (extremely small), sway back, and full hips. Padding to improve bosoms and hips was commonly used. The bodices of the period often incorporated fabric fullness in the front and sometimes blousing all around. The bodice was finished at the waist with a crushed band, belt, or peplum. Bodices for daywear all featured a high-standing collar, some of which flared out to frame the head. Necklines for evening might be a narrow square, heart-, or U-shape. The depth of the décolletage varied and the off-the-shoulder line disappeared.

Enormous leg-o'-mutton sleeves ballooned out from the shoulder and tapered dramatically from the elbow to the wrist. The shape was maintained with crinoline linings, pleated ruffles inside the sleeves, small pads worn at the shoulder, or whalebone hoops. Ruffles, lapels, and other trims accented the shoulder width and the narrow waist.

Skirts were cut in *gores* (triangular-shaped panels) to produce width at the hem without excess fullness at the waist and hip. Skirts were not excessively decorated and were worn over two or three

starched petticoats. Some skirts had extra fullness pleated into the center back. In about 1898 an unstiffened skirt appeared and gradually began to dominate dressy day and evening occasions. The stiffer skirt continued for tailored wear.

Bloomers appeared for women cyclists, although most women rode in skirts.

Hair was usually drawn up on top of the head in a bun or twist. A large, full style was created by adding false hair or pads over which the hair was dressed with a bun on the crown of the head in the style now called the *Gibson girl.*

Hats began fairly small and were seated squarely on the top of the head, attached securely to the bun with a long hat pin. As hairstyles grew larger, so did hats. Some styles reached quite extravagant proportions and were profusely trimmed with flowers, feathers, ribbons, lace, and veilings.

Earrings were out of fashion, but jeweled hairpins and combs were worn for evening. Wide, dog-collar necklaces of pearls, diamonds, or other precious stones were also popular for evening. Daytime jewelry was often limited to a cameo or other brooch centered on the front of the high collar. Lockets and chains were worn around the neck, and watches hanging from a small pin were worn on the left shoulder.

High-buttoned or laced shoes had pointed toes and spool heels. Low-heeled, laced boots were worn for sports, and evening shoes had spool heels and pointed toes with straps, bows, or buckles. *Lisle* (fine cotton) or wool stockings were commonly worn; silk stockings were a rare luxury for most women.

A variety of princess-style coats were worn by women. Shoulder-length and knee-length capes were worn over many day and evening ensembles. Linen dusters with large veiled hats were worn for traveling in open cars.

Edwardian (1900–1915)

GENERAL CHARACTERISTICS

Men's clothes differed little from those of the preceding period, although a general trend to less formal dressing continued. A square silhouette (broad, padded shoulders and straight body) was typical for men. New inventions like the zipper (used for shoes) and "man-made silk" (rayon, used for hose) began to find their way into fashion.

Women's clothes softened, sleeves became modest, and a soft, triangular silhouette developed. Later in the period the triangular-shaped skirt was reduced to a cylinder, producing a narrow, rectangular silhouette. Bodices and skirts were more often combined into dresses, and lighter construction techniques were employed. Tailored looks became more popular as women began to fight for voting rights and World War I loomed on the horizon. Top fashion designers experimented with unusual silhouettes.

Soft fabrics like crepe, charmeuse, chiffon, and batiste were popular for tea dresses and evening gowns. Dresses of all lace, or embroidered cotton combined with lace, were extremely fashionable for summer. Firmer fabrics were used for tailored wear.

Dress for Men

The stiff-front shirt was worn primarily with formal dress. Pleated-front shirts were worn with tuxedos, and soft shirts were appropriate with all other types of dress. Striped and colored shirts with white collars and cuffs were worn for less formal occasions. Detachable collars (the wing-tip, neckband, and rounded turndown) were still high and stiff. Attached turndown collars (with medium points) increased in popularity.

Although ascots and string ties were still worn, four-in-hand and bow ties were the most popular.

Collared vests matched business suits and were cut a bit lower. Vests of faille, brocade, or satin were worn with evening wear—black with tuxedos, white with tails. Matching or contrasting vests were worn with the cutaway and frock coats. V-neck sweaters were sometimes substituted for vests, and cardigan sweaters for jackets, in casual dress. Turtleneck sweaters and jerseys appeared in sportswear.

The square, loose sack coat influenced the shape and fit of the frock, cutaway, and tailcoat. Younger men neglected the frock coat and wore the cutaway for formal day occasions. The tuxedo was accepted for all but the most formal evening occasions. Blazers and Norfolk jackets were worn with matching or contrasting trousers for casual wear. Although frocks and cutaways might still be high cut, sack coats began to button lower.

Pegged trousers with pleats at the waist appeared on younger men. Most pants were creased, and some were cuffed. Belts began to replace suspenders except for formal wear.

Men's hair was close-cut and the center part went out of fashion about 1910. Side parts and *pompadour* styles (brushed straight back with lift in the front) were popular. Except for some small mustaches, young men were clean-shaven (thanks to the invention of the safety razor). Older gents retained the sideburns, mustaches, and clipped beards of their youth.

The gentleman wore a fedora or felt slouch hat with his business suit in winter and in summer he donned a straw boater or *Panama* straw (a high-crown, medium-brim hat of fine straw). The bowler or derby was also a popular hat, worn for a wide variety of occasions. Top hats were reserved for formal occasions.

High-top shoes were worn in winter, but *oxfords* (low-cut, front-tied shoes) were worn in summer. With cuffed pants some men chose colorful, patterned socks. Men's hose were made of wool, cotton, silk, and the new synthetic fiber, rayon.

Outerwear featured simple, long overcoats with velvet collars as well as shorter, lightweight topcoats. The *polo* coat developed from the "wait coat" worn by polo players.

Dress for Women

A wasp-waist corset was worn into the new century. The bust was lower than in previous periods; the abdomen, hips, and buttocks were flattened.

A variety of undergarments were available to meet the needs of season and fashion. Among them were union suits, camisoles, pantaloons, corset covers, short petticoats, chemises, and *combinations* (one-piece garments that combined corset cover or camisole and pantaloons). Silk undergarments gradually replaced cotton for fashionable ladies.

Bodices featured the *pouter pigeon* front, a soft blousing that puffed over the top of the belt and accented the full, low, mono-bosom look. Short, straight sleeves were acceptable for daywear. Shirtwaist and skirt combinations, tailored suits with matching or contrasting blouses, and a variety of day gowns were worn. Skirt lengths varied from long and trailing to ankle- or calf-length for sports.

Daywear might still have a high-standing collar, although it was not as tall and stiff as in the previous period. Afternoon and evening dresses might have simple square or round necklines. *Surplice* (wrapped look creating a V-neckline) necklines were revived. Neckties and stocks were adopted from men's styles to wear with shirtwaists.

Hair in the beginning of the period continued to be done in the pompadour style of the Gibson girl. Hair ornaments, combs, hairpins, barrettes, bows, flowers, and headbands were popular.

After 1910 a straighter silhouette developed and a high-waisted look became fashionable. The corset was more relaxed in the waist and aimed for a smooth cylindrical figure. The *dolman* or *kimono* sleeve (sleeve cut in one with the body of the garment) appeared on some garments. Soft, sheer overskirts and tunics returned to fashion.

Skirts were narrow and straight, sometimes with a slit up the front, back, or side to allow for walking. The *hobble skirt*, a pegged skirt—narrow at the bottom and full at the top—enjoyed a brief period of fashion. Wrapped skirts appeared. By the end of the period most garments were instep- or ankle-length. Many garments had long trailing panels, even if they were fairly short in the front. Designers experimented with new and unusual shapes, but most women settled into more practical styles.

By 1910 many women parted their hair in the center and dressed the sides in poufs. The back hair was curled or braided and twisted into a bun. False hair was added in the form of braids or curl clusters. Hairstyles diminished in size and height. Fashionable hair was often *marcelled* (set in tightly controlled waves) before being dressed into the prevailing style.

A wide variety of hats, many with elaborate trimming, were seen in this period. Early hats were of reasonable size and sat squarely on top of the head. In the middle of the period, hats grew larger and often tilted forward. A number of tall toques and large "lamp shade" hats could be found among fashionable headwear.

Large hats were held to the head with long ornate hat pins. Toward the end of the period, hats were generally smaller, often with tall, vertical feathers. Brims began to turn down over the face and many hats were worn at a dashing angle.

Jewelry included lockets, bracelets, rings, and watches worn pinned at the shoulder or on a fob at the waist. Toward the end of the period, the first wristwatches were designed.

High-top shoes with French heels were still worn. Pumps were worn in summer with day and evening dress, and oxfords were worn for most sportswear. Shoes had pointed toes and long vamps. Stockings were black, white, or matched to the dress.

Coats and jackets of various lengths were worn. Early coats were high-waisted and fitted; later styles were full and sometimes based on Eastern garments. Evening wraps were made of luxurious fabrics and trimmed in fur. Dusters or driving coats were still worn in open cars. Women wore cardigan and pullover sweaters for casual wear.

World War I and the Roaring Twenties (1915–1929)

GENERAL CHARACTERISTICS

The war brought about many military influences in civilian dress. Young men sought more comfortable clothing better suited to the faster pace of modern life. Coats had "natural" shoulders and high, nipped-in waists; pants were pencil slim. Military colors became popular in civilian dress.

To facilitate their participation in the war effort, women turned to practical, functional clothes. Corsets were made less restrictive or were abandoned; skirts were shortened; excess ornament and frivolous decoration were eliminated. Experiencing the freedom of these simpler garments produced a profound change in the attitude of women toward dress. Clothing henceforth was required to permit women to work, dance, and participate in a wide range of activities in relative comfort.

The slightly high waistline of the war years dropped first to the natural (although not cinched) waist, then to the lower hip. The silhouette of the early years was slightly wider at the bottom, but by the middle 1920s most dresses were rectangular, very little wider at the bottom than at the shoulders. A drooping, downward effect was produced in the look of clothes by the cut of the garment and the use of soft, lightweight fabrics.

Dress for Men

Men wore a one-piece cotton undergarment or knitted union suit. Except for formal wear, most shirts were soft and buttoned down the front. White was still the only proper color for business or formal wear, but colored and striped shirts were worn for casual and sportswear. Influenced by military styles, more shirts had attached,

turndown collars that were lower and soft. Four-in-hand and bow ties predominated.

Formal evening dress changed little, but by the 1920s tuxedos were acceptable for most evening occasions. Single-breasted sack suits were worn with matching vests, but the double-breasted coat was rarely seen with a vest. In summer the double-breasted coat or the suit coat and vest were often teamed with white flannel pants. Most coats were buttoned lower than before the war. Early coats had medium-width lapels, but by the end of the twenties, lapels were wide. A sport coat with pleats and a half-belt in the back joined the blazer and Norfolk jacket for casual wear. In the 1910s many coats were almost fingertip length, but in the early 1920s coats began to shorten.

Pants were either pencil-slim or full straight leg shapes. *"Oxford bags"* worn by college men were extremely wide. Many trousers had cuffs and all were creased. Depending on the season, white linen or tweed *plus fours* (long, full knickers) were worn for golf.

Most men were clean-shaven. Their close-cropped hair was worn slicked to the head, with a side or center part and very short sideburns.

The most popular hats for men were felt fedoras, slouch hats, and the *homburg*, a felt hat with a stiff curled brim and high creased crown. The derby decreased in popularity. Panama straws and the boater (also call the *sennit straw*) were summer favorites. Caps and canvas hats were worn for sports.

Spectator shoes, low-cut, string-tied shoes in black or brown and white, were very popular for summer and resort wear. Fashionable gents wore spats. High-top shoes were worn by older men.

Outerwear included the *Chesterfield* (tailored coat with velvet collar), the covert coat, the camel hair polo coat, and various topcoats. Outerwear was heavily influenced by military dress. A leather version of the officer's coat and jackets based on aviators' gear appeared. Every college man wanted a raccoon coat to wear when cheering for his team.

Dress for Women

The new elasticized foundation garment called the *girdle* was designed to streamline the abdomen, hips, and buttocks without cinching in the waist. A *brassiere* or a snug "bust suppressor" was worn to minimize the shape of the bosom. The two together produced the boyish figure deemed desirable. A sliver of silk slip covered the "foundations."

During the war simple suits with ample, though not full, skirts were common. Jackets were first high-waisted and slightly fitted, then loose and unfitted or "boxy." Dresses were slightly high-waisted with easy skirts. After the war the waistline dropped until in the early 1920s, the waist appeared to be very low on the hip. The whole silhouette was a narrow rectangle. The length of skirt hems started just above the ankle during the war and gradually rose to the

calf and finally hovered around the knees. Short skirts were fashionable for both day and evening wear, although many women never wore the shortest skirt lengths. Layers of fringe and all-beaded dresses were popular. By 1929 longer skirts created by the addition of hanging panels or uneven *handkerchief* hems were introduced for evening wear.

Blouses were long and worn over the skirts to create the low waist look of the late 1920s.

Day necklines were simple shapes, usually cut away from the neck. Many featured flat collars. Evening dresses were often sleeveless with scooped out V- or U-shaped necklines that left only thin straps across the shoulders.

Sleeves were slim and neatly fitted at the shoulder and many dresses were sleeveless with matching or coordinating jackets.

For the first time respectable women could cut their hair. Short, "bobbed" styles were the rage. Those women who were unwilling to cut their hair dressed it close to the head with the back hair arranged in a small neat bun on the nape of the neck. Both long and short styles featured side parts and Marcel waves.

Rouged cheeks, red "cupid's bow" lips, pale-powdered skin, and smoky-shadowed eyelids were fashionable in the later twenties.

Hats began the period as tall, "pot" shapes. As they decreased in height, they began to fit closely the shape of the head. The resulting helmet-like *cloche* sat far down on the head and had a small, asymmetrical brim. Large-brim hats also sat deeply on the head with the brim turned down.

Earrings, when worn, tended to be long and dangling, since the hair covered the ears. Long ropes of pearls or other beads were the most popular type of jewelry, and long scarves wrapped around the neck sometimes took the place of jewels. Wristwatches were more frequently seen.

Shoes with pointed toes, "French" heels, and laces or interesting strap arrangements were fashionable. Pumps, plain or with large buckles, were also worn. Spats, gaiters, and a few shoes that buttoned over the ankle remained. In the beginning of the period hose were still colored silk—black for day, pale colors for evening. By the end of the period, transparent flesh-tone stockings in real or artificial silk were fashionable.

Coats were straight, loose fitting, and slightly longer than the dress. Many coats "wrapped" and were held shut or had one button at the hip. Some were trimmed with fur cuffs and large, standing fur collars.

The Thirties (1930–1939)

GENERAL CHARACTERISTICS

For many the Depression put a damper on fashion. For those who could still afford to dress in style, men's clothes featured broad shoulders, a nipped-in natural waist, narrow hips, and straight, full, pleated trousers. The introduction of the forty-hour workweek gave the working man more leisure time and increased the demand for casual and sport dress. As each new sport craze developed, a new type of garment was developed to allow full participation in the sport. The increased development of sportswear in turn began to influence acceptable dress in the work place, a trend that continues to the present day.

A silhouette with a natural waistline returned to fashion. Smooth, flat hips and a soft, low-bosomed bodice also developed. Soft, draping fabrics were preferred. Dresses were usually cut on the *bias* (a diagonal to the straight grain of the fabric) to produce the desired clinging effect.

Zippers, previously used only on shoes or work clothes, now began to appear in fashionable clothing.

Dress for Men

Shirt collars were elongated, and four-in-hand ties were of medium width. Short-sleeved shirts of knitted or woven cotton appeared for summer casual wear.

Vests were still worn with single-breasted suits but were usually omitted with the more popular double-breasted suit.

The *English drape* suit was a major fashion development of the thirties. The ventless jacket was buttoned low, with wide shoulders, nipped-in waist, and wide, peaked lapels. The pants were pleated at the waist and tapered slightly to the cuffs. Many of the double-breasted examples were made up in pinstripe fabrics of black/gray or blue/gray combinations.

Linen and seersucker suits were popular for summer and resort wear. Corduroy pants and suits were popular on the college campus. Sweaters were worn for a wide variety of casual occasions. The white dinner jacket with shawl collar took the place of the tuxedo for resort and summer wear.

Hair continued to be close-cut and parted on the side, but many men now wore their hair in the pompadour style. Sideburns continued to be short. Most men were clean-shaven, but a few sported short, neat mustaches.

California life inspired a range of casual garments, such as the *cardigan suit* (collarless jacket), two-tone shirts, and Hawaiian print shirts and shorts. Ski wear allowing freedom of movement and warmth was developed as more and more people headed for the slopes.

The most popular hat was a felt *snap-brim* with pinched front and top crease. Most hat brims were wide and worn turned up in the back and down in the front. Homburgs, Panamas, *sennits* (boaters), and bowlers (derbies) were still worn. A new coconut straw hat with ridged crown and medium brim was introduced.

Shoes were natural or slightly tapered shapes with rounded toes. Most shoes were cut to just below the ankle and laced up the front. A slip-on moccasin or *loafer* was introduced in the late thirties. The saddle oxford was popular with younger men.

Outerwear included reversible coats (wool and waterproof duck), Chesterfields, leather jackets, and the trench coat.

Dress for Women

Undergarments were little changed. Slips became longer as skirts lengthened; many had bra-shaped tops.

Dresses were designed with shirring or pleats in the bodice to create a soft bosom effect. At the beginning of the period shoulders were small and natural. Necklines were simple and featured drapes, cowls, and soft collars. Sleeves sometimes had a bit of extra fullness at the top of the cap. Natural waistlines returned. A self-fabric belt was the usual waist finish.

Skirts dropped to calf-length for day, and once again evening gowns were floor-length, although many were shorter in the front. Most skirts flared either from the hip or just above the knee. Bias-cut skirts clung to the hips.

Suits were popular for daywear. Suit jackets fit snugly in the hips and bloused above the waist. Blouses with soft collars, jabots, or bows were visible at the neck of the jacket. Suit skirts were cut in gores or with pleats.

Long pants were worn by some women for sports or casual wear. *Lounging pajamas* were luxurious "at-home" attire.

Many evening gowns showed "classical" influence. Gowns were often simple in the front with a plunging back neckline, crisscrossed with straps. Simple, dramatic elegance was prized.

Hair was a bit longer than in the twenties, worn parted on the side and waved around the face. The ends of the hair were dressed in rolls or curls.

Hats continued for a time to fit closely to the head, but they became less deep. Toward the end of the period hats sat up on the head and were usually worn at an angle over the forehead. Hat veiling, spider-web fine, adorned many hats.

Many women copied the high, thin, arched eyebrows and dark red lips of the Hollywood movie queens. Even conservative women used face powder and lipstick.

Shoes had pointed toes and higher heels than in the twenties. Sandals were worn for casual wear, and high-heeled sandals in gold and silver kid were introduced for evening wear. Natural-color "nylons" with seams began to overtake silk stockings.

Coats were long or three-quarter-length, often with fur collars. *Boas* (long, narrow scarves) of fox or mink were worn draped around the necks of suits, coats, and evening wear.

The Forties (1940–1949)

GENERAL CHARACTERISTICS

World War II dominated the 1940s. As the conflict spread, all resources were conserved and given defense priority. Fashion excesses were out, rationing in. Two-pants suits, vests, trouser cuffs, and long skirts were deemed wasteful. New synthetic fibers were developed that soon entered the world of fashion. The broad-shouldered, drape suit for men continued in style, but gradually became less fitted in the waist and hips.

Military dress again influenced fashion styling for both men and women. As in World War I, women entered the work force in large numbers. Women's clothes took on a crisp, businesslike look. Shoulders broadened, defined waists returned, and skirts were shortened until they just covered the knees.

Dress for Men

Dress shirts had widespread, long-pointed collars. Toward the end of the war, shirts were made of parachute nylon. Sport shirts (often short-sleeved) were made in plaids, large prints, and solid-color gabardines. Factory workers often wore sport shirts and slacks instead of work clothes.

The popular four-in-hand tie was wide and was tied in a bulky "Windsor knot." Ties featured bold prints, some with hand-painted designs.

Two-piece, single-breasted suits without vests or cuffs were made during the war years. Lapels, while still wide, had less exaggerated points. Vents appeared in the center back or side back seams of jackets. Suits were made in a wide variety of plaids, stripes, tweeds, and flannels. The *Eisenhower* or *Ike* jacket was a waist-length jacket with shirt-type sleeves, button front, and patch pockets modeled after the military uniform worn by General Dwight Eisenhower. Separate sport coats appeared that could be combined with dress slacks or casual wear.

Pants were cut fairly full, pleated in front, creased, and cuffless. Hair continued close-cut with short sideburns. Most men were still clean-shaven.

Sportswear continued to flourish. Among the new garments to appear were Bermuda shorts, polo shirts, and zipper-front jackets.

Panama and coconut straws, homburgs, and Tyrolean hats were all worn, but the wide-brim, felt slouch hat was the most popular.

For outerwear "fingertip" coats (a short topcoat) were introduced. Trench coats remained popular.

Dress for Women

Shirtwaist dresses and "uniform" styles were popular. Large shoulder pads produced broad, square shoulders in dresses, suits, and coats. Skirts and blouses paired with sweaters became a practical way for many women to dress. During the war, skirts fit smoothly over the hips and flared to just below the knee. Garments were cut on the straight grain to conserve fabric. Asymmetrical garments enjoyed new popularity. Popular necklines included the sweetheart, V-neck, and shirt-collar styles.

"Teenagers," a new entity, wore blouses, sweaters, skirts, bobby sox, and saddle oxfords. Weekends were spent in blue jeans and dad's oversized shirt. Female defense workers wore uniforms, many of them coveralls. Some long, full pants and above-the-knee shorts were found in women's sportswear.

Hair was often shoulder-length. In one popular style the front and side hair was dressed in rolls away from the face and the back hair was rolled under and caught in a *snood* (a large hairnet). Other styles swept the hair up to a crown of curls on the top and forehead or let the hair hang loose from a side part to wave and curl about the face and shoulders.

Hats included turbans, toques, adaptations of men's styles, and whimsical concoctions of felt, veiling, and decorations. Hats were worn at an angle over the forehead.

Eyebrows were fuller and more natural in the forties, but powder and bright lipstick were still used.

Shoes were no longer pointed but followed the natural foot shape. Heels were thick and some were extremely high. Some shoes were built on thick soles called *platforms*. Strap sandals were sometimes worn for day as well as evening. The open-toe *slingback* pump (open heel with strap) was a popular shoe. Oxfords with stout heels were worn by more practical women.

Nylon stockings were extremely difficult to get during the war years. Cotton anklets and leg makeup were substituted.

Women wore trench coats and polo coats as well as full back, unfitted styles in long or short lengths (*toppers*).

After the war Dior introduced (in 1947) the "New Look." An attempt to return to more feminine fashions, the "New Look" featured natural shoulders, a pinched waist, and a long skirt. The skirt silhouette was either full and stiffened or the pencil-slim "straight skirt." In the next few years women all over the world dropped their hems and cinched their waists.

The Fifties (1950–1959)

GENERAL CHARACTERISTICS

The Ivy League, natural-shoulder style challenged the heavy padding and square shoulders of previous men's fashions and a slim, straight silhouette took over.

Dior's "New Look" was a major influence on the women's styles of the fifties. Women's clothes had either pencil-slim or full, *bouffant skirts* (full at the bottom supported by stiff, ruffled petticoats

called *crinolines*). Firm, structured undergarments were again required to produce the high, shaped bosom, small waist, and flat abdomen and buttocks in fashion.

New fibers (polyesters and acrylics) made big news in clothes for both men and women. Fashionable color schemes included neutral colors (gray, charcoal, black, navy) spiced with bright accents (red, lemon, pumpkin) and large areas of white.

Dress for Men

Dress shirts had narrow collars with small pointed or rounded ends. Button-down collars found their way from the college campus to business wear. Collar bars and tabs were devised to keep the collar neatly in place around the tie. Small patterns and pale pastel colors were fashionable in shirts. A wide variety of sport shirts were worn.

Ties decreased in width until some were barely 1½ inches wide. Bow ties were worn primarily for formal wear. Solids, stripes, and small patterns were popular.

The "natural-shoulder," unpadded coat made its appearance. After initial resistance, even older men accepted it in a modified version. Lapels narrowed to fine slivers on some jackets. Most coats had three buttons, although the top and bottom buttons were often left open. Coats were cut straight with little indentation at the waist. Sport coats were popular; "wash-and-wear" models appeared for summer. The *Continental* suit was more fitted, with a deeply rounded front opening and a high, two-button closure. Three-piece suits were rare, but plaid and fancy vests were occasionally worn.

After formal daywear (cutaway) was rejected as inaugural attire by President Eisenhower, its use rapidly declined. Jackets made of madras (bright-colored plaid cotton originally from India), batik, or other fancy fabric joined the white dinner jacket and tuxedo for dress occasions. Waist-length, zipper-front jackets of leather or fabric were popular for casual and sportswear.

Pants were cut straight and less full at the beginning of the period. Most trousers had pleats, creases, and cuffs. In the mid-fifties pants began to taper at the bottom and some uncuffed, flat-front pants appeared. Bermuda shorts, *deck pants* (calf-length sailing pants), jeans, and sport slacks were worn for casual wear. New active sportswear included stretch ski pants.

Hair was very close-cut with short sideburns, then combed away from the face with a side part. Some men retained the pompadour style of the forties, while others favored the short, military-type crew cut. Hair tonic was used to hold the style in place and give the hair sheen. Young men began to grow the side and top hair long and used hair oil to comb it to the back of the head in a style known as a "duck's ass."

Hats had narrow brims and lower, slightly tapered crowns. Many sported feathers or other small decorations. A plaid wool hat shaped like the snap-brim was popular for sportswear.

Car coats and other short overcoats were popular as more men drove their cars to and from the suburbs. Straight-cut raincoats of black or tan, some with zip-out pile linings, were versatile and practical. Trench coats were still popular. Dressy Chesterfields and simple wool topcoats were also worn.

Dress for Women

Brassieres were heavily structured and held the bosom in firm, high cones. Padding was added when needed. The *"Merry Widow"* was a lightweight corset with elastic insets and boning. Mid-hip length, this "long-line" bra could be worn with or without straps. Separate waist cinchers were also used to create the small, fashionable waist. Girdles were a necessity under straight skirts. Petticoats returned to fashion to support the full silhouette. Stiff horsehair, crisp taffeta, nylon net, or starched ruffles created the lower edge of these petticoats and sometimes three or four were worn together. Skirts were lower calf-length but began to shorten in the late fifties.

Shirtwaist (open down the front with shirt-style collars) and other simple dresses with fitted bodices and set-in, raglan, or dolman sleeves were popular for daywear. Collars were often large and stood away from the neck. Skirts were either bouffant or straight with *kick pleats* (a box pleat from knee to hem to allow for mobility). Bouffant skirts could be gathered, pleated, gored, or circular. Princess dresses, fitting tightly at the waist and sweeping to wide hems, returned to fashion. Starting from below the calf, skirts were shortened to just below the knee by the end of the decade.

Wide, stiff belts—matching or contrasting—were worn tightly buckled around the waist.

Suits followed similar lines: straight or circular skirts with hip-length fitted jackets or short "bolero" jackets. Suit jackets did not always match the skirt but were sometimes in a bright contrasting color. Coordinated separates (blouse, skirt, sweater, jacket, pants) became established as a classic way of dressing and increased in popularity throughout the twentieth century.

A brief fashion for the *trapeze* dress (a loose triangular-shape dress) and the *sacque-back chemise* dress (straight sheath with bloused back) foreshadowed less-fitted fashions to come.

Pants of all types were worn for casual wear: shorts (upper thigh), Bermuda shorts (just above the knee), pedal-pushers (upper calf), Capri or toreador (lower calf), and ankle-length.

Evening gowns were frequently strapless or furnished with small *spaghetti* straps. Draped bodices were fashionable and the bouffant skirt was often tulle or sheer organza. *Ballerina-length* (ankle or lower calf) was popular. Some evening wear required petticoats with lightweight hoops in the bottom.

Many women wore their hair short and close to the head. Straight-cut bangs were a popular feature. Young women wore the *ponytail*, all hair drawn high up on the back of the head and caught

with an elastic band. Longer hair was worn waved and curled about the shoulders or sleeked back into a "French twist."

Hats were small and fit close to the head at the beginning of the period. Hats completely covered with flowers were popular.

Makeup base, powder, lipstick, eye shadow, eyeliner, and mascara were commonly used. Bright red lipstick placed emphasis on the mouth. Dark lines were drawn around the eyes, and eyebrows were plucked to give a high arch.

Pumps were the most popular style of shoe. Pointed toes returned, and heels grew tall and very small at the bottom (*stiletto* or *spike* heels). Sandals, moccasins, oxfords, and "flats" were also available. Seamless nylon hose in black, taupe, navy, and flesh tones were worn.

Coats were either straight or full with "swingy" backs. The *topper*, a short wool coat, was worn for spring or fall. Car coats in corduroy, wool, or suede were available for women.

The Sixties (1960–1969)

GENERAL CHARACTERISTICS

Simple, clean lines in easy-care fabrics dominated the clothes of the sixties. Clothing for both men and women skimmed the body. New plastics and synthetic fabrics were incorporated into all types of clothing. Solid colors dominated the early part of the period.

The late sixties saw a revolution in men's clothing. Formality in dress was all but abandoned. Men began to wear bright colors for work as well as play. The "mod" style, "psychedelic" colors, and fantastic prints appeared as the "hippie" counterculture, rock music, and space exploration all had an influence on fashion.

Dress for Men

Men's shirts had moderate-length, pointed collars in the early sixties. Small stripes were popular. "No-iron" shirts of polyester and cotton or of cotton with a resin finish swept the market. Wider collars with long points came into fashion later in the decade. By the end of the sixties brightly colored shirts with French cuffs and large cuff links were worn. Shirts with stand-up collars and ties of matching fabric were also worn. Sweaters, turtlenecks, and knit shirts of all types were popular for a wide variety of occasions.

Ties began the decade as narrow, conservative neckwear and ended the sixties as wide (three to four inches), bold, brightly colored accents. Silk ties and matching handkerchiefs were worn even by conservative men. Some men substituted a silk scarf tied casually around the neck under an open shirt collar. Necklaces of beads or heavy chains with pendants were sometimes worn instead of traditional ties.

Traditional suits were lightly padded, single-breasted with medium-width lapels, straight and boxy in the body. Pants were slender with flat fronts and straight or tapering legs.

In the late sixties an array of new styles were created for men. Collarless, zipper-front suits; *Edwardian* suits (high-buttoned, pinched-waist, double-breasted suits); *Safari* jackets (belted jacket based on jungle gear); and new versions of the Norfolk jacket all appeared along with traditional sport coats in bright colors and plaids. The *Nehru* suit featured a jacket with a standing collar that buttoned to the neck without lapels.

Formal wear reflected the new freedom. Dinner jackets were styled in the Nehru or Edwardian styles, in brighter colors and varied fabrics (brocades, velvets). Shirts with ruffled fronts and cuffs were worn with lapel jackets.

Hair in the beginning of the sixties was neat and close-cut with short sideburns. By the mid-sixties sideburns began to lengthen and the "dry look" was in fashion. By the end of the period most men wore their hair over the ears and over the collar in the back in a loose, wind-blown look. Many young men wore their hair shoulder-length or longer and held it in place with a headband or tied it back in a queue. Full, bushy beards and mustaches were also common among the "hip generation."

Men's hats at the beginning of the sixties continued the small- and medium-brim styles of the fifties. Wider brims began to appear in the late sixties.

Late in the sixties short, square-toed boots and loafers with tassels or buckled straps became fashionable.

Topcoats and overcoats were short, between hip and knee. Early versions were mostly single-breasted; later ones were double-breasted with "Edwardian" shaping in the waist and chest. Zip-front reversible jackets were popular for casual wear.

Dress for Women

The early sixties saw a simplification of the silhouette for women's dress. Boxy suits with straight skirts, sleeveless dresses with coats or jackets, A-line skirts, and shifts were popular. The waistline became less important and skirts began to climb. Brightly colored plain and textured wools were popular. The *miniskirt* was first shown in the early sixties. Skirts so named were a minimum of two inches above the knee, and many exposed most of the thigh. By the end of the sixties, short skirts dominated the fashion scene.

As an alternative to the "mini," many women turned to pants. Pants suits were designed to be worn for work, play, and formal occasions. Jumpsuits and hostess pajamas were again in fashion. After some initial resistance, pants were accepted everywhere and became a staple wardrobe item even among conservative women.

Formal wear was styled along similar lines in fancy fabrics, often beaded. Cutouts and see-through sections revealed the body underneath.

Toward the end of the sixties, psychedelic colors and prints were used for dresses, hostess gowns, evening wear, and accessories.

Styles based on ethnic dress (gypsy, peasant, Mexican, American Indian, African, Russian) began to appear.

Denim began to dominate casual wear. Jeans were the full-time uniform of the young. Tight-fitting, worn, torn, and sometimes patched, jeans represented the anti-fashion, anti-establishment feelings of the hippies. The shape of jeans changed to a hip-hugging waist with bell-bottom legs.

Bouffant hairstyles of teased or backcombed hair were worn at the beginning of the period. Hair was shoulder- or chin-length. Headbands or large bows were worn across the top of the head, sometimes to disguise the addition of a "fall" of false hair. In the later sixties bouffant hairdos were replaced by short geometrical cuts. Hippie women wore their hair long and straight.

Fashionable hats were of solid-color, matching fabrics in small *pillbox,* cap, or helmet shapes. However, because they tended to depress the bouffant hairstyle, hats were no longer considered a necessity to a fashionable ensemble. Scarves tied simply around the head were frequently substituted. Hats never regained their former status as a required accessory.

The emphasis in makeup switched from the lips to the eyes. Lipstick colors were pale and often pearlized. False eyelashes were common, and eyes were heavily lined top and bottom.

Tights or panty hose reaching from waist to toe were worn with the mini-dress. Solid colors (often matching the dress), fishnets, ribbed, and other decorative knits were used in leg wear.

Shoes had low to medium, chunky heels, and they gradually developed from pointed toes to broad, square toes. Knee-high boots of vinyl or leather were added for winter. Boots were tight-fitting and zipped up the inside of the leg.

Cloth coats to match dresses were fashionable in the early sixties. Toward the end of the decade longer coats—*maxi* (ankle length) and *midi* (calf length)—inspired by nineteenth-century Russian styles became popular.

The Seventies (1970–1979)

GENERAL CHARACTERISTICS

The counterculture influences of the late sixties became mainstream fashion in the seventies. Romantic, "costume" looks inspired by many sources were popular. Blue denim was the most commonly seen fabric on both men and women. Casual styles invaded all occasions. Longer skirts returned, and a general softening occurred in women's clothes. A resurgence of interest in arts and crafts influenced the design of clothing that featured quilting, patchwork, and hand-woven effects. Clothes worn for active sports began to influence fashion. Although the great variety of clothing allowed for individualization of the wardrobe, most garments had natural shoulders and body-conscious lines.

Dress for Men

Undershirts were abandoned by many men. The athletic shirt and the T-shirt were worn alone as casual wear. T-shirts were printed with designs and slogans. Turtleneck sweaters were worn for almost any occasion. Dress shirts were bright, solid colors or bold stripes. Shiny, synthetic knit shirts were tapered for better fit and printed in bold, colorful designs. Collars were wide with long points.

Ties were very wide. Wide stripes and large floral and geometric prints were popular. Large bow ties were also worn. More and more men, however, abandoned ties for open shirts and gold chain necklaces.

Jackets were cut with wide lapels, two buttons, and nipped-in waist. Even business suits were made of polyester knits or denim and featured *saddle stitching* (decorative stitching). The Western influence could be seen in many garments. *Leisure suits* of polyester knits were popular. The jackets of these casual suits had "shirt" styling—tab fronts, wide collars set on a neckband, and shirt sleeves with cuffs. Patch pockets and yokes were usually topstitched with heavy, contrasting thread. *Safari* jackets were shirt-styled jackets with patch pockets and short or long sleeves.

Dress pants were cut slightly below the natural waist and had cuffs and creases. Casual, low-waist pants known as *hip-huggers* were worn with wide belts. Pants were tight-fitting in the waist, hips, and thighs, and then flared to a wide bell at the bottom. Denim and bright-colored knits were popular in pants. Jumpsuits based on workmen's coveralls enjoyed a period of popularity.

Toward the end of the seventies interest in more traditional men's styling revived. Vests and pleated-front pants were more often seen. Neutral colors, narrow lapels, thin ties, and suits with soft shaping began to reappear.

Traditional men's tailoring featured two basic styles: the *American cut* and the *European cut*. The American cut featured a soft-shoulder jacket with slight waist suppression, notched lapels (4½ inches wide), flap pockets, and vents at the sides or center back. The pants were straight. The European cut featured a close-fitting jacket with high armholes, nipped waist, flaring bottom, padded shoulders, wide lapels (five inches wide), and deep vents at the side or back. The pants were flared, and the suit often had a vest.

At the end of the period formal wear became less extravagant and more elegant.

Hair was frequently full and "dry" with long sideburns. Some men retained the very long styles of the late sixties. Mustaches and beards continued to be popular although they were sometimes neatly trimmed. By the late seventies neater, shorter hairstyles appeared, and sideburns began to shorten.

Boots and blunt-toed, heavy shoes were popular in the seventies. Shoes had thick soles, and some had platform soles an inch or more high. Some shoes were brightly colored and were decorated with

metallic leathers. By 1979 thin soles and tapered toes began to return. Sneakers were widely worn for casual wear.

Longer overcoats also returned—knee to upper calf.

Dress for Women

As a symbol of feminist independence, some women abandoned wearing bras. Others switched to soft, molded bras that provided only minimum support and allowed a lower, less-defined bosom.

Close-fitting sweaters and tops were popular. High waists, low waists, and natural waists all were possible. Most styles were soft, body-conscious shapes. Jackets had wide lapels and long, pointed collars. Romantic styles were based on the gypsy look, ethnic styles, and Victorian lingerie. Wraparound dresses in bright, printed knits and loose "tent" dresses were popular in the early and mid-seventies. Caftans were worn for hostess and beachwear.

Although the mini-skirt and the new *hot pants* (short shorts) remained fashionable, skirts began to lengthen, and some long skirts were worn. By the late seventies the majority of skirts dipped below the knee.

Hip-hugger or natural-waist pants with bell-bottoms were everywhere. Knickers, gauchos, and all styles of jeans were also worn. Straight, full legs with cuffs appeared in the late seventies. With the hip-hugger jeans and skirts, belts of leather or chain were worn.

Scarves tied around the head replaced hats for many occasions. Berets, caps, and some mannish hats were worn. The "gaucho" hat and Russian-style fur hats were also fashionable.

Natural hairstyles were in fashion. Blow-dry styles, short curly styles, blunt cuts, frizzed hair, Gibson girl, and French braids were all worn. Wigs were considered a fashion accessory and were very popular.

Dark, low-intensity lipstick colors were used with smoke-toned eye shadow. Many women abandoned makeup in the early seventies.

Platform shoes with blunt toes and wedge-heel shoes were popular. In the mid-seventies heels went up, platforms decreased, and a more natural toe returned. Tall boots were worn with coats and short pants.

Midi-length "Russian" coats and tailored capes were popular at the beginning of the period. Full-length, quilted down coats for sport and dress were worn.

The Eighties (1980–1989)

GENERAL CHARACTERISTICS

The eighties brought revived interest in traditional men's tailoring and styles. The more flamboyant styles of the seventies disappeared.

A variety of international influences began to impact women's fashion. Early romantic looks gave way to cleaner, bolder shapes and oversized, draped silhouettes. The fashions of the thirties, forties, fifties, and sixties each took a turn influencing current styles.

Neutrals and rich, jewel-like tones were favored and natural fibers returned to popularity.

Dress for Men

Dress shirts returned to medium- or narrow-width collars. Colored dress shirts in solids, stripes, and plaids were still popular, although colors were more subtle.

Medium- to narrow-width ties in pastels and medium intensities were worn. Plain or striped red ties and yellow ties with small dots were very popular.

Typical suit coats were less fitted, softer, less padded, and lower in the armholes. Lapels were medium to wide widths at the beginning of the period with some narrow lapels appearing later. A fashion for loose, unlined jackets with large shoulder pads appeared for fashionable young men in the mid-eighties.

Straight-leg, medium-width pants were worn by conservative men. *Baggies*, a loose trouser tapered toward the bottom, were popular with younger men. A preference for fifties-style tapered and tight-fitting pants was evident among the counterculture "punk" groups and spread to fashion in the mid-eighties.

Casual wear included loose-fitting sweaters, velour running suits, and sweat suits.

Many men returned to wearing classical black tuxedos, with color and pattern introduced in the cummerbund and tie.

Hairstyles became shorter and more neatly groomed. Many men returned to a close-cropped nape and cheekbone-length sideburns. Crew cuts, flattops, *spiked* hair (hair stiffened into points on the top of the head), and shaved heads were popular among those young people who were influenced by the punk movement. Some men wore long *shag* cuts in imitation of certain rock stars.

Large- and medium-brim hats returned to fashion but were infrequently worn.

Shoes tapered to natural shapes. Thin soles returned.

Dress for Women

Most women favored practical combinations of dress, jacket, skirt, pants, sweater, or blouse. Wider, padded shoulders returned to fashion. Clean, simple shapes evolved.

Fashion influences were more international. Italian designers contributed interesting knit fashions and tailoring. Japanese designers created unusual, loose, oversized, wrapped shapes. American designers developed practical and smart garments based on American classic looks. English designers contributed both traditional styles and eccentric dress. French designers continued to design high-fashion, body-revealing garments.

Skirt lengths varied but many were calf-length or lower. Prairie skirts layered with petticoats, *dirndl* (straight-cut, and gathered or pleated) skirts, and flared calf-length skirts were among the longer styles. Late in the eighties miniskirts again appeared. Short, straight skirts were worn with fitted, broad-shouldered tops sometimes with a peplum.

Pants went from straight cut to baggies to tapered leg. The calf-length, fitted styles from the fifties returned. Tight-knit leggings or pants worn with oversized, man-tailored shirts were popular. Loose-fitting sweaters were worn with skirts and pants.

Many women maintained a full mane of shoulder-length hair. Layered hairstyles were popular, and in the mid-eighties short, asymmetrical, or spiked styles were fashionable.

Small hats were worn at an angle over the forehead.

Large chunky necklaces, large dangling or button earrings, and bangle bracelets were fashionable.

In the early eighties makeup created the "natural look." Bright, clear lipstick colors returned in the mid-eighties.

Fashionable pointed-toe shoes ranged from flats to high, thin heels. *Sneakers* or *running shoes* were worn for sports, casual wear, travel, and sometimes business.

Quilted down coats in all lengths were popular. By the middle of the decade straight-cut wool coats with large shoulders were more fashionable. Large shawls and scarves were wrapped around the neck and shoulders.

The Nineties (1990–1999)
by Viviane Galloway

GENERAL CHARACTERISTICS

The corporate boom and dress-for-success fashions of the 1980s carried over to the early nineties. However, with the advent of casual days in the office and more people working from home, a less rigid style of dress known as business casual was introduced as the decade progressed. Active wear and sportswear become acceptable for a wider range of occasions. Entertainment and sports celebrities became fashion trendsetters and often developed their own clothing lines. With the Internet providing broader access to fashion trends around the world, a wide range of styles developed simultaneously, influenced by international cultures such as those of Jamaica, Japan, and Africa. Retro fashion with a strong Victorian, sixties, or seventies influence appeared early on in the decade, and mid-decade styles reflecting the thirties, forties, and fifties appeared. As a reaction to the heavily constructed fashions of the previous decade, designers from Europe, Asia, and the United States embraced minimalism, austerity, and deconstruction.

The eighties silhouette continued into the early nineties. Bright colors and color blocking, textured fabrics, and asymmetrical designs were popular with men and women. Sweaters with large graphic patterns and textures were popular. Black became a staple. Chunky gold jewelry was worn by both sexes.

Mid-decade saw the return of a more natural silhouette. Shoulders were still padded, but took on a rounder shape and gradually reduced in size. Fashion returned to classic, tailored lines, with natural fabrics in neutral and earth-tone colors draped softly over the body. At the same time, a rectangular silhouette developed, with fluid long-line jackets and fuller-legged pants for men and women, and both short, straight skirts and long, full skirts for women.

Improvements in polyester fabrics and blends made possible a wide range of fabrics that imitated higher-price silk goods such as charmeuse, suede, and crepe. Stretch fibers were added to denim and other woven or knitted fabrics for more comfortable and form-fitting fashion for both sexes.

Dress for Men

The decade started with updated classic styles like wool suits and separates in earth tones and textures. Men's dress shirts were more loosely fitted and made of bold colors and stripes, with a wide variety of collars. Contrasting white collars and cuffs were worn for an executive look. Ties, generally of medium width, were colorful and appeared in many patterns. Bow ties also were popular. Mixing patterns of shirt and accessories was acceptable although in the late Nineties there was also a fashion for wearing solid color shirts with matching ties and pocket squares. Vests, wool and knit, with higher closings regained popularity. Jackets were longer, some reaching to mid-thigh, with softer shoulders and large pockets. Lapels were cut in a variety of widths. Double-breasted jackets were common, and two- and three-button jackets were equally popular. Late in the decade suits were more fitted, and the four-button suit returned and the English skinny suit appeared. In urban areas suits with five or more buttons were also worn.

Rugby shirts, golf shirts, cricket sweaters, and loose sweaters with bold colorful graphic patterns were popular choices for casual wear. Earth-tone cotton shirts in prints or solid colors were worn. At the start of the nineties, trousers had double pleats and were slightly tapered. Mid-decade they were worn pleated or flat-front with a fuller leg. Chinos were acceptable for the more casual work wardrobe, and jeans could be worn for all but the dressiest of occasions. Parachute pants and brightly colored T-shirts were popular for casual wear. A parallel style of body-conscious clothing emerged, featuring fitted button-down shirts, tighter jeans and trousers, and closely tailored jackets. The hooded sweatshirt became a staple for all ages.

Casual shirts and pants were worn with dressier jackets in dark-colored corduroy or velvet for less formal affairs and for special occa-

sions. The dinner jacket was of a boxy cut at the start of the decade, but became more fitted mid-decade. Bow ties, vests, and cummerbunds were available in a variety of patterns, colors, and fabrics.

The Persian Gulf War led to the popularity of military-inspired fashion. Camouflage-patterned garments were especially popular, and eventually were made in brighter colors than the original army-issue items. Red, white, and blue appeared in active and sportswear.

Hairstyles were generally neat, with flat tops prevailing in the early nineties, replaced later by spiky styles. Some men kept the sides and back short, and the top longer, often slicking it back with gel. Later in the decade hair was worn longer, and wavy hair was accentuated with hair products. Men were bolder with their hair coloring. Men were clean-shaven or wore well-trimmed goatees, mustaches, or soul patches (a small growth of beard just under the lower lip). Men and women of all races cultivated dreadlocks (long, thin matted locks of hair all over the head).

Men wore gold chains and watches at the start of the decade, but favored silver jewelry toward the end of the decade. Men's rings and earrings became more acceptable.

Men wore sneakers, loafers, work boots, and hiking-style boots as casual shoes. Ankle boots were worn as casual and dress shoes. Spectators and round-capped dress shoes were seen throughout the decade. Late in the decade square-toed shoes and boots appeared often with crepe soles or molded rubber soles and heels.

Popular colors for men's coats were black, navy, gray, and camel. Coats were generously cut at the start of the decade. The 50s car coat returned mid-decade. The trench coat also had a relaxed fit. Loosely cut peacoats and field jackets, and polar fleece jackets were also popular. Leather jackets in a variety of styles were worn. Sporty fedora styles, tweed caps, and pork pie hats were in fashion. Baseball caps were worn with active wear and even dressier clothing.

Dress for Women

The decade started with a continuation of the inverted triangle silhouette of the eighties. Mid-decade saw the return of a more natural silhouette. Shoulders were still padded, but took on a rounder shape and were gradually reduced in size.

For business wear women favored matching separates of rayon, linen, suiting, or knit fabrics. Especially popular was the loosely cut, long-line jacket, often collarless. This was worn with trousers, short sheath dresses, or skirts. Boat-necked and scoop-necked shells were essentials. Separates were either solid or a mix of patterns: leaves, flowers, and paisley. Concurrently, a classic, tailored look developed featuring wool blazers, skirts, or trousers in solids, plaid, or tweed, and worn with men's-style dress shirts or turtlenecks. The mandarin collar was also very popular.

Skirts ran the gamut from very short to ankle-length. Elastic waistbands were common. Straight-cut, pleated, and gathered skirts were popular in all lengths. They could be worn with heavy black tights or tights in a coordinated color. Leggings were worn with longer gauzy skirts, dresses, long sweaters, or blazers. Later, matador or Capri pants of cotton or a stretch fabric were worn with cotton shirts or sweater sets. Pants were sometimes worn under short skirts, and blue jeans were worn for all occasions. The pant leg lost its taper, and the full cut, the boot cut, and even bell-bottom pant leg returned. Black or white jeans were also popular.

Dresses were still very popular. Cotton princess-line and shirt-dress styles, in plaid, large pastel floral, or paisley designs with jewel or V-shaped necklines with lace or crocheted collars were popular in the early nineties. Romper dresses and jumpsuits were worn early in the decade for a casual look. Bold black and white and Safari-inspired ensembles were also popular. Formal gown styles were very diverse including: vintage gowns, formal separates, and revealing gowns cut on the bias with extreme décolletage.

Gold jewelry was the most popular, although silver reappeared at the end of the decade. Big, chunky earrings, watches, and necklaces were worn, and large gold buttons adorned much clothing. Pearls were worn in the early nineties. Faux tortoiseshell was used for headbands and sunglasses throughout the decade.

Shoes in the early nineties were simple: plain round-toed pumps with medium heel and ballerina flats in a variety of colors. Both short and tall lace-up and slip-on boots were worn. As the decade progressed, women of all economic strata wore designer or "status" shoes of fine leather or satin featuring thin straps, beads, and sequins. Chunky heels and heavy soles appeared on all styles of shoes and boots. Work boots were worn with pants, skirts, and dresses. The "Mary Jane" and spectator shoe styles returned mid-decade. Bra straps and lacy décolletage could be seen peeking out from necklines and armholes. Underwear could be seen above waist-bands, but slips disappeared from most wardrobes.

Longer romantic hairstyles prevailed in the early nineties. Head-bands were worn for a classic look. A modernized shag or shorter haircut was worn, often with one or many decorative clips. Longer hair was often worn in a casual knot held by a large plastic claw or hair sticks. Women of color wore their hair in intricate styles featuring braids, ribbon curls, and twists, often artificial. A diversity of hair products allowed a greater variety of spiky, messy, curly, or smooth styles. Makeup was natural-looking, although the smoky eye was popular throughout the decade. Dark (almost black) shades of red were worn on the lips and nails in the middle of the decade.

Outerwear included wool coats in navy, gray, black, or camel. A looser cut, often with dolman sleeves, was a popular choice. Variations of the trench, barn, and peacoats were common. Parkas and ski jackets were worn, even on dressier occasions, as formal coats became less common. Fleece in vests and jackets became very popular in the second half of the decade. Cardigan coats were worn indoors and out. Felt hats with wide brims, men's-wear-influenced styles, and berets with sequins and rhinestones were often seen in the early nineties. Soft hats were favored for their versatility and were frequently worn with a pin holding up the brim. Later in the decade the cloche returned to fashion.

Young people began the decade in fun, modernized, men's-wear-inspired fashions, with oversized shirts, jackets, and vests. Vintage clothing was very popular, and brimmed hats were won by both sexes. As the decade progressed, a well-tailored look developed. At the same time, the emergence of hip-hop culture produced a style of its own: Clothes became very baggy, with boys' jeans worn at the lower hip, often exposing the tops of boxer shorts, and large fleece pullovers and sweatshirts prevailed. Bucket hats were popular, and baseball caps, "do-rags," and fuzzy billed caps were worn, often backward. Big chains were worn around the neck and were also used to attach wallets to the pants waist. Girls were influenced by popular dance troupes and wore baggy pants or short flared skirts with tight tops, often revealing the midriff. Large "door knocker" earrings were popular.

The Twenty-First Century (2000–2009)
by Jeanette Aultz Look

GENERAL CHARACTERISTICS

The twenty-first century brought the increased popularity of casual styles, not only for everyday clothes, but also as the continuation of business casual dress as first seen in the 1990s. With a relaxation of the social dress code, undergarments might either peek out from under clothing or sometimes break all the way out to outerwear. Clothing was often layered and, sometimes, informal clothing was mixed with formal pieces. All ages, social groups, and sexes commonly wore outfits consisting of T-shirts with mottos or graphics, jeans, and athletic shoes. People often participated in sports or wished to look as if they did, dressing in sportswear even when not engaged in these activities.

People dressed to be associated with a specific social group rather than by economic status, although the display of specific brand names could reflect that status. Fashion was often a revival of styles from the twentieth century, beginning with the late 1960s and 1970s in the early part of the 2000s, a fashion for 1950s clothing mid-decade, and a return to 1980s styles in 2007. These trends reflected the styles of the inspiring decade while retaining the silhouette of the 2000s. The Iraq war inspired military details in dress. Clothing and bags developed special pockets or straps for the array of portable electronic devices, like notebook computers and mobile phones, used every day.

Natural colors or neutral colors were popular, sometimes with a single, bright accent color, or color blocking. However, bright colors, especially blue, pink, and yellow, were popular early in the decade, then again toward the end in 2008. Fabrics included cotton and cotton-poly blends, wool, cashmere, some rayon, and polar fleece. Nearly everything included some stretch fiber. The fashionable waistline for pants and skirts was at the hip, or just above or below the hipbone. The silhouette was long and lean, with narrow hips and an undefined waist.

Dress for Men

Men increasingly dressed for comfort over style. Jeans and T-shirts were universal, as well as athletic-type clothing as fashion. Colors were subdued, usually natural or earth tones. Young men layered clothing and mixed formal clothing with informal pieces, such as a suit jacket paired with T-shirt and jeans. Young men and teenagers often allowed their brightly colored and patterned boxer shorts to show above their low-slung, hip hugging pants.

Business casual dress was increasingly common and even more informal after 2000. The standard business-casual outfit for men was either a *polo shirt* (a short-sleeve, collared knit pullover) or a button-front dress shirt without a tie, paired with tan cotton pants and leather shoes. Three- and four-button suits were mostly seen on higher-level businessmen and on certain professionals, such as lawyers, politicians, bankers, and financiers. The primary colors were black, gray, and blue, worn with brightly colored ties. African-American men wore suits more often, frequently in bright colors or bold patterns, tailored to be long and slim with five or more buttons. Sometimes suits and dress shirts were worn without ties.

Button-front cotton or cotton flannel plaid shirts were common. Knit sweaters, plain or with horizontal stripes, and pullover sweatshirts or zip-front hooded sweatshirts were popular in colder weather. Summer wear included special styles like the "Havana" shirt and the bowling shirt. Most common were T-shirts with graphics, logos, or mottos on them. Combinations of the aforementioned shirts might be layered and worn together.

Informality spread to previously formal occasions, too. The traditional tuxedo with satin lapels was still worn for black-tie occasions, but younger men often omitted certain parts of the ensemble (commonly the tie), or included an informal garment with the tux.

Pants were worn below the waist, usually resting on the hips, and fell straight from hip to ankle with the flat front being the most common. Jeans and *khakis* (tan, cotton pants) were worn for everyday, informal occasions. *Cargo pants* (cotton pants with extra pockets on the sides close to the knees) were popular for casual wear. Shorts were universal in summer, hemmed just above or below the knee. Corduroy pants were worn, usually gray, brown, or black, but sometimes in other colors like dark blue or hunter green. Possibly as a side effect of pants being worn below the waist, pants hems often touched the floor at the back and pooled over the shoes.

Sport fans of all ages and social strata displayed their enthusiasm for the local team or the wearer's college team by wearing a variety of garments (in particular, hats, shirts, or jackets) featuring the team's colors, logos, and mascots.

More men, especially in urban areas, became comfortable with finer grooming practices, like manicures and the use of specialized hair products. Hair was generally kept short, sometimes longer on top and clipped around the ears and necks, but long hair was acceptable among certain social groups. Shaving the head completely was also an acceptable option.

Athletic shoes, common for everyday and encompassing status brands endorsed by sports stars, were very important. Black or dark brown leather shoes, usually with a square-shaped toe and little decoration, were worn for business or formal dress. Most shoes had thick, rubber soles.

Men might wear waist- to mid-thigh-length leather jackets or shearling jackets. Modest wool coats in black, dark blue, or gray were worn for cold weather. Traditional raincoats and trench coats were still worn, although waterproof zip-front hooded jackets often replaced these styles. Team jackets and ski jackets were also worn as everyday coats.

Dress for Women

Pairing incongruent garments was also popular in women's dress: suits with knit wear, tuxedo-like shirts with jeans, or casual shoes with formal dresses. The layering of women's clothing allowed a fitted undershirt to peak out from a sweater at the collar, cuffs, and bottom. Sometimes skirts were layered over pants. Colors were generally soft and natural, with some bright and vibrant colors mixed in, usually shades with low intensity. Many fashions were inspired by ethnic dress, especially Chinese, Indian, and African traditional dress or fabrics.

Although panty hose began to disappear among younger women, colorful, opaque tights and leggings were common in winter. Women often wore colorful socks with patterns and pictures. The pushup bra from the 1990s was still worn, but equally common were soft, cotton jersey bras that created a natural-looking bosom. Lined skirts took the place of slip-and-skirt combinations, and many women allowed unlined skirts to cling to the body. Underwear was sometimes worn as outerwear; a full slip might become a dress, and bra straps or thong panties might be allowed to peek out from under clothing.

In many professions business dress saw the same slackening of formal standards for women as for men. Women might wear skirt suits, pant suits, or simply button-front shirts with plain cotton slacks.

Formal styles were extremely provocative. Low backs and décolletage were the norm. High-heeled sandals were worn to match the color of the gown, and often panty hose were abandoned altogether.

Dresses, though not worn often, were more common in summer. These dresses were made of lightweight fabrics or jersey knit in soft styles. Waistlines varied—the empire, the A-line with no defined waist, and the dropped waist silhouette. Wrap dresses returned to popularity.

Skirt waistlines were at the hips. Skirts were hemmed just above or just below the knee, or mini-length, while ankle-length skirts were generally reserved for members of conservative religious groups. Straight and A-line skirts were the most common. Jean skirts drifted in and out of fashion. Skirts might be of small flowered patterns, plaids, or solid colored. Ethnic patterns, especially African or Asian, were sometimes popular.

Most shirts were of fitted knit fabric, often with mottos or pictures on them. Horizontal stripes were sometimes popular, although solid colors were the norm. Long-sleeved fitted T-shirts were layered with sweaters or cardigans. Shirts were sometimes worn untucked and extended below the waist of the pant or skirt. Young women might wear midriff-bearing shirts.

Women's jeans were often tight-fitting at the thigh, with a slight flare in the lower leg, known as *boot cut*. A fashion for jeans, tight to the ankle and often worn with knee-high boots, appeared toward the end of the decade. Cotton khakis with straight legs and flat fronts were common. Lycra or spandex was added to most fabrics to allow for freedom of movement. Waistlines were at the hips or just below, usually referred to as *low-rise*. Corduroy pants in many colors were worn. Straight-leg or wide-leg pants were common for business. Calf-length pants, or pants that were rolled and snapped in place at the calf, were popular in summer.

Shoes were very trend-driven, but some styles were constant. For everyday wear, athletic shoes were common among all age and social groups, in similar styles to men, but often in brighter colors. Calf- or knee-high leather boots were worn with skirts or over pants or jeans. For business or formal occasions, ballet flats or high-heeled shoes with heels varying from one to three inches, occasionally up to four inches, might be worn, sometimes with pointed toes that extended far beyond the natural shape of the foot. Some other trends included calf-high shearling boots, molded latex clogs in bright colors, colorful Wellington boots, and cowboy boots. In summer, sandals with flat or high heels were worn. Like in the 1980s and 1990s, brand-name shoes continued to be popular, not only in formal styles, but also informal.

A woman's haircut and style was chosen specifically to enhance her face. Shoulder-length, layered hair was most common. Hair was often straightened with a blow dryer. Sometimes styles were purposefully messy, though great effort could go into such styles. Makeup was usually natural, with an emphasis on mascara and eyes. Lip color varied from year to year, but was predominately in natural colors to flatter women's complexions. Soft, neutral colors were used

in eye shadow. Sunless tanning creams became very popular, particularly among young women who no longer wore pantyhose.

Long, dangling earrings were popular and worn in both formal and informal occasions. Simple necklaces with pendants on delicate chains were common, but so were very long strings of beads that were wrapped around the neck or wrist many times. Large, bangle bracelets returned to fashion. Women might also wear jewelry inspired by their own or another ethnic group, especially African, Asian, or Celtic. Body jewelry, including nose and navel piercing, was no longer reserved for counterculture fashion. There was also a fashion for wide belts.

Most handbags had short handles, carried slung over one shoulder and clutched high under the arm. They could be quite large for everyday use and not necessarily coordinated with the outfit worn. Bags might also display the logo of a status brand. Formal handbags were much smaller, often coordinating with the outfit, while still having short handles slung over the shoulder.

Long overcoats in neutral colors were worn, although soft-colored wool and tweed coats reminiscent of the early 1960s came in and out of fashion. Quilted down coats were streamlined, and ski jackets might be worn for everyday in cold weather. Waterproof zip-front hooded jackets similar to men's styles were also worn, although traditional raincoats and trench coats could still be seen.

Selected Bibliography

Assembled by Shahrzad Khozein Haghjoo

Understanding Drama

Brockett, Oscar G., and Franklin J. Hildy. *History of the Theatre*. 10th ed. Danbury: Allyn, 2007.

Corrigan, Robert W., ed. *The Forms of Drama*. Boston: Houghton, 1972.

Jones, Robert Edmond. *The Dramatic Imagination: Reflections and Speculations on the Art of the Theatre*. New York: Routledge, 2004.

Molinari, Cesare. *Theatre through the Ages*. New York: McGraw-Hill, 1975.

Russell, Douglas A. *Period Style for the Theatre*. 2nd ed. Boston: Allyn, 1987.

Thomas, James. *Script Analysis for Actors, Directors, and Designers*. New York: Focal, 2004.

General Period Costume Research

Anthony, Pegaret, and Janet Arnold. *Costume: A General Bibliography*. London: Costume Society, V & A Museum, 1977.

Arnold, Janet. *A Handbook of Costume*. New York: Phillips, 1974.

Baines, Barbara Burman. *Fashion Revivals from the Elizabethan Age to the Present Day*. London: Batsford, 1981.

Barton, Lucy. *Historic Costume for the Stage*. New ed. Boston: Baker, 1961.

Batterberry, Michael, and Ariane Batterberry. *Mirror, Mirror: A Social History of Fashion*. New York: Holt, 1977.

Bigelow, Marybelle S., and Terry Patrick Bigelow. *Fashion in History: Western Dress, Prehistoric to Present*. Upper Saddle River: Prentice, 1997.

Blum, Stella, ed. *Ackermann's Costume Plates: Women's Fashions in England, 1818–1828*. New York: Dover, 1978.

_____. *Victorian Fashions and Costumes from Harpers Bazaar, 1867–1898*. New York: Dover, 1974.

Boucher, Francois, and Yvonne Deslandres. *20,000 Years of Fashion*. Danbury: Abrams, 1998.

Bradfield, Nancy. *Costume in Detail, 1730–1930*. New York: Costume & Fashion, 1997.

Brooke, Iris. *Costume in Greek Classic Drama*. New York: Theatre Arts, 1962.

Cassin-Scott, Jack. *The Illustrated Encyclopedia of Costume and Fashion: From 1066 to the Present Day.* London: Cassell, 2006.

Costantino, Maria. *Men's Fashion in the Twentieth Century: From Frock Coats to Intelligent Fibres.* New York: Costume & Fashion, 1997.

Cumming, Valerie. *Understanding Fashion History.* New York: Costume & Fashion, 2004.

Cunnington, C. W., and Phillis E. Cunnington. *Handbook of English Costume in the 16th Century.* 2nd ed. Boston: Plays, 1970.

Cunnington, Phillis, and Catherine Lucas. *Occupational Costume in England.* London: Adams & Black, 1976.

Ewing, Elizabeth. *History of 20th Century Fashion.* New York: Scribner, 2002.

Gernsheim, Alison. *Victorian and Edwardian Fashion.* New York: Dover, 1981.

Ghorsline, Douglas. *What People Wore.* Minneapolis: Dover, 2000.

Grimble, Frances, and Deborah Kuhn. *After a Fashion: How to Reproduce, Restore, and Wear Vintage Styles.* New York: Lavolta, 1998.

———, ed., *Fashions of the Gilded Age, Vol. 1: Undergarments, Bodices, Skirts, Overskirts, Polonaises, and Day Dresses 1877–1882.* New York: Lavolta, 2004.

———, ed., *Fashions of the Gilded Age, Vol. 2: Evening, Bridal, Sports, Outerwear, Accessories, and Dressmaking 1877–1882.* New York: Lavolta, 2004.

Grun, Bernard. *The Timetables of History: A Horizontal Linkage of People and Events.* New York: Touchstone, 2005.

Hope, Thomas. *Costumes of the Greeks and Romans.* New York: Dover, 1962.

Kybalova, Ludmila, Olga Herbenova, and Milena Lamarova. *The Pictorial Encyclopedia of Fashion.* Trans. by Claudia Rosoux. London: Hamlyn, 1970.

Lansdell, Avil. *Occupational Costume.* Aylesbury: Shire, 1977.

Laver, James. *Costume and Fashion: A Concise History.* London: Thames, 2002.

Meredith, Ray. *Mr. Lincoln's Camera Man: Matthew B. Brady.* New York: Dover, 1975.

Mirken, Alan, ed. *The 1927 Edition of the Sears, Roebuck Catalogue.* New York: Random, 1980.

Oakes, Alma, and Margot Hamilton Hill. *Rural Costume: Its Origin and Development in Western Europe and the British Isles.* London: Batsford, 1970.

Payne, Blanche, Jane Farrell-Beck, and Geitel Winakor. *History of Costume: From the Ancient Mesopotamians to the Twentieth Century.* New York: Addison, 1997.

Russell, Douglas A. *Costume History and Style.* Englewood Cliffs: Allyn, 1982.

Tozer, Jane, and Sarah Levitt. *Fabric of Society: A Century of People and Their Clothes.* Manchester: Laura Ashley, 1983.

Vincent, Susan. *Dressing the Elite: Clothes in Early Modern England.* New York: Berg, 2003.

Specific Costume Research

Boehn, Max von. *Ornaments: Lace, Fans, Gloves, Walking Sticks, Parasols, Jewelry, and Trinkets.* Boston: Ayer, 1972.

Colle, Doriece. *Collars Stocks Cravats: A History and Costume Dating Guide to Civilian Men's Neckpieces 1655–1900.* Emmaus: Rodale, 1972.

Cumming, Valerie. *Gloves: The Costume Accessories Series.* London: Anchor, 1982.

Cunnington, Phillis, and Cecil Willett. *The History of Underclothes.* Minneapolis: Dover, 1992.

Meyer, Franz Sales. *Handbook of Ornament.* Minneapolis: Dover, 2002.

O'Keeffe, Linda, and Andreas Bleckmann. *Shoes: A Celebration of Pumps, Sandals, Slippers and More.* Boston: Workman, 1997.

Speltz, Alexander. *Styles of Ornament.* Trans. and rev. by David O'Connor. Boston: Dover, 1959.

Taylor, Lou. *Mourning Dress: A Costume and Social History.* London: Allen, 1983.

Waugh, Norah. *Corsets and Crinolines.* New York: Theatre Art, 1970.

Wilcox, R. Turner. *The Mode in Footwear.* New York: Scribner, 1984.

———. *The Mode in Hats and Headdress.* New York: Scribner, 1959.

Elements of Design

Albers, Josef, and Nicholas Fox Weber. *Interaction of Color.* New York: Yale, 2006.

Bell, Ione, Haren M. Hess, and Jim R. Matison. *Art As You See It: A Self-Teaching Guide.* New York: Wiley, 1979.

Birren, Faber. *Creative Color: A Dynamic Approach for Artists and Designers.* Lancaster: Schiffer, 1987.

Edwards, Betty. *Color by Betty Edwards: A Course in Mastering the Art of Mixing Colors.* New York: Tarcher, 2004.

Developing the Costume

Anderson, Barbara, and Cletus R. Anderson. *Costume Design.* Belmont: Cengage, 1998.

Binder, Pearl. *Dressing Up, Dressing Down.* Winchester: Allen, 1986.

Ingham, Rosemary, and Liz Covey. *The Costume Designer's Handbook: A Complete Guide for Amateur* and *Professional Costume Designers.* 2nd ed. Chicago: Heinemann, 1993.

Lurie, Alison. *The Language of Clothes.* New York: Owl, 2000.

Pecktal, Lynn. *Costume Design: Techniques of Modern Masters.* Minneapolis: Watson-Guptill, 1999.

Russell, Douglas A. *Stage Costume Design: Theory, Techniques and Style.* Englewood Cliffs: Prentice, 1985.

Drawing and Rendering

Baker, Georgia O., and Helen R. Pullen. *A Handbook of Costume Drawing: A Guide to Drawing the Period Figure for Costume Design Students.* New York: Focal, 2000.

Edwards, Betty. *The New Drawing on the Right Side of the Brain.* Los Angeles: Tarcher, 1999.

Hogarth, Burne. *Dynamic Wrinkles and Drapery: Solutions for Drawing the Clothed Figure.* Minneapolis: Watson-Guptill, 1995.

Huaixiang, Tan. *Character Costume Figure Drawing: Step-by-Step Drawing Methods for Theatre Costume Designers.* New York: Focal, 2004.

Ireland, Patrick John. *Fashion Design Drawing and Presentation.* London: Batsford, 1970.

Kincaid, Elizabeth. *Paint Watercolors That Dance with Light.* New York: North Light, 2004.

Riegelman, Nancy. *Colors for Modern Fashion.* North Mankato: Nine Heads Media, 2006.

_____. *9 Heads: A Guide to Fashion Drawing.* North Mankato: Nine Heads Media, 2000.

Scanlon, Rory. *Costume Design Graphics: A Workbook in Drawing and Clothing Techniques.* New York: Costume & Fashion, 2000.

Simon, Mark. *Facial Expressions: A Visual Reference for Artists.* Minneapolis: Watson-Guptill, 2005.

Fabrics

Dryden, Deborah M. *Fabric Painting and Dyeing for the Theatre.* Chicago: Heinemann, 1993.

Kadolph, Sara J., and Anna L. Langford. *Textiles.* 10th ed. Upper Saddle River: Prentice, 2006.

Kafka, Francis J. *The Hand Decoration of Fabrics: Batik, Stenciling, Silk Screen, Block Printing, Tie Dyeing.* Minneapolis: Dover, 1973.

Textile Fabric Consultants, Inc. *Basic Swatch Kit.* La Vergne: Textile Fabric Consultants, 2007.

Tortora, Phyllis G., and Billie J. Collier. *Understanding Textiles.* 7th ed. Upper Saddle River: Prentice, 2008.

_____, and Robert S. Merkel. *Fairchild's Dictionary of Textiles.* 7th ed. New York: Fairchild, 1996.

Getting the Show Together
Patternmaking

Arnold, Janet. *Patterns of Fashion: The Cut and Construction of Clothes for Women c. 1560–1620.* New York: Drama Book, 1985.

_____. *Patterns of Fashion 1 c. 1660–1860: English Women's Dresses and Their Construction.* New York: Drama Book, 1977.

_____. *Patterns of Fashion 2 c. 1860–1940: English Women's Dresses and Their Construction.* New York: Drama Book, 1977.

_____. *Patterns of Fashion 4: The Cut and Construction of Linen Shirts, Smocks, Neck and Headwear, etc. c. 1540–1660.* New York: Macmillan, 2008.

Grimble, Frances, ed. *The Edwardian Modiste: 85 Authentic Patterns with Instructions, Fashion Plates and Period Sewing Techniques.* New York: Lavolta, 1997.

_____. *The Voice of Fashion: 79 Turn-of-the-Century Patterns with Instructions and Fashion Plates.* New York: Lavolta, 1998.

Handford, Jack. *Professional Patternmaking for Designers: Women's Wear and Men's Casual Wear.* New York: Fairchild, 2003.

Harris, Kristina, ed. *Authentic Victorian Fashion Patterns: A Complete Lady's Wardrobe.* Minneapolis: Dover, 2003.

_____. *59 Authentic Turn-of-the-Century Fashion Patterns.* Minneapolis: Dover, 1995.

Holkeboer, Katherine S. *Patterns for Theatrical Costumes: Trims, Garment and Accessories from Ancient Egypt to 1915.* New York: Costume & Fashion, 1993.

Jaffe, Hilde, and Nurie Relis. *Draping for Fashion Design.* Upper Saddle River: Prentice, 2004.

Joseph-Armstrong, Helen. *Patternmaking for Fashion Design.* Upper Saddle River: Prentice, 2005.

Levine, Arnold S., and Robin L. McGee. *Patterns for Costume Accessories.* New York: Costume & Fashion, 2006.

Waugh, Norah. *The Cut of Men's Clothes 1600–1900.* New York: Theatre Arts, 1987.

_____. *The Cut of Women's Clothes 1600–1930.* New York: Theatre Arts, 1987.

Sewing & Crafts

Ambrose, Bonnie A. *The Little Bodice Construction Book: A Workbook on Period Bodices.* New York: Costume & Fashion, 1995.

_____. *The Little Corset Construction Book: A Workbook on Period Underwear.* New York: Costume & Fashion, 1997.

_____. *The Little Hatmaking Book: A Workbook on Turn-of-the-Century Hats.* New York: Costume & Fashion, 1994.

Association of Theatrical Artists and Craftspeople. *Entertainment Sourcebook*. New York: ATAC. (See box 10.H.)

Croonborg, Frederick T, ed. by R. L Shep. *The Blue Book of Men's Tailoring*. Fort Bragg: Shep, 2005.

Cunningham, Rebecca. *Basic Sewing for Costume Construction: A Handbook*. Long Grove: Waveland, 2005.

Dreher, Denise. *From the Neck Up: An Illustrated Guide to Hatmaking*. Minneapolis: Madhatter, 1981.

Dryden, Deborah. *Fabric Painting and Dyeing for the Theatre*. Chicago: Heinemann, 1993.

Fernald, Mary, and Eileen Shenton. *Historic Costumes and How to Make Them*. Minneapolis: Dover, 2006.

Huaixiang, Tan. *Costume Craftwork on a Budget: Clothing, 3-D Makeup, Wigs, Millinery and Accessories*. New York: Focal, 2007.

Ingham, Rosemary, and Liz Covey. *The Costume Technician's Handbook*. 3rd ed. Chicago: Heinemann, 2003.

James, Thurston. *The Prop Builder's Mask-Making Handbook*. New York: North Light, 1990.

Lawson, Joan, and Peter Revitt. *Dressing for the Ballet*. London: Adam & Pitman, 1958.

Malcolm-Davies, Jane, and Ninya Mikhaila. *The Tudor Tailor*. London: Batsford, 2006.

Reader's Digest. *The New Complete Guide to Sewing*. Pleasantville: Reader's Digest, 2002.

Vogue. *The Vogue Sewing Book*. New York: Sixth & Spring, 2006.

Makeup

Baker, Patricia. *Wigs and Make-up for Theatre, TV and Film*. New York: Focal, 1993.

Corey, Irene. *The Face Is a Canvas: The Design and Technique of Theatrical Make-Up*. New York: Anchorage, 1991.

Corson, Richard, and James Glavan. *Stage Makeup*. 9th ed. Danbury: Allyn, 2000.

Delamar, Penny. *The Complete Make-Up Artist: Working in Film, Television and Theatre*. New York: Macmillan, 1995.

Mitchel, Doug. *Body Painting*. Minneapolis: Wolfgang, 2008.

Thudium, Laura. *Stage Makeup: The Actor's Complete Guide to Today's Techniques and Materials*. Minneapolis: Watson-Guptill, 1999.

Designing for Film

Chierichetti, David. *Edith Head: The Life and Times of Hollywood's Celebrated Costume Designer*. New York: Harper, 2004.

Cole, Holly, and Kristin Burke. *Costuming for Film: The Art and the Craft*. New York: Silman-James, 2005.

La Motte, Richard E. *Costume Design 101: The Art and Business of Costume Design for Film and Television*. Boston: Wiese, 2001.

Landis, Deborah Nadoolman. *Costume Design*. New York: Elsevier, 2003.

_____. *Dressed: A Century of Hollywood Costume Design*. Scranton: HC, 2007.

Leese, Elizabeth. *Costume Design in the Movies: An Illustrated Guide to the Work of 157 Great Designers*. Minneapolis: Dover, 1991.

Preparing for a Costume Design Career

Carter, David E. *Big Book of Business Cards*. New York: Collins, 2008.

Eisenman, Sara. *Building Design Portfolios: Innovative Concepts for Presenting Your Work*. New York: Rockport, 2006.

Jaen, Rafael. *Developing and Maintaining a Design-Tech Portfolio: A Guide for Theatre, Film and TV*. New York: Focal, 2006.

Linton, Harold, and Cesar Pelli. *Portfolio Design*. Boston: Norton, 2000.

MacDonald, Matthew. *Creating Web Sites: The Missing Manual*. Danbury: O'Reilly, 2005.

Mitchell, Scott. *Create Your Own Website*. 4th ed. Indianapolis: Sams, 2008.

Moody, James L. *The Business of Theatrical Design*. New York: Allworth, 2002.

Sussner Design. *Letterhead and Logo Design 10*. New York: Rockport, 2007.

Veen, Jeffrey. *The Art and Science of Web Design*. Berkeley: New Riders, 2001.

Societies Related to Costume

(See also box 10.H for unions and professional organizations.)

The Costume Society (UK)
www.costumesociety.org.uk
Publications: *Costume*
The Costume Society has as its aim the promotion of education in dress throughout the ages including contemporary dress.

The Costume Society of America
https://costumesocietyamerica.com
Publications: *Dress, The Journal of The Costume Society of America*
The Costume Society of America is an organization that works to advance the global understanding of all aspects of dress and appearance, to stimulate scholarship, and to encourage study in the field of costume.

Costume Society of Ontario

http://www.costumesociety.ca/
information@costumesociety.ca
Publications: *CSO NEWS, Costume Journal*
The Costume Society of Ontario is an association dedicated to exploring the design, development and deportment of fashion throughout the ages, the influence of dress on society, and the reflection of technology, culture and thought on fashion design and display.

Index

Bios of Interviewed Designers

Gregg Barnes (*Costume Designer*) Broadway: *Legally Blonde* (2007 Tony nomination), *The Drowsy Chaperone* (2006 Tony Award, Drama Desk Award, Outer Critics Award, Olivier nomination), *Dirty Rotten Scoundrels, Flower Drum Song* (Tony nomination), *Side Show.* New York: *Sinatra* (Radio City Music Hall), *The Wizard of Oz* (Madison Square Garden), *Radio City Music Hall Christmas Spectacular* (Principal Designer 1994–2005), *Cinderella* and *The Merry Widow* (New York City Opera), *Pageant* (The Blue Angel and London's West End— Olivier Nomination), *The Kathy and Mo Show*, Eliot Feld's *Behold the Man*, Judith Jamison's ballet *Sweet Release* (Alvin Ailey). Regional credits include: *Mame* (The Kennedy Center), *Lucky Duck* (San Diego Critic's Award), *Allegro* (Helen Hayes Award), and many others. Gregg was the first recipient of the Theatre Development Funds Young Master Award.

Judith Dolan is a Tony Award-winner costume designer (*Candide*) who also earned a Lucille Lortelle Award for *The Petrified Prince* and two Drama Desk nominations. She has designed the Broadway productions of *LoveMusik, Parade, Joseph and the Amazing Technicolor Dreamcoat,* and *Hollywood Arms*. Opera designs include *Idomeneo* for Wolf Trap Opera, Christholf Von Dohnanyi's *The Magic Flute* for The Cleveland Orchestra and Carlyle Floyd's *Willie Stark*. Dolan has designed for companies such as Dublin's Abbey Theatre, Theatre Clwyd in Wales, The Old Vic, the Alley Theatre, D.C.'s Shakespeare Theatre, Goodman Theatre, New York City Opera, and Houston Grand Opera. She has a Ph.D. in Directing and Design from Stanford University and is Professor in the Department of Theater and Dance at the University of California, San Diego.

William Ivey Long (*Costume Designer*) Broadway: *Nine to Five; Pal Joey*; *Young Frankenstein*; *Hairspray* (Tony, Drama Desk, Outer Critics Circle Awards); *Chicago.* Other New York credits include: *The Ritz, Curtains, Grey Gardens* (Tony award); *The Producers* (Tony, Drama Desk, Outer Critics Circle Awards); *Sweet Charity; A Streetcar Named Desire; La Cage*

Aux Folles (Hewes Award); *The Frogs; Little Shop of Horrors; The Boy from Oz;* Susan Stroman's *Double Feature* at the New York City Ballet; *Cabaret; Contact* (Hewes Award); *The Music Man; Annie Get Your Gun; The Man Who Came to Dinner; Swing; The Mystery of Irma Vep; Steel Pier; 1776; Smokey Joe's Café; Crazy for You* (Tony, Outer Critics Circle Awards); *Guys and Dolls* (Drama Desk Award); Madison Square Garden's *A Christmas Carol; Six Degrees of Separation; Assassins* (Obie Award); *Lend Me a Tenor* (Drama Desk, Outer Critics Circle Awards); *Nine* (Tony, Drama Desk, Maharam Awards); Robert Wilson's *Hamletmachine;* Leonard Bernstein's *A Quiet Place* and *Trouble in Tahiti;* Vienna State Opera, LaScala, Houston Grand Opera, and The Kennedy Center; Paul Green's *The Lost Colony;* Mick Jagger for the Rolling Stones' *Steel Wheels* tour; *Siegfried and Roy* at the Mirage Hotel; The Pointer Sisters at Caesar's Palace, Paul Taylor; Twyla Tharp; Peter Martins; David Parsons, Susan Stroman. He was inducted into the Theatre Hall of Fame in January 2006.

Martin Pakledinaz has designed costumes for numerous Broadway productions including the 2008 revival of *Gypsy, Kiss Me, Kate* (Tony award—2008), the revival of *Grease, The Life,* and *Thoroughly Modern Millie* (Tony award—2002). His work in dance includes pieces for the Mark Morris Dance Group San Francisco Ballet, Boston Ballet, New York City Ballet, and Pacific Northwest Ballet. He has designed opera and theater for companies throughout the U.S., Canada, Europe, and Japan. Awards include the Tony, Drama Desk, Obie, and Helen Hayes, among others. He teaches Costume Design at the Tisch School of the Arts at NYU.

Paul Tazewell (*Costume Designer*) Broadway credits include *In The Heights* (Tony nomination); *The Color Purple* (Tony nomination); *Hot Feet; Caroline, or Change; A Raisin in the Sun; Drowning Crow; Bring in 'da Noise, Bring in 'da Funk* (Tony nomination); *Elaine Stritch: At Liberty; On the Town; The Gershwin's Fascinating Rhythm;* and *Def Poetry Jam.* Selected Off-Broadway credits include *In the Heights, McReele, Flesh and Blood, Fame on 42nd Street, Boston Marriage,* and *Harlem Song.* For 18 years he has worked for theater, dance, and opera companies across the country and around the globe. His most recent work includes *Caesar and Cleopatra* and *Romeo and Juliet* for the Stratford Festival in Ontario, the world premiere of Toni Morrison's *Margaret Garner, Porgy and Bess* for Washington National Opera, *The Color Purple* First National Tour, *The Wiz* and *Memphis* at LaJolla Playhouse, *Jesus Christ Superstar* and *The Women of Brewster Place* for the Alliance Theater, and Christopher Wheeldon's newest piece at the Bolshoi Ballet in Moscow. Broadway revival of *Guys and Dolls* and *Ruined* by Lynne Nottage at Manhatten Theatre Club.

Mr. Tazewell has received three Helen Hayes Awards, The Lucille Lortel Award, The Jefferson Award, The AUDELCO Award, a Princess Grace Fellowship, the Princess Grace Statue Award, and the Irene Sharaff Young Master Award.

Catherine Zuber (Costumes) *South Pacific* (Tony Award), *The Coast of Utopia* (Tony Award, Outer Critics Circle Award), *Awake and Sing!* (Tony Award), *Edward Albee's Seascape* (Tony Award nomination), *The Light in the Piazza* (Tony Award, Outer Critics Circle Award nomination), *Dinner at Eight, Twelfth Night* (Tony Award nominations), *Ivanov* all at The Lincoln Center Theater. Other Broadway credits include: the Roundabout Theater production of *A Man for All Seasons, Mauritius, Crybaby, Little Women, Doubt, Frozen, Dracula, The Sound of Music, Triumph of Love* among others. Recipient: 2003, 2004 and 2007 Henry Hewes Award for Design, 2004, 2005 Lucille Lortel Award, 2004 Ovation Award, 1997 and 2005 Obie Award for Sustained Achievement. Other: Opera: *Romeo et Juliette* for the Salzburg Festival 2008, Austria, *Dr. Atomic* and *Il Barbiere di Siviglia* at the Metropolitan Opera, *The Ring Cycle* for San Francisco and Washington Opera, *Carmen* for the English National Opera, Fête des Vignerons 1999 Vevey, Switzerland. Upcoming projects include *Tales of Hoffman* for The Metropolitan Opera, *Impressionism and Ever After* on Broadway, *The Winter's Tale* and *The Cherry Orchard* directed by Sam Mendes for BAM, NYC and The Old Vic, London.